# SHOT
## AT
# DAWN

Executions in World War One by authority of the British Army Act

# SHOT AT DAWN

## JULIAN PUTKOWSKI & JULIAN SYKES

LEO COOPER
LONDON

First published in 1989 by
Wharncliffe Publishing Ltd

*Second impression 1990*
*Third Impression, new and revised edition 1992*
Leo Cooper Pen & Sword Books Ltd
190 Shaftesbury Avenue
London WC2H 8JL.

Copyright © Julian Putkowski, Julian Sykes 1989

*For up-to-date information on other titles produced*
*under the Leo Cooper imprint, please telephone or*
*write to:*

    Pen & Sword Books Ltd
    FREEPOST
    47 Church Street
    Barnsley
    South Yorkshire S70 2BR
    Telephone (24 hours): 0226-734555

ISBN: 0 85052 295 1

A CIP catalogue record of this book is available from
the British Library.

Typeset by Yorkshire Web, Barnsley,
South Yorkshire
*Printed in Great Britain by* Redwood Press Ltd

# Authors' Statement

In late 1989, when this book was first published, we called for the exoneration of all those who fell victim to British Army firing squads during the First World War. In anticipation of public interest in these cases, considered so sensitive that official records were declared secret for 75 years, the Ministry of Defence prepared a press statement with which they have sought to endorse their predecessors' judgement.

Although conceding that public attitudes have changed, with regard to circumstances which led to military executions, the Ministry contends that these matters are now history and that the Army is no longer subject to the same penal code. The Ministry also maintains that there are no grounds for setting aside the convictions, because they consider conclusive re-appraisals are no longer possible.

We maintain that such perspectives amount to a sustained defence of the court martial injustices and executions we have chronicled. *Shot at Dawn* provides substantial, annotated evidence of illegal irregularities and wilful disregard for mitigating factors, including defendants' ages, wounds and the effects of shellshock.

The Royal British Legion has championed the cause of these unfortunate men and their surviving relatives. Also, the authors have petitioned Her Majesty the Queen, and asked the Archbishop of Canterbury to intercede. Responses from the Ministry of Defence, Buckingham Palace and Lambeth Palace are still awaited.

We believe that few will read *Shot at Dawn* and conclude that these men deserved their fate, or that their shamed relatives should continue to endure the associated disgrace. Surely, the Ministry of Defence cannot continue to reasonably maintain that there is sufficient evidence to uphold these cases as sound convictions. Accordingly, we repeat our call for the Ministry of Defence to have the courage to admit these injustices, and to initiate procedures for exonerating all 351 men who were executed by the British Army during the First World War.

# Contents

British firing squad in action. The shooting is that of a spy in Belgium early in the war. [Penalty not inflicted by authority of the Army Act.]

# Foreword

In 1974 the publication of William Moore's book *The Thin Yellow Line* confirmed suspicion that the punishment meted out to soldiers in the Great War for offences like cowardice and desertion had been ruthless. Since as early as Christmas 1914 speculation and rumour had been rife that this was the case.

A more learned account of these events was published in 1983, when His Honour Judge Anthony Babington was permitted to examine the court martial transcripts which during the war were required to be kept, provided that he did not name the individuals concerned nor their units. The Judge's findings confirmed the worst misgivings that anyone had expressed. Army procedures had seriously jeopardised the prospects of a fair trial, and after conviction the defendant could not expect to be treated sympathetically. As well as legal irregularities Judge Babington also highlighted the absence of informed medical opinion, further prejudicing a soldier's prospects of justice.

However, he did not enquire deeply into the background of individual soldiers — tasks that had engaged our attention for some time prior to the Judge being granted access to the court-martial files. Some of the facts that emerged from our collaborative research were horrifying, and we consider their disclosure a necessity.

Judge Babington wrote a factual account of those questionable proceedings, based on access to official records. What his book accomplished was to let the actual records factually testify to the inequity of what happened. However, we are prepared to advance public awareness one step further, by the complete disclosure of the names of all individuals, their units, and the often appalling way in which they were sentenced to death. The elucidation of this information was not easy, but we have breached no rules of confidentiality, nor have we been granted access to any secret government archives. (Often referred to as closed records.)

After very careful consideration, a decision was reached (just prior to publication) to press for the complete exoneration of these men. Convictions should be quashed and the men pardoned. We are aware that a small number of these men whose cases we chronicle were desperate and worthless individuals — and a few were prone to violence. However, they were treated with contempt and did not receive even the rudiments of a just hearing.

We feel that it is redundant to complain that the setting aside of these convictions in any way devalues the memory of soldiers who served and died with honour, for many of those who faced the firing squads had long and sometimes distinguished service records. For example, author Desmond Morton points out that one of the executed Canadians (whom unfortunately it has not been possible to identify) had been awarded the Military Medal for a previous act of gallantry.

The cases described in this book relate only to soldiers who were subject to the British Army Act. They do not include men executed under the authority of the Indian Army Act. Nor does our work feature the execution of civilians, German prisoners-of-war, spies and foreign nationals sentenced by military courts abroad.

The predicament that confronted many of these condemned men was quite pathetic. In such cases it begs the question, were these the worst offenders that could be found of which to make purported examples? The suggestion is made here that in very many cases they were often unfortunate helpless victims, least able to help themselves. Often in poor physical health these ill-educated, inarticulate individuals were frequently exhausted through the strains of constant horrific trench warfare which drained their resolve – and ultimately their life blood. It is staggering, in an army numbering millions of soldiers that amongst those arraigned were so many from tragic backgrounds.

In a number of cases we know that the next-of-kin were never officially notified about the execution of their relative. Consequently, this book may be the first intimation they may receive. We regret if this is the case, but we hope that now the details have been publicly disclosed they and others will gain a better understanding of one of the most disgraceful episodes in British military history. These were the men who were shot at dawn.

# Introduction

In the early morning of 8 September 1914 a nineteen year old British Army deserter was shot by firing squad. He had been convicted just two days previously, in one of the swiftest disposals of a capital case during the war.

Just over four years later, on 7 November 1918, two London-born deserters faced separate firing squads. One was a 23 year old Jew who, after volunteering in March 1915, had been rejected as medically unsuitable for the army. However, the Londoner had been conscripted in April 1916, when medical requirements were lowered. The other victim, a conscript aged 32, was alleged to have a history of mental illness that similarly affected his family. Although these two offences and ultimate punishments occurred in different locations, in neither case did the soldier's medical record prevent him from being shot. The two were the last men executed on the Western Front before the Armistice.

The aforementioned men shared the same fate as no less than 312 men who were executed for military offences. Official statistics indicate, however, that they were only a minority, as 3,080 men subject to the Army Act had been sentenced to death between 4 August 1914 and 31 March 1920. In the region of 90 per cent of the death sentences passed during this six year period were commuted, including some which involved murder, which in any case carried a mandatory death penalty upon conviction. It would be wrong to suggest that even the total number of soldiers sentenced to death was large – it was not. In what proved to be ever-escalating carnage the daily average casualties were 2,000, including 400 fatalities.

The rationale, generally assumed to lie behind the army's use of capital punishment, related to the deterrent effect that the victims' fate had on their fellow soldiers. The dictum *pour encourager les autres*, that theoretically rationalised this practice was the subject of Judge Anthony Babington's book – *For the Sake of Example* – and merits critical evaluation.

The *pour encourager les autres* thesis, as it applied to the men of the British army during the Great War, presupposed that the structure and process of military discipline was universally consistent and predictable. The fate of those who were convicted and sentenced to death, if the deterrent aspect of the punishment worked, ought to have dissuaded other potential offenders from transgressing orders. However, if the punishment was effective then it was characterised by flawed judgements, inconsistent decisions and class bias.

During the war it was customary for details of recent offences and subsequent executions to be announced on parade. The very unpleasantness of an execution tended to ensure that it remained a very private affair. Enforced audiences, by order of a senior officer would seem to have been rare. The effect of such participation sometimes proved counter-productive. One assistant provost-marshal concluded that a mutiny was a likely outcome of arranging an execution in the presence of the condemned man's battalion. And another soldier claims that a mutiny did follow an execution. Another officer confided in his diary that he had refused to provide men to make up a firing squad, and another soldier, when detailed to join a firing squad, deliberately 'fired wide' when commanded to shoot the condemned man. Such actions probably served only to ease a soldier's conscience, and were no kindness to the victim. Those unlucky enough to survive the volley, occasionally only lightly wounded, faced moments of mental anguish as the officer in charge of the firing squad approached to administer the *coup de grâce* from point blank range.

The court martial panels that sentenced deserters to death often seemed to have little consideration for the predicament of the offender, who, after he had committed his crime then diced in an arbitrary lottery with death. Records relating to a number of these cases highlight just how arbitrary the decision to confirm a death sentence could be. The inference drawn from these records is that after the opening of the Somme offensive in July 1916, the judgement of Sir Douglas Haig was defective when he decided to have certain men executed. These records were compiled for Parliamentary consideration in the post-war review of the sanction of death sentence for military offences.

The suggestion that the Commander-in-Chief was solely responsible for the unfortunate demise of these men would be quite incorrect. Sir Douglas Haig, much maligned by previous authors for every conceivable disaster, was the final arbiter in a lengthy and complex legal military system. (Sir John French's command is less significant in comparison.) A more balanced view shows that unfortunate victims were 'snared' by an unforgiving military judicial system.

Whilst minor infractions of military discipline could be dealt with by the commanding officer of a malefactor's unit, the most serious crimes involving possible capital offences were dealt with via trials by court martial.

There were four types of courts martial: Regimental, District, General, and Field General. The Regimental Court Martial dealt with minor offences and the District Court Martial could only impose a maximum sentence of two years' imprisonment, but General Courts Martial and Field General Courts Martial dealt with offences which could result in a sentence of death.

General Courts Martial were far less frequently convened than Field General Courts Martial. Field General Courts Martial were a type of

British Army firing squad in action in Singapore 15th February, 1915. Victims were mutineers belonging to the 5th Light Infantry. The firing squad was drawn up from members of the Singapore Volunteers (European Company). [Sentence carried out by authority of the Indian Army Act.]    *IWM Ref: Q82506*

General Court Martial and allowed a considerable simplification of procedural matters and requirements, supposedly in the interests of military expediency. Less than than a dozen death sentences imposed by General Court Martial were confirmed and carried out in the period 1914-20.

Under the provisions of the Army Act a number of offences were punishable more severely when on active service. By far the greatest number of capital convictions for this type of offence was for desertion – over 260 shootings resulting during the war. However, the Army Act was quite clear on the point that deserting when under orders merely to go on active service also carried a similar penalty – although only a small number of such cases were recorded. Given that the most common capital offence was desertion, the army procedure for dealing with such offenders became well established.

Other than courts martial, the army also convened another type of tribunal – known as a Court of Inquiry. Such inquisitions were extremely common, and might enquire into any matter, from the trifling loss of a battalion bicycle, to the failure of a major attack. In the case of absentees, a Court of Inquiry would be convened at any period after 21 days from the reported disappearance of the soldier. At the hearing evidence would be given by witnesses with knowledge about the last known movements and sightings of the absentee. At the conclusion the court might then declare the soldier to be a deserter. This did not preclude the possibility of a charge of desertion being brought if the absentee was arrested within the 21 day period.

The offence of desertion was a crime in which the intent of the accused was all important. The length of absence was immaterial, but could of course be very relevant, as the absence of a soldier for months or even years, was good evidence that the man had abandoned his commitment. Conversely, if a soldier disappeared from the battlefront, and the same day was discovered in civilian clothing on board a ship about to sail for England, then this too was prima facie evidence that the man had deserted. Four men were also shot during the war for attempting to desert, and obviously evidence of their intentions was even more crucial in these cases.

As a matter of course details of deserters were circulated. In the United Kingdom such lists were sent to (military) record offices, and details were also sent to the police force for the district in which the soldier was last known to have resided. These details were processed, at least in part, by the editor of the *Police Gazette*, and a special supplement to this publication was produced detailing wanted men. It is also known that where available, photos were also circulated, often in the form of cards with information about an offender's associates, habits and aliases etc.

During the early years of the war, deserters arrested in the UK were brought before a court of summary jurisdiction (magistrates' court) before being returned to their unit for trial. Of necessity a prisoner would be returned with an escort. Later in 1917 this initial inquisitory examination in the UK was abandoned, consequently newspaper reporting of arrested offenders ceased.

Once back with his unit a soldier might be detained under open or close arrest, depending how desperate an individual he was. Although a Court of Inquiry might already have sat, a summary of evidence from witnesses was required to be taken before such papers could be submitted to a field officer who might then convene a court martial − usually this individual would be a brigadier-general.

The Army Act stipulated that a Field General Court Martial (FGCM) should consist of a minimum of three officers, one of whom, not below the rank of captain, should act as president. A sentence of death could not be passed without the concurrence of all the officers making up the Field General Court Martial panel. Trial by full General Court Martial was a much more formal affair with numerous provisions and requirements.

Prior to trial a soldier would be offered the assistance of an officer to act as 'prisoner's friend'. In essence the officer acted as defending counsel, although little is heard of legally qualified officers appearing.

Execution of a 'brigand' in Anatolia circa 1919 or 1920. [Penalty not inflicted by authority of the Army Act.]                                        (*F Baker Collection*)

Foolishly some men declined this assistance, although more often than not the officer was unskilled in advocacy. However, the army was not short of legally qualified practitioners amongst its ranks, and it is to its eternal shame that this asset was not utilised. (*The Times* on 12 December 1914 recorded that 1,150 solicitors and articled clerks were serving the forces, and on 18 December of the same year that 726 barristers were also serving. By far the vast majority of these lawyers were newly enlisted.)

The trial of many a soldier was carried out in improvised accommodation, with the battalion (or unit) adjutant acting as prosecutor. The charge would be read to the defendant, who would be asked to plead 'guilty, or not guilty?' However, following an unfortunate incident in 1915 an automatic plea of not guilty was always entered for a capital case, and then the court would proceed to hear whatever evidence there was — in full.

After the evidence of each prosecution witness the soldier, or his representative might then cross-examine that individual. Seemingly this was rarely done, and even less often effectively. At the conclusion of the prosecution case the defendant might call his own witnesses or give evidence himself. Undoubtedly unjust inference was drawn if a prisoner chose to remain silent, and those who elected to speak must surely have been subjected to an awesome ordeal. Little imagination is required to envisage the scenario of the ill-educated soldier on trial for his life, being led into making unfortunate admissions when questioned by his superiors, in their respective roles as prosecutor and judges.

Until the final year of the war a soldier could not expect immediately to be told the outcome of the court's deliberations. However, if the case was found not to be proved, and the soldier was acquitted, then he was told straight away. Consequently, in the absence of an acquittal, a soldier knew that he had been found guilty, although he had no indication as to the sentence, or whether any recommendation to mercy had been made in the case of a death sentence.

The powers of sentencing under the Army Act were wide. A commanding officer might, on his own authority, deal with minor matters of indiscipline. His powers included stoppages of pay, fines, and limited periods of detention and field punishment. This latter treatment caused much controversy, and two types existed, field punishment No.1 and No.2. With the former punishment, a soldier was kept busy with continual labouring duties and might be restrained in fetters or handcuffs. He was also liable to be attached to a fixed object − as additional humiliation. The fixing to a post, or sometimes a wheel, became known as crucifixion and might continue for a total of 21 days, during which the daily maximum period for such treatment was two hours. Additionally the attachment could not be carried out for more than three in any four consecutive days. In the case of field punishment No.2, the prisoner was not subjected to being tied to a fixed object, but underwent the other restrictions.

By way of a custodial sentence a court martial might sentence an individual to imprisonment. Such a sentence would invariably be carried out in a military detention centre in the theatre of operations. The maximum length of such a sentence was two years − and might be with or without hard labour.

More serious crimes attracted punishment in the form of penal servitude, and such a sentence was a minimum of three years. In the event that such a penalty was not suspended, the prisoner was returned to the United Kingdom to undergo his punishment. The ultimate sanction was of course the death penalty, which in all but an odd case was specified as being death by shooting.

Assuming that death sentences were imposed by officers overwhelmingly drawn from the upper classes, on soldiers who were predominantly of working class origin, the taint of class justice which accompanied the Edwardian civil magistracy cannot have been absent from courts martial.

Even had the more liberal 'temporary gentlemen' managed to dilute the generally atavistic perspectives of pre-war regular army officers, junior officers passing judgement in a capital case were likely to opt for the maximum penalty. To do otherwise was to solicit censure for lacking appropriate disciplinary zeal, and occasionally provoked a dressing down from a superior officer. A number of junior officers make mention of this pressure and one comments on the repercussion of his refusal to pass a sentence of death.

In any event, a FGCM panel could always assuage pangs of self-doubt caused by over-severe sentencing, by attaching to the written record of the proceedings a recommendation for mercy. This effectively passed partial responsibility along the chain of command, and eventually to the Commander-in-Chief. However, the palliative effect of such recommendations was likely to be useless.

A provision of the military judicial system dictated that following conviction in a capital case the papers from the case would be passed up though the army hierarchy (on its way to GHQ) with each General appending his recommendation.

In spite of Major-General Sir Wyndham Childs' (post-war) intimations to the contrary, commanders reviewing capital cases frequently seemed reluctant to commute death sentences. Judge Babington's reasoning, that confirming officers allowed death sentences to remain unaltered because court martial panels' judgements were passed in the full knowledge of all aspects of each case, is plausible — but the notion that court-martial judgements were fully informed and consequently reliable was wrong. The passage of time and the lack of reliable data does not permit a detailed appraisal of the reasons that motivated individual reviewing officers considering capital cases. However, it would be surprising if the reasoning would stand up to present day scrutiny.

At each stage of the post-sentencing procedure various comments were appended to the record of court-martial proceedings. Throughout most of the war this transcript was accompanied by the condemned man's conduct sheet. The review procedure progressed from the commander of the man's unit, usually a lieutenant-colonel or a major, via brigade headquarters. Once the brigadier-general had added his comments about the individual and his offence, the file passed on to divisional headquarters, where a major-general would carry out a similar task. Similarly, the corps and army commanders in their turn would read through the file and make a recommendation. The penultimate stage in the bureaucratic process of reviewing capital sentences rested with the Adjutant-General's department at GHQ, where court martial proceedings were checked by the judge advocate-general to ensure that the conviction was legally valid.

If the judge advocate-general did not quash the conviction for failing to meet statutory requirements, it then was up to the Commander-in-Chief to make the final decision whether the soldier was to live or die.

Although during the first few months of the war the documentary basis on which the Commander-in-Chief had to decide a condemned man's fate seemed to have been scanty, after April 1915 several other details enhanced information recorded in the court martial papers. These were a summary from the man's company commander regarding the condemned man's value as a fighting soldier; the opinion of a medical officer concerning the man's state of health; and a brigadier's report about the general state of discipline within the brigade and his opinion on whether an example was necessary.

It is quite clear that any of the aforementioned opinions were likely to materially affect the outcome of the review. One damning remark could have sent a man to his death, and on a number of occasions it did. In the lottery of death that accompanied court martial sentences and subsequent reviews there seems to have been little consistency. An arbitrary decision coupled with an offence committed at an inopportune moment could send a man to his death with sudden ferocity.

Although by far the vast majority of offenders were shot for desertion (268), a number of other crimes attracted the severest of sentences. Leaving aside murder (for which at least 37 sentences were carried out) the next most prevalent capital crime was cowardice, 18 shootings taking place for this offence. Other crimes included quitting posts (seven), disobedience (five), striking superior officers (five), mutiny (four − Western Front only), sleeping at posts (two), and casting away their arms (two).

Like many offences under military law a single act or omission could constitute more than one offence. For example refusing to go into an attack might be construed as cowardice as well as disobedience. However, cowardice was an offence that required an audience of witnesses, in order that testimony might be given at a subsequent trial. Consequently, if a soldier was seen to run away and hide during an attack, then that might be considered to be cowardice. However, if during an attack the soldier's whereabouts were unknown but a short while later he turned up in a back area, then that could be construed as desertion. The other offences for which the death sentence was imposed are perhaps self-explanatory. In the main text that follows the elements of these crimes are described in context.

The threat of being executed by firing squads composed of their comrades confronted soldiers of most nationalities who fought on different sides in the First World War. Direct comparisons are difficult to sustain but, amongst the Allies the French Army, numerically the largest force, seems to have resorted most frequently to the sanction.

In 1934 French journalists and ex-servicemen's organisations, campaigning for posthumous pardons and compensation, published horrific accounts of military injustices. They also reported that wartime executions officially sanctioned by French *conseils de guerre* (courts martial) officially totalled 1,637. Unofficial estimates, including summary executions, suggested a higher figure, approaching 2,500. However, more recent research suggests that approximately 2,000 death sentences were prescribed, but only around 700 *poilus* were shot.[1]

Execution of another 'brigand' in Anatolia, after the war.     (*F Baker Collection*)

The sanction of the death penalty in the Russian army was abandoned — although this perhaps was to be expected with the coming of the revolution. In the post-war period the United States' Order of Battle recorded its losses from military executions. It was recorded that 145 death sentences had been passed in the period beginning of April 1917 to the end of June 1919; however only 35 of these had been confirmed. Of those carried out, only ten related to the Western Front, the remainder being carried out in the United States. Whilst the percentage of sentences actually carried out is higher that those imposed by the British Army Act, the figures are not directly comparable as none of the Americans had been convicted of military offences. Their crimes mainly involved murder, often accompanying mutiny and occasionally rape. Eleven executions were solely for rape.

The German High Command structure, and subsequent destruction of military records, complicate comparative estimates. Nevertheless, in 1917 Prince Rupprecht of Bavaria recorded in his diary that the British Army deployed firing squads far more frequently than his own forces. Recently published estimates by a German military legal authority, suggests that the Prussians, Saxon and Wurtemberg armies followed Bavarian military-judicial policy. Only 150 German soldiers were sentenced to death by military courts, and only 48 were subsequently executed.[2]

Although Sir Douglas Haig had made strong representations for powers to inflict the extreme penalty upon Australian soldiers, the sanction was continually denied. Suggestion has been made that this decision was made because two Australian officers had been executed in the Boer War, under what were speculated to be somewhat dubious circumstances — without reference to the men's homeland. Consequently, such authority would not be granted. Such a hypothesis might not be without a grain of truth. However, it is believed that a major consideration was the Australian soldier's status as a volunteer, and that as such, these men should not be subject to the extreme penalty. Although no Australian soldier was executed it is not commonly known that in the post-war period, two Australian soldiers narrowly escaped possible capital sentences. The offenders were both murderers, and consideration had been given either to handing them over to the French civil authorities for trial under French law, or sending them to the UK to face trial under English law.

The other Dominions did not escape the sanction of the extreme penalty, with Canada 'heading' the shootings with 25 executions. And New Zealand had five men shot, including one for mutiny.

The miscellany of others who faced death sentences were four men from the British West Indies Regiment and an assortment of African troops, as well as native labourers (including Chinese) and also muleteers.

291 of those shot (including three officers) were serving in British regiments or units, and of these the vast majority (in fact 278) were executed on the Western Front. From the figure of 291, fourteen cases of murder (including one officer) can be deducted, leaving a total of 277 executions solely for military offences.

The average age of the offenders (of all types) varied little throughout the war years. (The authors have not been able to determine the ages of all those soldiers who were executed, but it is believed that the statistics that have been calculated are representative. Figures in brackets indicate the sample size.) The average age of the soldiers who were shot for all types of offences, was just under twenty-five-and-a-half years. (228) From the lowest average in 1915 to the highest in 1918, the maximum average yearly variation was only one-and-a-half years.

The average age of those shot for desertion was just over twenty-five years. (This figure is based on a determination of the ages of 177 out of the 264 men shot for this offence.) The average age of those shot for cowardice was just under twenty-six. (Based on 16 of the 18 men executed.)

Calculations of average ages in relation to the crime of murder are not statistically valid, as data is only available on 14 of the 37 offenders. However, there is some reason to believe that the soldiers (as opposed to non-combatants) shot for this crime were often a few years older than other types of offenders. Four soldiers shot for this offence were aged over thirty years.

One of the most worrying aspects about First World War capital courts martial is that over ten per cent of those soldiers executed had been unrepresented at their trials. Of these thirty-one men, twenty-six had been youths – i.e. under the age of 21. Furthermore, over two-thirds of those shot had previously been convicted of some serious crime, and

The execution post at Poperinghe — photograph believed to have been taken during the war.

hence were most vulnerable and most in need of assistance. At least 49 soldiers who were executed were under the age of majority, and as has previously been stated less that half were defended at their trials. The oldest soldier who was not represented at his trial was aged 26, and on average those declining assistance were aged twenty-and-a-half years. However, only four of the unrepresented soldiers were conscripts.

Leaving aside non-combatants who were subject to military law, the division of executed soldiers into different categories reveals the following statistics. (The percentages have been rounded-up.)

30 per cent were either Regular Army soldiers or Reservists i.e. they were, or had been, in the army before the war.

Three per cent were Territorials who had been in the army before the war.

40 per cent were volunteers who enlisted after the outbreak of war but prior to conscription. (These were British men who would eventually have been liable to be conscripted — had they not joined of their own free will.) This group might more accurately be described as Kitchener volunteers.

19 per cent were volunteers who joined (or were serving) in either Irish, Canadian or New Zealand units.

Nine per cent were conscripts. It might be wrong to assume that all conscripts were compelled to join the army against their own wishes. It is of course possible that a few were simply too young to join earlier, and had to wait to be called.

Although only ten of the men executed were pre-war Territorials (three per cent quoted above) 34 shootings had taken place in divisions comprised solely of territorial units — the remaining men having been enlisted on a different basis. However, by far the largest number of executions took place in New Army divisions — those formations raised specially for the war effort. Of course, by the end of the war the total number of New Army divisions far exceeded the number of divisions which, upon the outbreak of war, were formed solely from Regular units. A direct comparison between executions in New Army and Regular divisions is difficult. However, at the end of the war the number of Regular Army divisions only formed approximately one sixth of the mobilised British armies. The distribution of executions was, however, Regular divisions 119, New Army divisions 179. It is acknowledged that Regular divisions had been in action the longest, and that the substitution of Volunteer units in Regular Army divisions makes a direct comparison difficult.

Very few deserters who were shot were arrested in the UK. Of those that were, six had gone absent whilst at home, most of them being on leave from the front at the time, and eight had achieved the most difficult task of escaping across the Channel.

Very few of the convicted men would seem to have been married — although the authors have not been able to establish the marital status of all individuals. Enquiries show that at least 34 were married. It is thought however that fairly comprehensive details have been ascertained about the condemned men's previous behaviour, and statistics would suggest that 40 per cent had been in serious trouble before. At least seven of the condemned men were serving under false names, three of them being Irishmen. Of the remaining four, one man's true surname was literally 'Irish', another was a Cape Coloured labourer, yet another was serving with the New Zealand forces, and the final soldier was a mysterious person of Jewish origin.

Very few units from the army did not have men executed. The exceptions were: Grenadier Guards, Welsh Guards, Honourable Artillery Company, Bedfordshire Regiment, Royal Irish Regiment, Gloucestershire Regiment, Oxfordshire & Buckinghamshire Light Infantry, Shropshire Light Infantry, Monmouthshire Regiment, Cambridgeshire Regiment, Herefordshire Regiment, Hertfordshire Regiment and other miscellaneous small units. Similarly no men were shot from the Cavalry or the Royal Army Medical Corps.

In considering the percentage of the various British units in which shootings were carried out, 43 were Scottish, 24 were Irish and 15 were Welsh. The remainder (209) were English. Given that amongst the soldiers executed there was only a small amount of enlistment of men from one region (or country) in another's formations, the above figures can be considered to be national statistics. (Enquiries by the authors have ascertained that the extent of 'cross-enlistment' does not materially affect the above figures.) In considering the battalions raised in England recruitment from the north of England stands out as providing the largest percentage of victims for the firing squads. Units from Lancashire (and around) yielded 38, Yorkshire 28, and together with other formations from the north (not including Scotland) the total figure rises to 87 — approaching half of the English total. The regiment with the highest number of executions was the West Yorks (12) — followed closely by the artillery and the King's Royal Rifle Corps, both with eleven.

The reason why these northerners formed the majority of victims of the firing squads is unknown, but, like their southern, Canadian, and New Zealand counterparts — to quote just some — the soldiers received rough justice — when ultimately, at first light they were taken out and shot.

### NOTES

1 Le Crapouillot, *August 1934*; G Pedroncini, *Les Mutineries de 1917*.
2 M Messerschmidt, 'The German Military in the Age of Total War' (in *The German Military in the Age of Total War*, ed. W Deist).

# Chapter One

## *Regular blood*

The first sentence of death imposed on a soldier of the BEF was carried out in the fifth week of the war; and the condemned soldier was **Private Thomas Highgate** from Kent. He had been born in the little village of Shoreham, near Sevenoaks and had joined the Army in February 1913. Like many who enlisted for Regular Army service, the lad had joined up at the age of 17.

Highgate's battalion, 1 Royal West Kents, had been amongst the first to see action during the war. And following the retreat from Mons, after less than two weeks in action, the private had deserted. On the day that he went missing his battalion had started to move northwards, advancing towards the Aisne. Highgate, who was wearing civilian clothing, was discovered by a gamekeeper hiding in a barn. His uniform was concealed nearby. When questioned he said, 'I want to get out of it and this is how I am doing it.'[1] Amazingly the gamekeeper was an Englishman and an ex-soldier too.[2] Private Highgate was then arrested by the Gendarmes, who soon handed him over to the British Military Authorities.[3]

On 6 September Private Highgate was tried by Field General Court Martial (FGCM) on a charge of desertion. He was unassisted in his defence − presumably at his own insistence − it being hoped that he was made aware of his right to have an officer speak on his behalf. Consequently, without the assistance of an officer to act as prisoner's friend the private relied solely on the impartiality of the court's president. Not surprisingly Private Highgate was found guilty. The sentence imposed was that he would suffer death by being shot.

On the following day the punishment was confirmed by the Commander-in-Chief Sir John French. At dawn on the 8th, just two days after his arrest, 19 year old Highgate was shot by a firing squad from 15 Brigade.[4] Shortly afterwards, brief details of the case appeared in the circular known as 'Army Routine Orders'.[5] The theory was that such a disclosure would deter others.

In the post-war years the Imperial War Graves Commission was unable to locate Highgate's grave, and consequently he is commemorated on La Ferté-sous-Jouarre Memorial to the missing.

After the war the Army published lists of men who had died on active service. The records were produced in 80 parts by regiment or corps and were made available for sale, the volumes being called, *Soldiers Died in the Great War*. It was believed that these lists did not contain the names of those who had been executed during the war. Yet Highgate's name does appear, in part 53 which lists the dead of the Royal West Kent Regiment. The private's cause of death is given as 'Died of Wounds'.

The exact reason for the inclusion of Highgate's name is not known but it seems likely that the authorities, embarrassed by their predicament, sought to fudge the records and attempt a cover-up. It would also seem that they became confused by their own deception. The reason being that the information supplied by Army Records to the official registry of deaths states that Highgate had been 'Killed in Action'.[6] Private Highgate is not the only soldier who was shot to be commemorated in the volumes of *Soldiers Died in the Great War*. A total of 14 men appear in various volumes, with two regiments listing all men who were executed, suggesting that some regiments were either unaware of the exclusion directive, or that they preferred to ignore its existence.

Prior to the trial of Private Highgate, General Sir Horace Smith-Dorrien (commanding II Corps) had recorded in his diary that a number of incidents of straggling and looting were to be tried by court martial on the evening of 4 September. Whilst these cases did not include Highgate, on 7 September Smith-Dorrien recorded that two men had been executed that day, one for plundering and the other for desertion.[7] The deserter was undoubtedly Highgate – a mistake having been made concerning the date – but no details can be found about a soldier executed on 7 September for plundering, and during the war no man was put to death solely for this offence.

On 14 September Army Routine Orders again carried news of courts martial.[8] Two battalion commanders, Lieutenant-Colonel A E Mainwaring, 2 Royal Dublin Fusiliers and Lieutenant-Colonel J F Elkington, 1 Royal Warwickshire Regiment had been found guilty of 'behaving in a scandalous manner unbecoming the character of an officer and a gentleman'. The two officers had jointly agreed to surrender themselves and their troops to the Germans following a long retreat on 27 August. Both were sentenced to be cashiered. Two other courts martial also appeared in the same Routine Order. The offenders were a driver from the Army Service Corps and a private in the Dragoon Guards, both men had been convicted of sleeping on their posts. The two soldiers had been sentenced to death but the sentences had both been commuted to two years' imprisonment with hard labour.

The second execution of the war concerned the offence of cowardice. The soldier, **Private George Ward** of 1 Royal Berkshire Regiment, was charged following an incident on the Aisne. On 14 September Ward's battalion had been guarding the flanks during an uphill advance towards the Chemin des Dames. At around 9 am the enemy had opened up with shell fire and the advance had been checked. In the course of the bombardment Ward was seen to get up from his position and start to make his way to the rear. When challenged the soldier told his NCO that he had been hit by a shell burst.

The unwounded private reported back to his battalion six days later, and soon afterwards, on 24 September, he was tried at Oeuilly Farm. Unlike Private Highgate, Ward had an officer to act as prisoner's friend. Nevertheless it would seem that no defence was made. During the review procedure the court martial papers arrived on the desk of the Corps Commander Sir Douglas Haig. The General appended his thoughts to the papers. An example was required to prevent further cases occurring.[9] Sir John French concurred and Private Ward, aged 20, was executed at Oeuilly at 5.56 pm on 26 September.[10] It was very unusual that the shooting had taken place in the late afternoon. During the remainder of the war, almost all other executions took place at dawn.

The account of a supposed eye-witness emerged after the war. The story related that as the condemned man was being taken out to be shot he broke away from his captors and tried to escape. He was shot as he ran and was wounded, then brought back on a stretcher. The sergeant of the guard was then ordered to 'finish him off' as he lay wounded.[11] There is no official record to confirm or deny this story, although it seems improbable. After the execution Ward's body was buried south west of Oeuilly village — on the north bank of the river Aisne. However, after the war the soldier's grave was never located and he too is commemorated on La Ferté-sous-Jouarre Memorial to the missing.

What is astonishing about the case of Private Ward is that his offence occurred on his third day of active service. Ward had landed in France on 12 September[12] and the brief duration of his service, before committing the crime that would cost him his life, was the shortest of the war.

**Private Edward Tanner** of 1 Wiltshire Regiment was the oldest of the four British soldiers to be executed during 1914. At 33 he was nine years older than the average age of the others. Tanner had joined his battalion during the retreat from Mons and had seen action on the Aisne on three occasions before his battalion moved north to Flanders. The soldier had gone absent after recovering from a bout of dysentery. 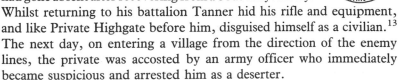 Whilst returning to his battalion Tanner hid his rifle and equipment, and like Private Highgate before him, disguised himself as a civilian.[13] The next day, on entering a village from the direction of the enemy lines, the private was accosted by an army officer who immediately became suspicious and arrested him as a deserter.

At his court martial, Tanner stated that his nerves had been shattered by the shelling.[14] The authorities were unsympathetic. The fact that the private had been arrested in civilian clothing was certainly noted by the court as an indication that the soldier intended to desert. In due course the execution was recorded in Routine Orders, although the date given was incorrect.[15] Private Tanner was shot at 7.10 am on 27 October, but after the war his grave was not located. Consequently he is commemorated on Le Touret Memorial to the missing, one of the many memorials that commemorate men whose graves disappeared on the Western Front.

The final soldier to be executed in 1914 was **Private Archibald Browne** of 2 Essex Regiment. Browne too was a veteran of August  1914.[16] His battalion had taken part in the retreat from Mons and had been in action at Le Cateau, the Marne and the Aisne. Once in Flanders, Private Browne had deserted during November 1914, after assisting a sick soldier to an Aid Post. Following the previous pattern, Browne had dispensed with his army uniform and assumed the appearance of a civilian.[17] But a few days later he was arrested by the French police after breaking into an unoccupied house in Hazebrouck. On 9 December the soldier was court martialled on three charges: desertion, plundering and finally, showing his desperate plight, escaping from arrest. During the trial Browne stated he had been captured by the Germans and escaped, adding that subsequently he had been looking for his unit.[18] His story was not accepted and at 7 am on 19 December 26 year old Private Browne was executed. Notification appeared in Routine Orders on Christmas Eve.[19] At this period in the war it was not uncommon for men who were under arrest to escape confinement. Browne's story that he had been captured by the Germans and had then escaped was not as incredible as might first be thought. Later in the war the unbroken trench lines from Switzerland to the sea made this event very unlikely, but in 1914 it was a real possibility and a number of such occurrences have been documented. In early 1915, when another soldier also claimed he had been captured by the Germans and had escaped, he too was executed.

As in the cases of the other men executed in 1914, the grave of Private Browne could not be found after the war, but today his name can be seen on the Ploegsteert Memorial to the missing.

The recent publication of an officer's diary from the Great War included details that a double execution had taken place in Rouen in 1914.[20] The diary entry was not made with the benefit of personal knowledge but from hearsay. Such rumours were very prevalent throughout the war, and extensive enquiries have failed to trace any such events. Consequently it must be stated that there is no foundation for this unsubstantiated yarn.

In spite of a considerable amount of trucing in Christmas 1914, some of which continued into the new year, the spirit of cordiality was not universally evident. On New Year's Day 1915 the Germans launched a number of attacks near Cuinchy, capturing a machine gun post and a handful of observation posts that stood in front of the main positions. It was not a good start to the new year, and the official historians later wrote, 'the depression of some of the troops during the winter of 1914-15 was evident. It was of the utmost importance as regards morale that our men should see that the enemy could be paid back in kind and was not going to have things all his own way.'[21]

Amongst those experiencing such depression were two Londoners from 4th Company, 2 Middlesex Regiment. **Private Sheffield** and **Private Ball** had gone absent in mid December and were shot early in 1915, in the first double execution of the war. The two privates had deserted after only six weeks on active service, going absent as their battalion made its way to the trenches prior to an attack on Neuve Chapelle. The two soldiers were discovered hiding under straw in a barn, and pretended to be French civilians.[22] The fugitives stood trial on the penultimate day of December when the prosecution alleged that the soldiers had 'attempted to desert'.

Presumably the close proximity of the two men to their unit determined that this would be the charge as opposed to the more usual charge of 'desertion'. (Strictly speaking the two men should not have been charged with 'attempting to desert' but with 'desertion'. Chapter 3, paragraph 18 of the *Manual of Military Law* explains the offence of attempting to desert: 'If a soldier commits an act which is apparently a prelude to, or an attempt at, desertion, although no actual absence can be proved, as if he is caught in the act of slipping past a sentry, or climbing over a barrack wall in plain clothes, he may be charged with an attempt to desert.') On 8 January the Adjutant-General of 8 Division received notification by telegram that the sentences had been confirmed, and the executions took place at 7.30 am on 12 January 1915.[23] Again details of the executions were circulated for the attention of potential offenders, an officer recording the notification in his diary.[24] Private Sheffield came from South Tottenham and was aged 26 when he died. Private Ball lived at Queens Park and was six years his junior. Although the Adjutant-General recorded the events in his diary, after the Armistice the graves were not found. Both men are commemorated on Le Touret Memorial.

In cases of desertion two aspects of the offence were likely to increase the likelihood of the death sentence being put into effect. Firstly soldiers who were caught wearing civilian clothing were regarded as clearly showing their intention to desert. It was considered far more serious for a soldier to be arrested in civilian clothing and without equipment than if he were apprehended in khaki and still in possession of his kit. In all cases of desertion hitherto, the soldiers had been arrested in civilian clothing. In the cases of Ball and Sheffield they had also compounded their offences by deserting to avoid service in the line. It was this second factor which was considered equally serious to a civilian disguise. Men who deserted specifically to avoid a dangerous or potentially dangerous duty ran the greatest risk of facing a firing squad − the duration of the absence was immaterial under such circumstances. To return to duty, even after a very short interval of time − a day or less, would not minimise the prospects of a death penalty being imposed. The fatal element was that the offence had been committed to avoid personal danger. This aspect − avoiding personal danger by deserting − is not far removed from the offence of cowardice. The differences were, firstly that the offence of desertion did not require an audience to prove the case, and secondly the crime did not have to be committed in action.

The first NCO to be executed during the war was a corporal in 2 Lancashire Fusiliers. **Corporal George Latham** was a regular soldier who had deserted at Le Cateau on 27 August. He was absent for several months and was eventually returned to his unit as a straggler.[25] The soldier again went absent for a further three weeks, until he was arrested on 21 December by the Military Police at Nieppe, where he was living with a French woman.[26] At his trial this 23 year soldier, who had a wife living near Birmingham, offered no explanation for his behaviour. On 22 January the corporal suffered the extreme penalty for his errant ways. Latham's grave was identified after the war and his wife decided on the inscription − *Rest in Peace*. The grave lies in plot 2, row F, grave 17 of Trois Arbres Cemetery, Steenwerck, France.

At the end of January 1915 a further double execution took place. Both men were in their twenties and were in 1 Irish Guards. **Private Thomas Cummings** and **Private Albert Smythe** had each served for a number of years before the war. Their battalion, which had been in action continually since Mons, was fighting in the Ypres Salient when in November 1914 the two men deserted. As in the previous case, a French woman had been harbouring the men. The duo had been unearthed by the Military Police during a raid on a barn.[27] After the trial the battalion commander added his comments to the proceedings, stating that Cummings was an excellent soldier, but that Smythe's reputation was disappointing. Nevertheless, both sentences were confirmed − and subsequently carried out on 28 January. The familiar notification soon appeared in General Routine Orders.[28] Neither man's grave was found after the war and both men are commemorated on Le Touret Memorial.

**Private William Scotton** pre-empted the war by enlisting in Middlesex Regiment at the end of July 1914. After a brief period of training the private was drafted to 4 Battalion which was serving in the Ypres Salient. At the end of December Scotton was convicted of going absent, yet a month later, on 23 January, he repeated the offence, his platoon having been warned for the trenches.[29] The private reported himself the next day, after his unit's return from the line, and was placed under arrest.[30] The court martial papers carried comments suggesting that the soldier was a weakling and that discipline in his battalion was bad — there was no recommendation to mercy. The sentence of death was carried out at Vierstraat on 3 February by a firing squad of eight men and an NCO from the condemned man's unit; and the whole battalion was paraded to witness the event.[31] The grave of Private Scotton, aged only 19 at the time of his death, was not discovered after the war and he is commemorated on the Menin Gate Memorial.

A third double execution took place in early February 1915, and the circumstances are surprising to say the least. The two soldiers were both privates in 1 Royal Scots Fusiliers who were charged with 'attempting to desert'. **Private Andrew Evans** was probably a Reservist. His Great War service had commenced in August 1914, and it is reckoned, based on his army number, that he was simply re-joining the colours. Private Evans was drafted to 1 Battalion on 10 October 1914.[32]

**Private Joseph Byers** however, had enlisted at the age of 17.[33] Anthony Babington in his book, *For the Sake of Example* mistakenly remarks that the first Kitchener volunteer to be executed met his end on 1 July 1915. This is not the case, Private Byers was the first Kitchener volunteer to be executed in the war. Byers enlisted on 20 November and received only a fortnight's rudimentary training in Britain before being despatched to France.[34]

Hence it can be seen that Private Byers had seen little service, as together with his comrade Private Evans the two men were tried on 30 January. The evidence indicated that they had been absent from parade, prior to their battalion proceeding to the front. Byers pleaded guilty to the charge, a decision that later was viewed with concern by the confirming officers and legal advisers. Subsequently instructions were issued that when a capital crime was involved, then irrespective of a soldier's wish, a plea of not guilty would be entered and the case heard as normal — with witnesses giving evidence on oath.[35]

One factor that the reviewing authorities omitted to consider further was that Private Byers was unrepresented at his trial. Perhaps an additional directive should have been issued that soldiers under the age of majority must be represented when on trial. Military indifference would seem to have had a rather blinkered approach to this equally serious oversight.

In spite of the deliberations the sentences of death on Privates Byers and Evans were very quickly confirmed, and the duo faced a firing squad at Locre on 6 February. Both the battalion war diary[36] and General Routine Orders[37] recorded the executions, but a rumour circulated that one man had not died instantly – and was eventually killed by a third volley.[38] Given that the story was true, it seems almost certain that the firing squad had been reluctant to shoot the young Joseph Byers, choosing deliberately to fire wide. Privates Byers and Evans are buried side-by-side in Locre Churchyard just yards from the Franco-Belgian border.

The month of January 1915 was also unusual for another soldier serving in 1 Royal Scots Fusiliers. The circumstances of the case are unique, and all the material facts have not come to light – however the soldier concerned was lucky to survive the war.

William Mitchell enlisted in the Royal Scots Fusiliers on 15 November 1906 and after the war broke out proceeded overseas on 6 October 1914 with 2 Battalion[39]. For a reason that is not clear, after a short period of service Mitchell was transferred to 1 Battalion.

Early in 1915 Private Mitchell ran away from the trenches during hostile operations, but was later captured. On 15 January he was tried on charges of both absence and cowardice before being sentenced to death. The resourceful soldier however escaped from custody, and denied the firing squad its prey.[40] Quite how long the private remained at liberty is not known, but it was almost certainly a number of months, maybe even years. The circumstances under which the soldier returned to duty are unknown, but it is clear that he subsequently served honourably.

During the time that Private Mitchell was absent the Suspension of Sentences Act came into being and it seems almost certain that upon his return to service, the soldier received the benefit of the Act's provisions. The official record (which it is believed was compiled in September 1916) states against the soldier's name, 'Escaped from custody. No intimation yet as to whether sentence [of death] is carried out'.[41]

In fact Private Mitchell never faced the firing squad, but he did not survive the war unscathed. In 1919 he was issued with a Silver Wound Badge for 'Services Rendered' during the Great War, the private having been discharged as 'no longer physically fit for war service',[42] on 6 April 1919.[43] Aged 32 on his discharge, William Mitchell was the only soldier to have cheated the firing squad.

On 30 January a private from 2 Royal Warwickshire Regiment was tried for desertion, although the evidence might well have warranted a charge of cowardice. Some considerable time previously, on 24 October, **Private A Pitts** had left his battalion and made off whilst under fire near the village of Zonnebeke – in the Ypres Salient.[44] Lying low, the private made his way to the coast, hoping to get to England. When he was captured at Boulogne on 12 January he gave false particulars in a vain attempt to avoid detection, but he was soon returned to his battalion to face a court martial. On 8 February Private Pitts was shot in Rue Bataille near Sailly-sur-la-Lys.[45] The location of his grave was subsequently lost and he is commemorated on the Ploegsteert Memorial.

At the end of January written orders, issued by the staff of 1 Division, showed that absenteeism was causing considerable administrative difficulties. The problem arose because soldiers were being reported as absentees, when in fact they had been attached to other units. In order to alleviate this problem, orders were given that at the end of each month units would submit details of all absentees to the APM. Subsequently, at the beginning of each of the following months, a list of such men would be circulated.[46]

Early in February five soldiers from 1 Cheshire Regiment were charged with quitting their posts. **Corporal George Povey,** together with four privates under his command, had been in a position in the front line near Wulverghem.[47] During the early hours of darkness on 28 January a German patrol had crossed no-man's-land, grabbed a sentry's rifle and escaped. In the following minutes, as rifle fire broke out, a rumour circulated that the Germans were actually in the British trenches. As a result Corporal Povey and his four men fled back to the support trench.

At their trial the group maintained that they had departed after hearing a shout to clear out as they had been overrun. When it was discovered that the British lines had not been overwhelmed Corporal Povey and the others were arrested. 23 year old Povey was sentenced to death and shot on 11 February,[48] and the privates were sent to prison.[49] After the execution had been carried out it was rumoured that the five had been asleep, and had been startled by the approaching German patrol [50] – which could have accounted for the party's panicky flight. As Corporal Povey has no known grave he is commemorated on the Menin Gate Memorial.

On 20 January 1915 2 Welsh Regiment were engaged in digging second line trenches near Béthune. Snow fell during the morning and in the appalling weather the regimental goat died of heart failure.[51] During the evening **Lance-Corporal William Price** and **Private Richard**

**Morgan** of 'C' Company got drunk and shot their Company Sergeant-Major.

Price was aged 41. Morgan was 32 – the same age as the victim, CSM Hayes. All of the men were old soldiers, with Hughie Hayes having enlisted as a boy soldier at the age of fourteen, before seeing action in the Boer War. Hayes' army service, of eighteen and a half years, ended when he succumbed to his injuries the day after he had been shot. (Béthune Town Cemetery register, gives CSM Hayes' cause of death as died of 'accidental injuries'.) On 28 January papers were sent to Corps HQ for consideration of charges of murder against the two men.[52] Under instructions from 1 Corps a General Court Martial was ordered for 6 February to hear the case.

The trial commenced at Lillers at 10 am with Captain Lyttleton, (Staff Captain, 5 Brigade) acting as prosecutor and with Brigadier-General Lowther presiding. Other court martial members were furnished from 1 Division. After considering the evidence guilty verdicts were returned and sentences of death passed. The Reverend Harry Blackburne (who later became the Canon of Windsor) was serving as a chaplain in 1 Division at the time. He had attended the men before their trial and did so again at their execution. Blackburne recalled how at the execution, he read the story of the Prodigal Son and prayed before the sentences were carried out.[53] All three men, the victim and his murderers, are buried in Béthune Town Cemetery. In 1929 an account by Robert Graves in *Goodbye To All That*, maintained that the company sergeant-major had been shot accidentally. The story continues that the two soldiers had intended to shoot their platoon sergeant, who it was alleged had been victimising the duo. Graves states that the French military governor was present at the execution and that the pair's last words were 'Stick it, the Welch' – the purported battalion rallying cry. Graves undoubtedly heard of the events second-hand, as he himself only joined the battalion in May 1915, and he described the offenders as two young miners. The same day that this double execution took place, 15 February, a soldier was shot at Locre for desertion. 20 year old **Private George Collins** of 1 Lincolnshire Regiment had been undefended at his trial.

In mid February the Commander-in-Chief expressed his concern about the increasing tendency of courts martial to impose the extreme penalty. In a confidential memorandum he specified a number of details, which in future, would be supplied with the court martial papers. Firstly, he wanted to know about the soldier's character, both as a fighting man and also in general, together with the man's length of service with the BEF. Secondly, the Field-Marshal wanted to know the current state of discipline within the condemned man's unit. Additionally, he wished to know whether the crime had been committed deliberately — with the intention of avoiding a particular duty. And finally, details were required from all reviewing officers commenting on why they thought the sentence should be carried out. The Commander-in-Chief had been at pains to point out that a soldier should not face a death sentence solely because he had gone absent following a drunken spree.[54] By coincidence, it has since been reported that just such a situation arose, immediately after the circulation of this memo.

In March 1915 two soldiers from 1 West Yorkshire Regiment were convicted of desertion and then were shot within a few days of each other. The first, **Lance-Corporal Alfred Atkinson,** deserted whilst in rest; the battalion being under orders to proceed to the front. In January of that year Atkinson had won a sum of money gambling and after a bout of drinking subsequently deserted.[55] After three weeks he was then arrested by the Military Police. At his trial the court was told that Atkinson was a good soldier — and previously of excellent character. As a result his sentence bore a recommendation to mercy. A soldier serving with the battalion at the time later confirmed this opinion, saying that Atkinson was 'a clean, smart , brave soldier, respected by all his comrades'.[56]

When General Sir Horace Smith-Dorrien reviewed the proceedings he was of the opinion that an example was required, and the sentence was confirmed. Labour MP Ernest Thurtle, was later presented with an eyewitness account of the final details:

*'The two men I selected for the firing party went with the adjutant.* [Presumably these two men formed only part of the firing squad.] *When they came back, tough characters though they were supposed to be, they were sick, they screamed in their sleep, they vomited immediately after eating. All they could say was: "The sight was horrible, made more so by the fact that we had shot one of our own men".'*

The other West Yorks deserter was **Private Ernest Kirk.** He too was executed by a firing squad from his own battalion. Both shootings took place at the Asylum at Armentières during the first week of March. The eyewitness again recalled the events:

*'I witnessed a scene I shall never forget. Men I had known for years as clean, decent, self-respecting soldiers, whose only offence was an occasional military "drunk", screamed out, begging not to be made into murderers. They offered me all they had if I would not take them for the job, and finally, when twelve of them found themselves outside, selected for the dreaded firing party, they called me all the names they could lay their tongues to. I remained with the guard for three days, and I leave you to guess what I had to put up with. I am poor, with eight children, I would not go through three more [sic] such sights for £1000.'*[57]

Lance-Corporal Atkinson and Private Kirk are both buried in Chapelle d'Armentières Old Military Cemetery.

In March 1915 a private in 2 Leinster Regiment was shot for desertion; and the soldier had also been court martialled for being drunk and disorderly. **Private Thomas Hope** had joined his battalion in September 1914 and remained with it for just over two months before deserting on 23 December. At the time the soldier was in the front line trenches at L'Epiniette and had been detailed to fetch rations from a dump in the rear.[58] It was snowing,[59] and Hope never returned from this task but was captured some six weeks later on 9 February – only a short distance away in Armentières. The private had adopted an unusual disguise, as he was arrested whilst masquerading as a lance-corporal of the Military Police, and had initially refused to give his name. At his trial, on 14 February, Hope told the court that whilst returning with the rations he had been captured by the enemy, successfully escaped, and had crossed back to the British lines. Private Hope was the second soldier to be executed who claimed such a feat. The accused explained away his presence in Armentières by saying that he was looking for his battalion. Significantly the young soldier was not defended at his trial.[60]

A more plausible reason for the private's desertion emerged when he informed the court that he had gone absent on impulse after hearing that his two brothers had been killed in action. (Private Hope was the first of a number of offenders who claimed that the death of a relative had contributed to the commission of their offence. However, research has shown that many deserters, executed in similar circumstances, did not make this fact known to the court.) Hope's record weighed heavily against him when it was revealed that he had two previous convictions for absence without leave. One in Cambridge, for which he had received 56 days' field punishment no.1, and on a second occasion (in France) for going absent during a march, for which he received months field punishment. As if the outlook was not bleak enough, the commanding officer, Major Bullen-Smith, appended a damning indictment to the proceedings, stating that Hope had made his mind up not to serve creditably and avoided all military duty. It was an example of just how influential a reviewing officer's opinion could be. On 27 February the soldier's fate was sealed when Sir John French confirmed the sentence of death.[61] Private Hope, aged 20, was executed on 2 March. The grave was not located after the war, but his name is commemorated on the Ploegsteert Memorial.

On 6 March a deserter from 2 Border Regiment was shot. His place of capture was a clear indication that he intended to soldier no more. **Private James Briggs** went absent on 20 January while his battalion were out of the line in rest. Later that same day they moved up into the trenches,[62] whilst Briggs quickly caught a train to the coast and 'stowed away' in the hold of a mail boat due to sail from Le Havre. His arrest came just two days after his flight and when questioned, he told a story about being directed from a hospital at Rouen, on to a hospital ship.[63] These details, brought out at his trial, were also complemented by a charge of escaping; and in due course the sentence of death was confirmed. Like the majority of previous executions the condemned man faced a firing squad of men from own battalion. An eyewitness recorded that Briggs displayed no fear and that, 'he marched to his death with a soldier's heart'.[64] The execution took place at 7.30 am on 6 March. After the war Private Briggs' grave was not found but his name is recorded on Le Touret Memorial.

On the following day **Private John Duncan** of 1 Cameron Highlanders faced a firing squad. The execution, like Private Ward's in 1914, was unusual in that it took place in the late afternoon – on this occasion at 5.30 pm.[65] Duncan, a Glaswegian, was an Army Reservist who had deserted after only one week in action. The soldier's name appears in the official casualty returns, recorded as died of wounds,[66] although he was killed by a firing squad from his own battalion.[67] After the war Private Duncan's grave was not found and he is commemorated on Le Touret Memorial.

March 1915 saw the first case of a soldier being executed where there would seem to be evidence that the condemned man was suffering from shellshock. Medical knowledge did not generally recognise the condition at the time, and **Lance-Sergeant William Walton** of 2 King's Royal Rifle Corps was doomed as a result. Walton, a veteran of the Battle of Mons, had deserted after the first Battle of Ypres in 1914. After about a month he took refuge in the house of a civilian in a small village near St Omer. Appearing to be wounded in the hand, he had called at the house and begged to be given a bed. At the beginning of March, as the result of a tip-off, Walton was arrested. Under interrogation he appeared to have difficulty in answering even elementary questions, but he eventually made a statement to the effect that he had undergone a nervous breakdown. At his court martial he repeated this defence – but to no avail for he was sentenced to death. Although medical observations were eventually ordered to be kept on the sergeant it is doubtful whether much examination actually took place.[68] Medical and military authorities seemed unsympathetic to his plight and he was shot on 23 March. Sergeant Walton, the most senior NCO to have been shot to date, was aged 26, and was buried in Longuenesse (Souvenir) Cemetery at St Omer.

# NOTES

1 WO93/49, Summary of First World War capital court martial cases.
2 Brigadier-General Count Gleichen, *The Doings of the Fifteenth Infantry Brigade*.
3 Major-General Sir Wyndham Childs, *Episodes and Reflections*.
4 Brigadier-General Count Gleichen, op cit.
5 Copies appear in WO95/25, War Diary of the Adjutant-General, GHQ.
6 Records of the General Register Office, London.
7 CAB 45/206. Diary of Sir Horace Smith-Dorrien.
8 WO95/25, op cit.
9 Anthony Babington, *For the Sake of Example*.
10 WO95/1361, Battalion War Diary.
11 Ernest Thurtle's pamphlet, *Shootings at Dawn*.
12 WO329/1, Index to the *Great War Medal Rolls*.
13 WO93/49, op cit.
14 Anthony Babington, op cit.
15 WO95/25, op cit.
16 WO329/1, op cit.
17 WO93/49, op cit.
18 Anthony Babington, op cit.
19 WO95/25, op cit.
20 *The Burgoyne Diaries*, published by Thomas Harmsworth.
21 Brigadier Sir J E Edmonds & Captain G C Wynne, *Military Operations France & Belgium, 1915*, Volume 1
22 Anthony Babington, op cit.
23 WO95/1680, War Diary of Adjutant-General, 8 Division.
24 *The Burgoyne Diaries*, op cit.
25 WO95/646, War Diary of Adjutant-General, II Corps.
26 Anthony Babington, op cit.
27 Ibid.
28 WO95/25, op cit.
29 WO93/49, op cit.
30 WO95/646, op cit.
31 WO95/1416, War Diary of 8 Brigade HQ.
32 WO329/2442, *1914 Star Medal Roll*.
33 Records of birth suggest that Byers was 17-years-old.
34 WO329/2442, *1914 Star Medal Roll*, gives the date of Private Byers' landing in France as 5 December 1914. The date of his enlistment has been deduced from known dates for soldiers with very close army numbers. There is no doubt that both dates are correct.
35 Anthony Babington, op cit.
36 WO95/1432, Battalion War Diary.
37 Copies can be seen in WO95/1449, War Diary of Adjutant-General, 4 Division.
38 *The Burgoyne Diaries*, op cit.
39 WO329/1, op cit. − note that Private Mitchell has two record cards.
40 WO93/49, op cit.
41 Ibid.
42 King's Regulations No.392 xvia − this included unfitness for medical reasons.
43 WO329/3036, *Silver Wound Badge Roll*.
44 WO93/49, op cit.
45 WO95/1636, War Diary of Adjutant-General, 7 Division.
46 WO95/1275, War Diary of 3 Brigade HQ.
47 WO95/1571, Battalion War Diary.
48 WO329/1001, *British War & Victory Medal Roll* states that Povey was also reduced to the rank of private for his crime.
49 Anthony Babington, op cit.
50 Memoirs of Lieutenant T E Rogers, Imperial War Museum, reference IWM, DS/MISC/81.
51 WO95/1281, Battalion War Diary.
52 WO95/1235, War Diary of Adjutant-General, 1 Division.
53 Harry W Blackburne DSO, MC, *This Also Happened on the Western Front*.
54 WO95/1091, A copy of the memorandum exists in the War Diary of Adjutant-General, Indian Corps.
55 Account given to Ernest Thurtle, and published in his pamphlet, *Shootings at Dawn*.

56 Ibid.
57 Ibid.
58 Anthony Babington, op cit.
59 WO95/1612, Battalion War Diary.
60 WO93/49, op cit.
61 Hansard, 20 January 1916.
62 WO95/1655, Battalion War Diary.
63 WO93/49, op cit.
64 Diary of an unidentified soldier of the Border Regiment. Imperial War Museum reference: Misc 550.
65 WO95/25, op cit.
66 *Soldiers Died in the Great War*, part 66.
67 Craig-Brown Papers, *Army Quarterly*, Volume 102 No.1.
68 Anthony Babington, op cit.

# Chapter Two

## *Lead us not into temptation*

During the second quarter of 1915 the execution rate dropped. Nineteen men had faced firing squads during the first three months, but this figure fell to fourteen between the beginning of April and the end of June. Excluding the soldiers who had deserted in 1914, those soldiers who were executed early in the new year had gone absent through a lack of resolve. No major engagements had taken place during the opening months – although winter in the trenches was an unprecedented hardship. The first deserter to be shot in 1915 as a result of any new initiative might equally well have been charged with cowardice. The execution took place in April.

Regimental pride would seem to have had little utility when yet another Guardsman fell victim to a harsh military regime. This time the battalion concerned was 2 Scots Guards. **Private Isaac Reid** had deserted during the attack on Neuve Chapelle on 11 March, before being discovered in the rear a few hours later. Evidence given at his  court martial reported that when questioned about his absence he had been inconsistent in his answers. Without any officer to assist him in his defence the court heard the soldier admit to losing his head during the fighting, before further stating that he regretted his actions. Reid's character was described as very good but adversely it was added that he was not a good fighter. Mercy was recommended – but none transpired.[1] The execution took place on Friday 9 April.

A graphic account was later published describing the scene as Private Reid was taken across the green at Laventie and executed against a tree[2]. The Guards were paraded to watch the execution and Reid's company commander was in charge of the battalion firing squad. (Stephen Graham's book, *A Private in the Guards* confuses a number of issues about Reid's offence. This is understandable because Graham was not serving with the battalion at the time of the soldier's death. Obviously he heard of the events second-hand. However, the details given concerning the execution appear accurate.) Reid was buried in Laventie Communal Cemetery and a few days later details of his execution appeared in General Routine Orders – where his name was incorrectly spelt as Reed.[3] In the 1950's the shortage of space for civilian burials at Laventie caused his body (together with the remains of 13 other men) to be exhumed and re-interred at St Omer.

**Lance-Corporal Joseph Fox** was the second soldier from 1 Wiltshire

Regiment to be executed during the war. Unlike the previous victim (in 1914) Fox was a young man of 20 attached to 3 Division Cyclists' Company when he deserted.[4] He was tried during April 1915 and executed at Dickebusch on the 20th of that month. Lance-Corporal Fox came from Chippenham and was buried in Dickebusch New Military Cemetery – Belgium. His grave carries the inscription, *'In loving memory of our dearly beloved Son, Gone but not forgotten'*. Fox is also commemorated in Chippenham on the Parish Church Roll of Honour and on the town War Memorial, suggesting that his parents were not told the true circumstances surrounding their son's death. At the time, however, the official army policy was to inform relatives of the true cause of death, and also to specify the offence.[5] On several further dates this policy was reviewed, although the military authorities were in somewhat of a dilemma, being divided over the type of notification to be used.

On the same day that Fox was executed another NCO of the same rank had been shot for desertion a number of miles further south. **Lance-Corporal William Irvine** served with 1 King's Own (Royal Lancaster Regiment) and had enlisted in July 1914. After two months training Irvine was drafted to France in mid-September,[6] but deserted a month later on 13 October, after his battalion had been in action at Meteren.[7] The soldier then made his way to Boulogne where he gave himself up to the authorities on 28 December. The NCO escaped from custody on 21 January and, using a false name, stayed at various addresses until he was arrested in Boulogne on 31 January. Irvine was a desperate, resourceful character and whilst awaiting court martial he escaped yet again – on 18 March.[8] At his eventual trial by Field General Court Martial Irvine faced two additional charges besides desertion – these were, stealing goods (the property of a comrade), and when in lawful custody attempting to escape. After spending his nineteenth birthday in custody Irvine was finally executed.

On 28 October 1914, two weeks after Irvine had initially gone absent, another soldier from his battalion had gone missing. **Private James Kershaw** was a regular soldier and had served in India before the war. Having fought in early engagements in 1914, Kershaw decided that enough was enough, and he deserted from his billet at Chapelle d'Armentières the day before his battalion was due to go back into the line.[9] The private then remained absent for a month, until detained on 29 November.

Kershaw seemed to have the same slippery abilities as his comrade Irvine, and whilst under arrest at Armentières he escaped on 3 December – after just five days in captivity. The fugitive decided that Paris was possibly a safe haven, but was arrested in the city on 2 January 1915. Still in the capital, he escaped again, only to be recaptured whilst using a false name. The prisoner was then taken to Rouen where he escaped for a third time on 11 February.

Like many of the more successful deserters Kershaw kept on the move, travelling northwards until he reached the Channel port of Calais. Here, on 26 February, his luck finally ran out when he was arrested for the last time, yet again using a false identity.[10] At his trial Kershaw claimed that he had a history of nervous trouble and heart failure.[11] Despite a medical examination, the soldier's fate had been sealed by his catalogue of ingenious escapes. Like his comrade, he too was condemned to be shot. Irvine and Kershaw, fellow soldiers in the same regiment, are both buried at Le Grand Beaumont British Cemetery, France.

Throughout the remainder of the war, the graves of those men who were executed have largely survived and only a small number are now lost. Those that have no known grave are commemorated on the appropriate 'Memorial to the Missing'.

The month of April 1915 also saw the first executions of artillerymen — dispelling any possible speculation that offenders from the infantry were alone in risking the extreme penalty for serious offences. **Gunner William Jones** of 43 Battery, Royal Field Artillery was shot for desertion on 20 April and five days later **Driver John Bell** of 57 Battery, Royal Field Artillery was shot for the same offence.[12]

The theory that one man could be selected to be shot as an example to others would seem to have been unsustainable when, on 22 April, the fifth double execution of the war took place. The condemned men, both privates from 1 Royal Welsh Fusiliers, had been convicted of desertion. Their names were **Private Penn** and **Private Troughton**. Penn had the rather unusual forename name of Major.

In May a further execution for murder took place after a Corporal killed a Lance-Corporal by shooting him in the back. **Acting Corporal Alexander Chisholm**, of 20 Army Troop Company Royal Engineers,[13] had been in charge of a small work force which included Lance-Corporal Robert Lewis, of 1 (Glamorgan) Fortress Company, REs. Whilst working at an aerodrome, Lewis who was a carpenter, fell out with Chisholm, who although in charge, was unskilled. Further animosity arose one lunch-time when Lewis blamed Chisholm for the loss of their billet. Lewis then accused Chisholm of falsifying pay records. Fellow Sappers from the same work detail were witnesses to the taunting. Whether Chisholm had been signing for other men's money was never revealed, but shortly before 1 pm on 4 May Chisholm shot Lewis outside the Estaminet du Pelican, in Bailleul. Mortally wounded, Lewis died 24 hours later. Although 31 year old Chisholm was sentenced to be hanged,[14] his death certificate indicates that he was shot.[15] The execution taking place at the Asylum in Armentières. The following month Chisholm received a posthumous Mention in Despatches revealing that prior to his offence he had been a good soldier.[16]

The second capital case for cowardice, and the first to occur in 1915, took place in May. **Private Oliver Hodgetts** of 1 Worcestershire Regiment was a regular soldier who had served on the Western Front since November 1914. His battalion had gained the distinction of being able to claim that it carried out the first 'trench raid' of the war — on 3 January 1915.

On the other hand the reluctant soldier left much to be desired. On two occasions — one during the Battle of Neuve Chapelle — Hodgetts had gone missing in the heat of battle. No retribution was meted out to the soldier, and on 9 May, prior to the attack on Festubert, he again went missing as his battalion prepared to go into action. On 12 May the private reported to a nearby unit claiming to have sprained his ankle, but when the doctor examined Hodgetts no injury was discovered.[17] Hodgetts was brought to trial on 22 May when the 20 year old was undefended.[18] His conduct sheet showed that he had been sentenced to 90 days' field punishment no.1 on 1 March of that year. His Commanding Officer Major G W St G Grogan (later Brigadier-General and holder of the Victoria Cross), added a damning comment to the proceedings by describing Hodgetts as a worthless fighting soldier — only intent on saving his own skin. Grogan also drew attention to Hodgetts' previous absences. Sir John French confirmed the sentence which was carried out on 4 June.

Later that month another young soldier — on this occasion aged 19 — was executed for desertion. **Private George Roe's** battalion, 2 King's Own Yorkshire Light Infantry, was amongst those that had seen heavy fighting in the Ypres Salient in 1915. After fighting on Hill 60 shortly after its capture the battalion was rushed to the very furthest extremity of the British line in a last-ditch attempt to withstand the German onslaught following the enemy's first use of poison gas. In the aftermath only 250 ranks remained, yet two days after the loss of Hill 60, two depleted companies were once again thrown into action on the Hill. No men came back, they were all either killed or taken prisoner.[19]

Such was the experience of Private Roe who had been on the Western Front since November.[20] Yet again, Roe's was a case in which a soldier was undefended at his trial. The court heard that until recently the private had been a good soldier with a character to match, and his Commanding Officer, Major C E Heathcote, added that Roe seemed to have lost his nerve. Following his conviction Roe was executed by a firing squad from 1 Royal West Kents, at 5 am on 10 June at Dickebusch Huts.[21] His body was buried nearby, but after the war was re-interred at Perth (China Wall) Cemetery, Zillebeke.

Two days previously the British had assumed control of the whole of the Ypres Salient. June was the only month during 1915 when no new divisions were sent to the Western Front — the current strength of the BEF being 22 infantry divisions. The low-lying ground in the Ypres Salient swiftly gained an evil reputation amongst soldiers during the First World War and it is not difficult to see why. During June another soldier fell victim to the firing squad; this time for cowardice during a gas attack. **Private Herbert Chase** had served with 2 Lancashire Fusiliers since the outbreak of war. He deserted shortly afterwards but was arrested in October only to escape; managing to avoid recapture until December. At his trial in January he was sentenced to three years' imprisonment, which he was serving when the sentence was suspended at the beginning of May.

Chase was sent back to his battalion, which had been posted to the Salient shortly after the first poison gas attack. On 23 May, after less than three weeks with his unit, the battalion was manning a support trench near Shell Trap Farm[22] when Chase complained to the men in his section that he felt unwell. At 2.45 am the next day the Germans launched a gas attack, following which Chase could not be found. A short while later the private was discovered a few miles behind the lines in a dazed and exhausted condition, lying by the side of the road. He was taken to a nearby dressing station where a doctor checked the soldier and declared him to be free from the effects of gas poisoning.[23] When these facts were reported a court martial was convened on 29 May and Chase was tried. His execution took place on 12 June at the St Sixtus Monastery, Proven.[24] Today visitors, on guided tours of the Monastery, are shown the place of execution, and the bullet marks against the Monastery Wall;[25] but until now the identity of the victim has been a mystery. Private Chase was a 21 year old Londoner from Fulham who was buried near the Monastery; but after the war was re-interred at White House Cemetery, St Jean.

A year later another soldier was shot for an offence committed in the Salient under almost identical circumstances.

In the middle of June 1915 a soldier was executed who had been absent since shortly after the earliest fighting of the war. Like the first soldier to be executed during the war (Thomas Highgate), the man was a private in 1 Royal West Kents. Both men shared the same forename, and had enlisted in 1913. **Private Thomas Harris** had been absent for nine months before being captured in May 1915 by the Military Police in Paris. At his trial on 12 June, Harris told the court that the sights he had seen at Mons and Le Cateau were more than his nerves could stand and he asked for leniency. (Army records indicate that Harris had previously been sentenced to 2 years' imprisonment with hard labour for absence − however, it is not clear how this could have come about unless he had been convicted pre-war.[26] The court were unsympathetic and his brigade commander, Brigadier-General C C M Maynard was later to comment that he considered the case a bad one and recommended that the sentence be carried out.[27]

Private Harris, aged 21, from Gravesend, was executed in the Ypres Salient on 21 June. In the same manner as Thomas Highgate, Private Harris is recorded in the official casualty lists − his cause of death being somewhat ambiguously given as 'Died'. [28] No other men were executed from this regiment for any offence, throughout the rest of the war.

In June 1915 the case of a private in 2 Leicester Regiment gave the impression that service in the trenches was not a prerequisite for a deserter. **Private Ernest Beaumont** absented himself on 14 March from a reinforcement draft travelling from Le Havre to his battalion. He was arrested in nearby Rouen on 4 May[29] although his court martial was delayed until 11 June. His battalion which was serving in France formed part of 7 Indian Division, and the soldier's execution took place on 24 June. In fact, as Private Beaumont made his way out of Le Havre he was merely re-joining his unit. Official records show that he had been in France since the previous October.[30] Private Beaumont was aged 27 and came from Cambridge. He is buried in St Vaast Post Military Cemetery, Richebourg L'Avoue, where the headstone on his grave carries the inscription, *'Gone but not forgotten'*.

During the first quarter of 1915 the average age of the soldiers being executed was 24.7 years. (This statistic has been calculated from the known ages of 15 out of a total of 19 soldiers who were shot.) During the period starting in April until the end of June the average fell to 22.3 years. (This statistic is based on the known ages of 11 of the 14 men.) Taking 1915 as a whole, the average age during this period was just over 25 years, although a good number of the convicted men (14) were under the age of majority.

In 1914 men had flocked to the colours in response to Lord Kitchener's call and in July 1915 the execution of a second such volunteer took place.[31] **Private William Turpie** enlisted on 9 September 1914 and had been posted to a Regular Army unit − 2 East Surrey Regiment − on

23 December 1914.[32] At the time that the volunteer went missing the battalion was serving in the Ypres Salient.

On 10 April whilst Private Turpie's battalion was marching up from Vlamertinghe to the trenches at Zonnebeke,[33] he was slowly making his way on foot to Boulogne. On the advice of a sailor he went to the British Consulate, where he managed to obtain a pass authorising his return to England.[34] However, during the Channel crossing Turpie changed into civilian clothing and threw his uniform overboard.[35] On his arrival at the port of Dover he evaded detection by the military authorities and took up lodgings at the Seamen's Rest Hostel in the town. The soldier spent two nights at the hostel before being arrested late one evening by Police Constable Stanford at the Priory Railway Station in Dover. He gave the police his correct name and address, but told them that he was a fireman on board a ship that crossed from Leith to Dunkirk. The absentee elaborated on this story by saying that his ship had been shelled out of Dunkirk and had been compelled to call at Boulogne, and that subsequently he had obtained a pass from the British Consul before returning to England. Detaining Turpie, the police made enquiries at his home address, and after further questioning Turpie admitted to being a deserter. Two days after his arrest Dover magistrates ordered that Turpie be handed over to a military escort and returned to his unit.[36]

At the court martial he faced on his return to Flanders, Turpie was unable to recall many details of the circumstances under which he had deserted, but he told the court that he had been infected with lice and sores and was receiving medication for dysentery when he decamped. However, no details have survived to suggest that the court made Turpie undergo any medical examination. Could Turpie's vagueness at his trial suggest that he was suffering from shellshock and may not have been responsible for his actions? At the very least, he seemed to have been in a physically debilitated condition. However, the court was unsympathetic.

An eyewitness recalled Turpie's execution – which took place on 1 July.[37] Twelve men were detailed to form the firing squad, three soldiers from each of the battalions in Turpie's brigade. The remainder of the four battalions were paraded in a hollow square to hear details of the offence and sentence announced by Turpie's Commanding Officer.[38] After the East Surrey's Colonel had finished his recital, the execution took place. Turpie, aged 24, was buried near Dickebusch, but later re-interred at White House Cemetery, St Jean. On the same day, 1 East Surrey Regiment was paraded to hear that four men in their battalion had been convicted of sleeping at their posts and were sentenced to death.[39] These sentences however, had been commuted. Exactly one year after Turpie's execution thousands of fellow Kitchener volunteers went to their deaths as the great Somme offensive opened with disastrous results.

On the day following Turpie's execution a Reservist with many years' previous service was tried for cowardice in the third and final such capital case to occur during 1915. **Rifleman Bellamy** originally joined the King's Royal Rifle Corps in 1898, but after several years' service had been transferred to the Reserve. When the war broke out he was called up and, in November 1914, was drafted overseas to 1 Battalion.[40] Bellamy's unit had taken part in the first large scale night-time operation during the war. At 11.30 pm on 15 May, 1 King's Royal Rifle Corps had advanced to the attack in the Battle of Festubert − in a sortie involving three brigades. One month after this attack, Bellamy found himself in trouble.

At the time of the offence 1 Battalion was serving in the trenches south of La Bassée, in an area that was the scene of constant mining activity.[41] Early in the morning of 24 June the Germans blew a mine under part of the battalion's trench system. The British rushed reinforcements to bolster the damaged defences and rapid rifle was ordered on the enemy lines. Bellamy, who was in a dugout, refused to come out and continued to remain below. On several occasions he was ordered to leave his dugout but each time he refused to obey.[42] At his trial the court heard that the soldier had told his platoon sergeant that he felt too shaky to stand on the fire-step. In his defence Bellamy said that the explosion of the mine had rendered him unaware of what he was doing and that, on two occasions in the past, he had suffered from nervous exhaustion. Whilst awaiting confirmation of the sentence of death Bellamy went before a medical board, but they were unable to detect any abnormal condition in the 34 year old.[43] At 3 am on 16 July 1 King's Royal Rifle Corps were paraded at the small village of Le Quesnoy, as final preparations were made for the execution. Bellamy's comrades did not see the execution, but a soldier recorded that they were still on parade nearby when they heard the fatal volley.[44] His body, which was buried near to the place of execution, was moved after the war to Brown's Road Military Cemetery, Festubert.

On the day before Rifleman Bellamy's execution the National Registration Act became law. Under its provisions every man and woman between the ages of 15 and 65 years of age had to register. Clearly the Government was fully aware that the supply of volunteers was diminishing. But the demand that women should also register, and that both sexes should register up to the ages of 65, is indicative that more than just recruiting was at issue. And the Government seized the opportunity to carry out an impromptu census. Registration commenced one month after the bill became law, and with great haste was completed just one month later – in mid-September. Whilst the statistics were being evaluated, one last scheme was brought forward under which men could voluntarily enlist.

In July 1915 another regular soldier claimed that the prolonged effects of warfare had unbalanced him. **Private Thomas Docherty** enlisted in  King's Own Scottish Borderers in June 1914, and had served with 2 Battalion since the early days at Mons.[45] Whilst in the Ypres Salient in February 1915 his brigade had been transferred to the newly arrived 28 Division. And during the following month, while under a heavy enemy bombardment, the private had deserted from the front line. Docherty remained at liberty for three months before being arrested, and during his absence avoided some of the worst fighting in the Ypres Salient during 1915. His battalion was in action twice on Hill 60, and between assaults helped repel the Germans who launched several poison gas attacks.

At his trial Docherty told the court that a shell had narrowly missed him, and that he had lost his memory and must have wandered off in a daze. His commanding officer described him as a well behaved individual, but added that Docherty was not particularly intelligent. The relevance of this comment is not clear, but whether the absentee's story was fact or fiction the court was unimpressed and he was executed on 16 July.

July also saw the trial and execution of a young soldier under very tragic circumstances. **Private Herbert Burden** added two years to his  real age in order to enlist in the Northumberland Fusiliers. He was really only 16 years old, but he told the recruiting officer that he was 18.[46] After training he was drafted to the first battalion of his regiment on 24 March, just before his seventeenth birthday.

In the summer of 1915, Burden's battalion was serving in the Ypres Salient, and while the unit was suffering enormous losses on Bellwarde Ridge in June, the young soldier had deserted. His freedom however was short-lived and he was court martialled on 2 July. This mere boy was undefended at his trial and, such were the casualties that had been suffered by his battalion, that no survivor from their depleted ranks could be found to give the youth a character reference.[47] Soldiers in his unit had been desperate to escape from the horrors of trench warfare and during the month of July the first case of a self-inflicted wound occurred in the battalion.[48] This involved a Kitchener volunteer and within the month two other volunteers emulated him.

Burden was executed on 21 July, although if deserting His Majesty's service was a capital offence, self-inflicted wounds were not, and during the following month four further cases occurred. Three were regular soldiers and one was a volunteer. (This pattern did not continue in later months.) For unexplained reasons Private Burden has neither a known grave nor is he commemorated on a memorial to the missing.[49] There is no indication, however, that this may have been anything other than an oversight.

If the initial capital cases of July 1915 are considered to be unfortunate and harsh, then the closing days almost exceed belief. With the benefit of hindsight it is difficult to imagine what was going through the mind of the Commander-in-Chief when he set the wheels in motion for what was to become the biggest execution the British Army would ever experience.[50] The five men condemned to be shot were all deserters, and what is extraordinary is that they were all from the same battalion. The theory that a single soldier could be shot for the sake of example would seem to have had no bearing in these cases. The battalion concerned was 3 Worcestershires and the most senior offender was an NCO.

**Corporal Frederick Ives** had gone absent on 15 September 1914 during the fighting on the Marne.[51] At the time of his offence he was already on remand for another offence, although the NCO had only been in France for just over a month.[52] Ives successfully avoided the military authorities until 24 June 1915, when he was arrested in civilian clothes by an officer from the Army Veterinary Corps.[53] The trial took place on 7 July, and in his defence Ives stated that the shell fire had caused him to lose his memory.[54] The court martial members, all of whom had front line experience, sentenced him to death but recommended mercy on the grounds that he might have been telling the truth — a rather surprising conclusion, that seemed to ignore the usual fatal implications of Ives' civilian dress and the duration of his absence.

The remaining four men from the battalion were tried exactly a week later. **Private Ernest Fellows** was a married man with children. He had re-joined his regiment on 29 September 1914 and was sent to France early in 1915. Anthony Babington maintains that Private Fellows was a volunteer. However, this does not seem at all likely, as his army number is considerably lower than many Regulars. It is far more probable that the soldier was a Reservist. Fellows was well regarded in his battalion — until he went missing in the middle of June. At the time the unit was resting, but orders had just been received that his battalion was to attack the enemy trenches the following morning. However, during evening roll call Fellows was discovered to be absent. At his trial he offered no evidence in his defence.[55]

Two of the deserters had gone absent together. **Private John**

**Robinson,** a Regular soldier with 13 years' previous service had been with the battalion since Mons.[56] His co-deserter, **Private Alfred Thompson,** was also a regular who had joined the battalion at the beginning of November 1914.[57] On 27 June Robinson and Thompson absconded after having been warned for duty that night in the trenches near Hooge — the Worcesters' war diary records that on 16 June the battalion had been in action near the village, where only limited gains had been made.[58] Shortly afterwards, on 5 July, the two men were arrested at Abancourt whilst sitting in a train bound for Rouen.[59] The statements of character that were appended to the court martial proceedings commented that both men were good soldiers, but that it appeared that they were suffering from nervous strain.

The fifth deserter was **Private Bert Hartells**, who had landed in France on 12 August 1914,[60] with the first troops of the BEF.

Matters of Army discipline were the responsibility of the Adjutant-General's Department and serving in the post of Adjutant-General, at GHQ, was Sir Neville Macready. Macready's son was also in the Army, serving as an officer in the Royal Engineers. On 24 April 1915 Lieutenant Gordon Macready had joined 8 Brigade as Staff Captain[61] and, when the Assistant Provost-Marshal fell ill, Macready junior was detailed to officiate at the executions of the aforementioned five men.[62] The officer's recollections about a number of the details are incorrect, but no other eyewitness account is known to exist. Macready maintained that one of the condemned men was an American, and that one was a well known boxer from the North East of England. Neither of these facts have been verified. Macready also stated that all of the offenders had been through ten months of war without a break, and that there were few survivors from the original battalion. Whilst the details about the service of the battalion and its casualties may well be correct, two of the men had been in action for a lesser period than Captain Macready recalled. It was also stated that had the Suspension of Sentences Act been in force at the time, then the men might well have been spared. In fact the Act had been passed on 16 March 1915, and was already in force when Macready joined 8 Brigade.

The five executions took place together on 26 July at the Ramparts at Ypres. It was a wet, windy morning as separate firing parties formed up for the unpleasant ritual. Private Hartells was the oldest at 32. Robinson was a year younger, and Ives a year younger than him. Fellows was 29 and Thompson was 25. Their average ages were five years higher than other soldiers executed in 1915. When the gruesome ritual was over the bodies were buried amongst the Ramparts, along with the many others who fell in the defence of Ypres.

The records of the Commonwealth War Graves Commission, together with the Great War Medal records and the archives of the General

Register Office, London, give the date of Corporal Ives' death as 22 July 1915. However, because Macready's account categorically states that there were five men executed together, and because no other execution on this scale took place, it has been assumed that the true date of Ives' death was in fact 26 July 1915. Similarly the *1914 Star Medal Roll* gives the date of death of Private Thompson as 21 July, whereas his death certificate shows 26 July. It is believed that both these discrepancies are clerical errors.

After the war when the concentration of many isolated graves took place, the five graves became separated, although they remain in the Salient. Corporal Ives and Private Fellows are buried at Perth (China Wall) Cemetery, Zillebeke, and Privates Hartells, Robinson and Thompson are buried at Aeroplane Cemetery, St Jean. The grave of Robinson has the inscription:

*'In loving memory of my dear son deeply mourned by father mother, sisters & brothers'.*

At the beginning of August a volunteer was shot who had accrued virtually as bad an army record as was possible during his period of service. **Private Evan Fraser** had enlisted in Royal Scots early in the war and was drafted to 2 Battalion on 27 December 1914.[63] On 21 April 1915 he was tried by court martial for desertion, and then sentenced to death. Six days later the sentence was commuted to ten years' imprisonment, which was then suspended. The private must have been one of the first soldiers to have been allowed a second chance under the Suspension of Sentences Act. He was certainly the first soldier to be executed who was under a commuted sentence of death.[64]

As a result of this suspension Fraser remained with his battalion under the threat of a ten year prison sentence if he did not behave. However, after a short while when the battalion was under orders to move up to the front line, he absconded. Fraser was arrested two days later in possession of a false pass, but while awaiting trial he escaped, only to be re-captured within 36 hours. On 19 June he again escaped but was seen lurking about a farm the next day. By giving false particulars he avoided detection, but was later confronted in a cottage wearing a cap without badges. Fraser put up a struggle but was successfully detained.[65] At his trial the private faced four charges, three of desertion and one involving a self-inflicted wound. Fraser was aged just 19 and had no 'accused's friend' at the hearing, but was acquitted on one charge of desertion. The young soldier was however found guilty of wounding himself, guilty of absence without leave and guilty of attempting to desert. 24 days elapsed between the court martial findings and Fraser's execution. On average, at the time that Fraser was shot, the period was only two weeks.

Much briefer consideration was given by the confirming authorities when reviewing the case of the first Jewish soldier to be executed. **Private Louis Phillips** lived in the West End of London — although  he had been born at Caistor, and chose to serve in the Somerset Light Infantry. In April 1915 he went to France with a draft of men destined for 6 Battalion who were serving in the Ypres Salient. During sustained and bloody fighting at the end of July he went absent for four days. At his court martial he said in mitigation that he had not received any letters from home for several weeks prior to committing his offence, and that this had caused him grievous concern. Sentencing him to death the court added a recommendation for mercy, on the grounds that Phillips had been suffering from mental worry.[66] Scant consideration was given to this recommendation and, at 4.20 am on 19 August, the Ramparts at Ypres were the scene of yet another execution.[67] Strangely this 23 year old volunteer is not recorded in the official casualty records — *Soldiers Died in the Great War*. Yet the only other soldier from the regiment to be executed (in 1916) is commemorated. A cover-up seems likely because Louis Phillips' death certificate records that he was killed in action. The soldier is also commemorated in the *British Jewry Book of Honour*.

Four days before the death of Private Phillips a captain in 10 Lancashire Fusiliers recorded in his diary that two soldiers serving in Yorkshire regiments had had their death sentences commuted. One man, a private in 7 East Yorks had been convicted of sleeping at his post, the other a ranker in 10 West Yorks, had been charged with using insubordinate language to his superior officer.[68] In fact the captain was mistaken (one would like to hope) as the offence of insubordination was punishable only by penal servitude.[69] Nevertheless the displeasure of the Commander-in-Chief was indicated in the fact that even when their sentences were commuted, both men faced five years in prison. (As well as sentences of death, all awards of penal servitude were also confirmed, or commuted, by the Commander-in-Chief.)

During the final quarter of 1915 the number of soldiers executed declined, continuing the pattern that had developed throughout the year. 17 British soldiers had been executed for military offences on the Western Front during the first three months of the year. This figure had dropped to 13 in the next quarter and then 14 in the third quarter. During the final three months of the year four soldiers were executed — all for desertion. (There were also four executions for murder in 1915 which were not included in the aforementioned figures.)

The first offender to be shot in the closing months of the year was a married NCO from Belfast. **Lance-Corporal Peter Sands** was serving with 1 Royal Irish Rifles (part of 8 Division) who were holding the front line in the low-lying land opposite the Aubers Ridge. No information has come to light about the NCO's offence except that he achieved a rare feat in that he successfully crossed the Channel. It is not known whether he then managed to cross to Ireland, but Sands was only the second deserter to be shot who had escaped from France.[70] The lance-corporal was executed at Fleurbaix on 15 September and his remains were interred in the churchyard there; but after the war the grave was not located. As a result he is commemorated in Cabaret-Rouge Military Cemetery, Souchez, France.

The case of a Kitchener volunteer executed in September revealed a number of aspects hitherto unseen in a capital case. **Private George Mills** was an East End lad who enlisted on 24 February 1915. Amazingly, after just three weeks, service he was dispatched to the Western Front as an officer's servant with 2 Duke of Cornwall's Light Infantry. His duties as a batman did not require him to go into the trenches and whilst his battalion was in the line he took the opportunity to go absent. In the town of Armentières where he was billeted, he stole the uniform of a lieutenant, together with a cheque book and some cash, before making off. Later in the Channel port of Boulogne the soldier was arrested masquerading as an officer.[71] Somewhat unusually Mills was not returned to his unit but was tried at Boulogne. The 21 year old faced charges of desertion, stealing and forgery but declined the assistance of an officer to defend him at his trial.[72] The Londoner declared to the court that he had only intended to slip home for a few days and then hoped to return unnoticed. The court was unimpressed by the soldier's deceptions, for Private Mills was shot at Boulogne on 29 September. It was the first case where the execution had been carried out some distance from the battlefields.

The first artillery men to be executed had been shot in April 1915, and as if to reinforce the point that serving with the artillery required the same adherence to Army Regulations, a further two men, both drivers, were executed in the autumn. Again the executions took place within a few days of each other.

**Driver James Spencer** joined 65 Battery Royal Field Artillery in April 1915 and was considered to be a good soldier. However, on 12 June, he deserted from a forward gun emplacement located about a mile away from the enemy. Spencer did not get far and was arrested on 4 August, and stood trial on 9 September. In reviewing the proceedings his Brigadier quite incorrectly added comments about Spencer's personal record stating that the commanding officer of 65 Battery believed that the convicted man had stolen a considerable sum of money from a ruined house in

Ypres. The Brigadier also speculated to the effect that Spencer had deserted in order to spend the money on wine and women. He concluded that Spencer was a deliberate skulker who should be shot.[73] Because 65 Battery was split up a fortnight before Spencer deserted it has not been possible to identify the Brigadier who appended the damning remarks. By the time that the sentence was confirmed Spencer's battery had moved its position to the Somme − to relieve the French. His execution took place on 29 September and Spencer was buried at Côte 80 French National Cemetery. However, it is possible that the date of the man's execution may be incorrect since Judge Babington maintains that the execution took place on 15 September.

In the second case involving an artilleryman the offender had been absent for eight months. **Driver Alexander Lamb** had been sent to France with a draft bound for 21 Battery, 2 Brigade Royal Field Artillery, in October 1914. On 19 October at Boulogne he absented himself from the train that would have taken him to the front. The soldier's liberty ended on 19 June when he was arrested in Calais, where he had been living with a woman. When searched Lamb was found to have civilian clothing in his possession.[74] For some reason which is not apparent three months passed before Lamb was brought to trial − but within a fortnight the sentence was confirmed and carried out. Driver Lamb was executed at Vlamertinghe, in Belgium, on 2 October.

September saw the trial of two men who had committed offences which had similarities with a number of previous cases, and yet revealed some new aspects. **Rifleman George Lee** and **Rifleman W Smith** enlisted in the Rifle Brigade in April 1915. The two men were old soldiers[75] and consequently were sent to the front after minimal retraining. Both men had served their time on the Army Reserve and in essence were volunteers. Lee had joined up under a false name, his correct surname being Irish, although the Army was not aware of the fact, nor that the 30 year old had served for 12 years in another regiment. Smith was 37, and had served in the Boer War. On 22 August their battalion, 2 Rifle Brigade, was in rest, when the two men got drunk and went absent. Six days later they walked into the British Consulate at Dunkirk and gave themselves up. Lee was dressed in a blue coat and dungarees and in his possession was a workman's pass.[76]

Committing offences when under the influence of drink was a matter with which the pre-war Army was very familiar. Perhaps because it was difficult to accurately distinguish between offenders who were drunk at the time of their offences and others who erroneously believed pleading inebriation would be a good defence, little credence was given to such a mode of defence. It is noteworthy that the two men chose to surrender to the British Consul, given that a previous soldier obtained assistance from the Boulogne Consulate. (See the case of Private Turpie, July 1915.)

At the trial of the two men the court heard that Lee was under a suspended sentence for a previous absence, but in mitigation the rifleman stated that he had a dependent widowed mother. However, after considering the evidence the court martial panel found both men guilty, but attached a recommendation for mercy on account of the men's previous good work in the trenches.[77] In due course the recommendations were ignored and the sentences were confirmed; being carried out on 3 October.[78] Lee's (Irish's) widowed mother lived at Salisbury, but never learned the truth about her son's death. A kindly member of staff at the Infantry Records Office fudged the notification of her son's death and told her that the soldier had been killed in action during the Battle of Loos. (This cause of death is recorded in the register of Sailly-sur-la-Lys Canadian Cemetery, France.)

The question of whether to tell relatives the stark truth when sending a notification in the case of a soldier who had been executed, was a difficult one for the Army to resolve. Later in the war the military authorities considered the issue in detail, but this did not stop an element of compassion being exercised, irrespective of any official War Office directive on the matter.

On 23 October, in the aftermath of National Registration, Lord Derby's scheme of enlistment came into operation. It was the final call for men to join the armed forces voluntarily, before the introduction of conscription. Derby's scheme allowed men either to enlist immediately, or to attest, and then at a later date when called, join their units. The system operated until 15 December by which time 2.1 million men had shown their willingness to serve their country. Unfortunately for the purposes of this book it has not been possible to ascertain whether any soldier who was ultimately executed, had joined under the second provision of this scheme — whereby a soldier could attest, and then later be called to join the Colours. Therefore it is just possible that a few men who in later chapters are labelled conscripts, might in fact have been 'Derby men'.

19 soldiers were executed during the second half of 1915, but only five of these cases occurred in the final three months. Between the beginning of July and the end of September, with one exception — a case of cowardice — all the offenders had been deserters. The average age of these men was 26.

The fourth and final case of murder, during 1915, occurred in November. Unlike previous trials for murder, the case was not heard by General Court Martial but by the less complex procedure — trial by Field General Court Martial. The defendant was a 28 year old Londoner who had volunteered to serve with the Royal Welsh Fusiliers. **Private Charles Knight** was serving with 10 Battalion, and had only spent a few days in the front line — his unit having landed in France five weeks previously.[79] On 3 November, Knight, who was drunk, came into his billet and started firing indiscriminately at men who were members of his platoon. In doing so he shot Private Alfred Edwards dead and wounded another man, before he was arrested by Company Sergeant-Major Fisher. As with previous offenders, the court gave no consideration to the fact that Knight was drunk, nor did they question whether in this inebriated condition the soldier was truly responsible for his actions.[80] Knight's trial took place on 6 November and he was executed nine days later.

The final capital case on the Western Front during 1915 was that of a man who had been absent for almost the whole year. And it was the last death sentence that Sir John French confirmed before he was replaced as Commander-in-Chief. The condemned man was **Private Graham,** a regular soldier with 2 Royal Munster Fusiliers. On 25 January 1915 his battalion had been serving in the front line trenches at Givenchy[81] when, immediately prior to a German attack he went absent. The private remained at liberty until 14 November when he was arrested by the Military Police in a brothel in Béthune.[82] Graham had attempted to disguise his real identity utilising a corporal's chevrons and a false identity disc. He also gave false particulars when questioned.[83] The deserter was tried at Béthune on 9 December, when additional charges of fraud indicated that he had been engaging in other crimes during his absence. The staff of the Adjutant-General, 1 Division, recorded the execution in their war diary, Private Graham being shot at 7.22 am on 21 December in the abbatoir at Mazingarbe.[84] The same bloody killing ground was to be the scene of many more executions before the war ended.

Although most of the bloodshed involving British and French troops during 1915 took place on the Western Front, an Expeditionary Force had also been landed on Turkish territory, and fighting was also taking place in other countries.

At the beginning of July 1915 a private from 'D' Company of West African Regiment was tried on two charges of cowardice together with one of quitting his post.[85] **Private Fatoma's** battalion had been fighting in the Cameroons where the convicted soldier was shot on 19 July.[86]

Earlier in the same month a British soldier serving at Gallipoli had faced a firing squad, although records concerning the individual seem somewhat confused. **Private Thomas Davis** was serving with 1 Royal Munster Fusiliers, a Regular Army battalion – and part of 29 Division. In the early hours of 21 June, Davis had been posted as a sentry to guard his unit's HQ, and during a routine check the duty NCO had been unable to locate the soldier. After an absence of three hours Davis was traced, and later faced a charge of quitting his post. The excuse Davis gave at the trial was that a bowel complaint had caused him to take to the latrines.[87] Although the prevalence of dysentery was considerable on the peninsula, greater account would seem to have been taken of the fact that the private had previously been convicted of other offences committed in the Dardanelles.

21 year old Private Davis was shot on Gully Beach at 5 am on 2 July.[88] Somewhat curiously, the day after his death, one of Davis' previous sentences (which unknown to the private had also been a sentence of death) was commuted to ten years' penal servitude. An account published 69 years after the event recorded that on 5 May 1915 Davis had been sentenced to be shot for cowardice, an offence which, it was stated, had occurred when the Irishman quit his post in the face of the enemy – (on a previous occasion).[89] It must be presumed that the promulgation of the already dead soldier's offence and his sentence, must have been inadvertent. The deceased soldier seems to have neither a known grave nor a memorial to the fact that his 'resting place' is unknown. Rather unusually, the records of medal entitlement do not list Private Davis either.

At around the same time, a New Zealand soldier – Private John R Dunn – was also sentenced to death at Gallipoli.[90] However, before the review procedure could be concluded the soldier had been killed in action.[91] The deceased soldier would seem to have been a strange choice of which to make an example, and such a sentence adds considerable weight to the hypothesis that men sentenced to death were often ill. After Private Dunn's death a diary that he had kept was published. The narrative showed the individual to be quite a cultivated man, and a Catholic who regularly attended confession. The New Zealander would seem to have been a good soldier, especially in action. However, in his diary, which ends a month prior to his death (and prior to his offence) he reports feeling unwell, and that he chose to rest on that day rather than harry the enemy.[92]

In the winter of 1915 the troops of the Mediterranean Expeditionary Force suffered the extremes of a harsh climate, and at this time a second execution took place. The victim, **Private Harry Salter,** came from Bridgwater in Somerset and was serving as a volunteer in 6 East Lancs – the only soldier to be executed in this regiment during the war. The account already published by Judge Babington differs in a number of respects with details discovered by the authors. Babington comments that Salter had landed at Gallipoli at the end of June 1915,[93] however the *Great War Medal Roll* Index states that the soldier arrived on 1 August. [94]

Again, the Judge recounts that Private Salter had deserted from the front line on 1 November, whereas the battalion war diary records that on that date the unit was in reserve trenches on Chocolate Hill, near Suvla Bay.[95] However, there is no disagreement about the fact that Salter had previous convictions – having been sentenced to one year's imprisonment for a previous offence of absence.[96]

At his trial Salter said nothing, but however reluctant the soldier might have been, no restraint was felt by his brigade commander who took the opportunity to speak his mind – to the detriment of the soldier.[97] 24 year old Private Salter was shot on 11 December 1915, just seven days before his battalion left the peninsula for good.

One final soldier, an NCO, was executed before the Dardanelles campaign was abandoned. The case is disturbing to say the least, and highlights those aspects of First World War capital courts martial that were so unjust.

The victim, **Sergeant John Robins,** was a Regular soldier who landed at Gallipoli as a corporal at the end of June 1915.[98] In the early hours of 10 August his battalion – 5 Wiltshires – suffered a disaster when, without warning, they were overrun by the Turks while the men were sleeping in their bivouacs. In the ensuing panic, those men who managed to flee left without their equipment, a situation that compounded their predicament when they found themselves trapped in a gully with no means of defence.[99] Nearly four months later, and after his promotion to sergeant, Robins found himself on trial for his life.

The fatal incident had occurred when the NCO had been ordered to accompany an officer on a patrol. Robins maintained that he was unwell and had refused to go. In consequence the sergeant had been ordered to report to the medical officer. After examining the soldier, the doctor prescribed some medicine and returned him to duty. However, Sergeant Robins maintained that he was still unwell, and he refused to accompany the officer on the patrol.[100]

On 8 December Sergeant Robins was tried on a charge of 'Wilfully disobeying an order given by a superior officer in the execution of his duty'.[101] The NCO still maintained however that he had been unfit for duty, and he related to the court that since serving in India he had suffered from fits which were aggravated by wet weather.[102] Whatever the cause of the sergeant's debility, his battalion's diary showed that during the month of December, 25 per cent of the battalion's strength was on the sick list[103] – adding weight to the likelihood that Robins was also unwell.

At the court martial hearing the doctor who had examined Robins did not give evidence, instead he submitted a written statement. The outcome of this fiasco was, that notwithstanding that the witness could not be cross-examined, this written deposition was improperly admitted as evidence.[104] In this unfortunate case, both medical and legal considerations are shown to be inadequate and illegal, particularly when the desperate soldier sought medical help, only to have the doctor turn prosecution witness. The Judge Advocate-General's department then failed to quash the irregular proceedings.

Sentence of death was promulgated on Sergeant Robins on New Year's day 1916, and at 8 am the following morning the execution took place on the beach at Cape Helles.[105]

A 20 year old serving with the 6 Leinsters in Salonika was the only 10 (Irish) Division soldier to be executed. According to Babington, **Private Patrick Downey** pleaded guilty to disobeying an order – to put on his cap. However, the officer who promulgated the sentence, Colonel F W S Jourdain, stated that the man had refused to enter the trenches. On hearing the sentence Downey was alleged to have laughed, saying, 'That is a good joke. You let me enlist and then bring me out here and shoot me.' He was executed shortly after 6 am on 27 December at DHQ Kerekoj. Hearsay suggests his death provoked uproar in the ranks of his division.[106]

During 1916 two executions took place outside Europe. On 3 April **Private N Mathews** of 3 South African Infantry Regiment, en route for France, was tried by GCM in Egypt and hanged.

The other executed soldier was **Private Aziberi Frafra** serving with the Gold Coast Regiment in German East Africa. Found guilty of casting his arms away in the presence of the enemy, Frafra was shot on 28 September.[107]

**NOTES**

1 Anthony Babington, *For the Sake of Example.*
2 Stephen Graham, *A Private in the Guards.*
3 WO95/25, General Routine Orders: copies of, included in the War Diary of the Adjutant-General at GHQ.

4 Ibid.
5 Army Council Instruction no.144, 14 February 1915.
6 Anthony Babington, op cit.
7 WO95/1506, Battalion War Diary.
8 WO93/49, Summary of First World War capital court martial cases.
9 WO95/1506, op cit.
10 WO93/49, op cit.
11 Anthony Babington, op cit.
12 WO95/25, op cit.
13 WO95/328, War Diary of 20 Army Troop Company, Royal Engineers.
14 Anthony Babington, op cit. As in the previous murder case, a General Court Martial was convened to hear the charge. WO93/49, op cit.
15 Records of General Register Office, London.
16 *London Gazette*, 22 June 1915.
17 Anthony Babington, op cit.
18 WO93/49, op cit.
19 Brigadier Sir J E Edmonds & Captain G C Wynne, *Military Operations France & Belgium, 1915*, Volume 1.
20 WO329/1, Index to the *Great War Medal Rolls*.
21 WO95/1558, War Diary of 2 King's Own Yorkshire Light Infantry.
22 WO95/1506, op cit.
23 Anthony Babington, op cit.
24 The entry in the War Diary of Adjutant-General, 4 Division (WO95/1449) relating to this event has been censored and removed to a 'closed' class WO154/28.
25 Rose Coombs, *Before Endeavours Fade*.
26 WO93/49, op cit.
27 Anthony Babington, op cit.
28 *Soldiers Died in the Great War*, part 53. His death certificate gives the true cause of death, although the country is incorrectly given as France.
29 WO95/181, Copies of General Routine Orders in the war diary of Adjutant-General, 1st Army.
30 WO329/1, op cit.
31 Anthony Babington, op cit. is incorrect about the first Kitchener volunteer to be executed. See the case of Private Byers executed early in 1915.
32 WO329/1, op cit.
33 WO95/2279, Battalion War Diary.
34 Anthony Babington, op cit.
35 WO93/49, op cit.
36 *Dover Standard*, 5 June 1915, 'Soldier's Serious Offence'.
37 Letter from W Barker ex. 2 East Surrey Regiment – Imperial War Museum, BBC Great War Series correspondence.
38 Barker op cit., states in his letter that all four regiments were paraded. At best he must mean battalions, although it would seem more likely that only the four companies in the condemned man's battalion attended.
39 Diary of Lance-Corporal Bolton – Imperial War Museum papers, reference IWM No.P262. These details were also published by Malcolm Brown in *Tommy Goes To War*.
40 Anthony Babington, op cit.
41 WO95/1358, Battalion War Diary.
42 WO95/181, op cit.
43 Anthony Babington, op cit.
44 Diary of Corporal A H Roberts, ex. 1/KRRC, Imperial War Museum reference 81/23/1.
45 Anthony Babington, op cit.
46 Records in the General Register Office, London, show that Burden was born at Lewisham in 1898.
47 WO93/49, op cit.
48 WO95/1430, Battalion War Diary.
49 Records of the Commonwealth War Graves Commission.
50 Following the mutiny by Indian soldiers of the 5 Light Infantry, in February 1915, at least 47 men were publicly executed in mass shootings. These, and similar sentences passed on Indian Forces in Europe and elsewhere, were carried out under the

authority of the Indian Army Act, and the numbers involved have not been included in the British Army's execution statistics. For a definitive account of the 5 Light Infantry affair see R W E Harper & H Miller, *Singapore Mutiny*.

51  WO95/1415, Battalion War Diary.
52  WO329/2451, *1914 Star Medal Roll*.
53  WO93/49, op cit.
54  Anthony Babington, op cit.
55  Ibid.
56  Ibid.
57  WO329/2451, op cit.
58  WO95/1415, op cit.
59  WO93/49, op cit.
60  WO329/2451, op cit.
61  WO95/1416, War Diary of 8 Brigade HQ.
62  Sir Gordon Macready, *In the Wake of the Great*.
63  WO329/1, op cit.
64  WO93/49, op cit.
65  Ibid.
66  Anthony Babington, op cit.
67  WO95/1909, Battalion War Diary.
68  Diary of Captain A H Thomas − private collection.
69  Army Act section 8(2).
70  WO93/49, op cit.
71  Anthony Babington, op cit.
72  WO93/49, op cit.
73  Anthony Babington, op cit.
74  WO93/49, op cit.
75  Anthony Babington, op cit.
76  WO93/49, op cit.
77  Anthony Babington, op cit.
78  WO95/181, op cit.
79  WO95/1436, Battalion War Diary.
80  Anthony Babington, op cit.
81  WO95/1279, Battalion War Diary.
82  WO95/181, op cit.
83  WO93/49, op cit.
84  WO95/1235, War Diary of Adjutant-General, 1 Division.
85  WO93/49, op cit.
86  WO95/5388, Battalion War Diary.
87  Anthony Babington, op cit.
88  WO95/4310, Battalion War Diary.
89  Christopher Pugsley, *Gallipoli: The New Zealand Story*.
90  Ibid.
91  *The Great War 1914-18, New Zealand Expeditionary Force Roll of Honour*.
92  Diary [of] The late Private J R Dunn.
93  Anthony Babington, op cit.
94  WO329/1, op cit.
95  WO95/4302, Battalion War Diary.
96  WO93/49, op cit.
97  Anthony Babington, op cit.
98  WO329/1, op cit.
99  WO95/4303, Battalion War Diary.
100  WO93/49, op cit.
101  WO95/4303, op cit.
102  WO93/49, op cit.
103  WO95/4303, op cit.
104  WO93/49, op cit.
105  WO95/4303, op cit.
106  Anthony Babington, op cit.; Jourdain Diary, National Army Museum; E Rogers, *A Funny Old Quist*; T Bennett (interview).
107  WO93/49, op cit.

## Chapter Three

### *Kitchener's men*

The first soldier to be executed on the Western Front in 1916 was a 19 year old deserter in 1 Northamptonshire Regiment. **Private John Dennis** came from Cheetham Hill near Manchester, and when tried stated in his defence that heavy shelling had affected his mind. However,  this argument did not convince the court who were later to hear that Dennis was under a suspended sentence of two years' imprisonment with hard labour for a previous offence of desertion.[1] (The account given by Judge Babington has maintained that Dennis was of previous good character.) Dennis' trial took place on 3 December and the subsequent 58 day delay in confirming and then carrying out the sentence was the longest of the war. On 19 December 1915 Sir Douglas Haig replaced Sir John French as Commander-in-Chief of the British Expeditionary Force on the Western Front. Private Dennis was the first of 253 soldiers upon whom Haig decided that the sentence of death would be carried out. (Eleven of these 253 death sentences were for murder.) Throughout the delay Private Dennis remained with his unit until at 7.10 am on 30 January 1916 he was executed by a firing squad of ten men from his battalion. The battalion war diary, kept on active service, recorded that it was thought to be the first case of an execution in the regiment since the Peninsular days.[2] Dennis was buried at Lillers Communal Cemetery, France.

On 7 February another regular soldier in 1 Division was shot for desertion. Unlike Private Dennis, who had been under sentence of death for nearly two months, **Private James Carr** of 2  Welsh Regiment was executed just over two weeks after his trial. Carr had no previous convictions on his conduct sheet but had compounded his offence by escaping whilst under arrest. 21 year old Carr was executed in the small French village of Auchel on 7 February and then buried in the Communal Cemetery nearby.

The first Kitchener volunteer upon whom Sir Douglas Haig confirmed a death sentence was a 20 year old private in 9 Black Watch. **Private John Docherty** had enlisted early in 1915, and on 21 June had been posted to 11 Battalion. Subsequently he was transferred to 'D' Company 9 Battalion before going absent in January 1916. His freedom however was short-lived — as he was captured the next day by the military police in Béthune. His case was brought to trial on 3 February and a week later he was medically examined. The two doctors reported that he was suffering from neurasthenia but they were unable to confirm or deny that the cause was shellshock.[3] This indifferent report was of no assistance to the condemned man for no heed was taken of its findings. The battalion war diary recorded the procedure that followed the confirmation of sentence:

'*On the morning of 14th* (February) *the Assistant Provost-Marshal notified the commanding officer that sentence of death had been passed and had been confirmed in the case of no.9672 Pte J Docherty of 'D' Coy. Crime, Desertion. And that the sentence was to be executed between 7 am and 8 am on the 15th. All arrangements were made and Pte Docherty was informed at 6.45 pm. (more than 12 clear hours before execution) . . .*

'*15th February. The sentence on Pte J Docherty was duly carried out at 7.12 am at the abbatoir Mazingarbe and he was buried in the civilian cemetery at that place.*'[4]

In the post-war years the War Graves Commission erected a headstone on the grave which bears the inscription from his relatives: '*Too dearly loved to be forgotten*'.

On 5 February the trial took place of another 20 year old soldier. Perhaps the fact that the private concerned had two previous convictions for absence, for which he had been sentenced to one year's imprisonment with hard labour, had convinced the soldier that it was futile to be represented at his trial. **Private William Hunter,** a native of North Shields, had served on the Western Front in 1 Loyal North Lancs since 4 January 1915.[5] His desertion a year later had been followed by two escapes from custody. Without representation at his trial, and with his previous antecedents, the outlook for Hunter looked bleak — especially in view of the fact that the court heard that he was of little value as a fighting soldier.[6] Nevertheless during the review procedure Lieutenant-General Sir Henry Wilson commanding 4 Corps saw fit to recommend that the sentence be commuted. Sir Douglas Haig did not concur and on 21 February Private Hunter was shot. The inscription on his grave in Maroc British Cemetery, France reads: '*To live in hearts we love is not to die*'.

Two more Regular Army soldiers with previous convictions were tried and executed during the month of February. The two, who were both from the same regiment, were tried on different days, and one was unrepresented at his trial. **Private Alfred Eveleigh** was born at Kingston-upon-Thames and enlisted in the East Kent Regiment late in 1905 at the age of 17. He joined his battalion with a draft of 21 other men on 28 January 1906. Five months later he was awarded a 2nd Class Certificate of Education. On 27 September 1906 he embarked for

South Africa.[7] **Private Robert Gawler,** who came from Blean near Canterbury, had enlisted a number of years after Private Eveleigh. The two men served together on the Western Front in 'D' Company. Both men had previous convictions for desertion and Private Eveleigh was under a suspended sentence of death. Private

Gawler had received a sentence of three months' imprisonment with hard labour, but had remained with the battalion when his sentence was commuted to field punishment no.1.[8] Gawler was not deterred, and deserted twice more before being court martialled on 10 February. At his trial he was undefended; but when the proceedings were reviewed, Brigadier-General C L Nicholson recommended that his death sentence be commuted on the grounds of Gawler's medical and family history.[9]

Private Robert Gawler

Three days after this trial, deserter Private Eveleigh was also sentenced to death. At 10 pm that night another private from the battalion who was missing, reported himself to the guard. The soldier had deserted at Dover when on a draft bound for the battalion. He had later changed his mind and decided to join his unit. He crossed the Channel and landed at Le Havre. From the port he marched to his unit who were serving in the Ypres Salient − a considerable distance.[10] The commanding officer of the East Kents recommended that this soldier should also be court martialled, but Brigadier-General Nicholson considered that he had shown considerable keenness. With two men currently under sentence of death the private was very lucky when the Brigadier decided to dispense with a trial. At 7 am on 24 February Privates Eveleigh and Gawler were executed at Burgomaster Farm, in the south-west part of the Ypres Salient. The firing parties were drawn from the ranks of their battalion. A soldier from the East Kents who was a member of the firing squad wrote to Ernest Thurtle MP after the war describing what happened.

'I think it was hard lines that I should have had to make one of the firing party, as he was a chum of mine . . . We were told that the only humane thing that we could do was to shoot straight. The two men were led out blindfolded, tied to posts driven into the ground, and then we received our orders by sign from our officer, so that the condemned men should not hear us getting ready. Our officer felt it very much, as he, like me, knew the fellow Eveleigh years before. Gawler I never knew, but his case was every bit as sad, he was only a boy.'[11]

The two men were buried near the farm but after the war, their graves were moved to White House Cemetery, St Jean − Belgium.

Private Gawler was aged 20 at the time of his death and Private Eveleigh 27.

Towards the end of February another soldier from the Northamptonshire Regiment was executed. He was the second man from 1 Battalion to be executed in 1916 and this was the fourth execution in 1 Division in just two months. No other soldier from the Northamptonshire Regiment was executed during the remainder of the war; indicating just how sporadic the use of the death penalty could be. Like his comrade before him, the doomed man's offence related to events in 1915.

On 7 October 1915 the battalion had taken over newly captured German trenches near Mazingarbe. After a preliminary bombardment the next day, the Germans attacked *en masse*. The battalion held its ground and the enemy were beaten back, after which the men were ordered to dig trenches and consolidate the positions. The next evening, the night of 10 October, the men were busy bringing up gas cylinders in preparation for an attack. **Private John Jones** sensing that more bloodshed was soon to follow, made off the next day whilst on sentry duty in a support trench.[12] The following month he was arrested in Béthune, but on 14 December he managed to escape by a subterfuge. He remained at liberty until 3 February and was tried a week later[13] He told the court that he had deserted because his platoon sergeant continually victimised him. His length of absence, coupled with his offence of escaping, weighed heavily against him. Other matters, of which the court took no regard, included the fact that he was only 21 years old and the father of a young child.[14] On 24 February Jones became the third soldier to be executed in the abattoir at Mazingarbe. Like the previously executed soldiers he was buried in the nearby Communal Cemetery, but for a reason that is not clear he is buried in an isolated grave quite separate from the other British military burials. The battalion war diary does not record the execution, and hence it would seem probable that he was shot by a firing squad comprised of men from a battalion other than his own. The burial officer may well have decided that, because of the manner in which he met his death, Jones should be buried separately.

The first case of murder that came before the new Commander-in-Chief was typical of the irrational behaviour that led to this type of offence. The offender was a driver recruited early in the war to serve in the horse transport section of the Army Service Corps.

**Private Thomas Moore** was born at Stockton-on-Tees and enlisted in the army at Darlington − the town where he had made his home.[15] Driver Moore had originally served with No.4 Company Army Service Corps but had later been transferred to No.197 Company. This company together with No.194 Company formed 24 Division Train and had responsibility for supplies in this 'New Army' Division. These two companies had been in France since the end of August 1915.

During the period that No.197 Company had been on active service a variety of offences had been committed by 'rankers', including drunkenness, theft and other crimes of a more serious nature. These had culminated on 1 February 1916 when a driver from the company had been sentenced to ten years' penal servitude, which had subsequently been commuted to two years' imprisonment with hard labour.[16]

On 11 February, 197 Company were billeted at Busseboom, a village in the southern part of the Ypres Salient — some eight miles from the front line. A heavy bombardment had commenced at dusk, but whether this contributed to the offence that followed is not known. However, at 11.35 pm Driver Moore shot a soldier from his own company who was billeted in the same hut. The victim was a Scotsman — Acting Farrier Staff Sergeant James Pick, who lived at Bannockburn. Fellow soldiers flocked to see what had happened but Pick was found to be dead. When Captain Thompson, a company officer, arrived on the scene he discovered that a crowd had gathered and that Driver Moore was still armed. When the captain intervened Driver Moore threatened to shoot him too; but Moore was successfully disarmed. At 11.45 pm the commanding officer of 24 Division Train, Lieutenant-Colonel F B Lord, arrived on the scene. He arranged for the custody of the prisoner and got stretcher bearers from No.74 Field Ambulance to take away Pick's body. Lord then started making enquiries, which took him some considerable time. He finally retired at 4.45 am. Later that morning Major T W Blakeway, the officer commanding 197 Company, started his own investigations and Driver Moore was remanded on a charge of murder.

The same day Major Hunter started to take a summary of evidence but this had to be abandoned because enemy aeroplanes were dropping bombs near the camp and this was distracting the witnesses. Colonel Lord also paraded 197 Company and gave the men a stern talking to. He reprimanded them about the incident the previous night, when no attempt had been made to disarm Moore and also about their behaviour in general. On 13 February the papers on Moore's case were forwarded to Division and at 6 pm the next day Colonel Lord was summoned to see Major-General J E Capper — General Officer Commanding 24 Division. The General expressed great dissatisfaction with the conduct of the men of 197 Company and ordered Colonel Lord to make arrangements for the General to speak to the men. Colonel Lord passed on the General's comments to Major Blakeway and a parade was ordered for the next day. At 5.30 pm on 15 February the whole company, including officers, paraded to hear the General rebuke them.

On 18 February Driver Moore was tried by a Field General Court Martial held in the lines of 197 Company Camp. The case continued from 10 am until 5.20 pm but no motive for the crime was disclosed. Moore did tell the court, however, that his mother was detained in a lunatic asylum, and in his defence he claimed that he too was insane.[17] But after the sentence of death was passed no steps were taken to assess his state of mind.

The authors have not had the privilege of access to the transcript of this (or any other) court martial and can only speculate on what events were considered during this relatively long trial. Perhaps the general conduct of the company came into question? Whilst it would seem unlikely that sentences of death for murder were put into effect to discourage others − in the manner in which such sentences where intended to deter deserters − it seems feasible that the record of indiscipline in this company attracted more attention than the consideration of whether the elements of this offence constituted murder, or the less serious offence of manslaughter.

At three minutes past four on the morning of 26 February the sentence of death was promulgated on 23 year old Driver Moore. At 5.30 am the company was paraded and the sentence was read out. Ten minutes later Driver Moore was taken out and shot by a firing squad drawn from his own company − lending weight to the theory that the severity of military discipline should be demonstrated to the victim's comrades. The execution took place as snow fell on Busseboom. The location of Moore's place of burial was recorded in the company's war diary but following the war it was never found. As a result Moore is commemorated on the Menin Gate Memorial to the missing. Moore's victim, Acting Farrier Staff Sergeant James Pick is buried in Poperinghe New Military Cemetery, Belgium.

The final execution in February 1916 took place under the most bizarre of circumstances. The victim, a young Irish lad, had eagerly enlisted in 9 Royal Irish Rifles.

Before the war **Private James Crozier** was an apprentice in a Belfast shipyard. He enlisted in September 1914 and 13 months later went to the Western Front with his battalion − who were part of 36 Ulster Division. The battalion served on the Somme in often trying conditions during the winter of 1915-16. At the time of his desertion, in February 1916, the battalion was serving in the front line trenches near the 'Redan' close to Serre.[18] After going absent Crozier walked a considerable distance before being admitted to a Royal Army Medical Corps field hospital. The court were later to hear the private say that he had not known what he was doing when he made off, being in a daze at the time and suffering from pains throughout his body. The doctor who performed the examination on Crozier stated, however, that the soldier was perfectly fit in mind and body. As a consequence the Ulsterman was returned to his unit and then court martialled on 14 February.[19]

Crozier had been retained with his unit when on 26 February the battalion were paraded to hear the sentence promulgated. The commanding officer then made preparations for the execution. Crozier was placed under close arrest and was visited by the chaplain whilst an execution post was placed in the back garden of a villa in Mailly-Maillet − a small village behind the Somme front. Private Crozier was plied with drink whilst the young officer in charge of the firing squad was ordered to dine with the commanding officer, the CO intending to prevent an alcoholic excess by the youngster in an attempt to render himself unfit to command the firing squad. Feelings ran high amongst the ranks, and the Assistant Provost-Marshal and the Military Police feared a mutiny with the firing squad refusing to shoot.[20]

Just before dawn on 27 February 9 Royal Irish Rifles paraded in the village. They marched towards the villa and halted alongside the wall that surrounded the back garden. The Assistant Provost-Marshal and the Military Police were absent, supposedly on the instructions of the battalion commander. Private Crozier was carried out, unconscious through drink, blindfolded and tied to the execution post. On the word of command a ragged volley rang out from the firing squad. The medical officer walked over and examined the body, but Crozier was not dead. The doctor stood back as the officer commanding the firing squad took aim with his revolver and fired a single bullet into the victim's head. The wall surrounding the villa prevented the whole battalion from seeing the execution, but as they stood to attention they heard the fatal shots.

Their commanding officer, however, witnessed the events; his name was Lieutenant-Colonel Frank P Crozier. The victim and his commanding officer were not related but the circumstances of the case are surprising. Frank Crozier, who was later promoted Brigadier-General, recalled many details concerning the young victim.[21] In 1914 the then Major F P Crozier, had recruited Private Crozier personally. J Crozier's mother was present at the recruiting office and had tried to dissuade her son from enlisting. She was unsuccessful but the major had told her that she need not worry because he personally would look after her son. Major Crozier did keep an eye on the young boy's progress, but following his court martial for desertion, as part of the procedure the battalion commander added his recommendation regarding whether the sentence should be commuted or not. However, Frank Crozier, apparently without the slightest hesitation, stated that he recommended the death sentence be carried out. In the aftermath of the execution Frank Crozier attempted to have the victim's name included amongst the list of casualties incurred on the field of battle. He was unsuccessful and as a result the victim's mother was notified that her son had been executed. This in turn meant that she would not receive the allowances normally payable. Private Crozier was buried in Mailly-Maillet, but re-interred after the war at Sucrerie Military Cemetery, Colincamps, France.

Two weeks prior to the trial of Private Crozier, Second Lieutenant A J Annandale, also from 9 Royal Irish Rifles, had been tried by General Court Martial for desertion. He was found guilty and sentenced to death but the proceedings were quashed on technicalities. Frank Crozier stated that these legal points were raised by Annandale's 'influential friends' and that had this officer been executed as opposed to Private Crozier then there would have been fewer regrets.

Another case of murder occurred early in 1916 when a private soldier killed an NCO. On 8 February, whilst out on rest, **Private Arthur Dale** of 13 Royal Scots, spent the morning drinking in an estaminet. Later the same day when the soldier was considerably the worse for drink, Lance-Corporal Sneddon, a friend of Dale's and a member of the same platoon, entered the estaminet and told the private to leave as he had already had enough to drink. Dale did so, and returned to his billet. A short while later the soldier was seen climbing into the loft of his billet whilst carrying his rifle. Soon afterwards a shot rang out and Lance-Corporal Sneddon fell to the ground mortally wounded.[22] Dale was brought to trial on 20 February, when the court heard witnesses state that the private had been very drunk. The two policemen who arrested him also stated that they had been unable to understand the prisoner's mutterings. No allowance was made by the court nor the reviewing authorities for Dale's inebriated condition at the time of the murder, and he was executed in the abbatoir at Mazingarbe on 3 March. The *Great War Medal Roll* Index shows that the 1915 Star medal was issued to Dale's next-of-kin. The record is marked 'Not to be recalled'. However, it is not recorded whether or not his British War and Victory medals were issued.[23]

A Scottish NCO who was executed in March 1916, was one of the very few deserters that year who discarded their uniform in an attempt to avoid detection. **Corporal Lewis,** of 12 Highland Light Infantry, deserted from his unit on 23 January whilst in rest at Noeux-les-Mines, having been warned for the trenches at the time. Desertion under such circumstances (i.e. to evade duty in the trenches) was an offence for which Sir Douglas Haig was frequently to confirm a sentence of death.

Lewis was arrested in civilian clothes at Thiennes on 10 February by members of 19 Durham Light Infantry who had recently arrived in France, and they noted the incident in their war diary – although they recorded that Lewis was a Canadian.[24] (Early in the following year the Durhams had three men executed from amongst their own ranks.) It would seem that Corporal Lewis told a number of differing stories, and at one time maintained that he was an American.[25] He was tried at Philosophe on 25 February and told the court that a few years before the war, whilst working in a factory in Canada, he had been blown up in an industrial explosion. As a result he had become prone to epileptic fits and loss of memory. Whilst under sentence of death Lewis was examined by a team of medical officers, but when their report stated that they were unable to confirm or deny the existence of such long-term intermittent 'after effects', Lewis' death sentence was confirmed.[26] Perhaps the novelty of his claim of pre-war injury coupled with his knowledge of Canadian accents and his initial attempt to claim to be an American when challenged, led the authorities to believe that his excuses were pure fabrication. The execution took place in the abbatoir at Mazingarbe, which was fast becoming the slaughter house of its pre-war days.

On 27 February the trials of two soldiers from the same battalion, 15 Royal Irish Rifles took place. It is significant that one of the men, who had a history of previous convictions, was unrepresented at his trial. **Rifleman McCracken** and **Rifleman Templeton** both came from Belfast and had served with the battalion since it arrived in France the previous October. McCracken, who was aged 19 years, and Templeton were both tried for desertion, the only military offence for which soldiers were executed during the first quarter of 1916. The court heard that McCracken had three previous convictions, two involving absence.[27] The duo were executed side-by-side on 19 March and were buried at Mailly-Maillet.

The execution of a Jewish soldier from the East End of London in March 1916 was indicative of just how scant the military's regard for human life could be. **Private Abraham Beverstein** was the only son of an East End family. Because it was considered dishonourable, in certain Jewish circles, to be a soldier Beverstein had 'signed up' under the false name of Harris. (Details of the use of this false name comes from the Commonwealth War Graves Commission register for Labourse Communal Cemetery. However, there is some doubt whether the name Beverstein was in fact the soldier's true family name. Worldwide enquiries have failed to trace any person with such a surname.) He had enlisted in 11 Middlesex Regiment in September 1914 and was sent to

Aldershot to do his training.[28] Once trained, Private 'Harris' had been detailed for duty at his Regimental Depot; however, when his battalion had gone to France the volunteer had successfully applied to join his comrades. He crossed to France on 31 May 1915.[29]

Two days before Christmas 1915, 11 Middlesex went into the front line trenches at Givenchy.[30] The next day, Christmas Eve, at 7.15 in the morning the Germans blew a defensive mine.[31] Considerable damage was done and many men were buried. And in the confusion the Germans 'rained down' a cocktail of shells, trench mortars and rifle grenades.

Although the exact date is not known, either in this mine explosion or a subsequent one a few days later, Private Beverstein was wounded in the back. He was admitted to hospital suffering from these wounds and also from shock. In due course the soldier's worried parents received the notification of their son's wounding on the official army form provided for such tasks. It read:[32]

*'Sir, Infantry Records Office, Hounslow. 15/1/1916*

*I regret to inform you that 11/1799, Pte.Harris A., 11th Battn, Middlesex Regt., G.S., is ill at 38th Field Ambulance, France, suffering from wounds and shock (mine explosion).'*

In his letters home Private Beverstein told of his progress in hospital and that he had been detained there until 19 January 1916, because he had developed a pressure sore on his heel.[33]

*'1st January 1916*

*Dear Mother,*

*I am very sorry I not did write before now, but we were in the trenches on Christmas Day and we had a lot to do. Also I was taken ill and I was sent to the hospital. I am feeling a little better, so don't get upset; also don't send any letters to the company, because I won't get them. Also you cannot send any letters to the hospital, as I won't get them. Dear Mother, do not worry, I will be all right. Hoping all of you are getting on well. I was only hurt in the back. I will try to send you letters every few days if I can to let you know how I am getting on. We get plenty of food in the hospital. Dear Mother, I know it will break your heart this, but don't get upset about it. I will be all right, but I would very much like to see you, but I will try my best . . .'*

*'6th January 1916*

*. . . I have been in hospital for nine days, lying in bed all the time, and now I have a sore heel . . . I had it cut to-day and it is getting on better . . .'*

*'20th January 1916*

*Dear Mother,*

*I am quite well, and I came out of Hospital on Wednesday.'*

Private Beverstein had been back with his battalion for less than four weeks when the incident occurred that was to result in his execution.

On 13 February the soldier had left his position in the front line trenches near the Hohenzollern Redoubt[34] and had made his way to one of the Company Headquarters in the rear. He reported to his Company Quartermaster Sergeant and stated that a grenade had burst very close to him and that he was suffering from shock. Believing him to be in a nervous condition this NCO told 'Harris' to report to the Medical Officer. Beverstein reported to the MO who examined him but found nothing wrong. As a result the private was ordered to return to the trenches. Beverstein however did not obey but made his way to a farmhouse in the rear where he took refuge. Shortly afterwards, whilst warming himself by the fire, an officer from another regiment came into the farmhouse, and suspecting that Beverstein was a deserter placed the lad under arrest.[35]

The letters sent home indicated that Beverstein was in trouble but did not disclose the serious nature of his predicament. Clearly the soldier did not realise that his life was at stake, but the letters relate, that at the time of his desertion, the private had been feeling unwell.

*'23rd February 1916*

*Dear Mother,*

*We were in the trenches, and I was ill, so I went out and they took me to prison, and I am in a bit of trouble now and won't get any money for a long time. I will have to go in front of a Court. I will try my best to get out of it, so don't worry. But, dear Mother, try to send some money, not very much, but try your best. I will let you know in my next how I got on. Give my best love to Mother, Father, and Kate.*

*From your loving son, Aby.'*

On 4 March when he was court martialled, Private Beverstein explained that on the day of his absence a grenade had exploded beside him, and this had been more than his nerves could stand. He added that he had then lost control. The court was unimpressed by this story and in spite of an unblemished army record the soldier was sentenced to death — and the finding was confirmed by the Commander-in-Chief. In the event that Private Beverstein's medical history sheet accompanied the court martial papers during the review procedures, then no more damning an indictment can be made against all who reviewed this case. Without doubt, the execution of this lad was a despicable mis-carriage of justice.

Private Beverstein's parents were left unaware of their son's predicament. The next communication which they received came from the Army. It was a official army form which carried a blunt message.

*'Sir, I am directed to inform you that a report has been received from the War Office to the effect that No.11/1799, Pte Harris, A., 11th Battalion Middlesex Regiment, G.S., was sentenced after trial by Court Martial to suffer death by being shot for desertion, and the sentence was duly executed on 20th March, 1916.*

*I am, Sir, Your obedient servant, P.G.Hendley, Lt-Col. ic. Infantry Records, Hounslow, 8th April, 1916'*[36]

Private Beverstein was executed at Labourse together with another man from the same 'New Army' Division. Once again the question arises of why two examples were required in a single division. Especially when both men were of good character.

Private Beverstein was recorded as being aged 21 at the time of his death – according to the Records of the General Register Office, London. However, some doubt exists as to the accuracy of these records which were compiled from army records. The soldier's age would have been calculated from his attestation form, and hence if the soldier had declared a false age on enlistment, then the error would have been repeated. In addition, army records of soldiers' ages are frequently inaccurate by one year. Information recorded by Sylvia Pankhurst would suggest that Beverstein's true age was 19. His mother, father and sister lived at 48 St Antony Street, Commercial Road, London. After the war Private Beverstein was commemorated in the *British Jewry Book of Honour* (under the name of Harris).

The other soldier executed with Beverstein was **Private Harry Martin** of 9 Essex Regiment. Martin joined 'A' Company of his battalion in early 1916 and had deserted when his battalion had been warned that they would soon be moving up into the trenches. Both men are buried in Labourse Communal Cemetery.

The last British soldier to be executed in March 1916, was arrested in the United Kingdom. Like the case of Private Turpie in the previous year, this soldier had successfully crossed the Channel; a considerable feat, the method of which the military authorities were always anxious to learn. Very few men ever succeeded, and there is reason to believe that the authorities were so intent on discovering escape routes that those who co-operated were normally treated leniently. The following case however, was hardly likely to attract the sympathy of the Commander-in-Chief.

**Private Charles Bladen** had served with both 10th and 11th Battalions of his regiment before returning again to 10 Yorks & Lancs,[37] and had deserted from his battalion at Armentières on 20 December 1915.[38] The previous day at 6.30 in the morning the enemy had blown two mines. In the subsequent fighting the Germans had attempted to occupy the craters – but had been repulsed.[39]

After successfully returning to England, Bladen enjoyed his liberty until arrested by the police in Hornsey (London) on 29 January when he was unable to produce a pass.[40] Although the deception was never disclosed to the court martial panel in France, when arrested in the United Kingdom, Bladen showed a resource hitherto unseen amongst the previous victims of the firing squad. He told the police and magistrates that he had merely overstayed his home leave — when in fact no such absence had been authorised. His ploy, that he might be released to return to his unit, only to desert again, was not however successful and the deserter was remanded for an escort. Realising his desperate plight Bladen tried three times to escape, but was brought back to Armentières for trial.

Bladen's battalion left the front line area to move into rest on 20 March,[41] while the 26 year old remained at Armentières under arrest. On 22 March arrangements were made for a contingent from the battalion to carry out the execution. Those detailed were the regimental sergeant-major, the provost-sergeant, an escort of one NCO, and two men. The firing squad included Bladen's platoon commander Lieutenant A W Lamond, one sergeant and 16 men — although it would seem likely that four of these men would have formed the burial party. This detachment was transported by bus some distance from Strazeele to Armentières on the eve of the execution. Their instructions required that the men need not be told in advance of the task required of them. However, as the orders given specified that the escort NCO must be able to identify the victim, at least one man certainly must have realised the task ahead.

At dawn the next day the fatal volley rang out at the Asylum in Armentières. Simultaneously the battalion, some miles away, were paraded for the sentence to be promulgated, whilst Bladen's body was removed for burial.[42] The remains of Private Bladen now rest at Cité Bonjean Military Cemetery, in the sleazy suburbs of the once famous town of Armentières.

The first Canadian soldier to be executed during the war was a French Canadian serving in the 14th Battalion.[43] In peacetime Canada had only a small army of some 3000 men, and **Private Auger,** whose first name was Fortunat, had been amongst the earliest of volunteers to enlist at Valcartier in September 1914.[44] Auger was a member of the first Canadian Division to land in France — arriving in February 1915. Three times during 1915 he went absent without leave. On one occasion Auger received a sentence of imprisonment, but this was suspended. In 1916 he twice evaded duty in the trenches.[45] However, his final absence resulted in a court martial on 15 March, at which he was sentenced to death. Canadian records indicate that many similar offences had been committed both in Auger's battalion and in particular, his company.

During the research for this book the authors have drawn on many sources for material. However, it has not proved possible to determine whether any of the Canadians who were executed were unrepresented at their trials. It is known that a number of the other soldiers were not, but this information has not been forthcoming concerning the Canadian cases. Although the transcripts of the Canadian courts martial would appear to be available for public inspection the authors have not been able to take advantage of this facility.

Eleven days after his trial Auger was executed at Steenwerck, near the border with Belgium. Although it is known that Private Auger came from Montreal, unfortunately his age is not disclosed. However, it is almost certain that the Canadian was not married.

Many of the decisions relating to capital offences on the Western Front later attracted critical attention. However, when a soldier under a commuted and suspended sentence of death was allowed UK home leave in December 1915, it is difficult to imagine why this concession was granted.

The soldier, **Private Edward Bolton,** a Regular in 1 Cheshire Regiment had, rather predictably, succumbed to temptation and remained at home. Some ten weeks after the date he was due back in France, the absentee was arrested at Ince in Lancashire, where he had taken up civilian employment under a false name.[46] Bolton was executed in Roclincourt Valley − on the Arras front − on 14 April.

In the final days of April 1916 three more privates were executed for desertion. They were all Kitchener volunteers who had joined up in the earliest days of the war. The trio were all serving in the trenches in the desolate mining area near Lens.

**Private William Thompson,** a native of Newcastle, had enlisted in 6 East Kents, and **Private Henry Carter** in 11 Middlesex. Both units were part of 12 Division, which had already seen two previous executions − just one month previously. Private Carter's unit, 11 Middlesex, was the same battalion as that in which the late Private Beverstein had served. And there were also a number of similarities between Beverstein's and Carter's cases. One of Ernest Thurtle's informants related that Carter had fled from the trench known as Vigo Street near Vermelles.[47] Seemingly a bombardment of six days and nights had been more than Carter's constitution could stand. However, the private was only one of several men who had deserted the battalion, which had suffered heavy casualties. Later a number of these absentees were arrested whilst hiding in a cellar. Although Carter was known in his company to be a bundle of nerves, it turned out that he alone was to be the scapegoat when problems of evidence led to the charges being set aside in four other cases. Unlike Beverstein, however, Private Carter had a poor record, his conduct sheet showing offences of a serious nature.[48] Carter had previously been absent without leave, disobedient, and had slept on his post. The two men earmarked to be shot at dawn were of differing ages, Carter being only eighteen-and-a-half and Thompson 27.

The third doomed volunteer was a Welshman who had been sent to reinforce a Regular unit − 1 South Wales Borderers − in November 1914.[49] Like others before him, **Private O'Neil** was led to the slaughter in the abbatoir at Mazingarbe.

Although the pattern did not continue after the Battle of the Somme commenced in July 1916, before the end of May yet another soldier who had crossed the Channel to freedom was executed.

**Private William Watts,** a pre-war Regular, was serving with 1 Battalion Loyal North Lancs when he decamped from near Mazingarbe on 20 November 1915.[50] Watts, a married man of 29, was arrested near his home in Liverpool on Christmas Eve 1915. What happened to Watts between his arrest and court martial is unclear. However, when he was tried (in France) in April 1916, he was also charged with an additional offence of: 'Conduct to the prejudice of good order and military discipline in that he, on the 6th March 1916, was apprehended at Liverpool when his duty required him to be with the 1st Battalion Loyal North Lancashire Regiment on foreign service'.[51]

Although Private Watts was of good character, he was executed on 5 May 1916. By virtue of his arrest in the UK his wife must have been aware that her husband was liable to be punished for his absence, but it is doubtful whether she was told the true cause of his death. Details recorded in the cemetery register, which were included at the request of the next-of-kin, state that he had been 'killed in action' − Commonwealth War Graves Commission register, Maroc British Cemetery − the inscription on the grave reads:

*'In loving memory of my dear husband on whose soul sweet Jesus have mercy'.*

On the day following the execution of Private Watts, another disturbing case was settled by firing squad. The young soldier involved was only 20, and had only recently arrived at the front. The conviction was for disobedience, and it was the first such case on the Western Front to end with an execution. However, the disturbing aspect of this case was the damning comment that the battalion commander, Lt-Col R B Morgan, saw fit to append to the proceedings.

**Private James Cuthbert**'s offence took place in the Ferme du Bois sector near Richebourg L'Avoué − low-lying marshy ground, entirely unsuited to the construction of substantial trench systems. Though it has not been possible to determine the exact date of Cuthbert's offence, it seems almost certain that the event took place in the second week of April 1916.

The battalion concerned was 9 Cheshires, and Private James Cuthbert was one of a party of eight men (including a corporal and a sergeant) who had been detailed for a wiring party under the command of an officer. Their allotted task was to erect barbed wire in no-man's-land. Understandably such tasks could only be carried out at night; however, on this occasion the brilliance of the moon worried the NCOs and men. As the party formed up, and before the arrival of the officer, the group discussed their fears, the sergeant expressing his opinion that he thought it unlikely that they would be sent out in such clear conditions. As the detail made their way towards the front line the men's grumbling continued and a consensus was reached that if they were ordered out into no-man's-land then they would all refuse to go. The instigator of this decision was never identified.[52]

Once in the front line, with no countermanding order, the party began to move out. However, only the officer and two NCOs advanced over the parapet, the eight rankers remaining in the trench. The officer and NCOs immediately returned to their trench whereupon the company commander appeared on the scene. He cautioned the eight men, pointing out that disobedience was an offence punishable by death. The company commander then ordered the party to follow him personally, as he would lead the wiring party. Private Cuthbert refused to go. Throwing down the gauntlet, he insisted that he would rather be shot than go out. At his court martial a prosecution witness – the company quartermaster sergeant – said that he had told those who refused to go out, to stand forward. He went on to say that the defendant and some of the others did so, but Private Cuthbert, conducting his own defence, adamantly denied performing such an action.

Eventually the party did move out (led by the company commander) but Private Cuthbert and two other privates remained in the trench. The depleted workforce, consisting now of only eight men (sic) all told, were successful in carrying out their task and returned without incident.

At the inevitable court martial the events of that fatal night were recounted, when the court heard about the men's informal agreement to refuse to go out. And it was alleged that the sergeant in the party had been the instigator.

One matter that the court did not consider was the ability and reputation of the subaltern originally designated to lead the party – perhaps a very apposite consideration. Surely it was significant that the company commander had taken over the task. Was the junior officer unfit to take the party out? In his defence Private Cuthbert maintained that he himself was unfit to go out.[53]

Cuthbert's conduct sheet revealed nothing more serious than being confined to barracks, however, he and his two comrades were all

77

sentenced to death. Damning comments were added to the proceedings by the battalion commander who stated that Private Cuthbert was considered to be an undesirable man who was likely to prove a source of corruption, and that the soldier's fighting value was not of a high standard. These comments revealed the commander's unparalleled bigotry – Cuthbert had only been with the battalion a short time. Such an assessment was manifestly unfair, given the brief period that the soldier had been on active service.

Perhaps a more balanced approach might have revealed a more complete picture. The offences of cowardice and disobedience are crimes that require the testimony of witnesses – if they are to be successfully brought to trial. The offence of desertion requires no such evidence, merely that a man made off and had no intention of returning.

In Cuthbert's case the witnesses were all members of the battalion. It is not difficult to imagine the scene in the officers' mess following the nocturnal episode in the front line. Two potential prosecution witnesses willing and able to recount the events to a receptive audience – perhaps with the junior officer keen to disassociate himself from any possible blame. The commanding officer attentive to every word – and keen to hear the names of those who erred.

Cuthbert was executed near St Omer on 6 May. His two comrades both had their sentences commuted to 15 years' penal servitude.[54]

The folly of this night time incident however did not go unrecorded by the battalion diarist. On 15 April 1916 he wrote: 'Weather fine with moonlight night, much work done, but too bright to wire in front.'[55]

Four days after Cuthbert's death a further Kitchener volunteer was executed. His battalion, 9 Northumberland Fusiliers, had been on the Western Front for ten months, during which time **Private Arthur Robinson** had received a sentence of ten years' penal servitude for desertion – which had later been suspended.[56] Although Robinson's death swelled the numbers of those shot for desertion, the executions that took place during the month of May were to display a diversity of offences which under the Army Act were punishable with death.

On 10 April 1916, 2 Battalion Highland Light Infantry, a unit in a Regular Army division, were resting in the village of Bruay.[57] As was the custom when out of the line, the soldiers were subject to kit inspections and drill. It was a routine that many felt somewhat tiresome after the rigours of trench life. During a rifle inspection one morning, a company commander criticised a soldier for having a dirty rifle and boots. The soldier, **Private Fox,** responded with a torrent of abuse, and threatened the officer with his rifle. Fox was swiftly disarmed by a sergeant, but proceeded to step out of the ranks and twice kicked the officer.[58] Although the blows were only to the knee the incident constituted, in military terms, a serious breach of the law. As a result Private Fox was charged with 'When on active service striking his superior officer, being in the execution of his office'.[59]

At his court martial Private Fox claimed that he had family troubles and that his requests for leave had been refused, although he had been on active service since November 1914. The stress he maintained, drove him to drink on the eve of the offence and he claimed he was still under the influence when he assaulted the officer. However, prosecution witnesses averred that he had been sober.[60] Perhaps the refutation of Fox's incapacity caused the court to take no heed of his claim of family problems. Although unrecorded in the court martial transcript, the reputation of the company commander concerned may well have been very material to the commission of this offence.

The execution of Private Fox went ahead at 4.35 am on 12 May at an unknown location and he is commemorated on the Arras Memorial to the Missing. His death personified the rigours of military law at their harshest, for the severity of the sentence was out of keeping with the offence. (During an interview with one of the authors in 1982, the then Judge Advocate-General, Judge Morgan-Owen, expressed surprise when he was informed that striking a superior officer was a capital offence during World War One, and consulted the Manual of Military Law to verify the allegation.) The issue did not embrace attempted murder but involved the pressures of active service and army 'bull' on a soldier apparently already burdened with family worries and a hangover.

Less than a week after the first execution for disobedience (on the Western Front) another soldier was shot for the same offence. The circumstances were entirely different, and evidence shows that **Driver John Hasemore** of 'A' Company 180 Brigade, Royal Field Artillery had decided to soldier no more.

Hasemore had previously served in the Navy before enlisting in the summer of 1915. His duties as a driver involved work with the many horses needed to transport the field guns and ammunition limbers. Many thousands of men had been enlisted since the outbreak of war to assist with transport for both the Artillery and for the Army Service Corps.

Hasemore's troubles had started with a sentence of 28 days' field punishment no.1 for disobedience. During the early morning of the first day of his sentence, he had refused to submit to being tied up and had been insubordinate to the bombardier detailed to administer the punishment. As a result he was confined in the guardroom. Later that day a sergeant ordered him to carry some horse rugs across to another building. Hasemore flatly refused, repeatedly asserting that he wasn't going to act like a slave.[61] Successive orders generated a similar response from Hasemore. Eventually attempts to put Hasemore to work were abandoned and he was placed under close arrest, but he continued to defy authority by refusing to march properly, eventually being dragged by the escort party.

After further punishment, Hasemore once again proved uncompromising in his attitude to military authority, and on one occasion lashed out with his feet as he was frogmarched into confinement.

At his trial on 30 April there was little that Driver Hasemore could say in mitigation or defence. Alleging that the bombardier had sworn at him and provoked the defendant, was a futile rebuttal to a catalogue of sustained anti-authoritarianism that included:

(1) 'When on active service, using insubordinate language to his superior officer.'

(2) 'When on active service, disobeying in such a manner as to show a wilful defiance of authority, a lawful command given personally by his superior officer in the execution of his office.'

(3) 'When on active service, using threatening language to his superior officer.'[62]

The sentence of death was carried out at Mazingarbe abbatoir on 12 May. 23 year old Hasemore was so far probably the most rebellious soldier to face a firing squad.

In May 1916 four men were executed who were all well above the average age of those convicted of capital offences. In the first case the sentence was only promulgated just prior to the execution. An audience of witnesses from Transport sections were present, presumably to ensure that details of the event reached all battalions in the division. The soldier concerned was **Rifleman Albert Parker** serving with 7 King's Royal Rifle Corps. His crime was a typical example of desertion committed with the intention of avoiding service in the line. 35 year old Parker admitted drunkenness at his trial but this did not mitigate his offence.[63] An eyewitness later recalled the promulgation of sentence and the execution that followed.

'*Then the prisoner's cap was taken off,* [this ritual is laid down in King's Regulations No.481, the cap being removed to prevent its possible use as a missile] *and he was told to take one pace forward, which he did. Then the APM commenced to read the papers . . .*

'*The man was then told to take a pace back again, which he did without a quiver − a braver man at that moment wasn't to be found in France. He was then marched away to the place where he was to be shot. We were then ordered to about turn, and the Brigade Transport Officer threatened us that any man who turned round would be put on a crime. So we stood in silence for what seemed hours, although only minutes. Then the shots rang out and one of the Yorkshires fainted, the strain was that great.* [A man from the 6th Battalion King's Own Yorkshire Light Infantry.] *Still we stood in silence until we heard another shot, which I afterwards ascertained was the doctor's shot to make sure he was dead.'* [The writer means the *coup de grâce* administered by the officer commanding the firing squad.][64]

The execution took place at Warlus, where Albert Parker, a Watford man, was buried in the Communal Cemetery — the only soldier's grave — dating from the Great War. His headstone now carries the inscription, *'Gone but not forgotten'*.

In the second case the soldier concerned was a 44 year old married man who was a Reservist. (In February 1915, a 41 year old man from this battalion — 2 Welsh — had been shot for murder. See the case of Lance-Corporal Price.) He was also the father of three children but none of these factors provoked sympathy for the deserter. At his trial the soldier pleaded with the court that it was unfair to expect him to be able to perform the same duties as men much younger than himself. He also expressed discontent because when rejoining the Colours he had only expected to have work behind the lines.[65] In due course **Private Thomas** of 2 Welsh was executed in the abbatoir at Mazingarbe.

However, not all soldiers who had enlisted on a regular engagement had seen long service. **Private William Burrell** had enlisted in Sussex Regiment in 1914 prior to the outbreak of war. On 10 November he embarked for France and joined 2 Battalion a week later. After less than two months' service Burrell went missing in January 1915, leaving the trenches near the 'Brickstacks' at Cuinchy.[66] He remained absent for some time before being captured, tried and sentenced to death. However, the sentence was commuted and he was sent to prison on 7 May 1915.[67]

On 4 April 1916, after serving just under eleven months, Private Burrell's sentence was suspended and he was released — returning to his battalion who were serving in the trenches at Loos. The soldier however did not intend to serve creditably — a month and a day after his release he was again tried for desertion. Perhaps one factor not known to the court was that a month prior to Burrell's release from prison his younger brother, a volunteer with 9 Sussex, had been killed in action in the Ypres Salient. (Private Ernest Burrell, G/3517, is buried in Menin Road South Military Cemetery, Ypres.)

21 year old William Burrell was executed at Mazingarbe just two days after Private Thomas. The two men are buried side-by-side in the Communal Cemetery Extension.[68] Burrell's imprisonment must have been known to his parents and it seems likely that they were told

of their son's execution as the inscription on the headstone of his grave reads:

*'The will of the Lord be done. Acts 21.14. Dad, Mum.'*

It is clear in several cases that have already been chronicled, just how detrimental to a soldier's prospects a damning statement made by a commanding officer could be. However, in a case in late May 1916 a favourable character reference, strongly extolling the fighting value of a condemned man, was ignored. The soldier concerned had joined the Royal Fusiliers at the age of 32, just five days before the outbreak of war.

**Private William Roberts,** known as Ted to his relatives, was drafted to 4 Royal Fusiliers in November 1914. His service was exemplary and on 16 June 1915 he was severely wounded in the head during an attack at Hooge in the Ypres Salient.[69] Private Roberts was one of 369 casualties suffered by his battalion that day.[70] After treatment and convalescence, the soldier returned on 20 September 1915 to his battalion, which was still in the Ypres Salient, in an area known as Sanctuary Wood. Five days later, bloody fighting broke out in the Salient as the British High Command attempted to draw enemy attention away from the Loos offensive — then taking place to the south.

As the diversionary attacks slackened Private Roberts slipped away from his battalion in the front line trenches at Hooge Crater. Unlike those who fled in the direction of the Channel Ports, Roberts remained just a short distance behind the lines. For quite a while he avoided drawing attention to himself until he was arrested on 4 May 1916 in the village of Brandhoek — just west of Ypres.[71]

While under arrest Private Roberts was kept in secure confinement at Locre, a small village on the Franco-Belgian border, but on 9 May he escaped — only to be re-arrested shortly afterwards. On 20 May he stood trial at Locre before a court martial staffed by a lieutenant- colonel and three captains.[72] Roberts' Commanding Officer described the Londoner as a good and plucky soldier, telling the court that the private had volunteered for dangerous tasks on a number of occasions. It is difficult to imagine what better testimonial could have been given. Nevertheless the reviewing authorities wasted little time, Sir Douglas Haig confirming the sentence a week later. It must be presumed that Roberts' length of absence, coupled with his escape, had negated the private's previous good service, and from a military view point he was now valueless.

At 3.45 am on 29 May a firing squad created another unfortunate 'example', the Medical Officer blandly recording that Roberts 'died of gunshot wounds'.[73]

In the early 1980s a story emerged that Private Roberts had been shot for habitually stealing the rum ration and drinking it himself.[74]

It would seem that the story was concocted to cover family embarrassment about this regrettable incident.

On 30 May 1916 two soldiers were executed in entirely contrasting circumstances. **Lance-Corporal James Holland,** a volunteer of previous good character, was executed for cowardice and quitting his post. Private Phillips, a regular, had been in France since 21 August 1914, and was a bad character. Holland's offence took place on the Arras front and Phillips' in the Ypres Salient.

Lance-Corporal Holland served with 10 Cheshire Regiment, and during the last week of April 1916 his battalion was holding the front line trenches in the Mont St Eloi sector. The area had previously been the scene of bitter fighting, and at 7.30 on the evening of 24 April the Germans blew a mine under the sector occupied by 'A' Company — burying several NCOs and men.[75] Two days later the battalion moved into Brigade Reserve, returning to the trenches on 2 May. During this tour of duty in the line Lance-Corporal Holland found himself in charge of a party of four men in an advanced sap close to the enemy's lines. The group had taken up their position early in the morning and had been instructed not to leave the position until ordered to do so, or until they were relieved. The party was also told that they could expect to be relieved after 24 hours.[76]

Later that day, at about 6 pm, the sentry on watch had seen two men, whom he believed to be French soldiers, approaching the post. He challenged them but received no response. As the pair entered the trench system the sentry realised that the intruders were in fact Germans. Lance-Corporal Holland, and three other privates in his party then left their positions and ran back to the main trench system. In the comparative safety of the British front line, Holland rushed into his company headquarters, reporting that the Germans had attacked and overrun their outpost.[77]

It rapidly transpired that the sentry on watch had remained at his post and the intruding Germans had hurriedly retreated. When the facts about the incident became apparent, Holland was arrested. On 18 May he was tried for cowardice and quitting his post. In his defence he stated that he had tried to report sick before going on duty and that he had been feeling unwell throughout the day. His Commanding Officer described him as an efficient NCO who had always performed his duties in a proper manner. As had occurred in a previous case — Private Roberts — the Commanding Officer's testimony did not save Holland. He was executed at 3.38 am on 30 May.

Details of Holland's offence and execution appeared as usual in General Routine Orders, and Captain Lionel Fergusson recorded the event in his diary — now deposited at the Imperial War Museum. Fergusson commented:

*'This punishment was not always carried out, in fact I do not know of another case in the Regiment. One cannot have but regrets about it but such a lot depends on the record of the man and I have known many that deserve shooting.'*[78]

Lance-Corporal Holland is known to have been of good character but he was in fact the fourth soldier from the Cheshire Regiment to be executed during the war. Two previous executions occurred in 1916 and one had taken place in 1915. Captain Fergusson's comments were also published by Malcolm Brown.[79]

Lance-Corporal Holland, aged 31, was originally a joiner's labourer, who regularly attended his local Wesleyan church in Northwich.[80] Holland's parents were not told the true cause of their son's death nor were the true circumstances revealed in the local press account which subsequently recorded his end.[81] The army chaplain who wrote to the lance-corporal's parents falsely intimated, 'Lance-Corporal Holland was buried in the debris from a shell which exploded in the trenches.'

The chaplain also remarked that Holland had been buried at Mont St Eloi, where a cross had been erected to mark his grave. The tombstone, which can be seen today in Ecoivres Military Cemetery, carries the inscription, *'His duty nobly done.'*

In the case of **Private Phillips** of 1 Coldstream Guards, who was executed for desertion on the same day as Lance-Corporal Holland, the

 chaplain who attended the execution also wrote to the next-of-kin. Little is known about Phillips except that he had served on the Western Front for 21 months and was under a suspended sentence of 10 years' penal servitude for a previous offence of desertion.[82] His case received the briefest of reviews. Six days after the trial the guardsman was executed.

The clergyman who attended Private Phillips was Captain T Guy Rogers MC, Chaplain to the 2nd Guards Brigade. During his wartime service from October 1915 to December 1916 Rogers regularly wrote home. In two of these letters he detailed the events surrounding the execution of Private Phillips. (Captain Rogers did not name Private Phillips in the letters.) The clergyman documented his feelings in what he clearly regarded as a most harrowing ordeal.

*'31st May 1916. Shall I tell you of the terrible experience I have just gone through (if so it must not go beyond the family circle of yourself and the Haslams). It has just fallen to my lot to prepare a deserter for his death, — that meant breaking the news to him, helping him with his last letters, passing the night with him on the straw in his cell, and trying to prepare his soul for meeting God: the execution and burying him immediately. The shadow was just hanging over me when I wrote the last letter but I tried to keep it out. Monday night I was with him, Tuesday morning at 3.30 he*

*was shot. He lay beside me for hours with his hand in mine. Poor fellow, it was a bad case, but he met his end bravely, and drank in all I could teach him about God, his father, Jesus his Saviour, and the reality of the forgiveness of sins. I feel a little shaken by it all, but my nerves, thank God, have not troubled me. Everyone has been so kind who knew of the ordeal. I will tell you more some other time. I want to get off it and away from the thought of it as much as I can.'*

Just over a week later Captain Rogers wrote again.

*'8th June 1916. I got your dear letter of sympathy today. I hear it is almost certain that the truth is told to the relatives, in the case of executions. (It was promulgated on parade.) I have written however, a careful letter in case this should not be so.'*

*'10th June 1916. I do value your letters so. I knew you would sympathise with me and felt cheered by the knowledge of it all the time in being called on to minister to that poor fellow before his death. I have not yet heard from his relatives.'*[83]

Private Phillips is buried in Wormhoudt Communal Cemetery, France, in a back area some distance from the battlefields.

Early in June 1916 a young volunteer was executed who had been unrepresented at his trial. It was very unusual for a soldier of good character not to have a 'prisoner's friend'. This only occurred in nine trials where the death penalty was carried out during the war. **Private James Archibald** of 17 Royal Scots was the last recorded case, and the only such case during 1916. However, Archibald's case was also unusual for another reason. The Scotsman was the first 'Bantam' to be executed during the war. The recruiting of Bantam battalions was authorised early in the war. It allowed men of otherwise good physique but who did not meet the minimum height requirement to be enlisted and serve together. The original height requirement was a minimum of 5' 3'', this was reduced to 5' for the purposes of recruiting Bantam battalions.

However, the case was also disturbing for another reason, Archibald's Commanding Officer, Lieutenant-Colonel R D Cheales, implied that soldierly qualities alone were not enough, and he commented that the private was considered to be of poor intellect.[84] This unfortunate remark, if true, did nothing to assist the 20 year old Edinburgh lad, who unaided had tried to conduct his own defence.

Six soldiers were executed during the month of June 1916. In five cases the condemned men were serving in Regular Army units, although two of the men were volunteers.

One Reservist, **Driver James Swaine** of 54 Battery, 39 Brigade, Royal Field Artillery, was a married man from Wealdstone in Middlesex. He was court martialled for desertion on 29 May 1916, when it transpired that he had overstayed his UK Christmas leave in 1915, and had not been arrested until the following April.

Although Driver Swaine had previously been of good character, a fellow soldier in 1 Division had not. **Private James Molyneaux** of 1 Loyal North Lancs, was serving under a suspended sentence of 10 years' penal servitude. His execution took place on 15 June and was the third shooting in the battalion in four months, the firing squad being found from Molyneaux's own unit.[85] Whilst it is difficult to imagine that there could be any consistency in a policy that generated successive executions in one particular unit, it would seem that the principle of deterrence was being exercised by HQ.

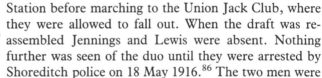

Two more Reservists who were executed towards the end of the month had both seen considerable army service, having enlisted early in the century. The two men, **Private John Jennings** and **Private Griffith Lewis**, had left Lancashire on 25 October 1915 on a draft bound for 2 South Lancs. In London the party left their kit at Waterloo Station before marching to the Union Jack Club, where they were allowed to fall out. When the draft was re-assembled Jennings and Lewis were absent. Nothing further was seen of the duo until they were arrested by Shoreditch police on 18 May 1916.[86] The two men were handed over to a military escort and then shipped out to their battalion which was billeted in a back area on the Somme. Their court martial took place on 20 June and confirmation of the two death sentences came quickly. Six days later, at 4 o'clock on the morning of 26 June, the sentences were carried out at the village of St Ouen – by a squad from the men's battalion.[87] Jennings and Lewis are buried side-by-side in Norfolk Cemetery at Bécourt-Bécordel, having been re-interred after the war.

Although both men had been absent for seven months the accounts given by Judge Babington, as well as the notifications appearing in General Routine Orders, both give the impression that Jennings and Lewis were new recruits. In fact this was not the case. The same incorrect conclusion – that Jennings and Lewis were fresh troops – had been drawn in 1925 during a Parliamentary debate on the Army & Air Force (Annual) Bill.[88] Jennings had previously served in France as a lance-corporal with his battalion, campaigning with the original BEF since 14 August 1914.[89] Lewis was also a veteran of the original BEF having landed in France on 15 September 1914. If Sir Douglas Haig thought that the executions of Jennings and Lewis would deter others from committing similar crimes, then he was wrong. On the day of the double execution, Private Richard Jones, No.10002, another August

1914 veteran, deserted.[90] There is no record that he was ever caught, but (like others) he forfeited his medals.

The *Medal Rolls* show an inconsistency that still persists today. Soldiers who were executed forfeited their medals, yet soldiers convicted of equally serious crimes, but who continued to serve after the suspension of their sentence, did not. The following examples are all men from 2 South Lancs who served with the original BEF and for whom medals were issued. Private Anderson, tried by FGCM for cowardice and sentenced to 7 years' penal servitude. Private Collins, sentenced to 5 years for desertion then killed in action on 4 August 1917. Private Kendrick, sentenced to 10 years' for cowardice then killed in action on 9 July 1916.

On 10 February 1925, Labour MP, Ernest Thurtle provoked the following Parliamentary exchange between himself and Secretary of State for War, Sir L Worthington-Evans. Thurtle was indirectly referring to the cases of Jennings and Lewis.

Thurtle: '. . . *number of men sentenced to death and executed for desertion while on active service in this country?'*

W-Evans: *'There were no men executed in the United Kingdom for desertion during the late war.'*

Thurtle: *'Is it not the fact that people who deserted in this country were executed for that desertion?'*

W-Evans: *'I was not sure what the honourable gentleman did mean by his question, and my answer is limited to those executed in the United Kingdom. I cannot give him the figures of those executed in France — if there were any — without a great deal of research, and I am not sure, at the moment, that the labour would be justified.'*[91]

The Secretary of State for War was of course, stalling. Fourteen soldiers had been arrested in the United Kingdom for an offence of desertion that subsequently resulted in their execution. More than half had deserted abroad before successfully negotiating the Channel, only to be arrested in the United Kingdom. The remainder had overstayed their home leave, or in the cases of Jennings and Lewis (exclusively), had absented themselves from a draft bound for overseas. However, no soldiers were returned to France and executed for any offence other than desertion.

Ernest Thurtle was not put off by Worthington-Evans' negative reply. A week later he raised the matter again, directly alluding to the cases of Jennings and Lewis.

Thurtle: '. . . *two private soldiers of the South Lancashire Regiment were arrested in London on 18th May 1916, for desertion in this country and were taken to France, tried, sentenced to death, and executed there . . state the reason why . . .'*

W-Evans: *'I am aware of the facts about these two cases as stated by the honourable member. The two men deserted at Waterloo Station from a draft proceeding to France to join their battalion. They were arrested together on the 18th May 1916, and were sent to France because it is ordinary practice to return a deserter to his unit for trial.'*

Thurtle: *'Does the right honourable gentleman think it is any less prudent to shoot these men in France than it would have been to shoot them in this country?'*

W-Evans: *'I am not expressing any opinion on the subject.'*[92]

On the penultimate day of June 1916, a Londoner who had volunteered soon after the outbreak of war, and who was serving in a Regular Army infantry battalion, was executed. **Rifleman Frederick Harding** of 1 King's Royal Rifle Corps deserted from a front line trench near Arras.

Had selection procedures been more rigorous in 1914, and if Harding had been truthful when he attested, then it is almost certain that the man would not have been accepted for army service. (Neither Harding's attestation form, nor his police record have been viewed by the authors. However, if he had been sentenced to imprisonment by the civil power before his enlistment, then he was required to make this known on his attestation form.) In a most unusual defence Harding virtually admitted to formerly being a tramp and beggar, who was prone to 'moving on'.[93]

His admissions prompted the authorities to make enquiries of the Metropolitan Police who confirmed his pre-war circumstances. (In normal circumstances details of a pre-war conviction would not have been admissible to the court – King's Regulation No.1919.) Following the trial Harding was medically examined. The check determined whether or not a soldier was physically and psychologically fit to undergo field punishment or hard labour. The medical board were of the opinion that Harding had a very low standard of intelligence but concluded that he showed no symptoms of mental illness.[94] The Commander-in-Chief was patently unsympathetic, and 21 year old Harding fell victim to both the army's inadequate enlistment screening, as well as his own personal failings. His execution was the last to take place before the Battle of the Somme commenced, and Harding was also the one hundredth victim of the army death penalty in the war. This total relates to all offences punishable under the Army Act, not just desertion, and also all theatres of operations, but does not include the Indian Army.

# NOTES

1 WO93/49, Summary of First World War capital court martial cases.
2 WO95/1271, Battalion War Diary.
3 Anthony Babington, *For the Sake of Example.*
4 WO95/1937, Battalion War Diary.
5 WO329/1, Index to the *Great War Medal Rolls.*
6 WO93/49, op cit.
7 Regimental Record book, East Kent Regiment.
8 WO93/49, op cit.
9 Anthony Babington, op cit.
10 WO95/1608, Battalion War Diary.
11 Ernest Thurtle, *Shootings at Dawn.*
12 WO95/1271, op cit.
13 WO93/49, op cit.
14 Anthony Babington, op cit.
15 *Soldiers Died in the Great War* − part 78.
16 WO95/2203, War Diary 24 Division Train ASC.
17 Anthony Babington, op cit.
18 WO95/2503, Battalion War Diary.
19 Anthony Babington, op cit.
20 F P Crozier, *A Brass Hat in No Man's Land.*
21 F P Crozier, *The Men I Killed.*
22 Anthony Babington, op cit.
23 WO329/1, op cit.
24 WO95/2490, Battalion War Diary.
25 WO93/49, op cit.
26 Anthony Babington, op cit.
27 WO93/49, op cit.
28 *The Dreadnought*, 22 April 1916.
29 WO329/1, op cit.
30 WO95/1856, Battalion War Diary.
31 WO95/1856, War Diary of 7 Sussex Regiment.(also)
32 Sylvia Pankhurst, *The Home Front.*
33 *The Dreadnought.*
34 WO95/1856, War Diary of 11 Middlesex.
35 Anthony Babington, op cit.
36 Guy Chapman, *Vain Glory.*
37 WO329/1600, *British War & Victory Medal Roll.*
38 WO93/49, op cit.
39 WO95/2158, Battalion War Diary.
40 *Hornsey Journal*, 4 February 1916.
41 WO95/2158, op cit.
42 Diary of J G Mortimer, Imperial War Museum, IWM:75/21/1.
43 Desmond Morton, *The Supreme Penalty: Canadian Deaths by Firing Squad in the First World War.*
44 Canadian Expeditionary Force, Nominal Roll of Officers, Non-Commissioned Officers and Men.
45 Desmond Morton, op cit.
46 WO93/49, op cit.
47 Ernest Thurtle, op cit.
48 Anthony Babington, op cit.
49 WO329/2669, *1914-15 Star Medal Roll.*
50 WO95/1270, Battalion War Diary.
51 Extracts from General Routine Orders, included in the war diary of 1 Royal Welsh Fusiliers − WO95/1665.
52 Anthony Babington, op cit.
53 Ibid.
54 Ibid.
55 WO95/2090, Battalion War Diary.
56 WO93/49, op cit.
57 WO95/1347, Battalion War Diary.
58 Anthony Babington, op cit.

59 WO95/1665, op cit.
60 Anthony Babington, op cit.
61 Ibid.
62 WO95/1665, op cit.
63 Ibid.
64 Letter from a Transport Driver in 10 Durham Light Infantry, sent to Ernest Thurtle MP after the war.
65 Anthony Babington, op cit.
66 WO95/1269, Battalion War Diary.
67 Record Book of 2 Battalion Sussex Regiment, Sussex County Records Office, Chichester, reference RSR MS 2/65.
68 The map reference of his grave was recorded − Record Book of 2 Battalion Sussex Regiment, Sussex County Records Office, Chichester, reference RSR MS 2/66.
69 North West Kent Family Historical Journal, March 1984.
70 WO95/1431, Battalion War Diary.
71 Letter from Lord Chancellor's Department to the next-of-kin. This letter does not make mention of the wound suffered by Private Roberts.
72 Ibid.
73 Ibid.
74 BBC *Sixty Minutes* programme 3rd or 4th November 1983.
75 WO95/2243, Battalion War Diary.
76 Anthony Babington, op cit.
77 Ibid.
78 Diary of Captain Lionel Fergusson, Imperial War Museum reference 77/166/1.
79 Malcolm Brown, *Tommy Goes to War*.
80 *Northwich Chronicle*, 10 June 1916.
81 Ibid and *Northwich Guardian*, 6 June 1916.
82 WO93/49, op cit.
83 Extracts from over 200 letters from Rev. T.G.Rogers MC, CF, Imperial War Museum, Misc.77/107/1.
84 WO93/49, op cit.
85 WO95/1270, op cit.
86 WO95/1665, op cit.
87 WO95/2250, Battalion War Diary.
88 Official Report 5th Series: Parliamentary Debates: Commons 1924-5: Vol.182: March 23 − April 9th, page 1385.
890 WO329/2458, *1914 Star Medal Roll*.
901 Ibid.
91 Parliamentary Debates: Commons 1924-5: Vol.180. Oral Answers, 10 February 1925.
92 Parliamentary Debates: Commons 1924-5: Vol.180. Written Answers, 17 February 1925.
93 *The Times* on 28 December 1914 published its annual review on 'Our Legal Poor'. The statistics for London showed that in 1914 pauperism was at its lowest level since the turn of the century. However, the drop of 1,399 cases was not significant as it represented only a one-and-a-third per cent reduction on a total figure of just over 100,000. Poplar had the highest percentage of paupers, with a ratio of 42.2 cases per 1,000 head of the population. This was twice the average for London. It would of course be incorrect to suggest that 1,399 paupers had successfully enlisted in the armed forces.
94 Anthony Babington, op cit.

# Chapter Four

## *And the meek shall inherit the earth.*

By the eve of the Somme offensive the BEF had built up a force of 54 British and Dominion infantry divisions with which to smash the Kaiser. In spite of careful preparations, including the provision of additional medical services, no one could have foreseen the scale and intensity of the slaughter which took place on the first day of the offensive. By mid-morning on 1 July it was bloodily self-evident that sheer mass of attackers was insufficient to overcome the withering hail of bullets from the determined German defenders. The official historian described the attackers' resolve:

*'No braver or more determined men ever faced an enemy than those sons of the British Empire who "went over the top" on the 1st of July 1916. Never before had the ranks of a British Army on the field of battle contained the finest of all classes of the nation in physique, brains and education. And they were volunteers not conscripts. If ever a decisive victory was to be won it was to be expected now.'*[1]

Now recognised as the blackest day of the British Army, 1 July and its casualties, which approached 60,000 men, reflected a nation's pride and sense of duty. For a small minority, however, the forthcoming ordeal by battle was to prove too much. Whether provoked by moral weakness or by sheer fright the unfortunates who deserted or ran away were regarded as 'expendable' by the British military commanders. The Somme was the proving ground of Kitchener's Armies, whose ranks also provided the majority of victims for the firing squads. Of the 79 men executed for military offences during and after the main battles on the Somme in 1916, five-sixths were serving in New Army divisions. (Period ending 31 January 1917.)

Whilst many of those who had been wounded and stranded in no-man's-land on 1 July were still struggling to crawl back to their trenches, the firing squads recommenced their deadly duties with a trio of victims. The executions, which all took place separately, had no connection with the activities or build-up to the Somme offensive. Similarly the circumstances of the cases would seem to have little in common – except perhaps, for the dubious mental condition of the condemned soldiers.

All three men were British, although **Trooper Alexander Butler**, formerly of the 7 Hussars, had re-enlisted in the Royal Canadian Dragoons at Valcartier, Canada, on 24 September 1914. Butler, a Londoner, served in 'B' Squadron Royal Canadian Dragoons – part of 3 Canadian Division. He was the only soldier serving with the

Canadian Forces to suffer the death penalty by sentence of a full General Court Martial.

The reason for trial before a more formal court was that Trooper Butler was charged with murder, having killed a comrade in the squadron by firing five shots into him. The trial took place on 24 June when the court heard that Butler had been behaving in a strange manner ever since he had suffered a bad fall from his horse.[2] The court expressed understanding, and while sentencing him to death recommended mercy. Sir Douglas Haig did not concur and the sentence was confirmed.

It is difficult to believe that someone involved in the review and confirmation procedure was not aware of the fact that blows to the head, such as might be sustained by a fall from a horse, could account for the rider's subsequent irrational behaviour. It must be presumed that the execution of Trooper Butler was a decisive remedy to a more complex problem. In more charitable circumstances Butler's uncharacteristic behaviour after his fall would have entitled him to an honourable discharge and a silver wound badge to match. (Silver wound badges were awarded to men who were discharged from the army as medically unfit. Interestingly recipients included men discharged with shellshock.)

In the case of a second soldier executed on 2 July, the man's mental state again came into consideration. **Private George Hunter** was an early volunteer who had been drafted to France on 24 August 1915[3]  and was serving in a regiment that hitherto had no man executed. During May 1916, 2 Durham Light Infantry were in the trenches near the canal to the north of Ypres[4] when Private Hunter went absent. At his trial on 22 June it was revealed that he had previously been punished for being absent on ten different occasions, and also had been convicted of carelessly wounding himself.[5] In his defence Hunter told the court that for the past 18 months he had suffered from a 'wandering mind'. Such a claim however was a poor attempt to justify the actions of the soldier. In fact Hunter had been very successful in his absence, being one of the very few soldiers who crossed the Channel and escaped to England.[6] After sentence of death had been passed his commanding officer noted on the proceeding that he thought Private Hunter was suffering from a mental abnormality, and recommended that he should be examined by a doctor specialising in mental diseases. However, rather callously, no notice was taken of his superior's statement and Hunter was duly executed in a back area of the Ypres Salient.

Little is known of the third and last soldier executed on 2 July. His army number would suggest that he was either a regular or a reservist who had gone to France early in 1915.

**Private John Smith** was probably in his late twenties. What, however, is extraordinary about his case is that he was the fourth man from his battalion — 1 Loyal North Lancs — to be executed in four-and-a-half months. Only one other man was executed from this regiment during the remainder of the war. The speedy imposition of this string of successive executions further substantiates the contention that death sentences were confirmed in an arbitrary manner.

On 9 July another soldier serving with the CEF was executed. **Private James Wilson,** like very many of his comrades, was actually an Irishman who had seen pre-war service with the Connaught Rangers before enlisting at Valcartier in September 1914.[7] On 13 June 1916 whilst his unit, 4th Canadian Infantry Battalion, was engaged in the re-taking of Tor Top (Hill 62) north of Mount Sorrell in the Ypres Salient, Wilson went absent in order to avoid service in the trenches.

In the summer of 1916 the first executions began to take place of men serving in Territorial Divisions. On 16 July two soldiers, from different units in 164 Infantry Brigade, 55 Division were shot for desertion. Although the division had only been formed in France in 1916, both battalions concerned had arrived on the Western Front in 1915 and had initially been allocated to 51 Division.

**Private Joseph Brennan** was a Merseysider serving in a unit comprised mainly of Irishmen — 1/8 King's Liverpool Regiment. (Private Brennan may in fact have been a wartime volunteer and not a pre-war Territorial.) His offence had taken place whilst the battalion was serving south of Arras, and his trial took place on the last day of June. The second soldier, **Private J Sloan** (who it is believed had enlisted as a Territorial before the outbreak of war) of 1/4 King's Own (Royal Lancaster Regiment), had been serving in support trenches during June, before being sent to a back area on a course of instruction.[8] During this training, which involved bombing with hand grenades, an eyewitness saw Private Sloan discard his equipment and make off. Six days later he was arrested in Rouen, and when questioned he stated that he had a pass to travel to the United Kingdom. His trial took place on the day before Brennan's, and in due course the small village of Barly on the Arras front was the scene of the twelfth double execution of the war.

The next soldier to be executed also served in a Territorial division, and it is believed, from his army number, that he was a Kitchener volunteer and not a pre-war soldier. He was also the first soldier to be executed as a result of direct involvement in the Somme offensive. **Private Arthur Earp** was serving with 1/5 Warwickshire Regiment — part of 48 Division. During the preliminary bombardment Private

Earp's platoon was holding the front line south-east of Hébuterne.[9] After two hours of enemy counter-barrage Earp had told his sergeant that he could stand it no longer and rushed away to seek refuge in a support line dugout. At his trial on 10 July Earp was charged with two offences, quitting his post and conduct to the prejudice of good order and military discipline. The court martial panel was told that Earp had shown signs of distress for some time prior to making off, and quite uncharacteristically the officers were sympathetic and recommended the private to mercy on the grounds of previous good service – adding that the ferocity of the bombardment was a further mitigating circumstance. The chain of command concurred with this recommendation until the papers reached the Army Commander, General Sir Henry Rawlinson.[10]

It was a testing time, the flower of the British nation had been in action for merely a few disastrous weeks. Perhaps in his brief deliberations, the Commander-in-Chief reasoned that this was a time to stand and fight, and hence he showed no mercy. Private Earp, from Birmingham, was executed at Bouzincourt on 22 July.

On 23 July, **Private James Cassidy,** a veteran of the Dardanelles campaign, faced a firing squad. His battalion, 1 Royal Inniskilling Fusiliers, had been part of the gallant 29 Division whose Gallipoli exploits had been widely recognised. (Private Cassidy had landed at Gallipoli on 25 May 1915 – Index to the *Great War Medal Rolls*.)

On 1 July the Irishmen were badly mauled in an unsuccessful attack south of 'Y' Ravine. Cassidy survived – somewhat briefly – unlike 568 of his comrades including the commanding officer.[11]

On 25 July another Canadian soldier was shot. Two of the three previously executed Canadians had seen pre-war military service, and by a rather unusual coincidence, so had **Gunner Frederick Arnold.** His inclusion amongst the victims of the firing squad is unique in that he was an American who had formerly served in the US Army.[12] At the time of his death Arnold was serving with 1 Battery, 1 Brigade, Canadian Field Artillery and his rank is given variously as driver, gunner or lance-bombardier.[13] Arnold's reason for deserting is not difficult to determine. At the beginning of April 1916 the Canadian Corps had taken over the front line trenches which extended from St Eloi, to north of Hooge – in the Ypres Salient. In June savage fighting had followed, when German gains were followed by Canadian counter attacks, the bitter dispute being enacted over the high ground which was coveted by both opponents.

It is difficult to imagine that Arnold's disappearance was more ambitious than simply to escape the horrors of the Salient. Nevertheless he was arrested at Boulogne wearing civilian clothes, although no information was forthcoming about any intention to cross the Channel. Rather unusually the artilleryman was not returned to his unit but was tried at Boulogne. As a result, Arnold's service record was not produced to the court, and speculation abounds that he might have fared better had this been available.[14] His execution at Boulogne was one of the few not carried out near the battlefront.

Anthony Babington incorrectly states that during the later part of 1916, all offences of cowardice culminating in executions were as a result of the most bitter fighting on the Somme. In fact, of the six offences, three were committed on the Somme, one in the Ypres Salient and two near La Plantin – north of the La Bassée canal. It is acknowledged that the latter two offences arose from actions designed to draw attention away from the Somme offensive.

On 30 June, as part of these diversionary activities, 39 Division had been ordered to attack a position known as the Boar's Head at Richebourg L'Avoué. The results were disastrous for the battalions involved, particularly the leading battalions of the Sussex Regiment. Further south, in similar territory, the first two offences occurred. In this sector the Germans had a prominent front line position known to the British as the Pope's Nose. The protrusion was the closest point to the British front line and an obvious target for aggression. Consequently XI Corps HQ ordered that a series of trench raids be carried out, the first of which took place on 4 June 1916.

On 11 June, 17 Sherwood Foresters took over the front line near the Pope's Nose. They were an inexperienced battalion like all the others in 39 Division, having only been in France since 7 March 1916. On the night of 3/4 July two battalions were detailed to raid the German trenches. The 16 Rifle Brigade would attack the Pope's Nose and a small party from 17 Sherwood Foresters would attack further south and guard the flank of their comrades. [15] In what must have been a rather unconventional arrangement, the raiders from the Sherwood Foresters were divided into two leading parties, led by NCOs, and two following, which were commanded by second-lieutenants. At 12.30 am the raid was carried out, the party returning one-hour-and-twenty minutes later. The battalion diarist recorded, 'Raid most successful'. This assessment however seems somewhat doubtful as Second-Lieutenant Bullivant was wounded (he died on 21 July), a private had been killed and another was missing. Additionally, all five NCOs had been wounded together with six privates, a total of 14 casualties from a complement of 50. Neither would it seem that the 16 Rifle Brigade fared any better, as the RAMC recorded the total casualties for the venture as 87, many of them being seriously wounded.[16]

On the following night a party — again from 17 Sherwood Foresters but led by a lieutenant — was detailed to go out and recover three portable bridges abandoned during the previous night's operations. Not surprisingly, as the court later heard from the officer, the whole party was in an extremely jittery state. Undoubtedly this was partly due to the fact that the battalion had already been in the line for 25 days without a break. The bridges were said to be about 75 yards from the German line and when the time came to move out into no-man's-land **Private George Lawton** refused to go. 36 year old Lawton, a married man with five children said it was certain death to go out on this mission and he remained in the fire trench.

On the following day, news of Lawton's disobedience had obviously not reached Brigade HQ, as Brigadier-General R D F Oldman DSO congratulated the Sherwood Foresters on their (previous) 'successful' raid. He continued saying how pleased he was with their fighting spirit, and that the raiders had brought credit to the battalion with their gallant conduct.[17] Lawton's offence was not unique, for in July another private from 17 Sherwood Foresters committed a similar offence.

At 1 o'clock in the morning, just three days after Lawton's offence, **Private Bertie McCubbin** had refused to go out into no-man's-land to occupy a listening post some 40 yards in front of the British parapet. The circumstances of the offence were very similar to those of Private Cuthbert (9 Cheshires) who was executed earlier that year — in May. Both offences occurred during moonlit nights, and in sectors of the line that were obviously very similar. The location where McCubbin was stationed had been fought over during the Battle for the Aubers Ridge (1915) and in places it had been difficult for the British to establish a continuous front line. As a result, in places there were positions that became known as 'islands' because of their isolation. Obviously manning such positions was extremely stressful and debilitating, as army doctor Lord Moran was later to comment[18]

These shortcomings however were not permitted to overshadow the perceived 'success' of the trench raid — as the Divisional Commander was recorded to have said of 17 Sherwood Foresters, 'the fighting spirit shewn was excellent'. Omitting the Corps Commander, the Army commander, General Sir Charles Monro was the next to pass comment. On 13 July he inspected the survivors of the raiding party and congratulated them on their work. 'He expressed himself as very pleased with their turn out and smart appearance, that they were very much steadier than when he saw them last.'[19] These comments were out of keeping with later remarks that he passed about Bertie

McCubbin. On 14 July Sherwood Foresters were relieved, and after a tour of duty lasting 34 days they went into rest.[20]

Away from the rigours and dangers of trench life military bureaucracy was invoked. Courts martial were convened and the process of military justice began. The charges in both Lawton's and McCubbin's cases involved cowardice and wilful defiance. George Lawton received a sympathetic hearing and a recommendation to mercy. He told the court that earlier in the war he had been buried for four hours after a shell had caused his dugout to collapse. (Lawton stated that this incident had happened five months previously. It is believed that this statement may be incorrect. If the private had crossed to France with 17 Battalion − which it is believed he did − then the unit had only been in France for just under four months. His error may of course have been inadvertent.) The court's concern extended to a recommendation that Lawton be subject to a medical examination, although ultimately it revealed nothing untoward about the soldier's health.

At his trial Bertie McCubbin pleaded that his nerves were also in a bad state. He said that if he had gone out into no-man's-land on that occasion, then his nervous state would have put his comrades' lives in jeopardy. McCubbin also explained to the court that he came from a large family. His father had been killed earlier in the war, leaving his mother to fend for six young children. The court sentenced Private McCubbin to death, but recommended mercy. Leniency for both cases was endorsed along the chain of command, until the proceedings were scrutinised by the Army Commander − General Monro. Commenting on the case of Bertie McCubbin he stated that soldiers who deliberately chose to avoid the dangers of soldiering would not be tolerated. Monro also recommended that Lawton's sentence be carried out. The Commander-in-Chief concurred with Monro's opinions.

On 29 July the two men were prepared for their final ordeal, the condemned cell being improvised at an advanced dressing station known as Lone Farm. At 9 pm a medical officer from 133 Field Ambulance recorded the events:

*'Preparations are being made at ADS for retention of two men, under escort, who are to be shot at dawn on 30th inst.'*[21]

The next day the executions proceeded as the ritual dictated, although an enforced audience was not in attendance. In fact it was strictly forbidden. Personnel from the Field Ambulance were ordered to remain in their quarters until the task was concluded.[22]

'Justice' had been heard, but not seen to be done. (Earlier in his book Jobson comments − probably of events circa March 1916 − on the 'monotonous' ritual of parading the men to announce the details of cases resulting in execution. It would seem that boredom rather than deterrence was the result. However, the requirement for this procedure was laid down in King's Regulations no.593.) Both men were buried in the little cemetery that adjoined the Advanced Dressing Station, but after the war they were re-interred at Brown's Road Military Cemetery, Festubert.

On the same day that this double execution was carried out another Canadian soldier was shot. Like the case of Lance-Bombardier Arnold of the Canadian Field Artillery who had been executed five days previously, the events took place at Boulogne. The unfortunate soldier was **Private John Roberts** of 2 Canadian Mounted Rifles.

J W Muirhead, a young officer recently commissioned into the Army Service Corps, recorded the case and its unusual twist of fate.[23]

'. . . in June 1916 I went to France and landed at Havre. I was soon sent to Boulogne where I spent a month. While I was there I was detailed to be an officer in waiting at a court martial which was hearing a case of desertion. The prisoner was a Canadian of 19 years, and as a volunteer had been sent to France with his regiment from which he had deserted and found his way to Boulogne.[24] Here he got entangled with a woman with whom he lived for several months. He might never have been arrested if he had not drawn his pay regularly from the Base Cashier.[25] He was sentenced to death and three weeks later he was shot . . .'[26]

Robert's long absence undoubtedly influenced the decision to confirm his sentence; as during this time he had avoided the carnage suffered by his battalion in the operations to recover Observatory Ridge in the Ypres Salient. His mother received a blunt notification of her son's demise.

'Madam,

With deep regret I have the honour to inform you that a report has been received to the effect that no.107526, Private Roberts J W was tried by Field General Court-Martial at Boulogne, France on the 15th day of July, 1916, on the charge of "when on active service deserting His Majesty's Service" and was sentenced by the Court "to suffer death by being shot." The sentence was duly carried out at 4.36 a.m. on the 30th day of July, 1916.

I have the honour to be, Madam, Your obedient servant, Frank Beard i/c Record Office.'[27]

The first soldier to be executed in August 1916 was yet another Canadian, of obvious French descent. **Private Come LaLiberté** enlisted in his home of Montreal in March 1915 and three months later sailed from Quebec with the first draft of reinforcements.[28] A year after his arrival in France his unit, 3 Battalion Canadian Expeditionary Force, was once again in the Ypres Salient when LaLiberté deserted. The battalion was billeted at Dominion Lines within the Salient, when at 4.52 am on 4 August, 25 year old Private LaLiberté was executed in front of his battalion — who had been paraded to witness the event.[29]

A week later a fourth soldier serving in a Territorial battalion was executed; and it would seem that Territorial soldiers had suddenly become the focus of the Commander-in-Chief's attention.

However, it is possible that the victim was a scapegoat from a division whose attack on 1 July had gone so disastrously wrong. Following the failure of 46 Division's attack on Gommecourt a Court of Inquiry had been held and the Divisional Commander, Major-General Montagu-Stuart-Wortley had been removed — even before the court's conclusions had been reached. His posting to a command in Ireland seems rather unjust, for his division had been given scant time to prepare for the attack.

The condemned soldier, **Lance-Corporal Frederick Hawthorne,** had landed in France as a private in March 1915.[30] In view of his abilities he was in due course promoted to lance-corporal. On 1 July his battalion, 1/5 South Staffs, assaulted the German trenches in the first wave. The divisional war diary recorded the scene. The German wire had only been breached in one place, and bodies cut down by German machine guns lay piled in the gap.[31] Fortunately a second assault was repeatedly postponed and eventually cancelled — for which the Corps Commander later demanded an explanation.[32] The attack on Gommecourt had been planned as a 'pincer movement'; with the 46 Division striking from the north and the 56 Division from the south. Although the latter division met with considerably more success than did the former, the grounds for continuing with a second assault were inadequate, given that 'Gommecourt' was only intended to be a diversionary attack designed to confuse the Germans. (Prior to 1 July 1916 consideration had been given to abandoning the Gommecourt attack in favour of retaliatory action to recover lost ground on Vimy Ridge.)

Anthony Babington states that the condemned man's battalion had suffered considerable casualties, but 1/5 South Staffs' war diary records that the losses on 1 July were 16 officers and 161 other ranks — two of these officers and 20 of the men were said to be suffering from shellshock.[33] When recorded by the division these figures were inflated to 16 officers and 190 other ranks.[34] There is reason to believe however that these figures were considerably exaggerated.

The casualty returns for 1 and 2 July for 139 Brigade — also part of 46 Division — were recorded at Division as 1085 all ranks. A few days later at the Court of Inquiry this figure had been reduced to 397. By way of an example (in a different regiment), the initial number of 1/5 Sherwood Foresters recorded as 'missing' was 232, but the figure was reduced to four by the time the Court of Inquiry took place! It would seem in fact, that overall casualties had been relatively light. Original figures being perhaps as much as two-and-half times the true numbers. (Fatalities in the ranks of 1/5 South Staffs for 1 July 1916 are recorded as 42 – *Soldiers Died in the Great War*, part 42 extracted details are reproduced in *Soldiers Killed on the First Day of the Somme* by Ernest W Bell.)

Casualties did not only occur from enemy action either; later that month one soldier in 1/5 South Staffs opted out with a self-inflicted wound. Further operations were planned for July – in the form of a night time raid on the German trenches. In charge of the rear section of the raiders was Lance-Corporal Hawthorne. But when the officer who was to lead the party appeared, Hawthorne complained. He argued that the night was clear and bright, insisting that it would be murder to go out under such conditions. In the confines of a battalion dugout, the raiders' rendezvous, the sentiment spread amongst Hawthorne's comrades, who began making the same representations. Eventually the party were persuaded to leave the dugout, but when the raiders left the advance trench neither Hawthorne nor his party followed.

The incident involving Hawthorne displayed parallels with what had occurred to Privates Cuthbert (May 1916) and McCubbin (July 1916). All three perceived the danger of detection by the enemy in the moonlight. One can only speculate about the soldiers' motives for remaining in the trenches, for it could have arisen from the men's respect for their NCO's assessment of the situation, or a keen sense of self preservation. However, neither allegiance to their officers nor the threat of a firing squad galvanised the men out of the trenches.

22 year old Lance-Corporal Hawthorne was tried on the last day of July. He was charged with cowardice as well as a rather unusual offence under section 5 (6) of the Army Act. Hawthorne's statement, made in the dugout before the aborted raid, that the good visibility made it murder to go out, gave rise to a charge of 'previous to going into action, using words likely to cause alarm or despondency'. No attempt was made at the trial to justify the corporal's actions, and a sentence of death was passed on him.

Anthony Babington has stated that during the confirmation procedure the brigade commander appended a highly prejudicial memorandum. This illegal addition presented the Brigadier's account of the aborted raid. The offender, Brigadier-General H B Williams had also been before a court during July. It had not been a court martial but a Court of Inquiry into the failure of the attack at Gommecourt on 1 July. (Both Brigadier-General H B Williams commanding 137 Brigade and Brigadier-General C T Shipley, commanding 139 Brigade, gave evidence before this court.) At the Inquiry the court had heard that Williams' brigade major had been more effective in command than the general himself had.[35] Was, therefore, the brigadier's vitriolic addendum an attempt to rehabilitate his own reputation as an effective disciplinarian in the eyes of his superiors?

Three Kitchener volunteers were shot in succession during the month of August. There was little or nothing which could be found to mitigate the offences of the first two.

The first deserter was a 24 year old with a very bad military record. **Private William Nelson,** of 14 Durham Light Infantry, had committed his offence in the vicinity of Ypres. The court heard that he had two previous convictions for absence, for which he had received a sentence of one year's imprisonment followed by a sentence of penal servitude for life.[36] By the time the Commander-in-Chief had determined Nelson's fate, the private's unit had travelled south to the Somme. He was executed at Acheux on the same day as Lance Corporal Hawthorne. It is interesting to note that Private Nelson's home town of Seaham Harbour had been shelled by a German submarine on 11 July. It is not of course possible to determine whether or not the soldier was aware of this incident, nor whether his possible concern had any bearing on his actions.

The second victim was **Private Allan Murphy** who had been absent from 9 Cameronians (Scottish Rifles) for six months. Not surprisingly Sir Douglas Haig confirmed his death sentence. Details of Murphy's offence and execution were published in General Routine Orders on 4 September 1916.[37] It appeared as item number 1771 and his case headed a list of five men, all of whom had recently been executed. Contrary to post-war instructions Murphy's death was recorded in the official casualty roll, as were all the soldiers who served in the Cameronians and who were executed.[38] In each such case, the cause of death was omitted.

In the third case the soldier was an NCO and a Bantam. (It is believed that the man was a Bantam, although Judge Babington has stated that the soldier enlisted early in 1916. Examination and comparison of his army number tends to indicate that he had probably enlisted early in 1915.)

**Corporal Jesse Wilton** was aged 40 and served in 15 Sherwood Foresters − part of 35 Division.[39] The sector of the line where his offence took place was the scene of much bitter and unsuccessful fighting. To the west lay British lines snaking through the shattered remains of Trones Wood; facing the Sherwoods were the enemy trenches at Guillemont. A couple of unsuccessful attacks had been made by both

Wilton's battalion and other units. The Foresters were hard pressed in their position and had eaten nothing for days. One officer jokingly ribbed a ranker, saying that the man would have to eat iron rations. However, the eating of iron rations was prohibited unless specifically permitted by an officer.

Hungry or not, Corporal Jesse Wilton and a number of men from his section were detailed to occupy a forward position in no-man's-land between Trones Wood and Guillemont. The position was considered to be of strategic importance and the task was all the more stressful because the party had been detailed to remain in the dangerously exposed spot for 48 hours. Whilst in this position the section had been under heavy fire, and just six hours short of the allotted time Wilton ordered the evacuation of the post. Details of the incident have recently been revealed.

*'It was at about this time that a corporal of Y company took his section of seven men out of the line* [Anthony Babington maintains that the party comprised ten men], *having had no rations for three days and being unable to stand up to the strain. Officers drew revolvers to control some dreadful moments when a panicky retreat began to spread . . . It is scarcely doubted that Colonel Gordon feared for the steadiness of his battalion.'*[40]

Lord Moran, an army doctor and later Winston Churchill's physician, knew the toll that manning such a position took of a man's constitution. He affirmed:

*'It is difficult to sustain the soldier's spirit in a lonely outpost; he is conscious of a sense of isolation. Between him and the main unit living further back in comparative security and comfort a gulf opens. His own fate is always in his mind.'*[41]

The execution of Corporal Wilton on 17 August led to a rumour and later a myth, the origin of which is not difficult to imagine. The story circulated that a corporal in 16 Cheshires (the unit is obviously wrong but 16 Cheshires and 15 Sherwood Foresters were brigaded together) had been tried by court martial and then shot for eating his iron rations without permission.[42]

As the Canadian Corps made its way down to the Somme battlefields in August, yet another of its soldiers was executed. Unusually the soldier had been shot for desertion, although the evidence suggested that he could have been charged with casting away his arms or possibly disobedience. **Private Reynolds** of 3 Battalion CEF had 'fallen out' on the way to the trenches. Throwing down his rifle, he adamantly insisted that he would not go to the trenches even at the point of a bayonet.[43]

On 8 August the court heard the unanimous testimony of Reynold's captain, platoon commander, and sergeant as to the soldier's former courage.[44] However, higher echelons were unimpressed. In the second week in August 3 CEF left the Ypres Salient and moved into rest near St Omer. The battalion war diary recorded that at 5.27 am on 23 August, Private Reynolds was executed at the Rifle Butts by a firing squad commanded by Lieutenant Gray. And at 9 am the battalion was paraded for promulgation of the sentence.[45] Private Reynolds is now buried at Longuenesse (Souvenir) Cemetery St Omer. His grave has an unusual headstone which commemorates not one, but two soldiers. The unusual headstone is not related to the fact that Reynolds was executed. The limited space available in the cemetery did not permit the erection of two headstones.

In the third week in August an execution took place in a Pioneer battalion − a type of unit which was allocated at the rate of one-per-division. Pioneering duties were of a labouring nature, including the movement of supplies, materials and trench stores as well as the construction of new trenches and the improvement of old ones. These tasks were frequently carried out at night, and were often hazardous.

In the same way that fighting infantry congregated prior to duty in the trenches, Pioneers also 'fell in', ready for the allocation of fatigues. At one such roll call **Private Peter Giles** of 14 Northumberland Fusiliers, was found to be missing, and he remained so for a week. During July, Giles' division, the 21st, had been engaged in the operations on the Somme, but shortly afterwards had temporarily been transferred northwards. On 24 August Private Giles was executed in a back area behind Arras.

On the day after Private Giles was shot another Canadian soldier was executed for murder. **Driver De Fehr** had served as a non-combatant on the Western Front for 16 months at the time the killing. He had originally served with 2 Canadian Divisional Train, Canadian Army Service Corps, but his duties had later altered and offered greater safety from hostile action. A further posting had dispatched him to 1 Canadian Reserve Park, a formation attached to GHQ. De Fehr's crime may have fulfilled many a soldier's fantasy when the Canadian shot his sergeant major in the back,[46] but in reality his actions, like those of his earlier counterparts, raises questions about the condemned man's sanity.

On the same day as Driver De Fehr's execution another colonial soldier was shot, when for the first time the firing squads turned their rifles on a New Zealander. During the war only five soldiers serving in New Zealand regiments were executed (Anthony Babington incorrectly quotes a figure of just two New Zealand soldiers being executed during the war, one for mutiny and the other for desertion) and although **Private Frank Hughes** was the first of these cases, he had also been the last of the five to enlist.

According to his service and medical records, Hughes was a strongly built individual – five foot four-and-a-half inches tall and weighing eleven stones. In pre-war life he was a labourer for a firm of builders in Wellington, New Zealand and had enlisted into 2 Battalion New Zealand Rifle Brigade on 16 November 1915 at Trentham at the age of 27. Hughes sailed from New Zealand on 4 March 1916 travelling with 10th Reinforcements, via Egypt and then on to France.[47]

On 28 April, the then Lance-Corporal Hughes (like most new arrivals Hughes relinquished his stripe) arrived at the New Zealand Infantry Base Depot at Etaples where he undoubtedly endured the rigours of training in the 'Bull Ring'. This infamous venue was often the scene of unrelenting cruelty at the hands of the bullying 'canaries' or instructors. After four weeks at the Base Depot Hughes was posted to the front, destined to serve with 2 Battalion Canterbury Infantry Regiment – near Armentières. Thereafter Hughes' military service was one long catalogue of military offences.

Hughes' company commander, Captain F Starnes was not impressed when, five days after the private's arrival, the soldier went absent from evening parade. The following day the commanding officer, Lieutenant-Colonel H Stewart, docked Hughes' pay for seven days after Company Sergeant Major Mitchell related the offence. When arraigned before his CO Hughes' character had been described as 'fair'. However, later that evening the private wasted no time in re-offending when he got drunk and was unfit to go on duty. And he compounded his misdemeanour by causing a disturbance after 'lights out' – and subsequently going absent from the early hours of the next day until mid-afternoon. Hughes' CSM again informed the commanding officer who prescribed a harsher penalty in the form of 28 days' field punishment no.2. Whilst this punishment did not entail being tied to a fixed object, it did involve loss of pay for the duration of the sentence. As Private Hughes' Army Service Record does not indicate otherwise, it may be assumed that he endured this sentence without further incident. It is possible of course, (or even quite likely) that he was sent away from his battalion to undergo sentence, or to a place where no written record was kept of any further indiscipline.

Less than two weeks after his field punishment had expired, Hughes went absent again. Two captains were witnesses at the subsequent Field General Court Martial on 26 July, when Frank Hughes was sentenced to a year's hard labour. The sentence was confirmed and suspended by Brigadier-General Braithwaite – two days after which, whilst in the front line near Armentières, Hughes promptly deserted again.

Hughes had gone missing whilst en route to the trenches, a fatally serious element in the charges which he subsequently faced after his arrest by military police in the early hours of 9 August.

The New Zealander was tried on 12 August. The president of the court martial was Major G G Griffiths, and Captains M Urquhart and W G McLean were members. The impartiality of the proceedings is questionable, for all three officers were serving in Hughes' battalion at the time of the trial.

By the standards of the time it is not surprising that the Commander-in-Chief confirmed Hughes' sentence, if only because of the private's disciplinary record. Hughes had been a soldier for about nine months, punctuated by two weeks' absence; he had neither been in action nor reported sick.

If his military record bears mute testimony of a wilful determination to disobey military etiquette, then contemporary recollections also provide evidence of what some of his comrades felt about the iniquity of his sentence.

A New Zealand officer, who subsequently witnessed the execution by firing squad of Private Hughes, recalled that the padre, a sympathetic captain named Kettle, had gone to offer the soldier religious solace on the eve of the shooting. The padre, shaking his head had complained to him:

'Can't do anything with him . . . He told me that I was a bastard, and to get the hell out of it. I can't do anything, but it's not right — they shouldn't shoot a man. A volunteer is a volunteer.'

Hughes was shot at the small village of Hallencourt, far away from the front line, on 25 August 1916. The execution was carried out by a firing party composed of a sergeant and ten Pioneers.[48]

Seven years to the day after General Sir Douglas Haig confirmed Hughes' sentence a clerk in the New Zealand Army Records Office was working on the issue of commemorative 'Death Plaques' that were to be mailed to relatives of deceased soldiers. Although it is clear that a plaque was made to commemorate Frank Hughes, his service record is marked, 'Shot by sentence of FGCM. Ineligible', so his plaque was handed to the Chief Clerk for disposal.

In early September General Routine Orders announced that a soldier from 51 (Highland) Division had been executed.[49] The extract recorded:

*'No.2057* **Private J Higgins**, *9th, attached 1/8th Battalion, Argyll and Sutherland Highlanders was tried by Field General Court-Martial on the following charge:-*

*'When on Active Service, Deserting His Majesty's Service.*

*'The accused absented himself from the fighting zone till apprehended, a week later, disguised, in the vicinity of a base port.*

*'The sentence of the Court was "To suffer death by being shot." The sentence was duly carried out at 5.33 a.m. on 26th August, 1916.'*

*The announcement gave away few details. The port concerned was not identified, and the description that Private Higgins had been arrested in disguise, conjured up a fanciful picture of elaborate subterfuge, but in fact Higgins was merely wearing riding breeches and wore no identifying badges.[50] After the war Higgins' death was also recorded in the official casualty records.[51] The cause of his death being given as 'died' — the term officially used to intimate that the soldier concerned had died accidentally or had succumbed to disease.*

*In recent years there has been speculation, fuelled by the reminiscences of Victor Silvester, that a number of soldiers from the Argyll and Sutherland Highlanders were executed during the war. Indeed Monocled Mutineer* authors Allison and Fairley stated that Silvester claimed to have been in the firing parties that carried out several executions of men from this regiment.[52] In fact Private Higgins is the only recorded case of a soldier from the Argyll and Sutherland Highlanders being executed during the war. It is also relevant to note that Victor Silvester only went to the Western Front on 1 October 1916, over a month after the execution of Private Higgins. (This date appears on Silvester's medals record card in WO329/1.)

The last soldier to be executed in August 1916 was a 19 year old serving in 1 Battalion Hampshire Regiment. **Private John Bennett** enlisted six weeks before the outbreak of war, but because of his relative youth he was not sent to France until November 1915.[53] During the earliest days of the Somme offensive Bennett had shown himself unable to display soldierly virtues. On 20 July he was sentenced to two years' imprisonment with hard labour after going absent. A short while later his division moved northwards to the Ypres Salient, accompanied by Bennett, who was now serving under a suspended sentence. For Bennett, however, the Salient held similar horrors to those being suffered by his comrades on the Somme.

The résumé of his offence, first quoted in General Routine Orders,[54] and subsequently in Parliament,[55] stated that Bennett had left the trenches during a gas attack because he was a coward. However, this did not convey the real horror of the soldier's plight. Private Bennett's battalion had in fact been subject to a night-time gas attack followed by a German raid. At 10.30 pm on 8 August (a dark and moonless night) the Germans had unleashed a poisonous cloud on the allies' position, and Bennett had fled to the rear. It is perhaps difficult to imagine the panic that ensued during such a terrifying incident — heralded by the sudden, startling noise of the 'gas gong'. A few hours later Bennett reappeared in the support trenches of his battalion. His flight from danger had not been imaginary, for the battalion war diary recorded seven men killed, and 46 more wounded — all from the effects of gas.[56]

At his trial on 16 August young Bennett was unrepresented, possibly indicating his disillusionment with war and military justice. In considering his character the court saw a statement written by the soldier's commanding officer intimating that under shellfire the private went to pieces.[57] His damning indictment confirmed exactly what Bennett's company sergeant-major had already told the court. Nevertheless during the review procedure Brigadier-General H C Rees compassionately recommended that the sentence be commuted. However, the Corps Commander, Lieutenant-General Sir A G Hunter-Weston thought otherwise. His militaristic mind caused unambiguous remarks to be appended to the proceedings. Cowards, he stated, constitute a serious danger to the war effort and the sanction of the death penalty was designed to frighten men more than the prospects of facing the enemy.[58]

Private Bennett's sentence was carried out at Poperinghe on 28 August, the shooting being the first and only one in the Hampshire Regiment. For some unexplained reason Private Bennett's death is recorded twice at the General Register Office in London. The cause of death is given in both cases as: 'Shot by sentence of F.G.C.Martial for Misbehaviour', to which is added on one entry, 'before the enemy'. The word cowardice does not appear. Bennett's grave in Belgium incorrectly shows the initial of his forename as 'I'. At the time of his death no soldier had been executed in 4 Division for over 14 months, but by a coincidence a predecessor from the same division had also been shot for cowardice. The offences were virtually identical. The other young soldier had also fled during a gas attack in the Ypres Salient. (See the case of Private Chase, 2/Lancashire Fusiliers, May and June 1915.)

Lord Moran commented, that in certain gas cases he had examined, hysteria had set in, 'implanted on the physical harm caused by the gas, which in itself was often trivial'.[59]

Viewed solely in terms of territory, the gains made on the Somme during the month of August had been derisory, especially when considering the cost in human suffering. Nowhere had the British advanced more than a few hundred yards. Yet even before the end of July 1916, the Commander-in-Chief had realised that the battle had been reduced to mere attrition. General Haig, however, was optimistic that by mid-September the German reserves would have been depleted sufficiently to allow the allies to gain the upper hand. The military strategy however was not that straightforward. There were other reasons for pursuing the offensive, not least of which was the continuing need to divert German resources northwards, and relieve pressure on the French at Verdun.

Whatever difficulties faced British commanders on the Somme at the beginning of September 1916, two soldiers who had gone absent on the eve of the opening day of the Somme offensive were to commit no further offences.

**Private Herbert Crimmins** and **Private Arthur Wild** were amongst the earliest of recruits to have enlisted in the 2nd Bradford Pals. The battalion, officially the 18 West Yorks and part of 31 Division, had travelled a devious route to the Western Front – via Egypt, from whence it had been recalled to France. No time had been wasted in ordering the battalion into the line once they arrived at the end of March 1916. From then until mid-June the battalion took its turn at serving in the trenches on the Somme. On 12 June they were relieved and moved into rest. As the great day for the new offensive approached the battalion prepared for the attack. Final preparations including a last hot meal had been made, when the offensive was postponed for 48 hours.[60] In the intervening period the battalion made a midnight raid on the German trenches. With the forthcoming offensive imminent the results were not encouraging when three-quarters of the raiders became casualties. As day broke on the eve of battle there was little for the men to do – except rest in their billets in the village of Bus-les-Artois. During the morning the men received instructions concerning their duties on the following day. Privates Crimmins and Wild being allotted tasks as ration carriers. At mid-day, after being ordered to parade that evening at 5.45, the men were dismissed.

With little else to do, Crimmins and Wild went to the local estaminet or café and spent their time drinking. Drink followed drink, and when the estaminet closed the two friends strolled away some three or four miles before falling asleep in a cornfield. At their trial the two men were unable to recall any further events until they awoke at dusk. Both men subsequently admitted to being afraid when they realised that they had missed their 5.45 pm parade. Admitting fear before a court martial was never a wise course of action.

Foolishly the couple made no attempt to re-join their battalion. Whilst back in the village of Bus-les-Artois the absence of the two men had been noted while final preparations were being made to go up the line. Eventually, at 8.45 pm, three hours after the parade, the battalion moved off. Their war diary recorded that the troops were in position, ready for the attack, by 4.30 am, three hours before zero. Whilst the battalion spent a restless night in the trenches Privates Crimmins and Wild took refuge 'under the nose' of the Commander-in-Chief. Walking away from the battlefront they found a billet for the night in the village of Beauquesne which also harboured the advanced General Headquarters of the British Armies in France.[61]

When 18 West Yorks went over the top on 1 July their casualties mirrored those of many other units that day. The commanding officer, Lieutenant-Colonel M N Kennard was killed, together with seven officers and 93 other ranks.[62] No ground was gained. On the following day, as the battalion reeled from the shock, a draft of 48 reinforcements arrived, but Crimmins and Wild were not amongst them. The two soldiers remained absent until 4 July when they surrendered to the Military Police at Vignacourt. In wandering some considerable distance away from the front the two men had stumbled across a checkpoint that controlled the movement of personnel to and from the restricted zone that sealed off the battlefront. The privates admitted their absence to the MPs and volunteered the exact time and date of their departure. Crimmins and Wild were placed under arrest until an escort could be provided to return them to their unit. Once back with their comrades the two offenders discovered that the battalion was out of the line in rest. And the unit remained in billets until 31 Division left the Somme and moved northwards taking over the trenches near Neuve Chapelle. On 27 July 18 West Yorks once again took their place in the trenches, and even at this late date no disciplinary action had been taken against the two men. Another Bradford Pal, Private George Morgan, later commented on the two men's attitude.

*'They laughed it off, they thought wandering away was just something or nothing . . . If it had been in England they would have got seven days CB.'*[63]

The two soldiers might well have thought the matter would come to naught, until on 21 August, while their comrades were in the trenches, the two men were court martialled. Herbert Crimmins and his defending officer made no cross-examination of the witnesses, instead he took the oath and recalled the afternoon's drinking, followed by sleep in the cornfield. Arthur Wild, however, knew better than anyone the benefits of cross-examining witnesses, but irrespective he had a very convincing defence. Under oath he told the court that during the month of June (on a date previous to his offence) he had been severely shaken by the explosion of a German trench mortar known as a 'coal box', which had detonated near him.[64] Under such circumstances Private Wild would have been perfectly at liberty to report sick. However, he told the court, he had not done so as his company commander had allowed him to rest. Wild's evidence, however truthful, was not always to his own advantage. When questioned by the court, why had he not returned to his battalion upon awaking? he replied, 'Because I was frightened of the consequences of my absence and also thought I would not be able to stand the noise of the guns.'

With the conclusion of Wild's evidence, the defence produced three witnesses all of whom were able to confirm that the accused had been suffering from shellshock early in June. One witness testified that on one occasion, after Private Wild's near miss, the accused had completely given way while going up the line and that the private had to be sent back down again. He added that Wild later appeared to have recovered, and that he had subsequently behaved well in the trenches.

The court's deliberations returned guilty verdicts in both cases and the panel proceeded to hear statements of the two men's character. The references could hardly have been better. Private Wild's testimonial was recorded as, 'very good', and Private Crimmins as, 'very good both in and out of the line'.

With death an everyday facet of trench warfare it would seem that such a blinkered finality was the only conceivable penalty that a court might impose for an offence of desertion. With the courts displaying little or no discretion in cases such as these, the penalty of death might just as well have been prescribed as the mandatory punishment required by the Army Act. One can only hope and speculate that the court martial panel assumed that the penalty would be reduced by a higher authority. (Anthony Babington also puts forward this hypothesis in his book.)

Recommendations to mercy were put forward for both privates. Crimmins received a strong recommendation to mercy on account of his exceptionally good character. Added to Private Wild's file was a strong recommendation to mercy on account of his nervous condition arising from the explosion of a trench mortar projectile.[65]

Sir Douglas Haig reviewed the proceedings on the first day of September. On cursory examination the offences were in themselves serious. What seems to have eluded the Commander-in-Chief was an ounce of mercy, the recommendations and character references being plain to see.

It is difficult to imagine what went through the minds of Privates Crimmins and Wild, when two months after their arrest they were informed that they had been sentenced to be shot, and that the sentences were to be carried out the next day. In 1981 an account from a former soldier in the battalion was published stating that the two men had been given the option of going 'over the top' or of being executed. It stated that the pair had opted to face the firing squad.[66] Whilst it is not possible to confirm or deny that such a choice was made available, it would seem very unlikely that it did occur. However, it is not inconceivable that had the two men been given the choice, that under the circumstances, they might well have chosen to go 'over the top'.

Over 70 years later it is difficult to believe that on 5 September 1916 Herbert Crimmins together with his friend Arthur Wild, a former serving officer with Bradford City Police Force, were taken out and shot by their own comrades.[67] Private Crimmins was aged 32 and Private Wild aged 24. Extensive enquiries have failed to reveal where the execution took place. However, both men are now buried in Vieille Chapelle New Military Cemetery, France, although they are not buried side-by-side.

Private George Morgan (who had also served in 18 West Yorks) maintains that the soldiers were reported as killed in action, but that their families had subsequently learnt the truth. (Neither Private Crimmins' nor Private Wild's name appears in the official casualty roll, *Soldiers Died in the Great War*, part 19.) Morgan maintains that many years later a letter appeared in a local paper enquiring about the fate of a private soldier. The soldier named had been one of the two executed Pals and the letter was from the dead man's sister.[68]

In post-war years Parliamentary attention was drawn to the infliction of the death penalty for military offences, and the cases of Crimmins and Wild came to note. Both trial transcripts were précised for official use and salient points were noted. The trials of these two men were the earliest of those in the war that received a close and detailed scrutiny in Parliament.[69] In the authors' opinion it is not idle to speculate that post-war interest in these cases was brought about by the belief that the judgement of the Commander-in-Chief had been defective when he had recommended the imposition of certain death sentences. (It would not be wrong to state that, with the many onerous responsibilities of the Commander-in-Chief, it would have been infinitely preferable for another person or body to have had responsibility for confirming death sentences.)

The executions of Privates Crimmins and Wild were amongst the most regrettable of the war, but years later the relatives of Arthur Wild added a few final words. They had an inscription placed on the headstone of his grave. It reads: *'Not forgotten by those who loved him best'*.

At the beginning of September a 30 year old Kitchener volunteer was sentenced to death. His case had a number of similarities to previous cases, and like Privates Lawton and McCubbin (July 1916) he was tried for cowardice as well as disobedience. The case also had a similarity with that of Private Wild, in that the soldier told the court that he had suffered from nervous troubles as the result of German projectiles; the difference in this case being that the soldier had previously been buried in a dugout. Yet another similarity with the case of Private Wild was that the offence related to the duties of a soldier when detailed as a ration carrier.

**Private James Anderson,** a Mancunian by birth, had enlisted in the King's Liverpool Regiment, and was serving in 12 Battalion — although at the time of his offence he was attached to 8 Loyal North Lancs.[70] His crime had been committed when his working party passed through an area being shelled. Before making off, Anderson had told the officer in charge that he was unable to stand the strain any longer. Far from fleeing, however, it was merely recorded that he walked away.[71] General Routine Orders number 1796 portrayed events in a much different light.

*'Misbehaving before the enemy in such a manner as to show cowardice. He left a working party, when under the enemy's fire, through fear for his personal safety.'*

Like previous condemned men, Private Anderson had a story to tell to the court about events that had occurred earlier in the war. However, his loss of relatives killed and wounded was more than eclipsed by a damning statement added by his Commanding Officer. The remark in this instance suggested that the accused considered disciplinary repercussions to be less risky than enemy shellfire.[72] Retribution was swift and on 12 September, just nine days after the trial, Private Anderson was executed.

On the next day another 30 year old volunteer was executed. **Private Charles Depper** had been sent to the Western Front as a reinforcement to 1/4 Battalion Royal Berkshire Regiment — a Territorial unit in 48 Division. Early in August 1916 he had deserted his comrades, prior to an attack on the Somme. Leaving his rifle and equipment in the reserve trenches at Ovillers, Private Depper made his way to Amiens, only to be arrested the same day.[73] General Routine Orders stated that he had deserted with the intention of escaping to England,[74] an admission made by the defendant, although the soldier's chances of realising such a goal were minimal. Foolishly Depper had told the Military Police that he was on his way to Rouen to catch the boat for England. The reason for his disaffection was that he was tired of serving in the trenches. On 14 August Depper's battalion was involved in an unsuccessful attack[75] and just over two weeks later the private was court martialled.

When the Commander-in-Chief's decision became known the unit was resting in the village of Beauval near Doullens. The battalion diarist recorded the offence, finding, and administrative details. At 6.10 am on 13 September, a wet morning, 'the execution was witnessed by 40 men of the battalion under the command of Lieutenant Hampshire the orderly officer of the day'. At a parade just after midday on the following day the commanding officer promulgated the sentence to his men. Whilst it hardly seems likely that news of the execution had not spread throughout the battalion, it is possible that full details of the actual offence were not known to the ranks, until disclosed during promulgation.

In the middle of September 1916 an Irish soldier was executed who had been on the Western Front for seven months. **Private Joseph Carey** had twice gone absent to avoid serving in the line, the eventual

cause of his downfall.[76] His offences had been committed
near Hulluch on the Loos battlefields, but by the time the
military bureaucracy had processed the papers his battalion,
Royal Irish Fusiliers, had moved to the Somme – his
execution taking place at Corbie.

The authors have not be able to determine a family connection but
another Private J Carey, (army number 23154), had given his life with
great gallantry two months after the battalion had arrived in France.
In this incident the heroic Private Carey had been a member of a five
man bombing party under an NCO. On 26 April 1916 the Germans,
under cover of gas, had launched an attack against the British trench
known as 6th Avenue in the Hulluch sector. Private Carey and his
comrades had held the Germans at bay for a considerable length of time,
denying entry to the British line. The small party eventually had to
withdraw, but not before Private Carey and a comrade had been killed
and all the other members had been wounded.[77]

In the middle of September a third soldier was shot in 29 Division –
a formation comprised mainly of Regular Army battalions. Like all
previous victims in the division, the man was a Gallipoli veteran serving
in an Irish battalion.[78] Although two-and-half months had passed since
the beginning of the Somme offensive the man was condemned for a
crime committed on 2 July. No reason for the delay in bringing his
case before a court has come to light, but it was only eight days after
the trial that the private was executed.

The soldier, **Private Albert Rickman,** was an original member of his
battalion, 1 Royal Dublin Fusiliers, and had landed
in France in March 1916. On 1 July the Fusiliers had
advanced at 8 am in the second wave attacking near
Beaumont-Hamel. Their experiences were typical of
events that day as murderous enemy machine guns
cut them down before they could even pass through their own barbed
wire. The casualties were estimated as eleven officers and 300 other
ranks.[79] On the following day the survivors held the British front line
near Auchonvillers, where they were engaged in gathering up the dead
and wounded and repairing the trenches. In the aftermath of the
disastrous bloodbath, 27 year old Private Rickman decided he had had
enough and deserted. His absence lasted until 20 July, when he was
arrested on the lines of communication.[80]

Six-and-a-half weeks passed before Rickman was brought to trial,
and in the intervening period his division left the Somme and moved up
to the Ypres Salient. A short while later the prescribed penalty was
recorded in the battalion war diary, when on 15 September 'Private
Rickman A of 'Y' Company was shot at 0600 for desertion'.[81]

On the day after, the third and final execution took place in the 31st

(New Army) Division. Unlike the disgraceful executions of volunteers Privates Crimmins and Wild, circumstances were different in the case of **Private James Haddock.** To start with the victim was a Regular Army soldier, (possibly on the Reserve upon outbreak of war) who had gone to France on 9 September 1914, some two years before his execution.[82] A native of Sheffield, Haddock was serving in the Sheffield City battalion − the 12th Yorks and Lancs, although his original posting had been to 2 Battalion. His military career was not without blemish. At the time of his final court martial he was serving under a suspended sentence of 20 years' penal servitude for a previous offence of desertion. His downfall had come about when, like many others previously, he had deserted on the way to the trenches. Five days later he was found some miles away trying to hide himself.[83]

Private Haddock's execution took place just eleven days after the shooting of the two Bradford Pals. Whilst Haddock's suspended sentence would seem to indicate that he, rather than Crimmins and Wild, was more deserving of the extreme penalty, it remains very questionable whether further death sentences were required as examples within such a short interval. The reason for suggesting that these decisions were made in an arbitrary manner was that throughout the remainder of the war no further 'deterrence' was supposedly required in this division.

Although the Somme was the scene of bitter fighting during the second half of 1916, those offending on its battlefields were often dealt with elsewhere. Nine soldiers were executed in September 1916 yet only one third faced firing squads near the Somme battlefront. **Private Peter Black** was an example of a soldier shot elsewhere. A private in the Black Watch (probably enlisted pre-war, as he had a previous army number of 2120), he was serving in 51 Highland Division − a division in which the sanction of the death penalty would seem to have been less arbitrary than in other formations. Private Black's record and offence had all the ingredients of a deserving case, although he had served in France since April 1915.[84] For a previous offence of desertion the soldier had received a sentence of death which had been suspended. Consequently, a subsequent offence committed prior to going into action, coupled with an absence of over one month, was unlikely to attract sympathetic attention.[85] The battalion war diary recorded that on the day prior to execution the sentence was promulgated on parade at 6 pm. The next morning, near the border between France and Belgium, 'C' Company was witness to the tragic event.[86]

The final soldier executed in September was a volunteer serving in a Pioneer battalion. 23 year old Londoner **Private Edward Card,** from Bow, had decided that the rigours and dangers of army life were not to his liking. Although the duties assigned to Pioneer units were usually of a more mundane nature, July 1916 had seen one company of 20 King's Royal Rifle Corps engaged as fighting infantry. A previous misdemeanour, also of desertion, had resulted in Private Card being sentenced to one year's imprisonment with hard labour. And his second offence, committed on the Somme, resulted in only one day's liberty. Escaping from the trenches whilst under orders to move up to the front line the soldier immediately fell into the hands of the Military Police in Amiens.[87] Card's trial took place on 9 September away from the Somme battlefields, and on 22 September, the abattoir at Mazingarbe, last used for an execution exactly four months previously, was venue for the grisly ritual. Private Card was the last British soldier to be executed there, a further execution of a Canadian in 1918 being the final act.

During the month of September the fighting on the Somme produced far greater gains, in terms of territory captured from the Germans, than had August. The area gained by the British being roughly equivalent to that captured during the first month of the offensive. The ruins of Mouquet farm and the fortress of Thiepval had at last fallen to the allies. Also Leuze Wood, High Wood, Lesboeufs, Flers and Courcelette had been taken. North-eastwards from Albert along the line of the old road the allies were 'hammering on the door' of Le Sars some four miles distance from Bapaume. A new weapon had been unleashed by the allies during the month by the introduction of tanks to warfare. Nevertheless the casualty figures had still been high, the terrifying effect of the crawling iron monsters having proved somewhat short-lived.

In the final quarter of 1916 thirty-five soldiers were executed on the Western Front — three more than the previous quarter. With one exception the offences were all of a military nature. Only seven of the thirty-five executed men were serving in Regular Army Divisions, perhaps indicating how Kitchener's New Armies had suffered from the fighting on the Somme. Of these seven men, one was a time expired soldier who had re-enlisted into his old regiment and another was a conscript. However, it would be incorrect to assume that all the other victims were volunteers, they were not. Events on the Somme had resulted in the exchange of men between the different types of battalions as well as between different regiments. As far as it is possible to tell, nine of the thirty-five men were either regulars or reservists.

Determining whether a soldier was a Regular, Territorial, Volunteer, etc., is a complex task. In many cases it has only been possible to ascertain a soldier's status after a lengthy study into the use and allocation of army numbers. However, a number of different criteria have been used to determine a soldier's enlistment status. It is not possible here to go into details about this method, which in itself is a complex subject.

Suffice it to say that large amounts of time have been allocated and vast quantities of data examined in order to obtain, in effect, very little materially. The 'spread' of executions between the differing divisions would seem to be fairly uniform, there being only two double executions, one in a Regular and one in a New Army Division.

Virtually all the victims were single men who were represented at their trials. Approximately two-thirds would appear to have been of previous good character and of the known ages (twenty men) their average age was twenty-five-and-a-half, the precise overall average of all those executed during the war.

On the first day of October 1916 a soldier was executed for a double killing. His case, the only strictly non-military capital crime in the quarter, remains somewhat of an enigma. The authors have been unable to ascertain any of the circumstances surrounding the offence or the identities of the victims. However, the military authorities themselves must have had some doubt about pressing charges of murder, as they also laid alternative charges of manslaughter. The offender was **Private Francis Murray** of 9 Gordon Highlanders − a Pioneer battalion.

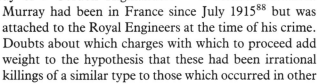 Murray had been in France since July 1915[88] but was attached to the Royal Engineers at the time of his crime. Doubts about which charges with which to proceed add weight to the hypothesis that these had been irrational killings of a similar type to those which occurred in other capital cases. Again it would appear that the man's mental condition at the time of the killings was perhaps questionable. Further speculation includes the possibility that at the time of the offences he was detached on some special duties. The reason for this speculation is that on the day of his execution his division was on the Somme, whereas the private was shot at Noeux-les-Mines, near Lens, much further to the north.

On 2 October another New Zealand soldier faced a firing squad. In fact **Trooper John Sweeney** was a Tasmanian born Australian who had joined the NZEF. Sweeney originally enlisted as a trooper in the Wellington Mounted Rifles in October 1914. [89] Six weeks later he was posted to the Otago Infantry with whom he embarked in December. After six weeks at sea the detachment arrived in Egypt. It would seem that Sweeney's military record is incomplete because for the next 18 months there are no entries, however it seems inconceivable that he did not serve at Gallipoli. [90]

Once on the Western Front the chronological record of Sweeney's service shows that on 17 July 1916, whilst at the Etaples reinforcement camp, he made his will. Of course such a task was mere routine for troops on active service. The following day he was posted to 1 Battalion Otago Regiment who were serving near Armentières. Sweeney's activities as a soldier in France however were short-lived and a week later he deserted. His absence was immediately noticed but his arrest was not effected for over five weeks. Private Sweeney rejoined his battalion on 11 September and four days later he faced a court martial. Second-Lieutenant W Bain and Corporal Simon were witnesses for the prosecution. A fortnight after the trial the Commander-in-Chief reviewed the sentence which was put in effect shortly afterwards. Private Sweeney was executed at 5.44 am on 2 October on the Somme battlefield where he had avoided serving.

Following Sweeney's death bureaucratic wrangling ensued concerning his pay and stoppages. At issue was kit that had gone missing at the time of his desertion and also the number of days for which pay was to be deducted because of his absence. Private Sweeney's father corresponded with the military authorities concerning his son's affairs and in due course a request to transfer the deceased's pension to his cousin Maria Wilson was granted. Payment however did not continue for very long as the unfortunate woman died on 12 August 1919. News of John Sweeney's tragic end and of his Australian origin was first disclosed recently in the New Zealand press.[91] The revelations revealed a further tragedy in the Sweeney family. In 1925 the soldier's father, Bernard Sweeney committed suicide just prior to the public announcement of the New Zealand wartime executions. A distraught man, he went off into the bush and poisoned himself with strychnine. The coroner recorded that Bernard Sweeney had been temporarily insane at the time. There was of course no reason why the coroner should have known that son John was Bernard's first child and a honeymoon baby — and that the loss had been compounded in 1918 when another of his sons had been killed in action on the Western Front.[92]

Thirty-seven year old John Sweeney, a volunteer serving thousands of miles from home has one other memorial, however. In the Turanganui area of Haurangi Forest Park a creek is named after him, where prior to World War One he worked with a bush felling gang.

On 3 October a double execution took place; the offences were identical, although they had occurred on different days. Only one soldier had previously been shot following conviction of a charge of striking a superior officer in the execution of his duty, a crime perhaps originally intended to encompass serious physical assaults. (It is noteworthy that all three men executed on the Western Front for this offence were Scotsmen.) However, both offences arose out of the most trifling of incidents that occurred in 72 Battery, 38 Brigade, Royal Field Artillery — part of 6 Division. The only evidence available to corroborate this affair has been chronicled by Anthony Babington in *For the Sake of Example*. The use of horse transport was of course vital to all belligerents throughout the war and it was during the everyday routine of battery life that the crimes occurred.

 In the first incident **Driver Thomas Grant Hamilton** had been accused by a second-lieutenant, of smoking during a stable parade. Not perhaps today a crime that would be considered a serious disciplinary issue, but when the officer subsequently refused to hear an explanation, Hamilton's temper got the better of him. As the second-lieutenant walked away Hamilton struck him four times. It was accepted in court that although the blows were to the body and head, none of them had been very hard; nevertheless coupled with a bad military record it was enough to cost the soldier his life.

Six days later **Driver James Mullany** of the same unit was amongst a party detailed to prepare a team of horses ready for the collection of  ammunition. The bone of contention in this incident, however, was that by performing this duty the men would miss their tea. Driver Mullany did not hide his displeasure at this prospect and swore soundly at his battery sergeant-major. Once placed under open arrest Mullany attacked his superior knocking him to the ground. In what would appear to be a deeply felt grievance he then set about punching the warrant officer on the ground. Fellow NCOs arrived on the scene and restrained Driver Mullany who, undeterred, continued his assault just as soon as the sergeant-major managed to stand up.

Both soldiers were tried on 20 September, being executed less than a fortnight later. The two men are buried in Ribemont Communal Cemetery Extension, a rather bleak spot on the Somme. Driver Hamilton has an inscription on his grave. It reads:

*'Ye babbling winds through silence sweep disturb ye not our loved one's sleep.'*

It was over two weeks before the next executions took place. In due course, on 18 October, two individuals were the victims in separate shootings. The circumstances of the cases, however, were disturbing to say the least. By coincidence the offences both involved cowardice, a comparatively rare offence.

The first soldier was yet another Pioneer – the fourth to date. **Private Albert Botfield** was aged 28 years and served in 9 South Staffs. The battalion had arrived in France in August 1915 and almost immediately the war diary recorded a number of irregular occurrences.[93] In October 1915 two men had received sentences of field punishment for using threatening language. On the following day three men received similar punishment having thought they were at liberty to wander into the local village. Early the next month another soldier had been arrested by the

French police for looting. Private Botfield however did not join the battalion until early in 1916. Upon his arrival in France the soldier had got off to bad start, when on 24 January a court martial had sentenced him to 90 days' field punishment no.1 for absenting himself from his reinforcement draft. Later that yea,r in July, Botfield and his comrades found themselves serving on the Somme.

Their allotted task was not pleasant as their diary recorded on 17 July, they were burying the dead, 1,532 corpses being interred in four days. At the beginning of August the men were busy digging trenches near the front line. However, on 8 August they were relieved from their duties and a short while later moved northwards to the comparative sanctuary of Ploegsteert Wood. After one month's stay they returned to the Somme, and were billetted at Bresle on 12 September. Six days later they moved up east of Albert into Bécourt Wood.

On the evening of 21 September three platoons from Private Botfield's company ('B') moved out for the evening's work. The party, comprising 146 other ranks, left at 6 pm. Their destination was a new trench system some three-and-and-half miles distant — and east of Pozières. Their route was comparatively direct, passing up Sausage Valley, to the side of Contalmaison Wood and then south of Pozières. As they approached their destination the Pioneers moved onto the high ground of the Pozières Ridge. Whether the party moved across the open or passed along the trenches is unclear. Evidence given at the trial however tends to suggest that the men were in the open. Similarly it is only possible to speculate about whether the group was observed by the enemy. Nevertheless when the party was within 500 yards of the intended place of work,[94] a shell crashed down just 25 yards from Private Botfield.[95] Evidence given at the court martial stated that the accused was seen to run away and that in a subsequent search he was not found.

The working party continued to their destination, and worked until 3.30 am. The diarist later recorded that they had completed 250 yards of digging. Three hours after the detail's return, Private Botfield was seen back in his bivouac near Bécourt Wood, and soon after, the disciplinary process began.

In the following six days the men from 'B' Company worked on the new trench. There is reason to believe that Private Botfield may well have been amongst the workers.

Private Botfield's trial for cowardice was held on 1 October. Although it has previously been stated that 9 South Staffs was a Pioneer battalion their war diary records that this did not exclude the men from danger. In the interval between the unit's return to the Somme and Botfield's court martial, a period of two weeks, the casualties suffered were: four other ranks killed, two officers and 65 other ranks wounded and one man reported as missing.

At the trial neither Private Botfield nor the officer acting as prisoner's friend thought to question any of the prosecution witnesses, a definite error of judgement in a capital case. Instead the defendant gave evidence on oath, rendering himself liable to cross-examination. Botfield told the court that after the shell exploded he jumped into a trench, adding weight to the theory that the party were in the open. There is no doubt however that this incident did occur in a very exposed position. The private continued that he had later attempted to rejoin his party but had met another soldier who must have given him incorrect directions. Botfield then admitted that he had sat down in the trench, fallen asleep, waking the next day at 4 am and then returned to camp. Under cross-examination, it was put to the defendant that he knew where the trench was that he was supposed to be working in, because he had worked there before. Private Botfield admitted that this was true and that he had worked there before.[96] This admission led to his eventual downfall and amazingly was untrue.

Although the battalion had been on the Somme earlier in the offensive the location at which the offence occurred had been in enemy hands at the time. Following the unit's return from the Ploegsteert area, no work had been carried out in the Pozières locality until the actual day of the offence. The battalion's very detailed diary shows this to be the case.[97] Hence Botfield's fatal admission was untrue, he had never been near Pozières before. It is possible that the private admitted that he knew the location of the trench because he had worked there subsequent to his offence. Doubt even exists as to whether the court martial panel was clear about the true nature of these trench digging operations. An official résumé, made from the court martial file, records the name of the trench concerned as Cable trench.[98] In fact the earthworks were just another trench dug for the purposes of carrying communication cables.[99] The official naming as Cable trench only occurred after completion.

One can only speculate that the ordeal of trial by court martial, coupled with the pressure of questioning, led to the soldier's false admission. In further cross-examination Private Botfield also admitted that, after meeting the soldier whom he asked for directions, he subsequently returned to his bivouac straight away. He agreed that upon his return he had not reported to anybody and had merely gone to sleep. Having admitted to the court that he had been lying he made a fatal statement. He told the court that he was nervous, and that was why he took so long to come home, and that this was also the reason why he did not try to go on to Cable trench after the shelling.[100]

Private Botfield made no statement in mitigation and perhaps unwisely called no one to give him a character reference. The court however did note his previous crime. Sir Douglas Haig confirmed the sentence of death on 14 October and three days later the prisoner learnt of his fate. At dawn on 18 October Private Botfield was shot at Poperinghe – his Division, the 23rd, had already left for the Somme battlefields.

On the same day a Regular Army soldier was shot on the Somme. The circumstances were equally disturbing. **Private Harry Farr** enlisted in 1910 in the West Yorks Regiment at the age of either 16 or 17; he told the recruiting officer, however, that he was three years older.[101] Farr was drafted to the BEF in November 1914 and joined the first battalion in the trenches at Chapelle D'Armentières.[102] The following March two fellow members of the battalion were executed for desertion. Two months later, whilst serving in the same sector at Houplines, Private Farr was evacuated suffering from shellshock.[103] Surprisingly it was five months before he rejoined his unit. Conditions at the front however had not improved during his absence and he now found himself serving in the Ypres Salient.

Nearly a year later during operations on the Somme, he committed his fatal offence. On the evening of 14/15 September Farr's battalion moved up into the front line near Guillemont. The private fell out and reported himself sick at the transport lines the next day. When the medics allegedly refused to examine him, he was ordered to accompany a ration party as they went up the line. Private Farr remained behind, and later that day was seen by a sergeant who had ordered his return to the line. Farr told the NCO that he felt unable to return to the front. The intervention of a corporal who had been detailed to escort the private was also unsuccessful, as was a forcible attempt to drag the soldier off.[104]

As 1 West Yorks went into action on 25 September Farr found himself a prisoner at Ville-sur-Ancre awaiting court martial.[105] The trial took place on 2 October and in spite of his earlier shellshocked condition in 1916, no medical examination was made. The location of Private Farr's place of execution is unknown, and unusually his grave was not identified after the war. He is commemorated on the Thiepval Memorial to the Missing, which overlooks the Somme battlefields.

The fifth and final soldier from the Loyal North Lancs to be executed was shot in October 1916. (The four other soldiers had been shot earlier in 1916 and had been serving in 1 Battalion.) Unlike his comrades, the offender was an early volunteer who was serving in a Territorial unit.

**Private Richard Stevenson** had joined 1/4 Battalion in France during May 1915. His service had been without fault until events on the Somme undermined his resolve. The offence had occurred at Fricourt on 7 September and his case had many similarities with those previously chronicled. At 2.30 pm on the day in question Private Stevenson had been warned that the battalion would move up to the trenches later in the day. Instructions were given that the men were not to leave camp, although no time had been stated at which to parade.[106] That evening at 7.30 the men fell in and Stevenson was found to be missing. Ten minutes later the 'Loyals' marched off towards Montauban, going into the line on the eastern edge of Deville Wood facing Ginchy.[107]

Four days later, at 9 o'clock in the morning, Private Stevenson was arrested in the village of Bussy-les-Daours in a back area. The soldier's downfall partly arose from an inconsistency in the first story that he told to his captors, and the defence that he made at his trial. Upon arrest Private Stevenson stated that when he left his company he had gone in search of a friend. He maintained that on his return the unit had gone and that he had not known where he was.[108]

Exactly one month after his capture he was brought to trial, by which time the division had moved to the Ypres Salient. Private Stevenson submitted a written statement to the court in which he admitted being warned for the trenches − later the same day − and also that he had been told not to leave camp. However, he pointed out, the limits of the camp had not been defined and that he had merely gone in search of his brother. He added that he had returned at 8.30 pm to find that the battalion had gone. Stevenson then confessed that he had lost his head and drifted away not knowing where he was going. He added finally that he was a young married man.

There would seem to be some doubt as to the officially recorded opinion of Stevenson's military value, Anthony Babington has stated that the soldier's fighting record was good. A résumé of the case, which was prepared during post-war Parliamentary attention, stated otherwise, the comment being that Stevenson had not got a good fighting record, and that he was extremely nervous when in action. His conduct was otherwise described as generally good.

On 25 October the town of Poperinghe was once again witness to punishment meted out for offences committed on the Somme when Private Stevenson was executed.

Two days later another soldier who had answered Lord Kitchener's call and had served in a Territorial battalion was executed. In yet another unfortunate case there would seem to be evidence to show that this soldier was not fully responsible for his actions. **Private Henry Palmer** was soldiering in 1/5 Northumberland Fusiliers − part of 50 Division. Probability suggests that he went to France in 1916, but no corroborative evidence has been found to confirm this.

Palmer's division had been in action in the Battle of Morval on 25 September 1916 and on 1 October the 1/5 Northumberland Fusiliers were engaged south of Le Sars − as part of a composite battalion. The war diarist recorded the attack which was conducted on a 300 yards frontage.[109] The weather was fine as the men formed up in the shallow assembly trenches. In places, cover was non-existent with men being left out in the open. Nevertheless the attackers were recorded to be in excellent spirits and following a very effective barrage, went over the top at 3.15 pm − zero hour.

Lance-Corporal Hadaway, a prosecution witness at the trial, recalled that he and Private Palmer had climbed over the parapet together.[110] However, the NCO had not seen Palmer again, although their company had halted twice and lay prone before reaching the objective. The war diarist recorded that he had seen the whole line of men disappear over the ridge, going out of sight as smoke from bursting shells obscured his view. The inference drawn by the court was that after going over the parapet Private Palmer went no further. Two-and-half hours after the commencement of battle both objectives had been taken, and all companies remained in the line, orders having been received that because of the success a further advance might be undertaken at midnight.

The court also heard that at noon the next day Private Palmer had been seen making his way up a communication trench, past Battalion Headquarters towards the front line, whereas the soldier had no reason not to be in the firing line at the time, his unit not having been relieved.

Again no cross-examination of prosecution witnesses took place, but the defendant gave evidence on oath. Palmer told the court that he had advanced in the attack but that he had been hit in the knee. He was however somewhat vague concerning his whereabouts at the time of this injury. He originally stated that his being hit had occurred half-way across no-man's-land, but later said he was injured whilst still in front of the German wire. Private Palmer was unable to explain what had hit him in the knee and admitted that there had been no lasting effects. In his original story Palmer stated that after the injury he had returned and stopped in the communication trench to rest himself, saying that the next day he had been unable to rejoin his unit because of hostile shelling. When questioned he agreed that the injury to his knee had not caused him to report sick, and he elaborated further by telling the court that when injured near the enemy wire he discarded his ammunition before making his way back to the British front line.

Palmer's military service record listed no previous serious offences and based on the court's recommendation it must be assumed that the soldier did not possess the ability to invent a convincing story, for the court strongly recommended mercy, on the grounds of his low intellect.

Private Palmer was executed at Albert on 27 October. Military indifference was such that nobody had even bothered to ascertain his age.

Towards the end of October three executions took place on the same day. One singly and the other two together at Rouen. A stranger line-up of victims it is hard to imagine. The double execution resulted out of charges of mutiny; the offences having occurred at the same establishment, but on different days. One of the two was a 30 year old Scottish Gunner in the Royal Field Artillery; the other was a 33 year old Australian citizen serving in the New Zealand Expeditionary Forces. The third soldier, **Private Elsworth Young**, aged 19, serving with 'D' Company, Nova Scotia Rifles, was convicted of desertion on 19 October and shot ten days later near Bully Grenay.

The offences of mutiny, the first of the war resulting in execution, had occurred at the military prison at Blargies, a locality midway between Rouen and the battlefront.

The Army Act laid down that sentences of penal servitude would be served in the United Kingdom;[111] however, lesser sentences were frequently served in prisons, camps and detention centres constructed or converted for use in the theatre of operations. It was not uncommon for serious offenders to serve part of a jail sentence before its suspension permitted them to be returned to the battlefront — it was at such a prison camp that the uprising occurred.

Wartime conditions for the average fighting soldier were harsh and dangerous. Consequently those who committed crimes could not expect to improve their lot, else others might well have chosen to join them. However, in imprisoning these men a balance had to be struck between a harsh regime and a humane one. When the inmates of Blargies prison decided they were being unjustly treated trouble broke out.

300 men were said to be imprisoned at Blargies[112] and on the afternoon of 14 August the men mutinied.[113] Their objectives, to improve conditions in the camp, had been fuelled by the knowledge that two days previously a number of Australians had had some of their grievances remedied following an insurrection.[114] The soldiers' complaints included the use of dietary punishment, leg irons and excessive zeal in administering field punishment. During such punishment it was said that some men had fainted whilst others had been blindfolded. The men's living conditions were also dirty and no proper provisions had been made for their laundry. A further restriction, the existence of which, if true, would seem to have been intended to create squalor, was that the inmates were only permitted the use of the latrines for 15 minutes a day. Allegedly only 14 latrines existed and their use was only available during the early afternoon. This being the case, the allocated daily usage per man consisted of less than 45 seconds a day.

About one fifth of the camp inmates joined in the initial protest. Already in leg irons they congregated together after the mid-day meal. When ordered to parade with the others they refused, demanding to see the deputy-governor of the camp. When this official (a captain) appeared, the prisoners began to insist on the removal of a number of restrictions including their leg irons. The captain however seemed disinclined to listen and when the men also refused to obey his order to parade, he decided that more, not less, restraint was required, and he ordered the rebels to be handcuffed. The disturbance then became a trial of strength as several prisoners battled to avoid being manacled. As tension mounted revolvers were drawn and bayonets fixed. Insults not bullets rained as the inmates taunted their captors − mocking the guards for being afraid to open fire.

With the handcuffing discontinued the mutineers were contained in an isolated compound, and during the course of the afternoon tempers cooled and prison routine was restored. How the ringleaders were identified is a matter for speculation however, seven men were arrested. (Judge Babington, who has had access to the court martial transcripts, says that it was believed that the seven detainees were the ringleaders.) Indicating the severity, or perhaps complexity of their offences, the trial took place by full General Court Martial on an unknown date. Five officers, their ranks varying from captain to colonel, were nominated to sit in judgement. A judge-advocate was also in attendance to advise on legal technicalities. In view of the fact that none of the defendants offered any defence, it is questionable whether the same importance had been attached to ensuring proper representation for the accused. The Rules of Procedure laid down that a defendant was entitled to be represented by a qualified barrister when being tried by General Court Martial. One need not speculate for long about whether the offenders were made aware of this provision. It should be noted, however, that the officer convening the court martial did have the power to refuse counsel leave to appear.[115]

Instead of mounting a proper defence the accused simply used the trial as a platform to air their grievances. It was a futile and poorly thought-out line of defence. The prosecution put forward a convincing case − men had refused to work, they had resisted arrest and they had threatened violence against the prison staff.[116] Rebuttal was needed, not complaint.

Sentences of death were passed on six of the seven defendants. **Gunner William Lewis,** late of 124 Brigade, Royal Field Artillery, was selected to be the scapegoat, his comrades received commuted sentences of between two and 15 years. At the place of execution his comrade in death came from an unusual background.

Four years after his death **Private John Braithwaite** was still causing the military authorities trouble. Not that the problems were insurmountable, merely that his assumed name of Jack, in which he had enlisted, was different from his real name and confusion had ensued in military records. (Braithwaite's military history record was sorted out on 24 September 1920.)

Braithwaite, a slight, nine stone individual, had enlisted at Dunedin, New Zealand on 29 May 1915. His posting had been to the New Zealand Rifle Brigade, where after three-and-a-half months it had been decided to re-examine him to determine whether he was fit for active service, his slight stature perhaps indicating a poor physique. In November 1915, when the military authorities discovered that his real forename was John they decided to have him re-attested in his correct name. It is difficult to see the logic in this requirement; however, the allocation of a second army number does throw light on the subsequent confusion. (Braithwaite's original army number was 24/58, his subsequent one 24/1521.)

In February 1916 Private Braithwaite arrived in Suez and was transferred to 2 Battalion Otago Regiment a month later. His promotion to lance-corporal on 1 April coincided with his admission to hospital with measles. However, a swift recovery on the fifth day was followed by his departure for France, just nine days after the onset of the illness.

A month after arriving in France, Braithwaite lost his stripe and two days' pay for going absent. On 13 June he received 60 days' Field Punishment for a second absence and associated minor offences. He escaped from the Field Punishment compound three times in a week to visit his mates in the line and was sentenced to two years' hard labour. On his way to prison, Braithwaite broke free from his escort, was recaptured and given a further two year concurrent jail sentence on 7 July.[117]

He was eventually lodged in the Blargies North prison, a tented compound near Abancourt. The circumstances which led to Braithwaite and three other Australians being sentenced to death on a charge of mutiny were summaried by Provost Staff Sergeant F E Shearing, who had been commanding a party of prisoners working outside the compound on 28 August. One prisoner, Private Little, had been insubordinate and Shearing was ordered to confine him.

'I had previously dismissed the section, except Pte Little, and the men went off to their tents which were a few yards away. I marched Little to the punishment compound about 30 yards away. He came quietly. On marching him to the gate of the compound, and before the gate was opened, Little shouted out to the Mess Orderly: "Bring my dinner over, this f.....g bag of slime is putting me inside". I opened the gate and told Little to go in; he refused to do so and made a good deal of noise. Whereupon the rest of the Section rushed over in a body, the four accused among them.'

Braithwaite had taken Little into his tent and the other three had been part of the hundred-strong crowd that proceeded to overpower Shearing. Later Braithwaite vainly explained:

'My motive in getting Private Little away to the tent was really to prevent trouble, as I had been given permission to petition General Birdwood on behalf of the Australian and New Zealand prisoners for release to go back to the front . . . and we were expecting an answer at any time.'

He pleaded, 'I do not wish to do my soldiering behind prison bars, but in the firing line where soldiers are wanted. The best I can hope for is a bullet in an honourable way . . . Give me a fighting chance.'

Sir Douglas Haig commuted all the death sentences except for the one passed on Braithwaite. He was executed alongside Gunner Lewis; the New Zealander became the fifth casualty and third fatality amongst six sons who had enlisted from the family of an ex-mayor of Dunedin.[118]

On 16 November 1916 a newspaper displayed a picture of a Bristol soldier who, it reported, had been killed in action.[119] In fact the unfortunate man had been executed by firing squad on the first of the month. The official attempt at covering-up the tragedy continued after the war, when his name was included in the official casualty rolls.[120] The full extent of the injustice however was not revealed until years later.

**Alfred Leonard Jefferies** enlisted upon outbreak of war. He had

Private Alfred Jefferies

gone to France with his battalion, 6 Somerset Light Infantry, on 21 May 1915 and was one of the first Somersets to be wounded during the following month. His return to active service was short-lived when in November of the same year, he was evacuated to hospital suffering from a nervous breakdown.[121] Following treatment, the most effective being simply rest, he returned to his battalion in the new year. On 18 August 1916 his comrades attacked Deville Wood, but Private Jefferies had previously gone missing, unable to stand the strain. Neither the length of his absence nor the date of his trial are known, but in the intervening period prior to execution, his brother was killed in action with the same battalion. (Arthur Jefferies, killed in action, 16 September 1916.) After the cessation of hostilities the city of Bristol decided to commemorate their dead. And in doing so they issued certificates of remembrance to the next-of-kin, and compiled a roll of honour to include as a permanent record when they published a chronicle of the Bristolian war effort.[122] By a strange twist of fate the name of convicted deserter Alfred Leonard Jefferies was included and a certificate issued. The same treatment, however, was not extended to his brother who had died an honourable death.

Continual fighting on the Somme was matched by a steady stream of deserters, of whom a number suffered the extreme penalty. On 2 November a second soldier from 1/8 King's Liverpool Regiment was convicted. The man was possibly a pre-war Territorial in this unit which contained many Irishmen. His demise was the fourth and final execution in 55 Division, all four shootings having occurred during a four month period.

**Private Bernard McGeehan** was an original member of his battalion which had landed at Boulogne on 3 May 1915.[123] During August 1916 his battalion had suffered considerable losses when an attack had been launched against Guillemont — 570 casualties resulted. Ten days later the assault was renewed with limited success, the village remaining in German hands. It was ironic, therefore, that towards the end of September Private McGeehan should desert before an attack — which in the event turned out to be successful, and in which very few losses were sustained. As with a number of other recent victims, the shooting took place at Poperinghe, whilst the division was serving in northern Flanders.

4th of November saw yet another execution in a Territorial division, and there were a number of similarities with the previous case. The soldier was a pre-war Territorial (not a volunteer), and had served with his battalion in France since they had landed on 18 March 1915.[124] After committing his crime on the Somme the private had been executed in Belgium. However, here the similarities ended.

Stepney-born **Private Robert Loveless Barker** (a rather unusual, and somewhat unfortunate forename) was serving in 6 London Regiment, and his previous army service had not been good. In fact he was serving under a suspended sentence of death.[125] During September 1916 his division prepared for the offensive and on the 14th struggled up Caterpillar Valley passing the latest new weaponry in the form of a tank, which had broken down and was blocking the way.[126] The next day the Battle of Flers-Courcelette commenced, the 6 London going over in four waves, two hours after the original assault. Heavy losses resulted and the remnants of the battalion, two officers and 100 men, occupied a position known as the 'Cough Drop'. For five days the depleted ranks remained in the front line whilst numerous others, each in turn, strove to drive back the enemy. Events proved too much for the 21 year old Londoner, whose behaviour resulted in him facing a charge of cowardice. Private Barker's trial took place shortly after the remnants of the battalion returned from the trenches, and for 36 days he awaited the

Private Harry MacDonald was posted to 12 West Yorkshire Regiment and was executed for desertion, 4 November, 1916. He was father of three children.

*(MacDonald Family Collection)*

outcome, and his fate. It was the longest interval between a trial and an execution to have occurred since Sir Douglas Haig had been promoted to Commander-in-Chief.

In December 1986, seventy years after the tragedy, a national newspaper carried a small news item relating that a pardon had been requested for an executed deserter.[127] The paper gave the man's name and outlined a number of details about the unfortunate victim.

The soldier concerned was **Private Harry [Henry] MacDonald**, a private with the South Lancashire Regiment.[128] In 1915 MacDonald transferred to the Duke of Wellington's Regiment and at the end of September he landed at Gallipoli as a reinforcement to 8 Battalion.[129] Accounts differ about whether he was actually wounded on the Peninsula, but there would seem to be no argument about the fact that he was invalided home suffering from frostbite. (When MacDonald's case was discussed in Parliament [*Hansard*, 12 December 1917] Philip Snowden stated that the private had been wounded. However, Babington's examination of the court martial papers found no such

*129*

record.) The account compiled in 1986 reported that MacDonald had recovered in the UK and that during a period of convalescence his wife had become pregnant before falling ill. A subsequent request by the soldier for an extension of leave on compassionate grounds was refused. The report continued that MacDonald then went absent as a result.

After being arrested MacDonald was sent to France and posted to 12 West Yorks who were serving in 3 Division – a Regular Army formation. At the beginning of July whilst serving on the Somme, MacDonald had been buried by the explosion of an enemy shell. The true nature of the resulting injury is not recorded,[130] however his treatment at the base, whether for shellshock or for wounds was brief, as the soldier was returned to his unit within a short interval. At the end of the following month Private MacDonald was sentenced to field punishment no.2 for being absent, although no motive has been disclosed for this crime.

It is only possible to speculate about the state of MacDonald's mental health, and his reasoning, when he absconded for a final time. However, besides his on-going field punishment and battle weary condition, other evidence also suggests that the soldier was unwell.

MacDonald's fatal crime had been committed away from the battlefields of the Somme. During the second week of September 1916 Private MacDonald had reported sick. The doctor's diagnosis and prescription typified the medical profession's unsympathetic attitude. 'Medicine and duty' was ordered and dutifully MacDonald returned to the trenches.[131] However, on 12 September whilst the battalion spent a fourth and 'very quiet day' in the front line trenches at Hulluch, MacDonald slipped away.[132] For a month he avoided the authorities, until arrested by the Military Police at Boulogne. A lack of identifying badges, coupled with a fictitious identity, were later regarded by the court martial as indications that the soldier had no intention of returning.

Once the trial of MacDonald was over his Brigade Commander, Brigadier-General H C Potter, appears to have been concerned about the condemned man's mental state and ordered a medical examination. The examination disclosed nothing un-toward about MacDonald. The absence of any medical 'excuse' seems almost to have compounded the crime, for when the Divisional Commander, Major-General C J Deverell, came to review the proceedings, he condemned the man as worthless and said that the soldier was of no fighting value.[133]

Thirty two year old father of three, Private Harry MacDonald was executed at Louvencourt on 4 November. The Reverend James H Jackman, chaplain in attendance wrote to his widow. The letter started: 'It is my painful duty to inform you . . .' By an unfortunate coincidence the clergyman had used the same expression that MacDonald's widow would have received on the blunt notification sent from an infantry records office, reporting an execution. (The letter from the Reverend Jackman to MacDonald's widow made no mention of the true cause of death.)

The travesty of justice had further repercussions. Because the unfortunate soldier had been executed, no pension was forthcoming to the deceased's widow who found herself having to depend on state benefits from the Keighley Board of Guardians' resources – military bureaucracy having the unfortunate effect of punishing the condemned man's family as well.[134] In 1917 Philip Snowden, Labour MP for Blackburn, raised the case in the House of Commons. No satisfactory answers were forthcoming from a Government unwilling to intervene.[135] Such complacency continued for nearly 70 years – on 30 November 1986 the Under-Secretary of State for the Armed Forces confirmed in writing that no pardon would be granted in the case of Henry MacDonald.[136] The craven response, doubtlessly drafted by some insensitive civil servant, merely stated that there was no new evidence on which to base such a consideration. Like their Great War predecessors, yet again the authorities sought a medical excuse to smother an injustice. The Under-Secretary admitted that present-day psychiatry might well have treated such men differently, but he continued by pointing out that no re-appraisal was now possible. Clearly the Ministry of Defence had examined MacDonald's court martial file as they pedantically pointed out that the deceased had previously been sentenced to field punishment no.2, not no.1, hence the prisoner would not have been liable to attachment in a fixed position. What a pity such technical niceties had not extended to events arbitrarily determined at the semi-formal courts martial that took place on the Western Front.

Towards the end of the first week in November a third Bantam was brought before a firing squad. The soldier concerned had seen action on the Somme, before his division (the 35th), had moved north to the Arras front. **Private John McQuade** had enlisted in 18 Highland Light Infantry, a unit also known as 4th Glasgow Battalion. Before his desertion the volunteer had previously been convicted of disobedience for which he received a suspended sentence of one year's imprisonment.[137] Private McQuade was executed at Habarcq behind the Arras front, on 6 November.

The frequency with which the death sentence was imposed during the final quarter of 1916 followed a pattern for which there is no obvious explanation. An analysis of the records shows that executions were always carried out during the first and last weeks of any month in the quarter; yet in the intervening periods there were occasions when no executions took place for some time. During the months of both October and December, over two weeks passed without the need for a firing squad, and during November eight days passed without an execution.

Whenever such events came to pass there were usually extenuating circumstances associated with the offence. The case of **Private William Hunt** was no exception. Hunt was a Regular soldier with two years' service on the Western Front. Originally he had landed in France on 9 November 1914 before being posted to 2 Manchester Regiment.[138] By coincidence he had previously been convicted of the same crime as Private McQuade i.e. disobedience, and had received exactly the same punishment, although in Hunt's case this had been commuted to 83 days' field punishment no.1. The recollections of an eyewitness to the private's execution recalled events surrounding the case, and these were published in the early 1970s – *The First Day on the Somme* by Martin Middlebrook, and the eyewitness later elaborated on some of the details.

The eyewitness, Private Paddy Kennedy, was serving with 18 Manchesters and recalled that Hunt was drafted to the battalion during the latter part of 1916. 30 Division had seen a lot of action in the opening month of the Somme offensive and during a subsequent operation Kennedy maintained that Private Hunt had become detached from his unit and had gone into action with one of the South Lancs battalions. Kennedy maintained that Hunt had become lost and, because the attack failed, it was decided to make an example out of Hunt. Kennedy had no personal knowledge of these events and his description is also clouded by the passage of time. However, what can be verified as correct is that Private Hunt was tried for desertion (the account given in Middlebrook's book incorrectly states that the offence was cowardice) on 22 October and that he was not represented or assisted by a prisoner's friend.[139] The commanding officer's comments, submitted to the court, stated that in his opinion, Hunt's behaviour was generally satisfactory. Later the Brigadier also recommended leniency for Hunt.

Private Kennedy recalled how news of the sentence was publicised. As was the custom the battalion was paraded for the promulgation. As the men stood to attention Private Hunt was ordered to step forward, then the sentence and confirmation were read out. Kennedy stated that he and five other privates were detailed to be the firing squad.[140] Once the sentence was known the Military Police were also in attendance to ensure the ritual's eventual performance. As was standard practice an attempt was made to get the soldier drunk. With the prisoner in a drunken state everyone's task became that much easier. Intoxication was also regarded as more humane for the condemned man. Private Hunt however refused drink, and as dawn approached on the following morning he was equally uncooperative. Refusing to walk, his escort dragged him downhill into a quarry, the place of execution. There they tied him, with arms and legs bound, into a chair. His final act of defiance was to refuse the offer of a blindfold.

Kennedy recalled that the firing squad had their rifles temporarily taken from them, so that a supposed blank round (which acted as palliative for troubled consciences) could be loaded into one man's rifle. The officer warned the firing squad to take care with their aim, as he did not wish to be the final executioner. Private Kennedy also mentioned that one man in the firing squad stated he knew the victim from their regular soldiering days and declared he wanted nothing to do with the execution, as Private Hunt was a good lad. The soldier's objection was ignored. With a white handkerchief pinned over the victim's heart, the unsteady firing squad took aim. The officer's worst fears were realised. Hunt was still alive when the officer stood forward and blasted the badly wounded private in the side of the head with his revolver. The grisly spectacle over, Private Kennedy and his comrades were left to bury the body and clean up the mess. The execution had been the first in 18 Manchesters and also the first in the division but others were to follow before this blood letting came to an end. Twenty year old Private Hunt was a native of Manchester, and seemingly an orphan. On the last day of November the local paper reported his death saying that Hunt had died of wounds.[141]

On 15 November, the day following Private Hunt's death, another soldier with previous Regular Army experience was shot. Once again an eyewitness recalls the event, although he is now aged over 100 years.

The victim, **Private Alfred Ansted** had been recalled from the reserve upon the outbreak of war. On 9 February 1915 he had been sent to France to 4 Royal Fusiliers.[142] Although a wound had necessitated a few months' hospitalisation Ansted had served for 15 months before going absent in May 1916. Shortly after his desertion another soldier from his battalion had been executed (see the case of Private W Roberts, May 1916) but Private Ansted continued to serve with his battalion while under a suspended sentence. In the following August when serving on the Somme at Guillemont, Private Ansted yet again went absent − after having been warned for the trenches. Although he did not venture far, he remained absent for over two months before surrendering to the Military Foot Police at Corbie.[143] At his trial on 5 November, the private attempted to excuse himself by telling the court that shellfire unnerved him. Should this have been the case, then little or no account would seem to have been taken of either his battlefield injury or his length of service.

A week prior to the execution, the Reverend Martin Andrews joined 4 Royal Fusiliers as replacement chaplain to Noel Melluish. (Melluish had won the Victoria Cross whilst serving with the battalion.) Andrews, then a captain, was an experienced soldier. He had served in the ranks as a private and stretcher bearer with 1 Australian Field Ambulance. The clergyman had been amongst the first to land at Gallipoli but the sights he saw on the Peninsula did not revolt him quite as much as the prospect of witnessing an execution. Andrews recalled the event well, because he was newly arrived and because the weather was particularly cold at the time. After the ritual was over, as they laid the body to rest, the Reverend Andrews remembers the pioneer sergeant telling him how Private Ansted had previously been a brave soldier.[144] Captain Andrews asked the NCO why he had not spoken up for the condemned man, and the clergyman raised the issue of executing soldiers with the Divisional Adjutant-General. Andrews told the AG that, in future, if any other soldiers were to face execution then he wished to defend the man at the trial[145] − acting as prisoner's friend.

Captain Andrews' offer − as a clergyman − to act as prisoner's friend was not unique. Michael Adler, the first Jewish chaplain to serve with the BEF, recorded that he too had acted as defending officer; and on occasions obtained the services of Jewish lawyers − serving in the army − to assist men who were in trouble.[146]

The passing of Private Ansted marked the eighteenth execution in 3 Division. Whether or not the intervention of Captain Andrews made any difference is not known, but only a further five men were executed in the division throughout the remainder of the war. Captain Andrews (later Canon) was badly wounded at Arras in the following year, although he recalled that the death of Private Ansted was not the only execution that he attended.

On the same day as Private Ansted's death, another soldier of diminutive stature was shot. His death confirms that the use of the death penalty was exercised in an arbitrary manner, rather than for the sake of example. **Private Hugh Flynn** had committed the same crime 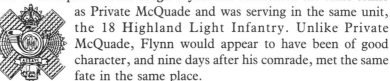 as Private McQuade and was serving in the same unit, the 18 Highland Light Infantry. Unlike Private McQuade, Flynn would appear to have been of good character, and nine days after his comrade, met the same fate in the same place.

The night of 17/18 November brought the first snow storm of the approaching winter and during the day the last major attack of the Somme offensive took place. The Battle of the Somme is perhaps best remembered for the appalling casualties on the first day, in reality this was but part of the cost. On average, throughout the offensive, casualties occurred at the rate of 3000 per day − the equivalent of three battalions a day. (The figure of 3000 relates to casualties of all types, sick, wounded and injured, not merely fatalities.) In context, deaths from disciplinary sentences look insignificant and might be considered so, were the circumstances of the victims not so tragic. Whilst records exist of soldiers being described as worthless individuals, very few details, other than pure conjecture, have ever emerged of many truly incorrigible individuals being shot.

When the weather brought an end to major hostilities on the Somme, the Commander-in-Chief issued instructions to General Rawlinson, commanding IV Army, and General Gough, commanding V Army, that they were to 'harass the enemy by every means possible' during the winter.[148] Offences arising from Somme battles however, were not all finally disposed of until 1917.

On 21 November another Canadian with experience of soldiering of the Somme met his end in front of a firing squad comprised of his comrades. **Private Henry Kerr** had enlisted in his home town of Montreal on 10 June 1915. Originally training with 60 Battalion he sailed with first reinforcing draft after ten weeks' training.[148] One year on the Western Front serving with 7 CEF, coupled with the ferocity of the Somme fighting was as much as he could stand. A fortnight after his trial for desertion, Kerr was shot in a bleak and windy spot near Vimy Ridge.

In the third week of November two NCOs fell victim to the extreme penalty. Little is known about either man, although both were deserters and had gone absent on the Somme. **Lance-Corporal William Moon** was a young volunteer in a division that had been heavily engaged before the Battle of the Somme had even commenced. Moon's departure had been followed by a divisional move to the Armentières front. The unfortunate twenty year old, who was serving in 11 battalion Cheshire Regiment, met his end near Bailleul. **Lance-Corporal George Hughes** is also believed to have been a volunteer. His age and length of overseas service are unknown, though it is clear that he deserted on the Somme. No battalion record has been found to confirm his execution on 23 November, although his unit, 7 Royal Lancaster Regiment, was stationed at the village of Warloy-Baillon where he is buried.

One of the last soldiers to be executed in November 1916 was a Gallipoli veteran.[149] He was also the first man to be shot in his regiment for desertion. (There had been three other executions in the Notts & Derby regiment, two for cowardice and one for quitting a post.) **Private William Randle** had served at the Dardanelles in 9 Sherwood Foresters, before the evacuation resulted in his drafting to the Western Front, and service with 10 Battalion. His execution took place behind the front, at the small village of Cavillon, west of Amiens.

The last soldier to be executed for an offence of cowardice on the Somme in 1916, was also a tragic individual. London born **Private Reginald Tite** came from a family of five. His elder brother, called Joe, lived at East Grinstead in Sussex and had joined the Sussex Pals in 1914. The more cautious Reg, however, had not enlisted until the end of October 1915. (Soldiers who volunteered for service in the Sussex Pals had very distinctive army numbers which were prefixed by the letters, SD/. This stood for South Downs battalions. The 'South Downers' were also known as 'Lowther's Lambs' after Colonel Claude Lowther who had been instrumental in their raising.)

Following the disastrous attack on the Boar's Head at Richebourg L'Avoué on the eve of the Battle of the Somme, large numbers of reinforcements were required to fill the depleted ranks of the 'South Downers', and it is almost certain that Reginald Tite was sent to France to 13 Sussex as a consequence. In due course the battalion, together with the other units in 39 Division, were sent to fight on the Somme. By the morning of 20 September the division had taken over the front line from Hébuterne down to the river Ancre in the south. Their positions looked out over battlefields where no gains had been made, in spite of continual fighting for over two months. On 5 October the division extended their lines further southward, taking over the trenches at Thiepval. After a continuous bombardment, and many sanguinary attacks the fortress village had recently fallen to the British forces. On the second and third days of the division's occupation of the famous Schwaben Redoubt, the Germans tried to regain control of their former stronghold. In spite of horrifying flamethrower attacks the Sherwood Foresters had repulsed every assault, and a week later the last German hold on the position was finally broken. The redoubt was a considerable asset, as those who held the vantage point commanded a strategic position, and on 15 October the enemy launched three further counter attacks with flamethrowers — all to no effect.[150]

Thus it came about that on a much contested battlefield 13 Sussex were ordered to launch an attack on another German position — Stuff trench. On 21 October, just after noon, the attack began and in the subsequent fighting Private Reginald Tite failed in his soldierly duties.

Tite was tried at Aveluy on 2 November. A previous conviction of four years' penal servitude for disobedience weighed heavily against the frightened soldier.[151] In the second week of November 39 Division left the Somme and moved to the Ypres Salient, and like many previous offenders, the condemned soldier was executed at Poperinghe.

Seventy years were to pass before the tragic family background of the 27 year old became known. Reginald Tite was the youngest in his family, yet tragedy had struck even before his birth. In 1886 an older brother had died, aged just 14 months. Reginald was born in May 1889, and 18 months later his sister of two years and eight months died, and that left a family of three boys. But once again fate struck a heavy blow when the boys' mother died, just before Reg's fourth birthday.

The execution of Reginald seemed to provoke the reaper of death, and once more family deaths started to occur. In February 1917 Joe, Reg's older married brother, died of wounds in Salonika whilst serving in a labour battalion. (Joe Tite trained with 13 Sussex in the UK [the same battalion that Reg was drafted to] but did not serve with them overseas.) In September of the same year a cousin, also called Reginald, was killed with 13 Sussex. And in April 1918 another cousin by the name of Ernest was killed, again with 13 Sussex. The two cousins had enlisted together and had consecutive army numbers G/17467 and G/17468. The death of Ernest in 1918 concluded the service of any Tite family member in the Sussex Regiment. Every 'Tite' that had served in the regiment (all of them volunteers) had now been killed.

Quite what the army authorities told Charles Tite, father of the executed soldier, concerning his son's death, is not known. Almost certainly it was not the truth. A death certificate issued in relation to the demise of the executed Reginald Tite gives his cause of death merely as 'Death'. An enquiry of the General Register Office reports that no other details concerning the cause of death are recorded in their archive. There is no reason to believe that this is not the case. The family Bible which was given to the authors by a friend of the family, incorrectly records Reg's date of death as 16 November 1916. It also has an altered entry in relation to the cause of his death. The original entry was 'died' but this was later changed to 'killed'. Neither gives the true cause of death, but the discrepancies do add weight to the likelihood that military officials did not disclose the true cause of death to the next-of-kin. It remains a mystery why the date of death is incorrect and also why the cause of death was altered. Although neither entry is correct, the change made does not substantially alter the meaning of the original cause of death.

The elder brother Joe, who died in Salonika, fathered two boys, both being born before the war. The eldest was named after his father, the younger after the uncle who was later executed. The naming was exact, Joseph Harry and Reginald Thomas. The names of the two dead soldier brothers lived on, but fate was not kind to the two boys either. Three years separated the two lads when shortly after the eldest's fourteenth birthday, their mother died leaving them orphaned. The boys were then brought up by their grandmother. A family friend recalls that the two were quite different. It is interesting to speculate whether the two might have been of the same character and temperament as their namesakes who fought and died in the Great War for civilisation.

The two boys didn't get on together. The eldest (Joe) grew to be a big strong man and a loner. Perhaps not unlike his father, who ended his days in a labour battalion. The younger, Reg, was smaller and the family favourite. He worked on the land, often ploughing with horses. It is said that he was work shy and frequently got the sack. Was this an indication of a family trait of disobedience?

The final irony came when Joe Tite, nephew of the executed man, joined the Regular Army and served creditably through World War Two. And later he gave further service, whilst serving in the Railway Police in Scotland.

When the *Official History of the Great War* was published it revealed that during its compilation, extensive enquiries had been made, in order to accurately quote the number of casualties that had been sustained. Its findings were sometimes surprising and raised as many questions as they answered. Recalling casualties on the Somme – up to the end of November 1916 – it quoted an unadjusted gross British figure of 419,654. Its narrative stated that from this total 'at least 5 per cent should be deducted for absentees at roll call who subsequently returned'. No further explanation was forthcoming, and it is only possible to speculate about the causes for this level of absenteeism.

The final month of 1916 opened with a double execution. The victims were volunteers serving in a division that had been heavily engaged in July, and both men had recently taken up new duties.

The two men were workmates who had enlisted together. Their battalion was the 3rd Manchester Pals, whose ranks had initially been filled with local clerks and warehousemen. Officially the unit was called the 18th (Service) Battalion, Manchester Regiment, a unit which had executed a private just two weeks previously. (See the case of Private Hunt.) Before the war **Private Albert Ingham** and **Private Alfred Longshaw** had worked together for the Lancashire and Yorkshire Railways. The pair were clerks in Salford Goods Yard. Enlistment in the army found the pals still together but serving as privates in No. 11 platoon, 'C' Company, 18 Manchesters.[152] The pair had travelled a devious route to reach the Western Front, as initially their division had been sent to Egypt where the two men had arrived on 18 November 1915.[153]

Private Albert Ingham

After service on the Somme the inseparable pair had been posted to their Brigade's

Machine Gun Company. Subsequent events have a certain familiarity, as the soldiers' actions included many of those that previous desperate men had tried. In the second week of October a warning order was given, in preparation for a move to the trenches. The two friends however decided to abscond, and made their way to the coast. With more success than many deserters, the privates avoided the military authorities and stowed away on a ship at Dieppe.[154] Quite how the soldiers' presence was detected is unknown, but the couple were discovered in civilian clothing hiding on board a Swedish ship. Private Longshaw stated that he was an American who had travelled via Spain. It was an unsuccessful ruse that had been tried before.

Convicted and sentenced to death the plight of the two men came to the attention of Private Paddy Kennedy — a participant in 18 Manchester's execution that had occurred the previous month. He recalled Private Longshaw's final farewell to his friend Albert — just prior to the fatal volley.[155] Private Kennedy's recollections are very interesting and only incorrect in minor detail. Kennedy recalled the promulgation of the sentences and stated that the two men had been arrested on board an American ship at Rouen — whereas in fact it was a Swedish ship at Dieppe. He also reported that the older man had received news that his wife was ill and had been refused compassionate leave. More correctly, it was the younger soldier, Private Longshaw who was married. Kennedy's statements, however, did suggest that the pair had deserted together because they were inseparable. Kennedy also maintained that both Roman Catholic and Church of England ministers made last-minute attempts to save the doomed men. Such unsuccessful pleadings had also been made in previous cases. News of the two soldiers' deaths reached their homes within the week. The evening paper first carried the news of 24 year old Private Ingham's death.

Private Alfred Longshaw

Mentioning his place of employment and his old school, it reported that he had, 'died of gun shot wounds'.[156] Strictly this was true, but must be viewed as part of an official cover-up. The paper also carried a picture of Albert Ingham, which together with the other details had been supplied by soldier's father. Two days later another evening paper commemorated Ingham's passing, adding that he had been an active worker at the Charlestown Congregational Sunday School.[157]

A week later, both evening papers reported the death of the other church-going soldier.[158] 21 year old Alfred Longshaw was reported as 'died of wounds'. His pre-war employment was mentioned, as was the fact that 'he joined the army on the outbreak of the war, and attended St Sebastian's Church for some years'.

For many years George Ingham, father of the executed soldier, was deceived as to the true cause of his son's death. He volunteered information to the (then) Imperial War Graves Commission for inclusion in the cemetery register — associated with his son's last resting place. On the father's instructions the Commission printed the details, that the soldier had 'died of wounds'. At a later date the Commission re-contacted the father, and asked him whether he required an inscription to be carved on the headstone of the grave. But in the intervening period George Ingham had learnt the truth. Enraged over the execution and deception he requested a unique inscription; and the content being true, the Commission did not decline. The headstone reads:

*'Shot at dawn one of the first to enlist a worthy son of his father'.*

Privates Ingham and Longshaw are buried side-by-side in Bailleulmont Communal Cemetery. The two comrades were also commemorated on the War Memorial at Salford Railway Station.

A rather unusual entry is recorded in the Index to the *Great War Medal Rolls*[159] concerning the reason for the non-issue of Ingham's and Longshaw's medals. The record states that the medals were destroyed by virtue of King's Regulation no.1743 of 1912, i.e. not having been claimed within ten years they could be destroyed. In fact the medals were forfeit by virtue of the Pay Warrant as mentioned in King's Regulation No.1761.

Also buried at Bailleulmont is Private Hunt who was also executed whilst serving with 18 Manchesters. A certain amount of confusion arose in Anthony Babington's account of the executions in 18 Manchesters. This occurred because Privates Ingham and Longshaw are recorded in the army court martial records as being in the Machine Gun Corps. Both 'Pals' however appear in other records as 'Manchesters' and have the Manchester Regiment's badge carved on the headstones of their graves. Another executed soldier was also buried in the same cemetery in 1918 — Private O'Connell. Private Kennedy later recalled the feelings of the men in the battalion concerning the executions — which he described as sickening. They resented what had happened, but had to remain silent.[160]

Another execution also took place on 1 December. The victim, also a volunteer, was **Private William Simmonds** who had been serving in 23 Middlesex Regiment. Details of the offence conformed to a familiar pattern. Following the soldier's absence whilst on the Somme, the private had been arrested, tried and then executed at Poperinghe. The 23 year old was the first soldier to be executed during the war whilst serving with 41 Division.

On 4 December another Territorial soldier was executed; and his army number suggests that he enlisted prior to the outbreak of war. Perhaps surprisingly, only five weeks had passed since a previous death sentence had been carried out on a volunteer serving in this battalion. And by coincidence, exactly one month had passed since the last 'Terrier' had been shot. The condemned man, **Private John Cameron** of 1/5 Northumberland Fusiliers, had been in France for just a year at the time of his offence.[161] Cameron's unit had fought a considerable number of actions on the Somme before he went absent. It can only be assumed that the strain of battle had undermind his resolve, as previously the soldier had been of good character.

The final Canadian to be executed during 1916 was a member of 1 Battalion CEF. 24 year old **Private John Higgins** had left his home on Prince Edward Island to enlist. The soldier's parents, however, were deceived about the true cause of their son's death. Although he too was shot for deserting, his next-of-kin were told that he he had died of wounds — cemetery register for Quatre Vent Military Cemetery, France.

On the same day that the Canadian died, another volunteer, an Irishman, received the same punishment. **Rifleman Samuel McBride** was serving in 2 Royal Irish Rifles — part of 25 Division. The Somme offensive had allowed little rest for the division, which had only left the region in October. McBride was one of the few soldiers shot towards the end of 1916 who was of bad character. A previous offence for absence had resulted in a sentence of two years' hard labour — which had been suspended.[162] On 7 December Rifleman McBride faced a firing squad from his own battalion at Hope Farm, on the northern edge of Ploegsteert Wood.[163]

Until December 1916 no member of the Royal Engineers had been shot for a military offence, although in May 1915 an NCO from the Corps had been executed for murder. The unfortunate man was a Pioneer in 212 Company, RE — part of 33 Division — a division which to date had had no man executed. Men serving as Pioneers had previously been executed but they were infantrymen carrying out pioneering duties. They were not members of the Royal Engineers. The soldier, **Sapper Ernest Beeby,** had deserted and successfully made his way to the coast. At a Channel port he joined a party of men on leave as they were about to board a ship bound for England. The Pioneer however was detected and placed under arrest.[164] Beeby's execution took place on the Somme at Albert on 9 December.

Another soldier faced a firing squad on 9 December, and on 10 December the ritual was repeated. Similarities existed between the two soldiers. They were both called Poole and they were both serving in Yorkshire regiments. But besides their 'common' offence of desertion, similarities ended there. **Private Harry Poole** of 7 Yorkshire Regiment was of the rank and file, but **Eric Skeffington Poole** was an officer.

Eric Poole was a 1914 volunteer. The military authorities however had considered him capable of greater responsibility, and on 3 May 1915 he was commissioned as a second-lieutenant in 14 (Reserve) Battalion, West Yorkshire Regiment.[165] The unit trained in England, supplying mainly 'other rank' reinforcements to the Western Front, but in May 1916 Poole was posted to 11 West Yorks in France. In the opening month of the Somme offensive Poole's Division, the 23rd, was engaged – 11 West Yorks being in action on 10 and 11 July. During this tour in the trenches the explosion of a German shell threw up a piece of earth which knocked the lieutenant unconscious. Later when examined by a doctor it was decided that the officer should be evacuated to a base hospital, as he was suffering from shellshock. In spite of hospitalisation and convalescence – in total lasting over a month – a consultant doctor decided that Poole's continuing symptoms rendered the officer unfit for active service at the front.

At Etaples Training Camp a week later, the recommendation that Poole should in the interim serve at the base, was overturned by a medical board who returned him to his battalion. In the middle of August, 11 West Yorks had left the Somme and travelled north to the area surrounding Bailleul. In the second week of September, the battalion and the newly returned Poole once again took to the blood soaked battlefields. On 5 October the unit was suddenly ordered to take over the front line that night.

Later, the court martial heard evidence that before the relief took place, Second-Lieutenant Poole had stated that he intended to see a doctor as he was not well. The court heard that the next morning, Poole had seen the doctor of a neighbouring battalion. After obtaining tablets for rheumatism, Poole had disappeared for two days; his absence during the move up to the trenches being the most fatal ingredient of his offence.[166]

On the day of Poole's arrest his battalion attacked north of Le Sars – on the Albert to Bapaume Road. Eventually the attack proved successful, although the West Yorks lost eight officers and 217 other ranks.[167] Ten days after Poole's arrest, the brigade commander, Brigadier-General T S Lambert sent a note to Major-General J M Babington, GOC 23 Division. The communication expressed the opinion that Poole ought to be sent back home rather than be court martialled, and it outlined the officer's previous shellshocked condition.

It has previously been suggested that, as a request had already been made to convene a court martial for Poole, it was then too late to prevent such an occurrence.[168] The authors however think that some consideration may well have been given to an alternative solution, the reason being that over a month was to pass between the date of the Brigadier's note and the eventual trial.

When the trial took place on 21 November, evidence was heard that the military policeman who had arrested Poole had found the officer in a confused state of mind. The battalion medical officer later confirmed that battle conditions might well have caused Lieutenant Poole to succumb to such a condition. Poole gave evidence at his trial, but was unable to present a plausible explanation for his presence so far from the line, other than his confused mental condition. It is surprising therefore, in view of his previous shellshocked condition and other conclusive evidence as to his unstable condition, that Poole was sentenced to death with no recommendation for leniency. Not surprisingly Brigadier-General Lambert suggested that the sentence be commuted. A recommendation that found favour, until Second Army Commander, Sir Herbert Plumer thought otherwise.[169] The inevitable medical board resulted, and as usual failed to appreciate the somewhat unfamiliar condition that could result from battle stress.

31 year old Second-Lieutenant Poole was executed at Poperinghe, where he now lies buried in the front row of the New Military Cemetery. He has an inscription on his grave that reads:

'Grant him eternal rest O Lord Jesu Mercy'.

Poole's grave incorrectly bears the badge of the Yorkshire Regiment; it should, in fact, show the West Yorks emblem. The deceased man's regiment is correctly shown on his death certificate, which also states, 'Shot for Desertion'.

Quite what the military authorities told Poole's relatives is unclear. But three weeks after the execution his brother, a Regular Army captain in the Royal Artillery, returned home. The dead man's relative was a career soldier with a number of years' service. Henry Reynolde Poole was commissioned in 1899. He served in South Africa and received the Queen's South African Medal, with five clasps' and the King's South African Medal, with two clasps. He returned to France in 1917 and received a number of honours, being Mentioned in Despatches (1/1/16) as well as receiving the Legion of Honour, 5th Class, the Distinguished Service Order and the Order of the British Empire. H R Poole retired from the army in 1920 and died in 1961 at the age of 84.

Poole's father was a mining engineer, who prior to the War had been Inspector of Mines in Nova Scotia's Department of Mines.[170] He later retired to the UK. It seems possible that Poole's father was unaware of the cause of his son's death, as the information he submitted to the War Graves Commission for inclusion in the register for Poperinghe New Military Cemetery included the phrase 'Died of wounds'.

With the approach of the winter weather and its associated problems, scarcely a moment went by without some new problem or development occurring on the Western Front. In spite of losses during the Somme battles, the Commander-in-Chief always had to be attentive to his French allies, whose demands upon the British Chief seemed to have been limitless. On 12 December, a request from the French to extend the British lines further to the south was acceded to, and the BEF took control of a further six miles of trenches, down as far as the village of Cléry. On the same day, the French Commander-in-Chief, General Joffre was replaced by the younger and more active General Nivelle. The appointment of the new general, whose enthusiasm for the offensive was considerable, was to prove disastrous in the new year, when widespread 'unrest' was to infect the French Armies.

With French politics a matter for speculation and continual surprise, the British Commander-in-Chief had more than enough to occupy his mind, especially considering the necessary preparations for the forthcoming offensive in the new year. It is not surprising, therefore, that towards the end of 1916, General Haig wasted little time before confirming a sentence of death on a young soldier who was a Special Reservist.

The condemned soldier's battalion had been involved in the assault on Deville Wood on 27 July, and the diarist from 22 Royal Fusiliers recorded the event. After just one week on the Somme, 'every available man of all four companies was thrown into the fight'.[171] The attack had been a success, although a statement made later was to maintain that one particular man had shirked from doing his duty. However, on this occasion **Private Charles Skilton** avoided disciplinary action, due to a lack of evidence.

As the fighting on the Somme drew to a close 2 Division was still in action. During the last week in October the Fusiliers' diary recorded just how bad the conditions could be. A week of heavy rain had turned the ground into mud. In the middle of November the battalion attacked the Quadrilateral, but reluctant soldier Private Skilton had gone absent in the interim. His trial took place on 9 December, when once again a disillusioned soldier declined the assistance of an officer to act as prisoner's friend. After the formal evidence had been given, the most dubious of documents was laid before the court. Major W J Phythian-Adams's statement said that, had evidence been available, then Private Skilton would have been court martialled for cowardice following the attack on Deville Wood in July. The major then continued with a character assassination – which ultimately proved truly fatal. Private Skilton was described as lazy, shirked fatigues in the trenches, and a man who was unreliable and useless.[172] It comes therefore as no surprise that the confirming authorities did not seek to reduce the prescribed penalty. 20 year old Charles Skilton was executed at 7.08 am on Boxing Day, in the small village of Yvrench.[173] For a reason that is unclear, his grave was not located after the war and consequently Skilton is commemorated on the Thiepval Memorial to the Missing. The village of Yvrench is 15 kilometres north-east of Abbeville and there is every possibility that the search for graves in post-war years was not carried out so thoroughly in this area, it being so far from the battlefront.

The final execution during 1916 was of a Scotsman who again was serving in a Regular Army division. 3 Division had served on the Somme in the opening two months of the offensive, but it returned again for the months of October and November.

**Private Peter Cairnie** of 1 Royal Scots Fusiliers had deserted in order to avoid taking part in a specific assault. The attack was to take place against objectives which, although assaulted on 1 July, had still not been captured.

On 13 November the village of Serre was attacked once more, although the battalion diarist recorded that any gains were untenable due to the mud. During the fighting the unit had sustained 201 casualties.[174] The folly of such ventures was emphasised when the official history of the war came to be written. It elaborated on the conditions, stating that in places the mud had been waist deep.[175] Private Cairnie was executed on 28 December, and like Private Skilton, is also commemorated on the Thiepval Memorial to the Missing. It is not known where the execution took place; however on this date the battalion was at Courcelles and it is possible that subsequent fighting might have destroyed the grave.

**NOTES**
1 Brigadier Sir J E Edmonds, *Military Operations France & Belgium, 1916, Vol. 1*.
2 Desmond Morton, *The Supreme Penalty, Canadian Deaths by Firing Squad in the First World War*.
3 WO329/1, Index to the *Great War Medal Rolls*.
4 WO95/1617, Battalion War Diary.
5 Anthony Babington, *For the Sake of Example*.
6 WO93/49, Summary of First World War capital court martial cases.
7 Canadian Expeditionary Force, Nominal Roll of Officers, Non-Commissioned Officers and Men.
8 WO95/2922, Battalion War Diary.
9 WO95/2755, Battalion War Diary.
10 Anthony Babington, op cit.
11 Brigadier-General Sir J E Edmonds, op cit.
12 CEF, Nominal Roll, op cit.

13 Sources: WO93/49, Commonwealth War Graves Commission, Desmond Morton, respectively.
14 Desmond Morton, op cit.
15 WO95/2587, Battalion War Diary.
16 Allan Jobson, *Via Ypres.*
17 WO95/2587, op cit.
18 Lord Moran, *The Anatomy of Courage.*
19 WO95/2587, op cit.
20 Lord Moran in *The Anatomy of Courage* quotes Sir John Fortescue, historian of the British Army saying, 'It is, I believe, a fact that even the bravest man cannot endure to be under fire for more than a certain number of consecutive days, even if the fire is not very heavy.'
21 WO95/2578, War Diary of 133 Field Ambulance, RAMC.
22 Allan Jobson, op cit.
23 J W Muirhead Papers, Imperial War Museum, reference no.P146.
24 Information supplied to the War Graves Commission, by the next-of-kin, indicates that Private Roberts was in fact 20 years old.
25 Private Roberts was also prosecuted for fraud.
26 In fact Private Roberts was executed 15 days after his trial.
27 *Sunday Star* – newspaper, Canada, 18 November 1984.
28 CEF, Nominal Roll, op cit.
29 WO95/3762, Battalion War Diary.
30 WO329/1, op cit.
31 WO95/2663, War Diary of the General Staff of 46 Division.
32 The cancellation of further assaults was considered by a Court of Inquiry. The transcript can be seen in WO95/2663, op cit.
33 WO95/2686, Battalion War Diary.
34 WO95/2663, op cit.
35 WO95/2663, Court of Inquiry transcript, op cit.
36 WO93/49, op cit.
37 Copies of (some) General Routine Orders can be seen in the war diary of the Adjutant-General, GHQ, WO95/26.
38 *Soldiers Died in the Great War*, part 31.
39 Evidence in Bacon and Langley's *Blast of War*, and the allocation of army numbers suggests Wilton volunteered in early 1915.
40 Ibid.
41 Lord Moran, op cit.
42 Hugh Dalton, diary, London School of Economics.
43 *Sunday Star* (newspaper, Canada) 18 November 1984.
44 Desmond Morton, op cit.
45 WO95/3762, op cit.
46 Desmond Morton, op cit.
47 Alphabetical Roll, New Zealand Expeditionary Force
48 Army Service Record: Private Hughes; eyewitness account quoted by Graeme Lay in his review of Christopher Pugsley, *On the Fringe of Hell – New Zealanders and Military Discipline in The First World War* (Hodder & Stoughton, 1991) page 122 *North & South*, May 1991.
49 WO95/26, op cit.
50 WO93/49, op cit.
51 *Soldiers Died in the Great War*, part 70.
52 Allison & Fairley, *The Monocled Mutineer.*
53 WO329/1, op cit.
54 WO95/26, op cit.
55 *Hansard*, 23 March 1925.
56 WO95/1495, Battalion War Diary.
57 WO93/49, op cit.
58 Anthony Babington, op cit.
59 Lord Moran, op cit.
60 WO95/2362, Battalion War Diary.
61 WO93/49, op cit.
62 Ernest W Bell, *Soldiers Killed on the First Day of the Somme.*
63 Malcolm Brown, *Tommy Goes To War.*

64 WO93/49, op cit.
65 Ibid.
66 Herbert Bradley quoted in the *Bradford Telegraph & Argus* Weekend Extra, 27 June 1981.
67 Arthur Wild's name, together with those of other police officers from the Bradford Force who had enlisted, appeared in the Bradford Weekly Telegraph on 3 September 1915.
68 Malcolm Brown, op cit.
69 Parliamentary attention is the reason for the inclusion of the trial transcript in file WO93/49.
70 WO95/26, op cit.
71 Anthony Babington, op cit.
72 Ibid.
73 WO93/49, op cit.
74 WO95/26, op cit.
75 WO95/2762, Battalion War Diary.
76 WO95/26, op cit.
77 WO95/1978, Battalion War Diary.
78 WO329/1, op cit.
79 WO95/2301, Battalion War Diary. These figures were surprisingly accurate. The official history of the war later stated the total casualties as 305.
80 WO95/26, op cit.
81 WO95/2301, op cit.
82 WO329/1600, *British War & Victory Medal Roll.*
83 WO95/26, op cit.
84 WO329/1, op cit.
85 WO95/26, op cit.
86 WO95/2877, Battalion War Diary.
87 WO95/26, op cit.
88 WO329/1, op cit.
89 New Zealand Military Service Records.
90 *The Sunday Examiner*, (Tasmanian newspaper) 14 June 1987, puts forward the same theory.
91 *Christchurch Star*, 12 October 1988, & *Wairarapa Times-Age*, 3 November 1987.
92 Christchurch Star, 24 October 1987.
93 WO95/2178, Battalion War Diary. This is one of the most detailed war diaries in the WO95 series and gives a most comprehensive account of the unit's activities.
94 Ibid. This gives the location as map reference X.6.a.2.6 on Sheet 57D SE.
95 WO93/49, op cit.
96 Ibid.
97 WO95/2178, op cit, records that from 16 to 20 September Botfield's company ('B') as well as 'A' Company had been working, together with 4 Royal Welsh Fusiliers, in Fricourt Wood.
98 WO93/49, op cit.
99 WO95/2178, op cit, records that the trench was dug two feet wide and six feet deep.
100 WO93/49, op cit., the name CABLE appears in capitals in this record.
101 Records at the General Register Office show that Farr was born at Hunslett (Yorkshire) in 1893. His death certificate however shows his age at death to be 26; there being a discrepancy of three years.
102 WO95/1618, Battalion War Diary.
103 Anthony Babington, op cit.
104 Ibid.
105 WO93/49, op cit.
106 Ibid.
107 WO95/2924, Battalion War Diary.
108 WO93/49, op cit.
109 WO95/2828, Battalion War Diary.
110 WO93/49, op cit.
111 *Toronto Sunday Star*, 18 November 1984; Army Act sec. 58.
112 Anthony Babington, op cit.
113 General Routine Orders, no. 1934.
114 The account here is taken from Anthony Babington's book.

115 Rules of Procedure, 1907, no.88.
116 General Routine Orders, number 1934.
117 *Christchurch Star*: 6.3.87; 31.7.89; NZ Military Service Records.
118 Ibid.; N Boyack, *Behind the Lines*, 1989.
119 *Bristol Gazette.*
120 *Soldiers Died in the Great War*, part 18. His cause of death is recorded as 'died'.
121 Anthony Babington, op cit.
122 *Bristol and the Great War.*
123 WO329/1, op cit.
124 WO329/2865, *1914-15 Star Medal Roll.*
125 WO93/49, op cit.
126 WO95/2729, Battalion War Diary.
127 *Daily Telegraph*, 16 December 1986.
128 *Keighley News*, 31 October 1986.
129 WO329/1, op cit.
130 Anthony Babington, op cit.
131 WO93/49, op cit.
132 WO95/1432, Battalion War Diary.
133 Anthony Babington, op cit.
134 *Keighley News.*
135 *Hansard*, 12 December 1917.
136 Letter from Roger Freeman to Gary Waller MP.
137 WO93/49, op cit.
138 WO329/1. op cit.
139 WO93/49, op cit.
140 Martin Middlebrook, *The First Day on the Somme.*
141 *Manchester Evening News*, 30 November 1916.
142 WO329/1, op cit.
143 WO95/1384, War Diary of the Adjutant-General, 3 Division.
144 '*Woodbine Willie – His Life and Times*', Anglia Television Production, 13 November 1983.
145 Interview with one of the authors.
146 Major-General Sir Ernest Swinton (Editor), *Twenty Years After.*
147 Captain W Miles, *Military Operations France & Belgium, 1916*, Volume 2.
148 CEF, Nominal Roll. op cit.
149 WO329/2751, *1915 Star Medal Roll.*
150 Captain W Miles, op cit.
151 WO93/49, op cit.
152 16th-19th Battalions Manchesters, A Record of 1914-18.
153 WO329/1, op cit.
154 WO93/49, op cit.
155 William Moore, *The Thin Yellow Line.*
156 *Manchester Evening News*, 7 December 1916.
157 *Manchester Evening Chronicle*, 9 December 1916.
158 *Manchester Evening News* and *Manchester Evening Chronicle*, 16 December 1916.
159 WO329/1, op cit.
160 William Moore, op cit.
161 WO329/2622, *1915 Star Medal Roll.*
162 WO93/49, op cit.
163 WO95/2247, Battalion War Diary.
164 Anthony Babington, op cit.
165 Army List.
166 Anthony Babington, op cit.
167 WO95/2184, Battalion War Diary.
168 Anthony Babington, op cit.
169 Ibid.
170 Nova Scotia, Street Directory, 1907/8.
171 WO95/1372, Battalion War Diary.
172 WO93/49, *Gunfire* No.18
173 WO95/1372, op cit.
174 WO95/1422, Battalion War Diary.
175 Captain W Miles, op cit.

# Chapter Five

## *You can't get away from the guns.*

*You may hide in the caves, they'll be only your graves, but you can't get away from the guns.* — Kipling

The new year of 1917 brought fresh hopes for the British commanders and their allies. Plans were made for new initiatives that they felt would prove decisive. Unlike the battles of attrition on the Somme, it was hoped to break away from the stalemate as seen in 1916, and drive the invader back. Once again however it was the French who dictated the location of the forthcoming thrust. In October 1916, even before the British attacks of the Somme had petered out, the French had conceived the possibility of an attack at Arras.

Although it would seem that the Germans had lost more men on the Somme than the French and British combined (the official history of the war quotes Germans losses on the Somme as 650,000), the Commander-in-Chief had calculated that future operations would require many additional men. Sir Douglas Haig knew that the serious manpower shortage would soon be partly alleviated by the arrival of new troops, but that it could also be improved by alterations to existing establishments. At this time the BEF comprised five armies, totalling 56 infantry divisions; and early in the year it was hoped to increase this number to 62 by the arrival of six second-line Territorial divisions as well as two Portuguese Divisions.

Additional alterations designed to produce more fighting men included the replacement of white soldiers, who were working on Divisional Ammunition Columns, by Indian troops. Similarly units comprised of white soldiers working on the lines of communication were to be replaced by coloured labour. Rather disappointingly, the calculations showed that these measures would only produce an additional 20,000 fighting men. On 6 February the Army Council agreed to the proposals and at a later date it was intended to extend the policy to the Army Service Corps, Royal Engineers and also the Royal Army Medical Corps. Two other innovations were also designed to release troops for fighting duties.

Firstly, large numbers of Chinese labourers started to be deployed on the Western Front, their strength having reached 50,000 by the end of the year. The other novelty was the arrival of the Women's Army Auxiliary Corps. They were administered by the Adjutant-General's department at GHQ, and it is noted that they were subject to military law.[1]

Two days after the official announcement of Sir Douglas Haig's appointment as Field-Marshal, the execution of a second officer took place. The case later attracted considerable interest.

In 1918, the weekly magazine *John Bull* commenced a series of articles, highlighting what its editor, Horatio Bottomley, thought was the truth behind the case.[2] The coverage provoked Parliamentary attention and eventually the House extracted a brief outline of the case, together with a few elements of the offence. A P Herbert, later to become a Member of Parliament himself, was a serving officer in the condemned man's division during the war. In 1919 he fulfilled an ambition to make known the inadequacies of defence representation during wartime courts martial. He did this by writing a novel entitled *The Secret Battle*, which, although intended to be fictional, included informed speculation about the military service and eventual demise of the unfortunate officer.

More recently, Judge Anthony Babington examined the case in depth.[3] He did this, firstly by reviewing the wartime attention and then secondly, based on the court martial transcript, outlining those events which can be substantiated. His conclusions were disturbing as well as unfortunate.

The condemned man was **Sub-Lieutenant Edwin Leopold Arthur Dyett.** He had been born in Cardiff on 17 October 1895, the son of a captain in the Merchant Navy.[4] Dyett had enlisted into the Royal Naval Voluntary Reserve on 24 June 1915.[5] In view of the fact that he did not serve at Gallipoli it seems unlikely that he went abroad until mid 1916 – as the Royal Naval Division did not land in France until May of the same year. Edwin Dyett had been commissioned as a temporary sub-lieutenant and was posted to the Nelson Battalion, part of 189 Brigade serving in the Royal Naval Division. Although the division had seen considerable action at Gallipoli, it was not until mid-November that they were once more thrown into the assault. At the court martial it was subsequently disclosed that, prior to the commission of his offence, Lieutenant Dyett had applied to be transferred to duties at sea, on the grounds that his nerves were unable to stand the strain of trench warfare.[6]

The attack of 13 November 1916 commenced at dawn, after having been delayed for several days by bad weather. The concerted thrust, launched by several divisions simultaneously, found the Royal Naval Division in action on the northern side of the river Ancre, and pressing towards the village of Beaucourt. On the right of the divisional front, the rear assaulting unit, on the left of the brigade, the Nelson Battalion – although Lieutenant Dyett had been left in reserve at the insistence of his CO.[7] At about noon when it became known that casualties in Dyett's battalion had been considerable, the sub-lieutenant and, another

Sub-Lieutenant Edwin Dyett

officer were sent forward as reinforcements. The pair reported to Advanced Brigade HQ and waited for an hour or so before being instructed to move up. Dyett, in a letter to a friend, later described the scene.[8]

*'There was considerable hostile artillery, gas shells and tear shells falling all round us, and snipers were all over the place; we had very narrow shaves more than once.'*

In the few remaining hours of daylight the two officers did not manage to locate their unit, muddy conditions as well as fog impeding their progress. In the darkness the two men parted company and continued their searches alone. Dyett, however, came across a fellow officer, Sub-Lieutenant William Fernie, who was in the process of organising the return of stragglers to the front. Both Fernie, an officer attached to Brigade HQ, and Dyett were of the same rank, and when Sub-Lieutenant Fernie ordered Dyett to follow his column to the front, to ensure that no one fell out, an altercation took place. Dyett refused, choosing instead to return to Brigade HQ for fresh orders. His action resulted in Fernie sending back a message to the effect that the sub-lieutenant from the Nelson Battalion had refused a lawful order. It has been stated by Basil Rackman (also a serving officer in the Royal Naval Division) that Sub-Lieutenant Fernie was universally disliked, and Horatio Bottomley, supposedly quoting from one of Dyett's letters (in *John Bull*, 23 February 1918), related that Dyett regarded Fernie as his one and only enemy. In the dark confusion of the battlefield Dyett came across a number of men from 'A' Company and together they searched for directions.

In letters that Sub-Lieutenant Dyett subsequently wrote he continually mentioned the state of his nerves,[9] indeed the court martial panel were to hear that he was a bundle of nerves quite unsuited to soldiering. With the realisation of the hopelessness of their task, Dyett and his party took refuge in a dugout.

In mitigation at the trial, the officer acting as prisoner's friend stated that on the following morning Dyett had reported to his brigade HQ; however, as the sub-lieutenant had declined to give evidence himself, the truth of the statement was never established. In answer to a question in the House of Commons it was stated that the officer had been missing for two days.[10] What has never been explained is why none of the men with whom Dyett took refuge were ever called to give evidence at the trial.

Whatever the truth of the situation, over a month after the attack on Beaucourt, Dyett was 'sick of waiting' for a decision on his conduct. In a letter to a friend, written in December,[11] Dyett displayed little apparent concern for his plight, indeed Bottomley suggested in 1918 that the loss of the officer's commissioned status was the worst that had been expected. The original article about the case in *John Bull* started a rumour that the sub-lieutenant had only had access to a defending officer for half-an-hour immediately before the trial. Later Parliamentary attention denied this, it being revealed that the two men had been in consultation for four hours between 11 am and 3 pm. Clearly enquiries had to be made of the Royal Naval Division staff in France to determine this, as the Under-Secretary of State had been unable to give the exact date, being unclear as to how many days prior to the trial the meeting had taken place.[12] What did emerge, however, was that Dyett had been represented by an officer with distinguished legal qualifications, but for some unexplained reason the accused had not handed over the summary of evidence until late in the consultation.

Dyett's trial took place by General Court Martial on Boxing Day, the first witness for the prosecution being Lieutenant-Commander Nelson RNVR from the Nelson battalion. Anthony Babington has commented that Dyett's 'distinguished legal representative' did more harm than good in cross-examining Nelson. However, the commander did confirm Dyett's request for a transfer, mentioned the sub-lieutenant's nervous state and confirmed his unsuitability for soldiering. At the conclusion of the prosecution case, Judge Babington noted, the court martial panel must have wondered what line the defence was going to take, particularly as Dyett declined to give evidence, and no defence witnesses were called. Indeed it would seem that, besides the suggestion that Dyett's nervous condition might have rendered him unable to control his actions, little defence was made, except the suggestion that the sub-lieutenant was neurotic and unfit for active service.

The members of the court martial panel would seem to have been commanders with first-hand experience of battle.[13] After imposing a sentence of death they were careful to recommend mercy on two grounds, firstly citing Dyett's youth and inexperience, and secondly, and more interestingly, that the prevailing conditions on the day of the battle were likely to have had a detrimental effect on any but the strongest of young men.

Major-General C D Shute, the divisional commander, recommended that the sentence be commuted; however, Lieutenant-General E A Fanshawe, commanding V Corps, together with General Gough, the Army Commander, both maintained that the sentence should stand. As was the custom, notification of the court's finding and sentence were not made known until a short while before the execution. A clerk at Brigade HQ Leading Seaman T Macmillan, later recounted his surprise when the order for the execution came through. Powerless to do anything other than pass on the instruction, the clerk later took the trouble to ascertain a few details about the case.[14]

When news reached the 21 year old lieutenant, he was playing cards with his fellow officers, it already being dark. With the padre already notified and on hand, the two men prepared for the ordeal, Dyett spending some of the time writing a final letter home. The clergyman later wrote to the officer's parents, Walter and May Dyett, stating how their son had met his end bravely. After the execution, on 5 January 1917, Edwin Dyett was buried in the communal cemetery at Le Crotoy. The village, a pleasant seaside resort, overlooks the estuary of the river Somme — a continual reminder of many wasted lives. The headstone on the grave of Edwin Dyett, in the unusual sand-covered cemetery, carries the inscription:

*'If doing well ye suffer this is acceptable with God I.Epis.Peter'.*

In the aftermath of the execution Leading Seaman MacMillan obtained the opportunity for a brief examination of the court martial file which passed through his office. What he saw confirmed his worst suspicions about the character and reputation of those involved. The clerk noted that there had been only two prosecution witnesses, one of whom had served at Gallipoli as a petty officer. The clerk commented that this officer had himself been of little value on the Peninsula, and, in MacMillan's opinion, the other witness was held in low regard. But the clerk also had another story to tell of events in the aftermath of the case. In October 1917 MacMillan's superior, Major R W Barnett, had been leafing through the list of officers nominated to be kept in reserve during a forthcoming attack. In the presence of the clerk the major deliberately made a point of altering the schedule, in order that the officer who had defended Dyett should now be detailed for battle. For a reason that is unclear the major would seem to have had a particular dislike of this officer; however, his scheme was thwarted when the advocate developed a fever and was evacuated to England. Major Barnett of the King's Royal Rifle Corps, however, was not so fortunate, being killed in action on 12 August 1918.

Dyett was the only member of the Royal Naval Division to be executed during the war. However, Douglas Jerrold, author of the history of the Royal Naval Division, commented in his autobiography — *A Georgian Adventure* — that when A P Herbert wrote *The Secret Battle*, the central figure was not in fact Sub-Lieutenant Dyett. Quite how Jerrold claimed to know this is not clear; he might well have been mistaken. Post-war speculation revolved around the suggestion that the decision to court martial, let alone execute, a member of the division was solely a political gesture. The unhappy soldier-sailor relationship eventually caused the influx to the division of a number of high ranking army officers (often guardsmen) as reinforcements. The suggestion abounded that the Navy's men were ill-disciplined; however, those serving in the division were fiercely proud of their naval traditions and deliberately strove to avoid compliance with army procedures.

A rebuttal, however, that Edwin Dyett was made a scapegoat to show the Navy's men 'who was boss', comes in the form of Major-General Shute's recommendation that the death sentence should be commuted. Shute, who it has been said, was intent on smashing naval traditions, and who would seem to have generated an unparalleled unpopularity for himself, would hardly have been the one to miss such an opportunity, had such vindictiveness been a motive.

In 1983 amazing revelations were exposed about the Dyett family's connections.[15] The executed sub-lieutenant was related, via his father's side of the family, to Sir John French who had been Commander-in-Chief when war had broken out. Further details revealed that both of the dead officer's grandfathers had been colonels, and that another relative had served with distinction in the siege of Lucknow. Clever detective work by the journalist located the deceased's sister, who suggested a motive for her brother's accuser. The story was that Dyett had made his 'one and only enemy' when he caught his fellow officer trying to admit women to their training barracks in Dorset.

Further revelations suggested that in post-war years the father's protestation had resulted in his son being exonerated, although it was not clear whether this meant the sub-lieutenant had been pardoned. The possibility is perhaps remote, although in 1981, information supplied to one of the authors by the Ministry of Defence stated that Dyett had been awarded the Victory and British War Medals for his services in World War One. If this medal issue was not in fact true, then clearly the present day requirement for a 'cover-up' exceeds any considerations of justice. A month after the newspaper's disclosures, another front page feature declared that files on World War One deserters were to be made available to the public.[16] The article even went as far as stating that the file on Edwin Dyett would be released by January 1985. No such events took place; any recommendations concerning early release of these documents must presumably have been shelved.

One further aspect of the Dyett case, as yet unconsidered, concerns the sub-lieutenant's status within the Navy. Under Naval law a sentence of death could not be carried out without the sanction of the Admiralty. And whilst there is no doubt that Dyett was also subject to the Army Act there is no reason to believe that any consideration was given to this additional requirement. There is little doubt that the consent of the 'Senior Service' was never obtained, nor would it have been given. Dyett may not only have been shot unjustly, but also illegally.

On 8 January a deserter from 2 Division was shot — a Regular Army formation in which the sanction of the death penalty had been used with some discretion. However, on this occasion, less than a fortnight had passed since an 'example' had been made. The condemned man's battalion, 1 King's Liverpool Regiment, had moved onto the Somme in mid July 1916, moving into rest after the Battle of the Ancre. **Private James (Joseph) Tongue** was Liverpool born and bred. (Records at the General Register Office differ with Army Records concerning Tongue's forename.) His passing was recorded after the war in the official casualty returns, listed simply as having 'died'.[17]

Although offences committed on the Somme continued to dominate capital cases, in the third week of January an unprecedented incident from the battlefields of Arras was concluded. It involved 35 Division, a formation comprised solely of Bantam battalions. It had fallen their lot to be the guardians of a part of the line that was frequently subjected to the detonation of underground mines.

At around 2 am on 26 November, Lieutenant Mundy of 19 Durham Light Infantry, together with **Lance-Sergeant Joseph Stones** left their trenches to patrol the edge of King's Crater.[18] As they passed along the lip of the crater they were set upon by a German raiding party who shot Lieutenant Mundy – Sergeant Stones thereupon dropped his rifle and made off. Without orders and assisted by a private from his battalion the sergeant then made his way towards the rear in order to give the alarm. However, the two men were detained by the military police at a battle stop.[19] In the meantime Corporal Stevenson went out and rescued the wounded Mundy, scattering the Germans in the process.

Although not attacked directly, in at least one section of the British line the sentries had also fled, and during the confusion the Germans captured a private. Amongst those who made off was a party of six men headed by **Lance-Corporal Peter Goggins** and **Lance-Corporal John McDonald,** all of whom ended up in the hands of the military police.

Meanwhile, under the command of Lieutenant Howes, a platoon of men moved up in an attempt to dislodge the foe. However, they discovered that the enemy had already retreated. The battalion diarist recorded that during the German raid another officer had been wounded, together with three other ranks.

In a very short space of time the battalion mustered nearly 600 men, and just three-quarters of an hour after the German raid, set out on a counter-raid on the enemy's trenches. Two second-lieutenants, together with a handful of other ranks, then entered the German lines, and without meeting any opposition bombed several dugouts. However, they did not locate their captured comrade. The battalion diary recorded the total casualties, for all these actions, as three officers and 14 other ranks.[20] However, the account by Sydney Allison has suggested that 25 other ranks were captured during the German raid.

In the aftermath of the night's activities, an explanation was required about the ease with which the Germans had penetrated the British defences. One relevant factor was that the line had been sparsely held because a gas release had been planned.

After a considerable delay Lance-Sergeant Stones was tried on Christmas Eve, on a charge of shamefully casting away his arms in the presence of the enemy. Also tried the same day were the six men, including the two lance-corporals who had fled from their posts. This group were charged with leaving their posts without orders from a superior officer, although they could also have been charged with the same offence as the sergeant, as they had not been in possession of their rifles when detained.

In the case of the sergeant, the court heard evidence from both the private who had assisted him to the rear as well as the policeman at the battle stop. Both confirmed that the NCO was in a nervous state and had difficulty in walking. It seems very unlikely that any member of the court martial panel had even the slightest inkling that in a shocked condition the soldier might not have been able to control his actions, particularly as the battalion doctor had merely reported that the accused was free of any organic disorder. In spite of a good fighting record together with a good character, the NCO received the maximum penalty.[21]

At the trials of the six men charged with abandoning their posts the court heard that an unauthorised person, who could not be identified, had called out to the men to retire. Although not directly attacked by the Germans, the party had fallen back. One account of the events records that the German raiders were all fluent in English, and hence it was possible that the bogus command might have come from the enemy.[22] The fact that the two NCOs were without their rifles must, however, have aggravated the soldiers' offence and all six received the same sentence as Sergeant Stones.

In reviewing the sentences, the opinion of the divisional commander, Major-General H J S Landon, would seem to have determined the final outcome, the NCOs — two lance-corporals and the sergeant — had their sentences confirmed. The General aired his prejudiced opinions about the two junior NCOs, noting on the proceedings that the pair were mentally and physically degenerate. The opinion that some of the reinforcements to 35 Division were degenerate was repeated in the official history of the war — *Military Operations France & Belgium, 1917*, Volume 1. The two lance-corporals, however, were original members of 19 Durham Light Infantry. The General was not the first commander to express such an opinion about Bantam soldiers. Indeed four days prior to the court martial, at a parade of a Bantam battalion in 35 Division, the Corps Commander, Lieutenant-General Sir A Haldane, had openly displayed his displeasure at their lack of stature. Rapidly passing through the ranks he brusquely identified the smallest and weakest, calling for their names to be taken before their dismissal from the unit.[23] Such arrogance was perhaps not unprecedented in the army, but such a display was unfitting for men who had enlisted voluntarily, sometimes in the face of considerable difficulty.

In the New Year when Sir Douglas Haig came to review the sentences, he commuted those imposed on the four privates to 15 years, which were then suspended. But an eyewitness recorded the final moments of the three condemned NCOs, shot on 18 January.[24]

*'Come out, you, ordered the corporal of the guard to me. I crawled forth. It was snowing heavily. "Stand here!", he said, pushing me between two sentries. "Quick march!" and away we went, not as I dreaded, to my first taste of "pack drill", but out and up the long street to an RE dump. There the police corporal handed in a "chit", whereupon three posts, three ropes and a spade were given me to carry back. Our return journey took us past the guard room, up a short hill until we reached a secluded spot surrounded by trees . . . Certain measurements were made in the snow, after which I was ordered to dig three holes at stipulated distances apart. I began to wonder . . . Could it be . . .? No, perhaps spies . . . perhaps, oh perhaps, only my fancy . . . The next scene a piercingly cold dawn; a crowd of brass hats, the medical officer, and three firing parties. Three stakes a few yards apart and a ring of sentries around the woodland to keep the curious away. A motor ambulance arrives conveying the doomed men. Manacled and blindfolded they are helped out and tied up to the stakes. Over each man's heart is placed an envelope. At the sign of command the firing parties, twelve to each, align their rifles on the envelopes. The officer in charge holds his stick aloft and as it falls thirty-six bullets usher the souls of three Kitchener's men to the great unknown. As a military prisoner I helped clear the traces of the triple murder. I took the posts down . . . I helped carry those bodies towards their last resting place; I collected all the blood-soaked straw and burnt it. Acting upon instructions I took all their belongings from the dead men's tunics (discarded before being shot). A few letters, a pipe, some fags, a photo. I could tell you of the silence of the military police after reading one letter from a little girl to "Dear Daddy"[25], of the bloodstained snow that horrified the French peasants; of the chaplain's confession that braver men he had never met than those three men he prayed with just before the fatal dawn . . . I could take you to the graves of the murdered.'*

Ernest Thurtle MP later recounted further details about this affair.

*'The victims of the above execution were a sergeant and two corporals of the Durham Light Infantry. Their Company had made an attack on King's Crater, near Arras, and captured it. The enemy counter-attacked and recaptured the Crater. The captain in charge was killed, and as he was dying he told his men to get back to their own trenches. [The rank is*

obviously incorrect, but Lieutenant Mundy who had been shot during the German raid, did die of his wounds. Perhaps his loss compounded the seriousness of the sergeant's offence.] *The next morning they were all put under arrest, and three NCOs were court-martialled, sentenced to death and shot at Roellecourt* [in fact the village is called Rollencourt]. *near St Pol.*[26]

In the last week of January, in some of the coldest weather of the winter, a deserter from the Somme was executed. (On 25 January 1917, the temperature dropped to 15 degrees Farenheit.) Like the two lance-corporals in the previous case, the victim had previously been convicted of quitting his post. However, that offence had not proved fatal, as on that occasion, the soldier had received a sentence of five years' penal servitude, which had been suspended. **Private John Taylor,** who had seen considerable action on the Somme with 15 Lancashire Fusiliers, was executed on 27 January.

On the following day a soldier serving in a Regular Army unit was dealt with in the same manner. His battalion, 1 Queens, had been transferred to a New Army division, and it is believed that the soldier was a Reservist who had been posted to France in the summer of 1915. The soldier does not appear in the medal rolls, consequently the above details have been deduced from records of soldiers with very similar army numbers.

**Private Frederick Wright** had served on the Somme throughout 1916 — with the exception of a brief period near Arras. His desertion from the horrors of the battlefields proved to be in vain, as he was returned to his unit to face death at the hands of his comrades.

Although just four days previously another soldier in 32 Division had suffered the extreme penalty, on the last day in January a 30 year old Scottish volunteer was similarly despatched. **Private Alexander Reid** had enlisted into 10 Highland Light Infantry early in the war. After service with this unit in 9 Division he had been transferred to 12 Battalion and in doing so had served in a second Scottish division, the fifteenth. The reason for the soldier's presence at 21 Infantry Base Depot at Etaples is unknown, but his posting to the 16 Highland Light Infantry was the last move that he would make.[27] Reid's battalion had taken part in the closing actions of the previous year's offensive, in an attack north of Beaumont-Hamel on 18 November. Unlike many other units, the division remained on the Somme, where the private was tried and finally executed. Puzzled by the untimely end to the soldier's life, his relatives had an inscription placed on the headstone of his grave. It reads:

*'Thy purpose Lord we cannot see but all is well that's done by thee'.*

The earliest shootings in February concerned two young offenders in 17 Division. The first soldier, a 20 year old infantryman, was of very bad character, whereas the artillery driver of a similar age was not.

**Private Ernest Harris** (known as Jack) was serving in 10 Lancashire Fusiliers under two suspended sentences, the later having been a sentence of death.[28] It is not perhaps surprising that after a third absence the Commander-in-Chief decided to implement the extreme penalty. Private Harris was the second native of Sheffield to be executed during the war.

Although many months had passed since the Somme offensive had been launched, the artilleryman who died alongside Private Harris had been absent for all that time. **Driver Robert Murray** landed in France in 1915, on the same day that the Battle of Loos commenced[29] and somewhat surprisingly had been granted home leave after only nine months on active service. Following his return to 81 Brigade, Royal Field Artillery, Murray had made off, but instead of trying to escape to England he had travelled to the south of France. Besides enjoying the milder climate the driver had availed himself of other amenities, taking up residence with a prostitute. Following a quarrel with her English lodger, the woman had reported the absentee to the French police.[30] The two men died side-by-side on 3 February.

On the day following this double execution, a soldier aged over 40 who had served at Gallipoli was shot. The private, who had deserted near Armentières, was married and came from Scarborough.

**Private James Crampton,**[31] a Reservist, had re-joined the colours in 1914 and was posted to 6 Yorkshires.[32] In July 1915 the unit sailed for Gallipoli, landing at Suvla Bay a month later. After four-and-a-half months on the Peninsula the battalion was evacuated, landing in Egypt six weeks later. On the opening day of the Somme offensive, the unit arrived at Marseilles, and shortly afterwards Private Crampton was transferred to 9 Yorks & Lancs. On 16 August 1916, when detailed for work in the front line with the Royal Engineers, the soldier made off.

With little apparent motive or plan, the private remained nearby until arrested in Armentières three months later — without equipment. At his trial Crampton sought to convince the court that his behaviour was not normal, and consequently that he must be ill. Witnesses he called, however, confirmed no more than the fact that he was a loner.[33] A medical examination, carried out after the trial, of dubious value in any regard, did nothing to suggest that any alteration to the sentence was required.

On 6 February a pre-war Territorial soldier was despatched by firing squad. **Private Benjamin Hart,** of 1/4 Suffolk Regiment, had shown himself to be a bad soldier having received a previous sentence of five years' penal servitude for an offence of desertion.[34] Details about the 22 year old soldier were recently published. The account shows a sympathetic approach from an officer in the condemned man's unit.

*'The day after our establishment in the line at Clery an unpleasant thing happened. There was a man in the battalion who had run away on numerous occasions. His intelligence was low and he could not stand war at all. After, I think, the sixth occasion when he had collected some twenty years or more "penal servitude" from various courts martial, I made him my servant so that he shouldn't have to go in the line. Officers' servants were always left behind at transport lines − I can't think why. The unfortunate man then proceeded to run away from transport lines. He was court-martialled and condemned to be shot. We were ordered to supply a firing party. I sent a chit to OC Companies to supply a few men each − wondering what would happen. As I expected, everyone refused to do it and I wasn't going to press the company commanders on the subject. I rang up Brigade and had a rather heated conversation about it and finally the poor chap was shot by someone else − perhaps a well-fed APM, such as C E Montague describes.[35] I had to write to the man's mother.'[36]*

In 1916 Private Hart's unit had served for many months on the Somme and in the autumn of 1917 his elder brother was killed at Passchendaele whilst serving in 11 Suffolks.[37]

Not all soldiers who faced a firing squad during this period had been in action for a long time, neither had they necessarily been anywhere near the front line at the time of offending. On 29 December 1916, **Rifleman William Murphey,** a Kitchener volunteer, had joined 5/6 Royal Scots whilst they were in rest at Pernois.[38] Seven days later, during a march towards the front the soldier deserted.[39] Yet at the time the group were near La Vicogne, some considerable distance from the front, and they had not gone into the line until five days after the soldier's departure.

In the middle of February 1917 the tragic case of a young regular army soldier came to a conclusion. **Private Frederick Stead** enlisted into the Duke of Wellington's Regiment in December 1913, and his death, over three years later, was the only disgrace of this type to besmirch the regiment during the war. Stead had gone to France at the end of 1914, as a reinforcement to 2 Battalion which had been heavily engaged in the first Battle of Ypres. In the middle of January 1915 the young soldier was admitted to hospital with diarrhoea but returned to duty four days later. After a similarly brief period back with his battalion Stead was again hospitalised but this time classified 'NYD' – not yet diagnosed. His condition resulted in his evacuation to the UK and only when the Somme offensive loomed was he returned to France.

Stead joined his old battalion towards the end of May 1916. However, before the end of the month he was admitted to No.10 Field Ambulance suffering from debility. With manpower at a premium the luxury of convalescence could not be afforded and he was discharged to duty the next day. A fortnight later working parties had to be found for duties on the Somme where, six weeks later, the soldier was again admitted to a Field Ambulance – this time with a sprained ankle. The injury resulted in Stead's evacuation to No.9 General Hospital at Rouen, before transfer to No.6 Convalescence Camp at Etaples. On 26 July Private Stead was considered to be fit for duty and was transferred to No. 34 Infantry Base Depot, where he endured a week's training in the 'Bull Ring'.

Returned to his battalion, Stead discovered that his comrades had moved into rest behind the Ypres Salient. Such peace was not to last and in October the unit, now back on the Somme, moved up ready for a final push towards Bapaume. On 10 October Stead was wounded whilst serving in the trenches near Lesboeufs. His admission to a Casualty Clearing Station the next day revealed the nature of his injury, 'GSW right hand' – a gun shot wound in the hand.[40] The likelihood is that the wound was self-inflicted. In particular, Stead's subsequent return to duty on the very next day, would seem to suggest that the soldier had not exercised enough care to ensure a lengthy absence from the line. Brief though his two day recovery had been, Private Stead had avoided a most costly day in action – 12 October 1916. On that day, whilst the soldier made his way back to the battalion, his comrades had unsuccessfully attacked Le Transloy – 342 casualties resulted.[41]

A week after his return, Private Stead went absent;[42] his freedom however was short-lived, for one month after the date of his departure he was tried and sentenced to death. Following a delay of three weeks, Stead ultimately learnt of his fate – only to hear that the sentence had been commuted to five years' penal servitude and suspended. On the next day, during very cold weather, Stead and his comrades were ordered to move up the line, leaving their reserve position at Frégicourt and relieving the Essex Regiment. Private Stead never did so, and was arrested two days before Christmas, whilst trying to escape from the controlled area behind the battlefront. By coincidence the day of Stead's departure was the third anniversary of his enlistment in the army.

Stead's second court martial took place on 11 January 1917. Like other soldiers who had faced trial with an already tarnished record, the private declined the assistance of an officer to defend him. Such foolhardy action perhaps reflected the disillusionment and despair of men who ultimately resigned themselves to accept what fate would bring. The soldier's morose outlook would seem to have extended to continual silence throughout the trial, as he chose not to question any witnesses, nor to say a single word in his own defence.[43] In spite of the soldier's previous conviction, his commanding officer, Lieutenant-Colonel A G Horsfall, gave a very fair account of the private's service. Recording that the soldier had always performed his duties satisfactorily when in the trenches, the CO continued by expressing his concern that Stead appeared to be slightly backward.

As a consequence the court ordered that the prisoner be sent to 21 Casualty Clearing Station for examination by an army neurologist. For some reason the court martial record and the soldier's army record do not concur about where this examination took place. 21 CCS was in Third Army, yet the court martial record maintains that Stead was examined by a Fourth Army neurologist. It would seem that the dumb soldier was at least a little more open with the medic, as the doctor reported that there was 'No evidence of feeble mindedness or other mental defect'.[44] 'NAD' was the official medical opinion of the soldier's condition − i.e. nothing abnormal detected.

With Stead's blatant display of indiscipline and non-cooperation, it is perhaps not surprising that the sentence was confirmed. The 20 year old was executed at 6.50 am on 12 February.

On the following day the British forces extended their lines yet another ten miles further southwards. But during the final two weeks of February, no volley rang out at dawn with any other intention than to drive the enemy back. However, when a German withdrawal did take place the retreat had been planned for some time. On 17 and 18 February British attacks took place against the village of Miraumont and three days later the Germans began to withdraw from their front line positions along the Ancre. A month later saw Bapaume occupied, and by 5 April a new enemy line had been established.

At the beginning of March two deserters were executed in completely contrasting circumstances. Perhaps the only similarities were the soldier's ages, and the fact that their battalions were both serving in 30 Division. However, **Drummer Frederick Rose** had been missing for so long that during his absence his battalion had been moved within divisions. Until his untimely demise, Rose had been amongst the most successful in avoiding the military authorities.

Drummer Rose was a regular soldier in 2 Battalion Yorkshire Regiment and had deserted on 18 December 1914.[45] At that time, his unit was moving up to the trenches near Fleurbaix, for an attack that was due to take place later in the day. Ironically it was cancelled.[46]

Absentee Rose, however, took no steps to flee the country. But during his court martial, details of his residence in the two years' that he had been missing emerged. Apparently the soldier had been living with a woman in Hazebrouck. The capture of Drummer Rose came about when a neighbour reported his presence to the police.[47]

In the case of the second soldier — **Private Ellis Holt** of 19 Manchesters — there was a fundamental difference. Holt was a volunteer with a previous conviction recorded against him — a suspended sentence of two years imprisonment with hard labour — for desertion. Private Holt's battalion had served on the Somme during the summer of 1916 — before moving to the Arras front for the winter. The simultaneous execution of the two soldiers did not go unrecorded, although the diarist heard of the events secondhand.

'*5.3.17. Yesterday the APM of the 3rd Division, Mellor, who always acts for Trousdale[48] when the later is away had a bad time.* [This comment that Mellor had a bad time is interesting, as 3 Division had executed 19 men up to this date.] *He had to be present at the shooting of two deserters first thing in the morning and that is a horrid business as you can well imagine.*'[49]

Private Holt, a native of Salford, was 22 at the time of his death and Drummer Rose a year older.

During March one other soldier was shot who was serving in the ranks of a Regular Army battalion within a New Army division. **Private John Rogers,** a volunteer in 2 South Lancs, had, somewhat unusually for a capital crime, deserted whilst actually in the trenches. More commonly a soldier would desert when warned for, or when actually moving up to the trenches. Once again the final events were recorded in the battalion war diary. On 8 March the sentence had been promulgated, and at 6 am the next morning, during very cold weather, the sentence had been carried out 'by a specially selected party under the command of Second-Lieutenant I W F Agabeg'.[50]

Three days after this shooting, trouble of a more serious nature broke out in Russia, in the form of revolution. This rebellion eventually culminated in the abandonment of hostilities on the Russian front, although it was over a year before the Germans took advantage of the released manpower. Transferring their divisions from the Eastern Front, the Central Powers mounted their final offensive in the west in March 1918.

On 24 March 1917, another volunteer was dealt with by firing squad. **Private William Bowerman** was a Londoner serving with 1 East Surreys. A married man of 38, he had a previous conviction for absence, and was serving under a two year suspended sentence.[51] His offence had occurred in the Béthune area, although the battalion had served on the Somme in July and September of the previous year. Rather unusually, the grave of the deceased soldier was not located after the war, and as a consequence the private is commemorated on the Loos Memorial to the Missing.

Another soldier also in his thirties was executed three days later, after absconding from a nearby part of the line. During February **Private Arthur Hamilton** and his battalion – 14 Durham Light Infantry – were serving in the Cambrin sector, when prior to duty in the front line trenches the soldier went absent. Shortly afterwards Private Hamilton was seen buying provisions in a distant village, but it was a week later before he was arrested in the Channel port of Calais. Compounding his offence by giving false particulars, there was little defence that the soldier could make, having been arrested so far from his unit.[52] In mitigation of his offence Hamilton claimed that he had been medically unfit for duty at the time of his crime, stating that he had been suffering from bronchitis and trench feet.[53] Private Hamilton, aged 31, was shot at Noeux-les-Mines, becoming the second soldier in his battalion to suffer the extreme penalty.

Twenty soldiers were executed during the first three months of 1917, three-quarters of them volunteers. Only four of the executions had taken place in Regular Army divisions, emphasising the fact that volunteers in New Army divisions who had fought on the Somme were still being brought to account. On the final day of March a young soldier with considerable experience of battle found his way into the statistics. The details given by Judge Babington differ occasionally from the information that has been obtained by the authors, although there are still a number of issues which remain unresolved. The charges actually involved two soldiers, both from the same regiment, who offended together and were arrested together, but for some reason that remains unclear, were executed on different days.

The battalion concerned was 5 Dorsets and the earlier of the two recruits was **Private William Anderson**. This soldier had arrived in Gallipoli on 22 September 1915, a month after his unit had originally landed.[54] Anthony Babington maintained that Anderson's comrade and fellow offender had also served at Gallipoli but no record has been found of this being the case, based on an examination of the Medal Rolls and Medal Records Index. The Judge also maintains that the soldiers were of good character, but records show that a fortnight after landing on the Peninsula, Private Anderson was tried by Field General Court Martial for disobedience and sentenced to three months' field punishment no.1.[55] Such a sentence is of particular interest, because it highlights the possibility that a soldier might be killed or wounded by enemy action whilst undergoing punishment.

Before the expiry of his sentence Private Anderson and his battalion were evacuated from Gallipoli to the island of Mudros, and later to Imbros. On one of these islands the soldier again found himself in trouble. On this occasion Anderson received a sentence of 112 days' detention for absence. Still under sentence the soldier and his battalion moved on to Alexandria (in Egypt) where the remainder of the sentence eventually expired. On the third day of the Battle of the Somme the unit set sail again, arriving six days later at Marseilles en route for the Western Front.

Private Anderson would seem to have learnt his lesson, and in the final week of September 1916, a year after his initial baptism of fire, the battalion moved up in support of an attack on Mouquet Farm on the Somme, and 'did valuable work in bringing up bombs'.[56] Anderson's eventual downfall came about from his absence on New Year's Day 1917. As the battalion moved up into support trenches on the left bank of the river Ancre, south-west of St Pierre Divion,[57] Private Anderson and his comrade made off. Whilst their battalion attacked unsuccessfully near Beaucourt the two men escaped together across the Channel to England. The two both lived in Barking near London and made their way home. On 30 January, whilst still wearing their uniforms,[58] the pair were arrested in their home town. (For some reason which is unclear the records to which Anthony Babington has had access suggest that the two men were arrested at Folkestone).

Private Anderson's trial took place on 9 March and it is assumed that the two men were tried together. The delay in bringing the cases to court adds weight to the belief that deserters who successfully crossed the Channel were interrogated in an attempt to discover their escape route. Any information disclosed by captured deserters enabled the army to tighten security. Although such questioning was very likely to have taken place, no record exists to confirm such a procedure. In previous cases where a man's conduct sheet already showed a number of convictions, the soldier had often declined the assistance of an officer to act as prisoner's friend. Private Anderson did likewise, and one can only assume that, based on past experience, he considered the assistance of little value.

21 year old Anderson was shot at Beauquesne on 31 March, but in 1935 his remains, together with those of the two other soldiers buried in the communal cemetery, were re-interred in Gezaincourt Communal Cemetery Extension.

All of the soldiers shot by firing squad during the period beginning of April to the end June 1917 were convicted deserters. They numbered 15 in total and with one exception were all infantrymen. With one further exception, all were privates or equivalent ranks. Although the Somme battles were some time distant, a handful of cases still related to crimes committed during those sanguinary days. Clearly though, with the number of executions dropping by 25 per cent, compared to the previous quarter any further legacy of those Somme battles was fading away. With one third of the executions being either of regular soldiers or in regular battalions, those men who had volunteered and fought so bravely on the Somme no longer provided the bulk of the victims. Half of those shot had a variety of previous convictions recorded against them. Three conscripts were also shot, one in April and two in June.

The first three executions all took place in Regular Army divisions. Little information has come to light about **Sapper Frederick Malyon** of 12 Company Royal Engineers. It is known that at the time of his offence he was attached to the Royal Field Artillery, and his army number would suggest that he was well above the average age of those executed for military offences. No details have been discovered about his desertion, the only further information being that he was shot at Noeux-les-Mines on 4 April.

On the day that America joined the war a Reservist in 1 West Yorks was executed. **Sergeant George Gleadow** had originally enlisted in the East Yorks Regiment in 1906, and had gone to France in January 1915. In 1916 he had transferred to the West Yorks and held the rank of sergeant at the time of his death.[59] The NCO had gone missing in October 1916 whilst his unit was engaged in operations on the Somme. During the following two months whilst masquerading either as a senior NCO or an officer he had fraudulently cashed a number of cheques. When arrested in Amiens in January 1917 Gleadow's disguise proved far from inconspicuous, as he was wearing the ribbons of the Victoria Cross, together with those of the Distinguished Conduct Medal and the Military Medal.[60]

Quite what caused the delay in bringing the sergeant's case to trial is unclear, but when the court eventually sat to hear the evidence the soldier recounted an unlikely story. Gleadow told the court that when on leave he had been wounded in the head and taken to a French hospital for treatment. Unable to give any further details and without witnesses to confirm such events his story had been treated with incredulity. Before Gleadow's execution, he was however examined by two doctors. Although they found a small scar on the soldier's head, it was their joint opinion that the wound was not recent.[61]

Easter Monday 1917 (9 April) was recorded by the official historian as 'one of the most successful days of the war'.[62] 14 divisions were in action on the first day of the Battle of Arras – exactly the same number as had been involved on 1 July 1916. However, the initial gains made at Arras were far more promising, and by the third day of battle, the casualties suffered were only roughly one third of those inflicted on the opening day of the Somme offensive.

On the second day of the new offensive, a conscript in a regular battalion suffered the extreme penalty. **Private William Robinson** had gone absent at the beginning of March in order to avoid taking part in an attack. His freedom had been short-lived, as later in the month he was brought to trial. No entry has been found in the war diary of 1 Sherwood Foresters to record the soldier's death, nor the locality at which the event took place.[63] But today the private's remains lie buried in Peronne Communal Cemetery.

On the following day a Canadian soldier fell victim to army style justice. **Private Eugene Perry** was just 21 years old at the time, and was serving in 22 Canadian Infantry Battalion. The unit was unusual in that French was the spoken language. Perry was unmarried and had been a labourer in civilian life. He had attested in his native New Brunswick in October 1915, and sailed for England a fortnight later. Eight months of training improved the youngster's physique, and in mid June 1916 he was drafted to France. After further training he was posted to the front in July, and served creditably until February of the following year.[64]

Once Private Perry committed an offence events happened swiftly. On 21 February the Canadian received a sentence of 28 days' field punishment no.1 for a brief absence. Three days into his punishment, an even briefer absence cost Perry his life, when the private went missing between 3 pm and 9.45 pm.

Two days after his 21st birthday Private Perry was tried at Petit Servins for desertion, and on the eve of the Battle of Arras the Commander-in-Chief considered the soldier's fate. As the battle commenced the condemned man's battalion did sterling work. Going over the top as 'moppers up' they brought in 500 German prisoners to the POW cage at Aux Rietz. 11 April however brought an unpleasant task for the men: at 5.30 am a party from the battalion formed a firing squad for the execution.[65] During his military service Private Perry had only been absent for a total of fifteen-and-three-quarter hours – yet he was executed. Youth had not excused him, but his death became the first in pattern that did not go unnoticed. Perry's execution was the first in 22 Battalion, but four others were to follow. The significance of the execution of five soldiers, all from a French speaking battalion, did not go unrecorded.[66] During the war only one other Canadian unit had more than one man executed from its ranks – 3 Battalion. This unit had two men shot on different dates in August 1916.

A week after the commencement of the British offensive at Arras, the French launched their own assault on the Aisne. The attack later became known as the Second Battle of the Aisne, or the Nivelle Offensive – after their new Commander-in-Chief. The Frenchman's elevated status had come about after his success, late in 1916, in driving the Germans back at Verdun. However, his leadership was short-lived, as one month after the launch of the offensive the new commander was removed from his post, leaving behind him a chaotic situation, as the French armies openly displayed their contempt of military authority.

To date, the accounts which have been given of these events in the French armies show only a sketch picture of what went on. The mutinies, often described as 'serious unrest' or 'collective indiscipline' remain shrouded in mystery. The French authorities, clearly keen to cover-up such matters, have kept the records secret, perhaps a surprising decision in view of the fact that in post-war years a number of courts of cessation were held to clear the names of a number of French soldiers who had faced firing squads.[67]

The British official history of the war makes mention of the French mutinies, although the details given portray events in such generalities that it is doubtful that the account is comprehen-sive.[68] Considering that the malaise did not disappear until the final year of the war, it is an over-simplification merely to state that, lack of leave, drunkenness, poor medical facilities, coupled with the occasional red flag waving, could have nullified the effectiveness of such a large fighting force.

The first of the 119 recorded cases of collective indiscipline was said to have occurred on 29 April, with two thirds of such disturbances occurring between 25 May and 10 June.[69] All but nine of these acts of indiscipline were said to be serious, but the official account suggests that occasional arson was the most serious occurrence, with other disturbances including stone throwing and window breaking. Surprisingly in an army with such a marked contrast between officer and *poilu*, attacks on officers were rare, although in June railway officials and military police reported being abused.

Although the mutinies eventually subsided, such a return to normality did not occur without concessions from the High Command. A generous leave allocation was granted, which in itself was costly – if only in terms of the reduction in fighting strength. Another event worthy of note was that in November 1917 a brief escalation of trouble amongst French troops was caused by the Pope's actions in advocating peace, which he compounded by suggesting that the belligerents should attend the Socialist conference in Stockholm. Perhaps, however, the most interesting aspect from a disciplinary view point, was that Pétain the new Commander-in-Chief, decided to remove from the ranks those bad characters who were serving under suspended sentences. In what was clearly an alteration in policy the French commander must have considered that the resultant manpower loss was out-weighed by the damage being done by disruptive elements. The new decision must also have taken into account the possibility that soldiers might commit offences with the hope of a custodial sentence resulting in their ultimate escape from the horrors of trench warfare. Early in 1915 the British Government had brought in the Suspension of Sentences Act solely to prevent prison sentences from becoming an alternative to service in the line.

In the third week of April a second soldier from 5 Dorset faced a firing squad. 21 year old **Private John Lewis** had deserted with his comrade Private Anderson. The authors have found no evidence that Private Lewis served at Gallipoli, only that Private Anderson had done so. (See the case of Private Anderson − March 1917.) Both men lived in Barking, London, where they were subsequently arrested. It is not clear why the two 21 year olds who served together, deserted together and were arrested together, should be separated in death. Certainly it is unusual that the pair were executed on separate dates. Assuming that a mistake has not been made concerning the location of his grave, then Private Lewis was shot at Forceville, behind the Somme battlefields on 19 April.

On the following day an execution took place in 4 Canadian Division, whose ranks until then had been spared the extreme penalty. The victim was a 21 year old from Toronto with a bad military record. **Private Harold Carter** enlisted in 59 Battalion in March 1915 and sailed for England at the beginning of the following year.[70] On the Western Front the soldier served with 73 Battalion but deserted and was sentenced to 10 years' imprisonment, which was then suspended. However, a while later he repeated his crime with fatal results.

On the same day another execution took place − the victim being a Scotsman who was a Regular soldier − the fourth consecutive soldier to be shot at the age 21. **Private Joseph Ferguson** had enlisted in the ranks of the Royal Scots Fusiliers in October 1913. For reasons that are unknown the members of his chosen regiment would appear to have had a propensity for committing military offences.

Major-General Sir Wyndham Childs wrote in 1930 that conscripts were more likely to desert than regular soldiers since career soldiers enjoyed an *esprit de corps*.[71] The General's theory would seem to be in question when applied to the Royal Scots Fusiliers, the Scotsmen being prone to offending irrespective of the terms of their enlistment. (The authors have compiled this brief study from an examination of the British War & Victory Medal rolls for the regiment. WO329/991-993. No suggestion is made that the record of this regiment is any worse than any other. A full examination of the records of all regiments would be impossible.) A total of 527 men (not officers) in the regiment, at some time during their military service committed a crime for which they were liable to forfeit their medals. The crimes ranged from the seemingly insignificant offence of fraudulent enlistment (the military did not consider it so) to cowardice and desertion. By far the vast majority, however, re-earned their medals for subsequent good service. (Medals could be re-submitted for issue by virtue of Army Council Instruction, no.75 of 1921.) Nevertheless, at the very least, these offenders amounted to a staggering one man in every 69. The true percentage would in fact be higher than this figure, because not every soldier in the sequence of army numbers examined, saw service. Some would have completed their time on the reserve, some would have been discharged unfit and a number would have been transferred. Of course, outsiders would have been drafted in as well.

The statistics quoted must be seen in context and it is not possible to make generalities with any certainty. For example, in considering the number of offenders one must remember that deceased soldiers always had their medals issued — unless shot for a military crime. It is a matter for speculation whether dead soldiers committed more or less offences than those who survived. However, there must certainly have been a number of bad characters amongst them, hence increasing the overall percentage of offenders.

General Child's theory, however, is worthy of further consideration. In the Royal Scots Fusiliers, in a sample of 100 men who were probably mainly Reservists aged 30 plus, approximately one in three committed some crime or other.

Those least likely to offend were the last of the regulars to enlist prior to August 1914, and also the earliest of the volunteers. Of course it is possible that the reason that they did not offend is that they were quickly killed, maimed or taken POW, never having time to commit crimes. A group of volunteers that enlisted in the first half of 1915 would seem to have the worst record, with upwards of 40 per cent offending. Unfortunately it has not been possible to draw any conclusions from the data on the conscripts. It would seem that either not all the army numbers were issued, or that the men were transferred, only having served with the Royal Scots Fusiliers for a short period.

The condemned man was atypical, being a Regular soldier with little pre-war service. Private Ferguson had been drafted to the first battalion of his regiment on 22 September 1914.[72] In the following year the soldier had been wounded and returned to England. Upon recovery he commenced the first of a number of deceptions when he fraudulently re-enlisted. Although his sentence for this crime is not known, the date of his conviction is recorded as 20 October 1915.[73] Returned to his battalion in France the private continued his crimes, but in a more serious manner. Twice Ferguson was convicted for desertion, and on a second occasion received a sentence of death.[74]

Serving under two suspended sentences the soldier had expended any chance of further leniency, when in October 1916 he deserted again. The crime was serious, as at the time Ferguson was attached to the Royal Engineers who were engaged in tunnelling operations on the Somme.[75] For three months the private avoided the military authorities until 27 January 1917, when he was arrested in Ribemont — a village behind the battlefront. The military policeman had caught Ferguson masquerading as a war hero, for he wore the ribbons of the Distinguished Conduct Medal, the Legion of Honour together with an armful of wound stripes.[76] It comes therefore as no surprise that the Commander-in-Chief decided to end this continual and sometimes irrational behaviour. Private Ferguson was shot at Wanquetin on 20 April, just two weeks after a soldier in the West Yorks had suffered the same fate for similar deceptions.

When next a firing squad despatched a victim the battle of Arras was almost over. The unfortunate soldier was an Irishman who was serving under an assumed name, **Private Thomas Hogan,** having enlisted in the Royal Inniskilling Fusiliers in the name of Thomas Murphy.[77] He was the first Irishman to be executed in 1917, and at 31 was older than most of the other deserters shot at this time. Hogan had been posted to France soon after his enlistment, landing in France on 18 March 1915.[78] His posting was to a Regular battalion −2 Royal Inniskilling Fusiliers; however, at the end of 1915 the unit was transferred to 32 (New Army) Division. The Irishman served for over two years without apparently committing any serious offence. Hogan's execution on 14 May was the fourth such sentence carried out in 32 Division −all of them in 1917. In the three previous shootings, one victim was serving in a Lancashire regiment and the other two in Scottish units. By coincidence the previous victim in the division had also been named Murphy, although the army incorrectly recorded his name, the man's true surname being Murphey.

On the following day another 'first' took place, although the event did little credit either to those responsible or to the victim. Until that day no soldier in Lloyd George's 38 (Welsh) Division had suffered the extreme penalty, and the shooting was the first of a Welshman in 1917, the 'men from the hills' having served creditably on the Somme in

1916. With the exception of Sub-Lieutenant Edwin Dyett, with the tenuous connection that he had been born at Cardiff, no Welshman had been executed as the result of the Somme fighting.

**Private George Watkins** was a Reservist who had been recalled at the outbreak of war. He had originally enlisted in 1904, so it is likely that he was aged about 28 when he rejoined his regiment. With no time for re-training the Welshman had gone to France with the earliest of drafts, landing in France on 13 August,[79] and shortly afterwards served with 2 Welsh at Mons. In the following year he was twice wounded, returning each time to active service − although he was subsequently posted to 13 Battalion. After fighting on the Somme in 1916, Watkins' division moved to the Ypres Salient, where in December the veteran soldier went absent. For three months he remained at liberty until arrested the following March.

In Watkins' case yet another unexplained delay occurred before the hearing took place. The Welshman was able to boast a fine record of service, but the length of his absence proved to be his undoing. The soldier pleaded that family troubles had led to his uncharacteristic behaviour, but the utterings proved to be in vain. The scene of his crime, the Ypres Salient, became his final resting place.

The third and final execution during May was that of a young regular soldier. In January 1914 **Private Samuel Cunnington** had enlisted into the Royal Warwickshire Regiment. His service in France had not been without blemish, as on 21 January 1916 he had been tried by District Court Martial for desertion − and sentenced to 28 days' detention. Six months later, as 2 Battalion moved up to take part in operations on the Somme, the soldier went absent.[80] With considerable luck he enjoyed his freedom until the end of the year.

In yet another puzzling case, no reason is evident to explain why Cunnington was not brought to trial until 29 April 1917. Seemingly, the only likely possibility was that the soldier had escaped before an earlier trial could be held. This suggestion arises because the miscreant was charged with two offences of desertion.[81]

In what was a very unusual occurrence at a court martial, a French woman gave evidence for the prosecution. She told the court that the accused had lodged for some time in a hut near her house. With the soldier being in uniform she had initially thought that his presence was legitimate, and she had often given him food. As time progressed, doubts began to cross her mind, leading to the woman and her husband reporting the facts to the police.[82]

Private Cunnington had a previous conviction for desertion, but on that occasion he had received a lenient sentence. It is therefore surprising that he chose to be unrepresented at his trial. Clearly he must have sensed the gravity of his offence, having been absent for so long. Nevertheless his choice suggests that the soldier sensed, or did not care, what fate awaited him. The unlucky soldier, aged just 20, was shot at 6 am on 19 May.[83] The execution was the first to take place in 7 Division for over two years.

At the beginning of June a young conscript with a bad military record suffered the extreme penalty. **Private Charles Milligan** had enlisted in February 1916 into the Cameronians (Scottish Rifles). Once in France the soldier had committed his first offence of disobedience in October of the same year. The resultant sentence of one year's imprisonment with hard labour was obviously suspended, as early in 1917 the private was again convicted for the same offence – but on this occasion received the more lenient sentence of 42 days' field punishment no.1.[84] The young soldier's battalion was part of 15 (Scottish) Division and was engaged in the opening day of the Battle of Arras, as well as on a number of days thereafter. And it was at this time that Private Milligan went absent – just as his unit was preparing to attack. The soldier's freedom was short-lived, and five days later he was arrested.[85]

A court martial disposed of Milligan's case on 5 May when once again a soldier with a bad record chose to be unrepresented. The Scotsman's unfortunate admissions included one that, at the moment he fled, he had been unable to control his actions. His commanding officer, Lieutenant-Colonel A C Stanley-Clarke, was very fairminded in his written statement to the court. He recorded that Milligan's conduct 'has not been good on the whole', although there is 'nothing to his discredit in the field'.[86] The brigade commander however, was not so charitable about the 20 year old. He recommended that the sentence be carried out, adding that men even younger had been known to do their duty in the past.[87] Private Milligan's death on 3 June 1917 was later recorded in the official casualty rolls, but no cause of death was stated.[88] Although the Glaswegian received such commemoration, in post-war years the Imperial War Graves Commission were unable to locate his grave. But in later years the diligent staff of the Commission did identify his remains, which today lie in Canadian Cemetery No.2 at Neuville St Vaast – near Arras. Rather strangely, and by way of an oversight, Private Milligan had initially been commemorated on the Menin Gate Memorial to the Missing. In fact the correct location would have been on the Arras Memorial.

The second soldier to be shot in June was a Londoner and a Kitchener volunteer. **Private John Fryer** had enlisted in the East Surreys and was serving in 12 Battalion under a suspended sentence of two years' imprisonment. Following a second offence of desertion, the usual procedure of trial, review and confirmation, culminated with orders for Fryer's execution being issued to a battalion officer. On 13 June, Lieutenant R A Brearey, together with a sergeant and ten men, made his way to Poperinghe. The next day their grim task was the shooting of the 23 year old private from 'D' Company.[89]

A further conscript with an unenviable reputation was also dealt with in the same month. **Private Arthur Allsop** of 12 King's Rifle Corps first committed a crime before enduring anything more rigorous than training in France. His conduct sheet showed that on 14 November 1916 (whilst in the UK) he had been convicted of desertion, receiving a sentence of 112 days' detention, and on 12 March the following year, had been sentenced to death.[90] How-ever, considering that the private had committed his second offence whilst at a base camp, it was not surprising that the death sentence had been commuted to five years' imprisonment, before being suspended.

Unfortunately, during Allsop's first tour of duty in the front line he went absent. His defence was a familiar one; he related that his brother had recently been killed in action and that his mother was ill.[91] Once again the battalion members were required to perform the grisly ritual, with an unusually high ranking officer taking an active part. At a court martial it was usual for the adjutant of a unit to act as prosecuting officer, and at executions it was also the norm for a junior officer to command the firing squad. Although the name of the prosecuting officer has not been traced, it was certainly unusual when either the battalion commander or his second-in-command were involved in a shooting. Major G Aylmer minimised his chances of having to administer the *coup de grâce* by selecting a firing squad from the battalion snipers. The event was recorded in the war diary as having taken place at 4.15 am on 15 June.[92]

As the war progressed the percentage of those soldiers executed who were already serving under a suspended sentence increased. An exception to this rule was an Irish soldier who also claimed to have family problems. **Private J Wishard** disappeared between Hazebrouck and Bailleul, when on his way to join 7 Royal Inniskilling Fusiliers. He was arrested three weeks later at Boulogne, but escaped and assumed a civilian disguise. Twelve days later whilst still in Boulogne, Wishard's luck ran out.[93] The story he later told to the court was that his child was ill.[94] Domestic worries did not seem to impress the military hierarchy — with the inevitable result. The Irishman was shot on 15 June in the small village of Merris — near Hazebrouck. Although it was recorded that his body was buried in Merris churchyard, after the war it proved impossible to verify the location; consequently Private Wishard is commemorated in Cabaret Rouge British Cemetery near Arras.

The last soldier to be executed in June was a 25 year old volunteer, whose case was the first to occur in a Territorial division during 1917. Additionally, prior to this shooting, no man had been executed in 56 (London) Division.

**Private James Mayers** had been sent to France in September 1916[95] as a reinforcement for the BEF, whose ranks had been depleted by vast losses incurred on the Somme. The volunteer had proved himself a poor soldier, and had been sentenced to death for quitting his post.[96] On that occasion Mayers, a Londoner from the East End, was fortunate, and the sentence was suspended. A fellow soldier with the 13 Londons – the Kensingtons – later recalled the events that led to Mayers' downfall.

*'After one rather trying tour in the trenches, we came back to a quiet village and one chap chose this opportunity to desert and hid in a nearby wood. After a day or two he was caught and condemned to death. A small tin lid was handed to me to paint white. The firing party marched off next morning, the tin disc fixed to his chest, and he was shot. The sentence seems very savage, but was customary, as desertion or cowardice has to be dealt with drastically in warfare, not only to discourage waverers, but to prevent the spread of panic. In this case the sentence was very drastic, as the offence was not actually committed "in the face of the enemy". In fact he may even have got away with shell-shock if he had disappeared during battle.'*[97]

At the beginning of July disciplinary matters dating back several months were still being attended to, and two Canadian soldiers were 'weeded out' to be the examples. A never to be repeated event occurred, when the two Canadian privates were shot on the same day. The soldiers were both in their early twenties and many similarities exist between the two cases.

**Private Gustave Comte,** a native of Montreal, had enlisted in September 1915 and had landed in England in June of the following year. By trade Comte had been an industrial worker, and although small – five feet three-and-a-quarter inches high – he was strongly built. His first misdemeanour typified the restrictions of service life, when four days after his arrival in the UK the private was confined to camp for a week – for being unshaven on parade. On the next day the sentence was doubled, when the soldier was deemed to be improperly dressed on parade.[98]

Private Comte joined 22 Canadian Infantry Battalion in France midway through the Battle of the Somme, and until the winter served without blemish. Scant details exist about his first offence on active

176

service, nevertheless the authors are of the opinion that the crime was rare. On 29 December Comte was sentenced to 21 days' field punishment no.1, for 'irregular conduct whilst a sentry' on Christmas day. The offences of sleeping on post, quitting post or being drunk can be discounted, as charges under the Army Act already existed for these crimes, nevertheless it is a matter for speculation whether or not Private Comte had been fraternising with the enemy.

On 2 January 1917 – just the fourth day of his punishment – Comte went missing, a six hour absence adding seven days to his field punishment. In early April, prior to the assault on Vimy Ridge, Private Comte decamped for his longest ever absence; and not being captured until May he avoided the bloodshed of the Arras offensive. The deserter was kept in close confinement, and tried at Grand Servins on 6 June. Sir Douglas Haig considered the case on the penultimate day of June.

The second Canadian deserter had joined the army on 10 June 1916, just two days after his fellow countryman had landed in England. In due course, when **Private Joseph LaLancette** landed in England, his comrade was sampling – for the first time – life in the trenches. LaLancette was a tall, slightly built individual, who had been a tailor in civilian life.[99]

Private LaLancette was drafted to France in November 1916 – just before the end of the Battle of the Somme. Later that month his first offence was to dodge off from his draft which was bound for an entrenching battalion – remaining absent for over a day. The weakling, who would undoubtedly have found the digging heavy going, escaped lightly, suffering only two days' loss of pay. In December 1916 the private was despatched to lighter duties at the divisional laundry, yet before the end of the year he was returned to 22 Battalion and was again in trouble.

The nature of the soldier's crime appears to be similar to that committed by Private Comte, both offences occurring roughly at the same time. Two days prior to Christmas, Private LaLancette went missing. It must be assumed from the charge that he was on sentry duty at the time, as the soldier was charged with 'being absent from the trenches from 4 pm to 8 pm causing another man to take his place'. A fortnight's field punishment no.1 resulted, and immediately after its expiry the fragile young soldier was admitted to a Canadian Field Ambulance suffering from PUO, or Pyrexia of Unknown Origin – an all encompassing term, used to describe illness where the patient suffered with a temperature, with possible sweating and shaking, for which there was no clear diagnosis. The sick soldier took over ten days to recover, and it is small wonder that prior to the Battle of Arras he again chose to go absent.

Private LaLancette's capture, detention and court martial followed closely that of his comrade — the case being heard the day after Private Comte's. On 3 July 1917 the small village of Aix-Noulette, in the shadow of Vimy Ridge, was venue to the double tragedy. At 4.45 in the morning the crash of two volleys rang out, killing 21 year old Joseph LaLancette and his comrade Gustave Comte, just one year his senior.

On the same day that the two Canadians had been executed, a Londoner who had volunteered for army service was shot. **Rifleman Walter Yeoman** enlisted in May 1915, but had not been posted to the Western Front until the 13 January 1917.[100] Amazingly Yeoman had served with 12 London Regiment for less than four months, when in April he went absent for a second time. On the first occasion the soldier's sentence of death had been commuted to 15 years.[101] However, after deserting again, Yeoman's second death sentence was confirmed. The 22 year old was shot on 3 July, without having even completed six months on active service.

On 4 July a second double execution took place, both soldiers having seen many months of service. **Private John Barnes** had been posted to France on 29 September 1915 as a reinforcement to 2 Royal Sussex Regiment[102] which had been engaged at Loos. He also served with 12 Battalion (Southdown) before being transferred to 7 Battalion. However, the soldier was not of good character, as he was already under a suspended sentence of 15 years' penal servitude for desertion when, on 10 June 1917, he repeated his crime.

Although it is clear from Barnes' army number that he was a volunteer, some doubt exists about the second soldier. The logical inference, based on this man's army number, is that he had enlisted during the early period of the war. It is not possible to be certain, however, and it is thought that **Private Robert Gillis Pattison** might have seen pre-war army service. The soldier's surname is incorrectly spelt Paterson in army records. Pattison's second forename is seemingly unique, yet the only Pattison, (in fact spelt Paterson) in the Index to the *Great War Medal Rolls*, had previously served in the Indian Army as a gunner.[103] It is difficult to offer any explanation why Pattison appears to have the army number of an early volunteer, yet seems to have previously served in the Indian Army. The likelihood of the records of two individuals becoming mixed up is thought to be very remote, given the unusual forename.

Private Pattison served on the Western Front with 7 East Surreys, and it was recorded that he was the first soldier in his unit to suffer from shellshock.[104] The onset of Pattison's disability is recorded to have occurred on 5 March 1916, and it is not difficult to visualise his predicament, given that at the time his unit was serving opposite the Hohenzollern Redoubt. This area was the scene of constant mining and counter mining as the belligerents cratered the wasteland in vain and bloody attempts to gain a slight territorial advantage. The battalion diarist gave a graphic account of hostilities in the week following the private's illness.

The diarist recorded that on 6 March the Germans put down a heavy bombardment, and just after midnight they exploded a mine under the trenches to the right of the British line. The following night the enemy made three raids against the British front line. On 10 March, the enemy carried out a night-time bombing raid, which was followed the next night by the detonation of another mine. At the end of the week the British 'blew in' three German mineshafts during defensive operations.[105] If such conditions were typical, then it is not surprising that men succumbed to shellshock.

It is not known on what date Private Pattison returned to duty, but what is surprising, given the soldier's shellshocked condition, is that during the very same month (March), he was convicted of desertion and sentenced to 84 days' field punishment no.1. Somehow Pattison managed to maintain control of his nerves for over a year — until the Battle of Arras loomed. On 2 April 1917 his battalion went into the front line, and a week later were in action on the first day of battle. The soldier stuck it, but on 3 May prior to an attack, his nerves gave way. He reported to the battalion doctor, whose examination culminated with instructions to return to the line.[106]

It would be an understatement to say that the medic failed in his duty. One time army doctor Lord Moran described how during the war he came to judge when a man was finished, when a soldier could no longer be of any use until rested and recovered.[107] On 4 May Private Pattison was arrested by the military police in Arras. The account given by the policeman at the court martial indicated that Pattison was displaying symptoms of shellshock.

It is not known whether Private Pattison was medically examined whilst in confinement, but if he was, then the medical profession once again failed to recognise the soldier's confused condition.

Privates Barnes and Pattison were shot at Arras on 4 July. Barnes was aged 24 and his parents lived at Littlehampton — where their son is now commemorated on the local war memorial. His grave in France carries the inscription, 'He giveth his beloved sleep'. Pattison was aged 23, his parents living at Cramlington in Northumberland.[108]

On the following day an Irish soldier, also aged 23, was shot. **Private Robert Hope** was the eighth soldier to have served at Gallipoli whose subsequent posting to the Western Front resulted in an offence of desertion followed by execution. Additionally Hope was masquerading under an assumed name. A previous individual, Private Hogan, shot in May 1917, had also served in the same regiment – Royal Inniskilling Fusiliers.

Hope had enlisted in the name of Hepple, although doubts about the need for such a falsehood exist, as some army records show the name spelt as 'Heppel'. The soldier's service in Gallipoli had been short-lived, as he landed on 13 November 1915,[109] only a few weeks before the entire battlefront was evacuated. Hope served with 1 Royal Inniskilling Fusiliers – part of 29 Division – and during 1917 the troops fought at Arras. No details have emerged concerning Hope's character, nor the circumstances under which he deserted. However, his untimely end on 5 July came when his battalion had been transferred to the Ypres Salient.

In the second week of July a conscript with a bad military record was executed. **Private Denis Blakemore** was a native of Bicton, Shrewsbury and was the fourth conscript to face a firing squad during 1917. The soldier's first absence resulted in a death sentence which had been suspended. Therefore in June 1917, when he repeated the crime, the outlook was bleak.

The offence had occurred in the run-up to the attack on the Messines Ridge, when 8 North Staff were due to assault Wytschaete. At this time, when under orders to advance, Private Blakemore went absent from the assembly trenches. Like many previous deserters the soldier sought refuge in the Channel ports, presumably looking for a route to escape to England. After 18 days Blakemore was arrested in Boulogne, whilst masquerading as a member of the Army Service Corps.[110] The 28 year old conscript – the eldest to face execution – was shot at Locre, near the Franco-Belgian border, on 9 July. Private Blakemore's grave carries the simple inscription, *'Thy will be done'*.

*It would be wrong to assume that Regular Army soldiers were normally mature in years. The average age of the Regular Army soldiers who were executed during the war was just over 24 years. This figure is based on the known ages of 61 of the 81 Regular soldiers known to have been shot. One young Regular, serving in 7 King's Royal Rifle Corps, was shot during the second week in July. At his trial 23 year old* **Rifleman Frederick Barratt** told the court that he had soldiered with the original BEF, during which time he had been wounded and left unattended for five days. The rifleman continued that his constitution had never recovered, and that he became terrified when under fire.[111]

Clearly, however, such fear did not always keep the soldier awake, as in March 1916, Barratt had been sentenced to three years' penal servitude for sleeping on his post.[112] His trial for desertion took place on 21 June, when once again a disillusioned soldier chose to be unrepresented. Although the offence had occurred on the Arras front, his execution took place on the Somme. On 10 July, 8 Rifle Brigade furnished a firing squad to shoot the unfortunate Barratt. The diarist of the Rifle Brigade noted that it was the first time that his battalion had been called upon to provide such a squad.[113] Barratt's execution was the fourth in his division (14 Division), and strangely the shootings had alternated between 7 King's Royal Rifle Corps and 6 Somerset Light Infantry, both having had two men shot. Throughout the remainder of the war, no other man was executed in this division for a military offence, although in 1918 a soldier was shot for murder.

It has previously been stated that for some unknown reason executions were often more prolific during the first two weeks in any month. July 1917 was no exception, as the final execution took place on the 12th of the month.

Two previous executions had taken place in 56 (London) Division, one in June and the other, earlier in July. Like the previous victims, **Private William Benham** was a volunteer serving in this Territorial division. Unlike his predecessors Benham appears to have been of good character prior to his desertion. He had served with 1/3 London Regiment since April 1916,[114] and it must be assumed that a year later during the Battle of Arras, he absconded. The soldier's end came at 4.37 am on 12 July, when he faced a firing squad comprised of his battalion comrades.[115]

**NOTES**

1 Captain Cyril Falls, *Military Operations France & Belgium, 1917*, Volume 1.
2 *John Bull*, 23 February, 2 March, 16 March & 23 March 1918.
3 Anthony Babington, *For the Sake of Example*.
4 Records of General Register Office, London.
5 Ministry of Defence, Naval Archives, Hayes.
6 8 November 1916 is the date given for this request – *John Bull*, 23 February   1918.

7 Further details of the Dyett case all come from Anthony Babington's book unless otherwise footnoted.
8 *John Bull*, 23 February 1918.
9 Letters to a friend on 13th & 26th December and quoted in *John Bull* on 23 February 1918.
10 *Hansard*, 14 March 1918.
11 *John Bull*, 23 February 1918.
12 *Hansard*, 14 March 1918.
13 *John Bull*, 23 February 1918, stated that the President was a Brigadier- General.
14 Unpublished memoirs of Leading Seaman T MacMillan.
15 *The Times*, 20 August 1983.
16 *The Times*, 19 September 1983.
17 *Soldiers Died in the Great War*, part 13.
18 The account given here is based on the war diary of 19 Durham Light Infantry, WO95/2490, and the account related by Sydney Allison in *The Bantams*.
19 Anthony Babington, op cit.
20 WO95/2490, op cit.
21 Anthony Babington, op cit.
22 Sydney Allison, op cit.
23 Ibid.
24 The account was published by Ernest Thurtle, *Shootings at Dawn*.
25 If the account of the eyewitness is correct then this letter must have come from the daughter of 28 year old, former labourer, John McDonald. 21 year old Peter Goggins, a miner in civilian life, had only married in 1915. 25 year old Joseph Stones was not married.
26 Ernest Thurtle also exposed details of this case in his book, *Military Discipline and Democracy*.
27 WO329/1633, *British War and Victory Medal Roll*.
28 WO93/49, Summary of First World War capital court martial cases.
29 WO329/1, Index to the *Great War Medal Rolls*.
30 Anthony Babington, op cit.
31 Confusion arises in army records concerning the spelling of the private's surname. In a number of documents the name is incorrectly recorded as Grampton. This incorrect name is also engraved on the headstone of his tomb.
32 WO329/1600, *British War and Victory Medal Roll*.
33 Anthony Babington, op cit.
34 WO93/49, op cit.
35 C E Montague, *Rough Justice* (fiction).
36 Memoirs of Captain Stormont-Gibbs, *From the Somme to the Armistice*.
37 Commonwealth War Graves Commission register, Tyne Cot Memorial.
38 WO95/2392, Battalion War Diary.
39 Anthony Babington, op cit.
40 Army Service Record.
41 Brigadier-General C D Bruce, *The History of the Duke of Wellington's Regiment*.
42 Anthony Babington, op cit, gives the date as 19 October.
43 Ibid.
44 WO93/49, op cit.
45 Ibid.
46 WO95/1659, Battalion War Diary.
47 Anthony Babington, op cit.
48 Major R C Trousdale, APM, VII Corps.
49 Major C L A Ward-Jackson, Camp Commandant to VII Corps, Letters to his wife 1915-18, Imperial War Museum, reference 78/22/1.
50 WO95/2250, Battalion War Diary.
51 WO93/49, op cit.
52 Ibid.
53 Anthony Babington, op cit.
54 WO329/1, op cit.
55 WO93/49, op cit.
56 Captain W Miles, *Military Operations France & Belgium, 1916*, Volume 2.
57 WO95/1820, Battalion War Diary.
58 WO93/49, op cit.

59  WO329/1, op cit.
60  Anthony Babington, op cit.
61  Ibid.
62  Captain Cyril Falls, op cit.
63  WO95/1721, Battalion War Diary.
64  Canadian Army Service Records.
65  WO95/3822, Battalion War Diary.
66  D Morton, 'The Supreme Penalty' – article in *Queen's Quarterly*, 1972.
67  P. van Passen, *Days of our Years*.
68  Captain Cyril Falls, op cit.
69  Ibid.
70  Canadian Expeditionary Force, Nominal Roll of Officers, Non-Commissioned Officers and Men.
71  Major-General Sir Wyndham Childs, *Episodes and Reflections*.
72  WO329/2442, *1914 Star Medal Roll*.
73  WO329/991, *British War & Victory Medal Roll*.
74  WO93/49, op cit.
75  Anthony Babington, op cit.
76  WO93/49, op cit.
77  Commonwealth War Graves Commission register, Ham British Cemetery, France.
78  WO329/2704, 1915 Star Medal Roll.
79  WO329/1, op cit.
80  Anthony Babington, op cit.
81  WO93/49, op cit.
82  Anthony Babington, op cit.
83  WO95/1664, Battalion War Diary.
84  WO93/49, op cit.
85  Anthony Babington, op cit.
86  WO93/49, op cit.
87  Anthony Babington, op cit.
88  *Soldiers Died in the Great War*, part 31.
89  WO95/2634, Battalion War Diary.
90  WO93/49, op cit.
91  Anthony Babington, op cit.
92  WO95/2120, Battalion War Diary.
93  WO93/49, op cit.
94  Anthony Babington, op cit.
95  WO329/1926, *British War & Victory Medal Roll*.
96  WO93/49, op cit.
97  J F Tucker, *Johnny Get Your Gun*.
98  Canadian Army Service Records.
99  Ibid.
100  WO329/1924, *British War & Victory Medal Roll*.
101  WO93/49, op cit.
102  WO329/1247, *British War & Victory Medal Roll*.
103  WO329/1, op cit., states that Private Pattison had his 1915 Star medal issued by the Government of India.
104  WO95/1862, Battalion War Diary.
105  Ibid.
106  Anthony Babington, op cit.
107  Lord Moran, *The Anatomy of Courage*.
108  Commonwealth War Graves Commission register, Faubourg d'Amiens Cemetery, Arras.
109  WO329/2703, *1915 Star Medal Roll*.
110  WO93/49, op cit.
111  Anthony Babington, op cit.
112  WO93/49, op cit.
113  WO95/1896, War Diary of 8 Rifle Brigade.
114  WO329/1908, *British War & Victory Medal Roll*.
115  WO95/2949, Battalion War Diary.

## Chapter Six

### *Far, far from Wipers I long to be.*

The final day in July marked the beginning of the third Battle of Ypres. The British had made some progress during the previous month, when the enemy had been driven from their vantage point on the Messines Ridge. In later years it was suggested that the opportunity had been wasted, as the gains might have been exploited with a good chance of success. Whatever other criticisms arose from the slaughter in autumn 1917, no suggestion could be made that the drive towards the Passchendaele Ridge had been other than the work of a determined Commander-in-Chief.

Predictably, on 31 July it started to rain — and it continued for three days and nights, almost without stopping. As a result, access across the shelled area, to and from the front line, became very difficult, as a swamp up to 4,000 yards wide had to be negotiated. The problem however was short-lived, and although the Flanders offensive is remembered for the appalling conditions, caused in part by the weather, in fact considerable periods of drought occurred.[1]

On 1 August, as the battle for Pilkem Ridge raged, a Kitchener volunteer was executed. Exactly one month previously whilst in billets in Locre, **Private Frederick Broadrick** had deserted from 11 Warwicks when warned for a working party. The soldier fled straight to Calais where he was arrested five days later.[2] Perhaps in view of the fact that the private was already serving under a suspended sentence of death for a previous offence of desertion, it is not surprising that on the second occasion it was decided to confirm the penalty. Private Broadrick was executed at Dranoutre, near the border between France and Belgium.

Although the fighting in the Ypres Salient was proceeding with much ferocity, a lull occurred in the execution of offenders, until 19 August. On that date a conscript and a colonial were shot in separate executions.

The overseas soldier was an Australian, although he was serving in a New Zealand Regiment. The man was serving under an alias, but unfortunately the authors have not been able to determine his true identity. **Private 'John King'** was a miner by trade and had enlisted in the Canterbury Infantry Regiment at the end of 1914; and during the later part of his military service the private alternated between being ill and going absent. It is questionable whether he should ever have been passed as fit for military service, or perhaps, subsequently, whether he should have been discharged as unfit.

Early in 1915 Private King sailed from New Zealand, travelling via Egypt to Gallipoli, where he landed in May. Three months later he was invalided from the Peninsula with a crushed finger, and when other medical problems developed, he remained in Egypt. During 1916 King trained with his unit — until 26 May when he went absent. No punishment would seem to have been inflicted, and on 10 July he crossed to France with 1 Battalion.

Shortly after King's arrival at the New Zealand Infantry Base Depot at Etaples, the Australian was taken ill with dysentery. It was nearly two months before he recovered, and his previous complaint — haemorrhoids — must have seriously aggravated his condition. Private King's medical examination sheet — completed at the time of enlistment makes no mention of this complaint. It is of course possible that this examination was carried out in a most superficial manner. Private King rejoined his unit on 22 September, but ten days later went missing. His punishment comprised 28 days' field punishment no.2, but half-way through his ordeal the soldier repeated his offence. Surprisingly, an absence of just 20 minutes doubled King's punishment. Shortly after the completion of the punishment the soldier fell ill with influenza. His recovery took ten days but upon returning to the battalion — two days prior to Christmas — Private King got drunk and deserted. The Australian was brought to trial in January 1917, just one of three occasions on which he was tried for absence during the first five months of the year. King's service record is a curious combination of crime, punishment and illness. For in spite of his regular absenteeism, he often served his field punishment before re-offending.

King's behaviour however became all too much when in May he had escaped after being arrested for absence. The court heard that on 21 April 1917 he had gone absent and remained so until 1 May. Interestingly, King was found not guilty of desertion, but guilty of being absent without leave — proving that serious offences could be defended successfully. Brigadier-General W G Braithwaite confirmed King's sentence of one year's imprisonment with hard labour, and on 22 May the soldier was informed of his fate. However, three days later an error of judgement was made by General Sir Herbert Plumer, commanding Second Army, who suspended the sentence. Private King must have been delighted, and five days later he celebrated by deserting.

Five weeks passed before a Court of Inquiry declared Private King to be a deserter.[3] However, the evidence before the court offered a possible explanation for the soldier's behaviour. Initially the court heard that Sergeant Thompson of King's Company (12th) had ordered searches to be carried out for the missing private, and had passed a description to the military police. The second witness, Corporal J A Smart, gave further information, stating:

*'I am in the same platoon as Private King and he was absent from round-about 9 pm May 30th. About a fortnight after, I met two men who said they had seen King in Steenwerck. I do not know the names of these two men. About a week later Private Wells of our company told me he had seen King near Nieppe. Private Wells is now in hospital. I reported the facts to Mr Barton, then o/c 12 Company and a search party was sent to look for King. King is an Australian and associates with Australian troops a great deal. I felt convinced that King would be in the vicinity of Steenwerck, Nieppe or Erquinghem'.*

A further witness gave details that Private King was with his fellow countrymen who, of course, were not subject to the extreme penalty. Private G Boswell stated:

*'I know Private King well by sight and about 8.15 pm on June 4th I saw King entering the Church Army Hut at ........... I spoke to him, but as I was in a hurry I did not say much to him. He said he was well, and having a good time. He was wearing a steel helmet and his ordinary New Zealand uniform. I did not notice any badges, he was with Australians.'*

Private King and two other absentees were ultimately arrested at 10 pm on 23 July by Sergeants Hots and Hainsworth of the New Zealand Military Police. King stood trial on 5 August before Major Shepherd, president of the court martial and Captains L G O'Callaghan and J P O'Sullivan. The story that King related to the court was that during his absence he had spent all his time drinking.[4] Indeed the evidence given would suggest that the Australian was probably an alcoholic. However, genuine medical ailments were rarely considered mitigating factors, and events moved swiftly as three days after the trial Sir Douglas Haig confirmed the sentence of death. Private King's execution, on 19 August, was carried out by his battalion at 5.30 am, and his body buried in Trois Arbres Cemetery, in the village of Steenwerck where he had roamed. 32 year old King left three children, who were in the care of his mother in Australia.

A member of King's battalion recorded in his diary the death of the soldier, whom he described as a 'waster'.[5] Official records are ambiguous concerning the issue of the deserter's war medals. One account states that the medals were to go to his mother, the other states no medals were to be issued. Irrespective of this final decision, the case of Private King is surely disturbing.[6]

The conscript shot on the same day was **Private Frederick Loader**, a soldier with 1/22 London Regiment. The battalion, which was a Territorial unit and part of 47 (London) Division, had seen action on the Somme the previous year; and when it moved from those battlefields, it came to the Ypres Salient and went into the line near Hill 60. On 7 June 1917, the opening day of the Messines offensive, the battalion had attacked the Bluff[7] and it was at this time that Private Loader went absent. Once again the condemned man was serving under a suspended sentence of death for a previous offence of desertion.[8]

On the following day, 20 August, a Territorial soldier was executed who had spent the majority of the war in another theatre of operations. **Private Arthur Mitchell** had landed at Helles on the Gallipoli peninsula on 5 May 1915.[9] His battalion, 1/6 Lancashire Fusiliers, was one of four Fusilier units from Lancashire which had landed simultaneously. The battalions were all part of 42 Division, and did not arrive on the Western Front until March 1917.

Evidence given at Mitchell's trial stated that the private had gone absent prior to a tour of duty in the trenches. He had then been arrested nine days later when working in a field. The soldier had discarded his uniform and was wearing blue trousers and a French police bonnet! Whilst perhaps it did not substantially detract from the conspicuous nature of the absentee's chosen headgear, the court did hear that the private had shaved off his moustache.[10] The unfortunate soldier, who like so many, had endured hell on earth at Gallipoli, was executed at Achiet-le-Grand, mid-way between the Somme and Arras fronts.

In the third week of August a sixth soldier was shot from the 15 (Scottish) Division. **Private James Michael** was a volunteer serving in 10 Cameronians (Scottish Rifles), and his death came just ten weeks after that of another deserter from the same battalion. Early in the summer of 1917 Michael's comrades had taken part in the fighting in the Salient, whilst the reluctant soldier had made off. The inevitable execution was recorded in the unit's history, the diarist noting that it was the second case in the battalion.[11] Private Michael was shot at Poperinghe, becoming the twelfth victim to die in front of the firing squads in this Belgian town immediately behind the Ypres Salient. Like the previously executed deserter from the battalion Michael was commemorated in post-war years in the regiment's casualty roll.[12] Both victims were natives of Glasgow and by chance the two names appear on the same page of this official record. No cause of death is recorded for either soldier.

At the end of October 1917 Philip Snowden MP asked a question in the House of Commons about a soldier who had been executed two months previously.[13] The condemned man was **Private Stanley Stewart** who had been a Special Reservist serving with 2 Royal Scots Fusiliers. The terms of enlistment of these peacetime soldiers required very little of the volunteers, many of whom were comparatively old for fighting troops.

Their training was often minimal and they were certainly not held in high regard by the British Army Regulars.

Private Stewart, however, was a young man, and had landed in France on 10 November 1914.[14] In the following month the soldier received a 'Blighty' wound, and was invalided home suffering from shellshock.[15]

Philip Snowden maintained that Private Stewart had been returned to active service when still in a state of nerves.[16] Unfortunately the date of the soldier's return to the Western Front is unknown, although the date of his initial absence is given as 25 July 1917. Whilst under arrest Private Stewart escaped when the explosion of an enemy shell near to his place of detention caused havoc. At his trial the soldier told how he feared enemy gunfire, and his statement that for four years he had been resident in a lunatic asylum did nothing to enhance the reputation of special Reservists. Private Stewart was the seventh execution victim to claim a history of mental illness.

Seemingly, Stewart was not medically examined,[17] and although the soldier had no history of previous offences, the Commander-in-Chief decided to confirm the sentence of death. Private Stewart aged 21 was shot at Kemmel on 29 August. In post-war years his mother had the following inscription carved on the headstone of his grave – it reads:

*'Fondly remembered by a sorrowing mother'.*

In the early 1960s an abortive attempt was made, prior to the public release of the army war diaries from the Great War, to remove any material giving details about courts martial or disciplinary matters. The practice was known as 'weeding' and was, and still is, routinely carried out to thwart the inquisitive. During this time-consuming procedure the war diary of Adjutant-General, 30 Division[18] was examined, and a reference to the execution of Private Stewart removed. The censor's work however, was all in vain, as a roughly scribbled note in the diary which included the aforementioned details, was overlooked.

On the penultimate day of August, three soldiers in different Yorkshire regiments were executed. Two of the men, serving in 17 Division, were shot in a double execution. This division had already had five men executed during the war, and yet another victim from its ranks had served at Gallipoli.

**Private Walter Neave** enlisted in the West Yorkshire Regiment in April 1915, and in November of that year he landed on the Peninsula as a reinforcement for 9 Battalion, just a few weeks before the evacuation.[19] The soldier arrived on the Western Front during the Battle of the Somme, only to be wounded at Hébuterne during September. It was 1917 before Neave was deemed fit again for active service, but on 26 July he decamped. Unfortunately for Neave, a previous suspended death sentence, also for desertion, proved a very relevant consideration, and on 30 August he was shot alongside 21 year old **Private Thomas Watts,** a deserter from 7 East Yorks. Watts was a volunteer and native of Houghton-le-Spring (County Durham) and prior to his offence had been of good character.

The final soldier shot that day was **Private Albert Parry** from 2 West Yorks. Little is known about Parry except than he was a deserter, and the eighth soldier to be executed in his division (8 Division). His army number would suggest that he was a conscript. It must be presumed from his place of burial that the execution took place in a remote spot behind Armentières — within yards of the Franco-Belgian border.

Nine soldiers had been executed in July and the same number in August, but in September, with the continuing offensive in Flanders, the figure increased to twelve. In spite of the fine weather which was enjoyed for the first three weeks, the month started badly when, on 5 September, three deserters were shot for offences which had occurred in the Salient. The executions took place separately, two of the men being northerners and one a Londoner.

**Rifleman John Hyde,** a conscript from Bow, in London, was serving in 10 King's Royal Rifle Corps — part of 20 Division. The date of his offence is unknown, but his battalion had been in action in both July and August 1917.[20] Seemingly, the soldier had no previous convictions of a serious nature, nevertheless this did not save the unfortunate man.

26 year old **Private James Smith,** from Bolton in Lancashire, was soldiering in 17 King's Liverpool Regiment, after previously serving in the Lancashire Fusiliers at Gallipoli. Smith's division (30th) had been serving in the Ypres Salient since May 1917 and had been in action on the first day of the autumn offensive.[21] Private Smith was brought to trial on 22 August when he faced charges of both desertion and disobedience.

Only one week had passed since another soldier in 30 Division had been executed; and as in the previous case, Smith was executed at Kemmel. Private Smith's death was the seventh and final execution in this division.

On the same day — 5 September — a volley rang out from a firing squad in Poperinghe. The soldier, **Private Joseph Stedman** was aged 25 and came from Liverpool. Stedman's case is unique for a number of reasons. Firstly he was the first soldier from a machine gun company to be executed. Secondly his unit, 117 Company Machine Gun Corps, was serving in 39 Division, in which previous executions had only been carried out for cowardice; three such shootings had occurred, and the

death of deserter Stedman was the last execution in the division. Finally and most amazingly, is the inscription on the headstone of his grave. Clearly it suggests that the soldier's parents were deceived. It reads:
*'He died for King and Country may he rest in peace Amen'.*

Another soldier with an inappropriate inscription on his grave was shot at Vlamertinghe (mid-way been Ypres and Poperinghe) on the following day. **Private Edward Delargey** was a young conscript who  had been called up in 1916. Army life would not seem to have been to his liking, as on 18 July 1916 he was sentenced to 112 days' detention.[22] Anthony Babington has stated that the soldier joined his unit in France in January 1917, and hence we must assume that the above sentence (which was imposed by District Court Martial) occurred in the United Kingdom.

Delargey was posted to 1/8 Royal Scots, which was the Pioneer battalion in 51 (Highland) Division. At the beginning of 1917 the battalion was engaged in constructional activities on the old Somme battlefields. In early January they had been building roads, tramways, dugouts and shelters, as well as working at a sawmill, and on wiring parties.[23] Not all activities however had been directed towards the war effort, as after a week in supposed rest, during which time the men had been building huts while it was snowing, a twelve man party had been detailed to build a steeplechase course at Divisional Headquarters.

It was at about this time that Private Delargey joined the battalion, and for the final two weeks of January he spent his time in rest.[24] At the end of the month the unit moved to the Arras front, where the first two weeks in February were spent building roads and repairing trenches. The tasks proved very difficult, as frost hampered the work. However, this caused little problem for the young soldier, as during this time he had been admitted to a field ambulance where he stayed for one week.[25]

On 15 February, shortly after his discharge, Delargey had been given a pass to a village just two miles away, whereupon the opportunist deserter promptly disappeared, remaining absent until arrested on 6 August some ten miles from Arras.[26] Unfortunately the scant details available to the authors have not revealed the full circumstances of the absentee's arrest. However, the evidence given at Delargey's trial perhaps suggests that he had been under surveillance, as some details of the private's movements were put before the court. Further evidence to the soldier's discredit was that when challenged Delargey had lied, and also that he had been improperly dressed. It must be assumed that little defence was made, as Delargey was unrepresented at his trial — the second Scottish soldier during the year to decline such assistance. The trial took place in the Ypres Salient — where the 19 year old was ultimately shot on 6 September. The puzzling inscription on his grave reads,

*'He died that we might live Gone but not forgotten'.*

The same day, but further behind the line at Poperinghe, another volley rang out, creating an unfortunate 'example'. The victim was **Sergeant John Wall** of 3 Worcs. Wall had enlisted in 1912 and had served on the Western Front from the very beginning, having arrived in France as a lance-corporal on 12 August 1914[27] – the first day that any British troops landed. The sergeant had fought with his battalion in every engagement,[28] and therefore must have been aware of the execution of five comrades from his unit, who were shot in 1915.

During August 1917, 3 Worcesters had been in action near the Bellwarde Ridge, at which time the sergeant had disappeared during an attack. At his trial no motive was disclosed for this uncharacteristic behaviour, and author Anthony Babington comments that after such a lengthy period of active service the soldier's mental faculties warranted the fullest investigation.[29] Unfortunately, such an examination did not take place. When 22 year old Sergeant Wall was shot he became the fourteenth soldier to die in front of a firing squad at Poperinghe. The inscription that his parents had placed on the headstone of his grave is undoubtedly appropriate – *'For ever with the Lord'*.

On 8 September GHQ issued an administrative directive concerning offenders who claimed to have been wounded. It reads,

*'Whenever a soldier who is convicted of desertion and sentenced to death, has stated that he has been wounded, or where, in the absence of any such statement, there is reason to suppose that this is the case, particulars of the casualty will immediately be obtained from the Deputy Adjutant-General 3rd Echelon by the convening officer.'*[30]

The records centre to which the memorandum referred was situated at Rouen and acted as intermediary between the units in the field and the infantry and other record offices in the UK. The size and complexity of this operation is today largely forgotten. However, all records pertaining to individuals whether sick, dead, or wounded went via these offices to Britain. Considering that on average throughout the war, 2,000 casualties were suffered every day, including 400 killed,[31] some idea of the scale of the operation can be envisaged. Clearly from the provisions of this directive copies of individuals' service records were kept in France, and from these such information could be extracted. During the compilation of this book no indication has emerged that 3rd Echelon ever failed in this task.

On 12 September three more soldiers were executed, again at separate locations. All of the offenders had deserted from the Flanders battlefields and two of the men were believed to be Regular soldiers. **Private John Abigail** was serving with 8 Norfolks, a battalion that had suffered a large number of casualties on 1 July 1916. Eleven officers and 334 other ranks were the quoted figures for the unit, which that day had been in action north of Carnoy.[32] In the aftermath of that grisly day Private Abigail had deserted, only to be captured and sentenced to ten years' penal servitude, which had then been suspended. Events in the Ypres Salient in 1917 once again proved too much for the soldier, and on 24 August Abigail was once more before a court martial. It must be assumed that the soldier was indifferent to his fate, or perhaps doubted the likelihood of an acquittal, as he declined the assistance of an officer to defend him. Abigail's execution took place in the remote village of Esquelbecq — there being only one other British soldier buried in the village cemetery.

In the case of the second Regular soldier, the condemned man had gone absent on two previous occasions. Initially **Private William Wycherley** had overstayed his UK leave by seven weeks — an offence for which he might well have been shot in any case. His punishment for this crime is unknown, but a while later he deserted once more, as his battalion — 2 Manchesters — were on their way up to the front line. Again the soldier received punishment, the severity of which is unknown. The official record continues that on 25 June 1917, Wycherley complained of feeling sick, just before going over the top, and disappeared.[33]

Wycherley's battalion was part of 32 Division which, on 20 June (just five days before the alleged offence), had taken over the inner sector of the Nieuport bridgehead, near the sea. At this time no offensive operations were planned from these positions, indeed defensive fighting was the main consideration, orders having been issued that the line was to be held at all costs.[34] Examination of army records has failed to disclose that any trench raiding was planned on the day of the supposed offence,[35] and consequently the nature of the intended operation remains unknown.

Two days after his departure Wycherley was arrested at Etaples, where he gave false particulars as to his identity.[36] What is slightly puzzling about the place of the soldier's arrest is that Wycherley passed up a selection of possible safe havens on his way to Etaples. However, the 24 year old married man, with a wife in Cheetham Hill near Manchester, was returned to the northern Belgian coast to be shot. The execution took place at Coxyde on 12 September.

The final soldier executed that day is believed to have been a conscript. **Private Charles Britton** of 1/5 Warwicks had deserted at the beginning of the autumn offensive. The soldier had been absent from a company parade prior to moving up to the trenches, and ironically had been arrested on 16 August — the beginning of the Battle of Langemarck in which his division, the forty-eighth, had had a hard fight in the attack against St Julien. In accordance with King's Regulations No.593, the army commander, General Sir Hubert Gough, ordered that details of the offence, finding and sentence be read out on parade as soon as possible.[37]

On 14 September a married man from the Midlands with the most appalling military record faced a firing squad at Poperinghe. **Private George Everill** was aged 30 at the time, and it is thought that he was probably a Reservist. The soldier's initial crimes had been ones of defiance; however, in 1917, offences of absence joined the charges.

It is not known what brought about the change that converted Private Everill from a placid to a defiant soldier, but he had landed in France in May 1915[38] and served without confrontation until 16 March 1916, when his first offence had been dealt with by FGCM. The charge was using insubordinate language to a superior officer, a crime for which he received a sentence of one year's imprisonment with hard labour. Like the remainder of his punishments, the sentence was suspended. Five weeks later Private Everill was sentenced to ten years' penal servitude for wilful defiance; however, this was considered to be excessive and the penalty was commuted to two years. Given that no further entries were made on the soldier's conduct sheet for nearly a year — in the period following his second conviction — it seems likely that Everill was imprisoned, perhaps for nine months.

On 8 March 1917, Private Everill was sentenced to one year's imprisonment for being absent; this however was commuted to 90 days' field punishment no.1. Shortly after the expiry of this sentence, the soldier was convicted of using threatening language to a superior officer. However, the subsequent sentence of three years' penal servitude was commuted to another 90 days of field punishment.

After serving his punishment for two weeks Everill was once again before a court martial. The charge was disobedience showing wilful defiance — the penalty doubled Everill's sentence.

The court martial that ultimately led to Private Everill's death sat on 3 September, and at the time Everill was serving with 1 North Staffs. Details of the court martial record have been available to the authors and are quoted below.

The charge was:

'*that on 24th August 1917 after being warned to hold himself in readiness to proceed to [the] forward area with a view to taking part in active operations [the defendant] absented himself till apprehended by No.28 Examining Post on 25 August 1917.'*

In accordance with an army directive of 1915, a plea of not guilty was entered and the court proceeded to hear the prosecution case.

*'At Dickebusch at 2.30 pm on 24th August, 1917 [the] accused was warned personally by Sergeant Harper to be ready to move at any moment with [the] Battalion which was in Divisional support and under orders to stand to. [The] Accused was at the time a prisoner in the guard tent having been sentenced to 90 days F.P.No.1 by Field General Court Martial on 29/7/17.* [Natural justice would dictate that such a prejudicial disclosure should not have been made during the prosecution case, but should only have been made known if and when the soldier had been convicted.] *About 3.30 pm the same day the guard and prisoners were warned by the NCO i/c Battalion Quarter Guard to be ready to move up the line at any time. At 6.30 pm the same day the guard and prisoners fell in behind 'A' Company and were ordered to sit down and take off their equipment. [The] Accused was then present. At 7 pm when [the] guard and prisoners were falling in to follow 'A' Company the accused was missing having left behind his rifle and equipment. [The] Camp was then searched and [the] accused not found. At 12.30 am on 25th August 1917 [the] accused was stopped by No.28 Examining Post at Wippenhoek without rifle and equipment or pass and when questioned stated that he had broken arrest when under detention at Reninghelst.'*

During this evidence Private Everill did not question a single witness, nor did he make any statement. Perhaps such omissions indicate just how inadequate (or even non-existent) defences were, even when assisted by an officer. Not surprisingly, Everill called no evidence in an attempt to suggest that he was of good character. The court made no enquiry as to the private's age, and in due course Sir Douglas Haig reviewed the proceedings and confirmed the sentence.[39]

It is suggested that Everill's wife, with whom it is likely he had only limited communications during the war due to loss of privileges, may never have learned of her husband's fate, because information she volunteered to the War Graves Commission indicated that her husband had been killed in action. A simple epitaph is displayed on his grave in Poperinghe New Military Cemetery which reads:

*'Thy will be done from his loving wife and children'.*

On 19 September a conscript who originally had been posted to a Territorial unit before being transferred to a Service battalion was executed by firing squad. **Private Leonard Mitchell** had served in 1/5 Yorks & Lancs — part of 49 (West Riding) Division — before being posted to the 8th battalion of this regiment.[40] The soldier had an unenviable reputation to live down, being under a suspended sentence of death for an offence of desertion.[41] However, Private Mitchell did not conform, and decamped from the Ypres Salient when the dangers of active service became too great for his constitution. His execution took place in the small village of La Clytte, some distance away from the front.

On the day that the Battle of the Menin Road Ridge commenced a very young colonial soldier was shot. It was over two years since a soldier as young as 17 had been lined-up before a firing squad, and again the victim had seen only brief service.

**Private Herbert Morris** lived in Jamaica and had joined the British West Indies Regiment during a recruitment drive between November 1916 and March 1917. 6 Battalion had trained at Swallowfield Camp, Jamaica, before embarking from Kingston at the end of March, and then arriving at the French port of Brest on 17 April. The battalion had been struck down with disease, even before they landed in France, with some men dying at sea. During the final fortnight of April, eleven men died from either measles or pneumonia, amongst them an officer. At the same time, an outbreak of mumps had occurred, and the whole unit was also treated for hookworm, as well as receiving the routine typhoid inoculation.[42] After one month in which to acclimatise, 6 Battalion, together with two other British West Indies units, was sent to the Ypres Salient.[43] Although the troops were not fighting units, their duties on the lines of communication of the Fourth Army were not without danger, and at the end of June the battalion suffered its first fatalities from enemy action.

Private Morris was tried for desertion in September, when he told the court that he could not tolerate the sound of gunfire. In the soldier's favour, the court heard a good character reference, including the opinion that the defendant was considered to be of higher intelligence than his platoon comrades.[44] Details have not emerged about whether the military authorities were aware of the soldier's true age, it would certainly seem unlikely, and further to their discredit that they did not enquire.

On 20 September Private Morris was shot, and then buried in Poperinghe New Military Cemetery, in a row that was fast becoming filled with executed deserters. Next to him lies Private Everill, and just beyond two other offenders. Although a soldier from a British West Indies Regiment had previously been executed in a different theatre of operations, Private Morris was the only soldier from his regiment to be shot on the Western Front. He was also the only British West Indian soldier to be shot for an offence not involving violence.

During the research for this book, the authors have been unable to discover whether or not Private Morris was black. Certainly the battalion NCOs were white, however the question of whether any whites served as privates is unclear. No eyewitness account or rumour has been unearthed about the execution of a black soldier on the Western Front, although it would seem likely that details of such an unusual event would have spread quickly − perhaps suggesting that Morris was not in fact black, but white.

The final soldier to be executed during September was a Reservist serving in the Lincolnshire Regiment. **Private Charles Kirman** had landed in France with 1 Battalion on 13 August 1914[45] He had been wounded that November and again in July 1916 − before deserting from 7 Battalion during the summer of 1917.[46] There was little that Kirman could tell the court, except that his constitution had been undermined by long service. However, to the soldier's discredit was a previous con-viction for absence that had resulted in a one year prison sentence.[47] In due course Sir Douglas Haig confirmed the sentence, and the 32 year old married man from Portsmouth was shot at Arras on 23 September.

# NOTES

1 Brigadier Sir J E Edmonds, *Military Operations France & Belgium, 1917*, Volume 2.
2 WO93/49, Summary of First World War capital court martial cases.
3 The Army Act, section 72, and King's (!) Regulations no.673, required that a such Court of Inquiry should be held after 21 days, or as soon as possible.
4 *Christchurch Star*, 13 October 1988.
5 Diary of Signaller Felix Rodney.
6 All details concerning the case of Private King come from his army service record.
7 WO95/2743, Battalion War Diary.
8 WO93/49, op cit.
9 WO329/2673, *1915 Star Medal Roll*.
10 WO93/49, op cit.
11 WO95/1918, Battalion War Diary.
12 *Soldiers Died in the Great War*, part 31.
13 *Hansard*, 31 October 1917.
14 WO329/2442, *1914 Star Medal Roll*.
15 Anthony Babington, *For the Sake of Example.*
16 *Hansard*, op cit.
17 Anthony Babington, op cit.
18 WO95/2315, War Diary of Adjutant-General, 30 Division.
19 WO329/1, Index to the *Great War Medal Rolls.*
20 WO95/2115, Battalion War Diary.
21 WO95/2334, Battalion War Diary.
22 WO93/49, op cit.
23 WO95/2857, Battalion War Diary.
24 Ibid. Once again the war diary of a Pioneer battalion gives a most detailed account of life on active service.
25 Anthony Babington, op cit.
26 WO93/49, op cit.
27 WO329/2451, *1914 Star Medal Roll*.
28 Anthony Babington, op cit.
29 Ibid.
30 WO95/939, War Diary of the Adjutant-General, XVII Corps.
31 *Soldiers Died in the Great War* − information on the dust covers of J B Haywards' 1988 reprints.
32 WO95/2040, Battalion War Diary.
33 WO93/49, op cit.
34 Brigadier Sir J E Edmonds, op cit.
35 WO95/2392, Battalion War Diary.
36 WO93/49, op cit.
37 WO95/954, War Diary of the Adjutant-General, XVIII Corps.
38 WO329/1, op cit.
39 WO93/49, op cit.
40 WO329/1600, *British War & Victory Medal Roll.*
41 WO93/49, op cit.
42 WO95/495, Battalion War Diary.
43 Brigadier Sir J E Edmonds, op cit.
44 Anthony Babington, op cit.
45 WO329/1, op cit.
46 Anthony Babington, op cit.
47 WO93/49, op cit.

# Chapter Seven

## *There is a limit to the number of good men.*

*'There is a limit to the number of good men any race can furnish.'* –
Lord Moran.

At the beginning of October a Regular soldier who lived in Leicester yet was serving in a Scottish regiment was shot for desertion. **Private Ernest Mackness** was already under a suspended sentence of death for desertion when he repeated the offence, and in doing so avoided a close encounter with the enemy.[1]

On 22 August 1917, 1 Cameronians (Scottish Rifles) had moved into the trenches at Nieuport, but the relief was hardly completed when the Germans attacked. The front line positions comprised a series of posts, and 'hand to hand' fighting commenced. Two days later the British retaliated, gaining some territory from the enemy; the victory was short-lived, however, as two nights later the Germans counter-attacked expelling the Scotsmen.[2]

25 year old Private Mackness had avoided such unpleasantness by going absent, and on 1 October he paid the penalty; the execution took place in the remote village of Blaringhem. Together with four other executed men from the Cameronians, Private Mackness' passing is commemorated in the official casualty rolls, although once again no cause of death is stated[3].

In 1978 the publication of a book led to speculation that following a mutiny at Etaples in September 1917, a systematic hunt had been organised until the ring leader had been traced, ultimately to die in a bizarre post-war shoot out. The central figure was Percy Toplis, who was portrayed as a rebel from a lowly background who enjoyed considerable success as an impostor and womaniser. A decade later the story was serialised for BBC television. The broadcast was accompanied by much speculation about the accuracy of the events depicted. Little evidence came to light to substantiate the yarn, which consequently must be treated with suspicion.[4] Other accounts, one of them fictional, have described the Etaples mutiny with some accuracy. Henry Williamson, in his novel *Love and the Loveless*, correctly records both the rank and regiment of the main offender; and further, an ex-military policeman recalled that a terrible riot had been *prevented* by the tact of senior officers.[5]

Only one soldier was court martialled and executed as a result of the Etaples mutiny, and whilst Percy Toplis was portrayed as the 'Monocled Mutineer', the real-life character who faced a firing squad can accurately be described as the Miniature Mutineer. The life story of this unique individual is fascinating, not only in what has emerged during research about the soldier, but also in what has remained undiscovered about this very unusual character. The man was an adept liar, initially without success, but that soon changed. He masqueraded as an Englishman, an Irishman and also as a Scotsman — but in fact he was Welsh. His deceit was convincing, and even after his death the true facts did not emerge until now — some 70 years later.

The disturbance at Etaples in the autumn of 1917 has previously been described by authors Gill and Dallas, and based on their balanced account, the relevant aspects are recalled below.[6]

The tinder box of discontent was set alight by a chance occurrence on Sunday 9 September. In the afternoon a rumour circulated that New Zealand troops were intent on settling an old score with the military police, seemingly as a result of a past injustice. As such threats were not uncommon, little heed was taken of the warning. However, the gathering of troops on the camp-side access to the three arch bridge leading to Etaples resulted in the arrest of a New Zealander. Although the military police soon released the man, who seemingly was an innocent party, the situation had been inflamed. With swelling crowds the atmosphere at the bridgehead became unruly as the revellers pressed forward towards the forbidden town of Etaples. In the mêlée a Base Depot policemen, Private Reeve, fired a revolver, mortally wounding a Scots soldier and injuring a civilian. Infuriated by this incident, the crowd hurled stones at the Assistant Provost-Marshal, forcing the mounted officer to flee.

4,000 men were said to be party to the initial disturbance, of which only a quarter were present in the town during that evening. Amongst these intruders were a group who went out of their way to locate the Base Commander, Brigadier-General Thomson.

The Camp Adjutant later recorded that his chief had been unceremoniously paraded through the town, shoulder high. Another party of about 70 passed through the town and made their way to the river bridge that separates the fishing port of Etaples from the exclusive resort of Le Touquet and its Paris Plage. The attractive seaside amenities were the exclusive retreat of officers and those frequenting the hospitals there.

As the party approached the bridge they were confronted by a mixed picket, commanded by a captain and four other officers. The intruders however passed with ease, as the picket proved ineffective. Upon the return of the rebels, the captain was urging his men to do their duty when an outsider interrupted. Normally the man would have remained inconspicuous, had it not been for the display of his rank as corporal and the action that he proposed. The NCO addressed the picket suggesting that they take no notice of the captain, whom, he continued, should be thrown in the river with a stone round his neck.[7]

Although no such action was taken the captain noted the suggestion, and detailed a trusted party to detain the NCO should he happen to return. Later that evening an arrest was made and the corporal secreted in a safe quarter. That night the mob returned to camp and, surprisingly, training recommenced the next day.

Disturbances continued all week, with the majority, including excursions into the town of Etaples, occurring during the afternoons. The indiscipline gradually died down, but for the arrested corporal events were to move swiftly. Bundled away from the scene of his crime the NCO was removed, away from the possibility of sympathetic intervention that might have secured his release. Safely away, the corporal stood trial for his life on the very day after his misconduct.

Clearly the NCO had had little time to consult with the officer who was to defend him at the trial. And in due course none of the prosecution evidence was challenged, instead the corporal relied on the soldier's oldest defence – that he had been very drunk at the time. Such a suggestion however proved to be futile, when all witnesses except one, declared that the NCO had seemed to be perfectly sober.[8] With a sentence of death imposed upon him, the corporal's fate passed into the hands of the Commander-in-Chief, and even he, with the court martial file in front of him, knew little about the offender's true character.

**Corporal Jesse Robert Short** was born on 4 July 1886 at Nantyglo in Wales and was the son of a coal miner. In working life he followed in his father's footsteps until an encounter with Company Sergeant-Major J C Nesbitt who recruited the young man to the army. Short enlisted in January 1905 and commenced his catalogue of deceptions. The eighteen year old told the recruiting officer that he had been born in Durham, before enlisting for nine years with the Colours, and three on the Reserve. However, after just three months with 1 Battalion Welsh Regiment the new recruit went absent. His brief four day absence earned Short a sentence of 21 days' imprisonment with hard labour, and stoppages of pay to match. The private was released on 18 May, and exactly seven months later – to the day – was discharged as incorrigible and worthless.

Jesse Short must have gained an affinity for soldiering or, perhaps more likely, army life had numerous advantages compared with the spartan life of a coal miner. Consequently on 6 October 1906, a certain Jesse Morris swore an oath of allegiance to his King and joined the South Wales Borderers. The deception however was short-lived and was compounded by additional crimes. Three charges were proffered, one relating to his enlistment, another concerning desertion from his newly chosen regiment, and finally the loss of equipment. The penalty was 56 days' imprisonment with hard labour and a discharge with ignominy.[9]

The convicted soldier returned to civilian life and coal mining, although he moved to Felling, in the county of Durham. Five years after his discharge from the army, Jesse Short married a girl one year his senior. Dinah was the daughter of a coal miner, although the fathers of both partners had died before the wedding — perhaps an indication of the hazards of their underground occupations.

When the First World War broke out, three years after the marriage, veteran soldier Short was eager to enlist. There was one small problem however; he was literally too short! Jesse was a slight, 9 stone individual, only five feet three inches tall — too small for the requirements of the army in 1914. When Short had originally enlisted, in 1905, he had weighed only 8 stone, an army diet and training having improved his physique. Imagine then his delight, when on 5 November 1914, height requirements were reduced (for a second time) to 5' 3'. Almost straight away Short rushed to the recruiting office and enlisted in the Northumberland Fusiliers.

Thoughtful Jesse Short realised, however, that the military authorities might once again identify their previous outcast. So consequently he told a few untruths in order to avoid drawing attention to himself. Short lied about his age, stating that he was a year younger than he was, told the army that he was a Scotsman, and joined a battalion of Irishmen — 26 Northumberland Fusiliers (Tyneside Irish).

Short enlisted in 26 Northumberland Fusiliers on the first day of recruiting, although how he managed this remains a mystery, as the Tyneside battalions were ethnically disposed. (It has been possible to deduce that Short enlisted on the first day of recruiting by an analysis of the allocation of army numbers in the battalion. Hence approximately 750 men enlisted in the battalion on the first day of recruiting, and the further down the alphabet the man's name the higher his regimental number.)

The details of Short's service in France and Flanders are somewhat contradictory. Anthony Babington has stated that the soldier was a Regular with eight years' service, and presumably this information came from army records.[10] It is however completely at odds with UK civilian records and also with deductions based on his army number. Short's army number was prefixed 26/, a wholly reliable indication of the fact that he enlisted as a Kitchener volunteer into 26 Battalion. No cases have ever come to light of Regular soldiers being re-numbered in 1914 with Service battalion numbers. The only way a soldier might get such a number was to fraudulently re-enlist. No evidence has come to light that Short did this, and in any case records show that pre-war he was a civilian.

Further doubt is thrown on the accuracy of Babington's version of the soldier's army record as he states that Jesse Short went to France in November 1915. Only two battalions of the Northumberland Fusiliers landed that month, the Sixteenth and Seventeenth. 16 Northumberland Fusiliers landed at Boulogne on 22 November and 17 Battalion, who were pioneers, had landed at Havre the day before. No corroboration exists to confirm that the soldier ever served with either unit.

Jesse Short almost certainly went to France with 24 Northumberland Fusiliers (1st Tyneside Irish) in January 1916. At that time he held the acting rank of corporal, and must have transferred from his original battalion whilst serving in the UK.[11] Furthermore it is almost certain that Short served on the Somme in 1916 and survived unscathed. 70 of the men who had enlisted with Short in 26 Battalion were killed on 1 July 1916 alone. The reason why it is thought that the corporal came through the ordeal without injury is that, had he ever left the battalion, for whatever reason, the likelihood was that he would not have been returned to the same unit. Additionally the official records show that Short was still serving with his battalion on 10 August 1917 when it was amalgamated with 27 Battalion to form 24/27 Northumberland Fusiliers.[12] Hence between that date and the fateful Sunday, just over a month later, something occurred to cause the corporal to be present at the Etaples base. The most likely event was that Short had been wounded or had fallen sick. However, whatever his ailment, the NCO must have recovered and been convalescing at the time of his offence, as he was soon due to be posted back to the front. Events at Etaples undoubtedly overtook such duty as he was present during the mutiny. The final entry on Short's record shows a posting to 8 Northumberland Fusiliers. There can be little doubt however that this was Short's final posting, and one that never materialised.

The diminutive soldier was shot at Boulogne on 4 October 1917, but his unfortunate wife was spared the agony of public disclosure of the disgraced circumstances under which her husband had died. Jesse Short had seemingly served without blemish during the Battle of the Somme, and any soldier who served on those battlefields during 1916 had endured immeasurable hardship and suffering. Yet one rebellious outburst on a Sunday night in Etaples, when a few ill-chosen words labelled him as a mutineer, were to cost the soldier his life. How ironic therefore that Short's wife should choose the inscription for her husband's grave:

*'Duty called and he went forward ever remembered by his wife and children'*

On the same day a volunteer in the King's Royal Rifle Corps was shot for desertion. **Rifleman John Woodhouse** was already under a suspended sentence of death when, prior to an attack during the Battle of Langemarck, the soldier made off.[13] The absentee's subsequent actions were predictable, as he fled for the Channel ports with unrealistic intentions. Sixteen days later Woodhouse was found crouching under a hedge near Calais, and like numerous previous deserters, he tried to lie in an attempt to avoid detection. On this occasion the story was that the soldier had lost his way after returning from leave. Woodhouse's battalion, the 12th, had had a man shot just the previous June for desertion, and his division, the Twentieth, also suffered a similar fatality during September.

On 9 October a division which had previously had one man shot for murder and another man shot for desertion, completed the sequence of the common military crimes with a case of cowardice. The circumstances were unusual and perhaps unique.

Indicating the diversity of nationalities serving in the Canadian armed forces, **Private Dimitro Sinizki** was a Russian serving in a foreign army. The young labourer had been born at Kiev, enlisting at Winnipeg at the beginning of December 1915. Over nine months later the private arrived in England, where another five months were to pass before he was posted to the Western Front. Sinizki joined his battalion − 52 Canadian Infantry Battalion − on 24 February 1917 and exactly six months later he committed the crime that cost him his life.[14]

On night of 24/25 August Sinizki's battalion had been moving up to the front line at Sains-en-Gohelle (Vimy Ridge) when the soldier refused to continue and sat down in the communication trench. The private had made known his unwillingness to serve in the trenches prior to this act of defiance, and as a consequence was being escorted up the line. Nevertheless any remonstrations with the soldier were in vain, and during the review procedure that followed Sinizki's trial a comment was appended to the proceeding suggesting that the case was one of the worst in the Canadian Corps.[15]

The young Sinizki, however, was of good character, the only blemish on his record being an excursion to the VD hospital at Aldershot, when he had contracted gonorrhoea. The 22 year old spent his last moments detained in Winnipeg Camp in the Bois des Alleux − near Mont St Eloi. The Russian was shot at 6.11 am on 9 October, and it is almost certain that he was buried in one of the two cemeteries that adjoined the wood. The cemeteries have now disappeared, and their burials have been concentrated into the nearby Ecoivres Military Cemetery. The mistaken diarist for 3 Canadian Division recorded that the execution had been the first to take place in the division.[16] In fact it was the third and last execution that took place in the division.

On the following day another foreigner, but from a different clime, was shot as the result of his unruly behaviour. **Mahmoud Mohamed Ahmed** was one of 500 Egyptian labourers who rioted on 16 September

1917. The work force had been recruited to carry out labour intensive tasks including loading and unloading ships, in this case at Marseilles. The cause of the labourers' discontent is said to be that they had been under the mistaken impression that their service in France was of limited duration, whereas in reality the men were not free to go until the end of hostilities.[17]

As a consequence, on the morning of 16 September Camp Fournier was in turmoil when the men refused to work. British and Indian troops were called in to restore order, and during the afternoon the labourers returned to work, although their transit and work was overseen by an Indian Cavalry guard.[18]

According to a previously published account, the evening of 16 September saw the worst violence of the day, which resulted in injury to at least one British officer.[19] During the disturbance Ahmed, who seemingly had been inciting others to attack the officers, struck Second-Lieutenant A G Turley on the head with a stick, knocking him unconscious. Turley was rescued, but Ahmed, now in possession of a rifle and bayonet, issued a challenge, threatening to kill anyone who would come out and fight. However, when Ahmed was tackled by three NCOs from his homeland the violence ended and the labourer was detained in custody.[20]

Ahmed was tried on 28 September on a charge of joining in a disturbance of a mutinous nature. The labourer's previous record of indiscipline certainly weighed against the likelihood of a reprieve, which in the event never materialised. Ahmed was shot at No.8 Rest Camp on 10 October, and enquires of the Commonwealth War Graves Commission have failed to locate either a grave or a memorial that commemorates his passing.

By far the largest number of soldiers executed during the 1917 Flanders offensive were men serving in New Army divisions. The 15 (Scottish) and 18 (Eastern) Divisions standing out, as each had four men executed during this period. On 16 October volunteers from both of these formations were shot.

 Another young soldier who was convicted of desertion at this time was a lad from Kent. **Private Frederick Gore** had enlisted in 1915 at the age of sixteen and had served on the Western Front for two years, during which time he had been convicted convicted on three occasions. The private, who was serving with 7 East Kents, had deserted twice, and also been convicted of cowardice. Consequently the young soldier was serving under two suspended sentences of death.[21] Private Gore, aged 19, was shot at Poperinghe, being the seventeenth and last soldier to be executed in the town during the war.

Two Scottish volunteers shot on the same day faced firing squads at Arras. **Private Norman Taysum** had originally been an army cyclist before a posting in June 1916 transferred him to 9 Black Watch. The second soldier was **Private Thomas Ward,** a married man serving in 8/10 Gordon Highlanders, a battalion which surprisingly had been formed by the amalgamation of two units as early as May 1916. Details of the soldiers' crimes are not known to the authors – although both men were deserters. Private Ward was aged 23, and his partner in death was two years his senior. Norman Taysum has the inscription on his grave, '*Rest in Peace*'.

One of the oldest soldiers to face a firing squad at his time was a Londoner who had seen 15 years' army service. Although **Sergeant William Alexander** had been born in the capital, his enlistment in the King's Royal Rifle Corps had taken place at Manchester, near where his mother lived. After one year's training the former labourer was posted to South Africa where he earned the Queen's South African Medal with two clasps. He returned home in June 1904, having decided to extend his service to eight years. Eleven months later Alexander was promoted lance-corporal and shortly afterwards received his second good conduct badge. For some unknown reason during 1908 he reverted to the rank of private at his own request, and nine months later, having served his time, was transferred to the Army Reserve. During his service career Alexander had not been idle, being awarded both second and third class certificates of education, as well as a certificate in chiropody.[22]

In March 1911 William Alexander requested permission from the army to reside in Canada. This requirement for a Reservist to state his place of residence was contained in King's Regulations, no.373-6. The request was granted, and in December 1912 Alexander was finally discharged from his liability to be recalled. However, little time passed before war broke out, and on 24 September 1914 the old soldier rejoined, enlisting in the Alberta Regiment.[23]

On the Western Front Alexander served with credit, the Commanding Officer of 10 Canadian Infantry Battalion speaking well of his ability after the fierce fighting at Mont Sorrel (Ypres Salient) in 1916. However, in September 1917 during the fighting on Hill 70 near Lens, a tragic incident occurred. Alexander, who was then a company quartermaster-sergeant and acting platoon commander, handed over command of his party to a corporal, telling the junior NCO that he had been wounded. Unfortunately the corporal's advancing patrol was wiped out, leaving Alexander to account for his actions. Surprisingly the sergeant continued to claim that he had been wounded, but when examination proved this not to be the case, Alexander was placed under arrest.[24]

In 1934, the publication of the memoirs of one-time Senior Chaplain to First Canadian Division revealed details of an execution,[25] and the chronological order in which the book was written would suggest that the victim was William Alexander. The text gives very few clues which assist in the identification of the prisoner, and hence it is not possible to be certain that the man was CQMS Alexander.[26] The chaplain recalled the desperate attempts he made in trying to save the soldier's life, including visits to two senior officers.

Canon Scott's recollections were not wholly accurate, as he recalled that the army commander had suggested that only the Divisional Commander had the authority to halt the execution. Scott perhaps stated army commander when he meant brigade commander. Another anomaly occurs in that the chaplain recalled the victim saying that he had been orphaned since the age of eleven. And whilst this might just have been a 'hard luck story' it was certainly not true of William Alexander, as his mother had been alive when he originally enlisted at the age of 20.

Canon Scott's attempts however were in vain and the clergyman continued to describe the events leading up to the execution.

In due course the guards entered the condemned man's cell, handcuffing the prisoner and placing a gas helmet over his head – with the eye pieces facing to the back. At the place of execution the victim was seated on a box, and his hands were tied behind a post which had been driven into the ground. During the final moments the firing squad waited – facing the other way in order to minimise their anxiety. The prisoner requested that the gas mask be removed but the suggestion was declined, perhaps mercifully so for the victim. The object of covering the head was so that the firing squad might not see the victim's face; such mental anguish in past cases had caused men deliberately to fire wide.[27] Officiating at the execution was the assistant provost-marshal. His duties included recording the time of the soldier's death. 37 year old Alexander died at 5.57 am on 18 October,[28] and was buried in Barlin Communal Cemetery Extension, in the mining district near Lens.

The recorded number of married soldiers who were executed increased to a maximum during 1917, with no less than 14 being shot. One such man who was shot in a double execution was **Rifleman Frank Cheeseman,** a conscript serving in 18 King's Royal Rifle Corps. Cheeseman had previously been convicted of absence, for which he had been sentenced to one year's imprisonment. The rifleman's companion in death came from an unusual unit for a deserter. **Sapper Arthur**

**Oyns** was serving in 50 Field Search Light Company, Royal Engineers – part of Fourth Army troops. His unit, together with others, was engaged in trying to deter enemy night-time bombing, which during the later part of 1917 was proving to be somewhat troublesome. Unlike the rifleman, Oyns was of good character, and came from a respectable background – his father being a customs official. The two deserters were shot together on 20 October; Sapper Oyns being aged 31, and the infantryman two years younger. Rifleman Cheeseman has an inscription on his grave – it reads, *'Rest in the Lord'*.

By a strange coincidence a second soldier put to death during the Flanders offensive had also served in the British Army before emigrating to Canada – later to enlist in the Canadian Expeditionary Force. **Private Thomas Moles** was a native of Brompton Ralph, a tiny village in Somerset, and during his residence in the UK had served in the Somerset Light Infantry.

Moles enlisted with the CEF in August 1915 and two months later sailed from Montreal. On the Western Front the private served in 54 Canadian Infantry Battalion which was part of 4 Canadian Division. Nearly two years had passed since the soldier had left his new homeland to fight in a European war, when on 4 October 1917 Moles was tried for desertion.

The inevitable execution took place at the prison in Ypres on 22 October, and 28 year old Moles was buried in the nearby cemetery. The cemetery was once known as Ypres Prison Cemetery, but after the war it was renamed to Ypres Reservoir Cemetery. The alteration presumably came about through deference to relatives' feelings, thus avoiding any possible misapprehension about the circumstances under which their kin died. Only three executed men are amongst the 2,602 burials. The private's grave now carries the inscription requested by his mother: it reads, *'Grant us thy peace Lord'*. Moles' mother, who had re-married, also had her son's name added to the Roll of Honour in the village church at West Chinnock, near Crewkerne in Somerset.

On the same day an early wartime volunteer was also shot. **Private Ernest Worsley** had enlisted in 1914 and been posted to France in July 1915.[29] By a chance of fate the soldier's reinforcement draft followed in the footsteps of another soldier who was to die before a firing squad. Worsley had gone to France exactly five weeks after Private Beverstein (served as Harris), who was shot on 20 March 1916. Like Private Carter, who was executed in April 1916, these two soldiers had fought with 11 Battalion Middlesex Regiment. Clearly the deterrent value of such executions was limited, although Private Worsley had been transferred to 2 Middlesex.[30]

In the autumn of 1917, during duty in the front line trenches Worsley had been sent out of the line to draw rations. Instead, the soldier had run off, only to be arrested in Calais six days later – without equipment.[31] Very few soldiers were aware of the difficulties involved in obtaining an illicit passage across the Channel, but nevertheless it is significant just how many deserters were arrested near the Channel ports as they vainly attempted to achieve the near impossible.

In the winter of 1917 Mr Outhwaite, Labour MP for Hanley, asked the Under-Secretary of State for War whether or not shellshock victims were likely to suffer a relapse if returned to duty in the line. It is perhaps significant that Private G Everill, executed on 14 September 1917, came from Outhwaite's constituency. The reply, 'speaking generally', was 'no'. Mr Macpherson was then asked if he would take steps to ensure that no soldier who had been seriously wounded or invalided with shellshock, should suffer the death penalty. The wording of Outhwaite's question did in fact specifically mention the offence of cowardice, although it would be fair to assume that the meaning included desertion. The reply was to the effect that the Secretary of State was not in a position to give such an undertaking, but he tried to allay the House's concern by stating that he personally knew that the Commander-in-Chief gave the most careful consideration to such matters. Macpherson continued by saying that, only recently, 'to take one particular case', the condemned soldier had been medically examined.[32] The minister was clearly misleading the House, as it has since been stated that between 20 July and 11 October 1917, only three of the 32 soldiers tried between these dates and who subsequently were executed had been medically examined.[33]

In confirmation of Outhwaite's worst suspicions, a private who had not been medically examined, and who claimed he was suffering from acute depression, was tried on 11 October. The soldier had also been wounded on the Somme in 1916.

**Private Frederick Turner** was a volunteer who joined his local Territorial battalion before going to France in 1915. 6 Northumberland Fusiliers saw considerable action and on 11 September 1916 Private Turner was wounded.[34] In August of the following year the battalion was serving on the Arras front when Turner absconded from a reserve trench leaving his equipment behind. He was arrested six days later, but a month afterwards escaped. A few days later Turner was discovered in the first class compartment of a train bound for Calais. When the police entered his carriage Turner bolted out of the opposite door, but was detained.[35] At his court martial Turner claimed that he was suffering from acute depression, and he stated that he had been serving in France for 20 months without leave – although seemingly he had been of good character.

On 23 October, 31 year old Turner was executed in the Ypres Salient, and after the war his grave was moved to Bedford House Enclosure Cemetery, where the headstone now carries an inscription which confirms the plea made by the soldier at his trial.

*'I came to Jesus as I was weary and worn and sad I found in him a resting place'*

As is perhaps fitting a soldier with such long service, he is commemorated in the official casualty rolls, his cause of death being simply given as 'died'.[36]

In September 1917, the mounting numbers of soldiers reporting sick without any recognised signs of illness caused the army to review its position with regard to the medical condition which today might be called battle fatigue. In doing so they had a specially prepared form drawn up (Army Form W3436) and 10,000 copies were printed. The form, which was marked 'urgent and confidential', was to be rendered in the cases of officers and men who, without any visible wound, became unable to soldier on because of physical illness resulting from active service in the line. The form detailed nine different questions, which when answered gave some idea of the nature of the illness and how it came about.

One of the earliest soldiers to have his illness recorded on such a form was a private from 7 Leicesters who had reported sick on 1 October. The soldier's condition was described as tremulous and emotional, although this was not a good description as it did not include his confused state. The man had few recollections, only that after leaving a shell hole near Hell Fire Corner he had heard a shell coming which blew him up. He recalled nothing else, except that he remembered being led down the road by another soldier.

In fact, as his commanding officer added, the incident had not happened at Hell Fire Corner but at Black Watch Corner, where a five hour bombardment had been suffered. The soldier's condition did not seem to be in doubt, and he was classified as suffering from a shellshock wound and evacuated.

The scant details on the army form, however, gave a very poor picture of the soldier's predicament. He was a married man of 28 who had served in the army for nine years. Prior to the war he had been in India, and in October 1914 had gone to France. In 1915 he had been invalided home with malaria, but a year later returned to France. In July 1917 he had been wounded, but in the incident described above, he had in fact been blown up and buried in a trench − remaining unconscious for two hours. Unlike the brief description on army form 3436, the private shook all over, stammered, was agitated and tired out. His condition had not improved, and with his memory gone the soldier found he was unable to concentrate. The private's stammer was very bad and additionally he was unsteady on his feet – perhaps partly due to his blurred vision. Over a year passed before the soldier was considered fit for release from hospital, and by then the war was all but over.[37]

This private's case history makes a mockery of the statement that Mr Macpherson, Under-Secretary of State for War, made to the House when he blandly assured MPs that shellshocked soldiers usually recovered and could be returned to full duties.[38] The Leicesters private was discharged to agricultural duties only.

The behaviour of men whilst off duty was sometimes as surprising as their actions when under fire. One such case occurred in October 1917 when the man concerned could well have expected his crime – if it was such – to go undetected. The Welshman had achieved every deserter's dream, he had successfully crossed the Channel and escaped. He was only the third condemned man to have performed this feat during 1917, and his was the final cross-Channel escape of the war (that ultimately resulted in execution).

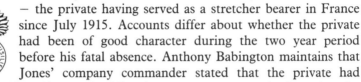 **Private William Jones** was a volunteer in 9 Royal Welsh Fusiliers – the private having served as a stretcher bearer in France since July 1915. Accounts differ about whether the private had been of good character during the two year period before his fatal absence. Anthony Babington maintains that Jones' company commander stated that the private had proved himself a good soldier; however, army records show that the Welshman was serving under a suspended sentence of death for desertion.[39]

Whatever the truth, Private Jones disappeared on 15 June 1917 whilst taking a wounded man to the dressing station. The next the army heard of him was on 4 September when he surrendered to the assistant provost-marshal at Bristol. He told the officer that he had been wounded at the front before being evacuated to England. Evidence given at the trial supposedly discredited this story. Quite why Jones gave himself up is not known. The proliferation of his family name would certainly have made his detection difficult. In fact it would have been distinctly to the man's advantage not to use an alias.

Had Jones chosen to remain absent, then an impression of the difficulty in identifying the absentee can be gained from the problem that faced the authors in positively identifying which W Jones had been executed in 1917. In fact 40 W Joneses alone died whilst serving in the Royal Welsh Fusiliers that year.[40] The authors were only able to identify the victim by a process of elimination. The 40 names (and numbers) obtained from the General Register Office were checked against *Soldiers Died in the Great War*, part 28 – Royal Welsh Fusiliers. This particular part does not list soldiers who were executed.

Private Jones was shot on Kemmel Hill on 25 October,[41] his motives still a mystery.

In the run-up to the final assaults on Passchendaele, events behind the lines were also proving more bloody than usual. Twenty soldiers were executed during the month of October, the highest figure at any time during the war; and all the offences were of a military nature. On 27 October two men were executed separately. One man was a volunteer and the other a conscript. Unfortunate circumstances surrounded both victims.

The volunteer, who was the elder recruit, was serving in 10 Cheshire, part of 25 Division which had first had a man shot in May 1916. **Private Ernest Bryant** had been serving with the battalion at the time, and had been wounded in both legs shortly afterwards, during the opening month of the Somme offensive. The injury had incapacitated him for some time, his inevitable return to the Western Front taking place the following February.[42] The next month whilst engaged in training exercises the soldier made off, remaining absent for four months until arrested in an unused convalescent hut at Boulogne. He was returned to his battalion, and at the end of July, just prior to going into the line, Bryant absconded again. The soldier's second taste of freedom was, however, short-lived; he was arrested at Bailleul nine days later when again he gave false particulars about his identity.[43] Perhaps the soldier's pre-war occupation as a gentleman's servant indicated that the 33 year old was of too mild a disposition for soldiering; nevertheless, neither this nor his former injuries persuaded the Commander-in-Chief to interfere with the court's sentence.

It was uncommon at a capital court martial hearing for a soldier aged under 21 to present his case without the aid of a defending officer, unless the defendant also had previous convictions for some crime or other. Such a soldier was brought to trial on 8 October.

**Private Charles Nicholson** had enlisted in the Yorks & Lancs Regiment, and served on the Western Front with 8 Battalion. The young soldier had first shown his contempt for military authority in June 1917 when he had been sentenced to one year's imprisonment with hard labour for desertion. However, the sentence was commuted to 90 days' field punishment no.1, although the private did not complete it. A month after the first court martial Nicholson was convicted of being absent without leave, the sentence, which was later suspended, being two years' imprisonment with hard labour. It was not long before Private Nicholson went missing again, only to be arrested once more and brought to trial.

In what must have been a unique misfortune, two days after the trial that sentenced the private to death, Nicholson's twin brother was killed in action in the Ypres Salient.[44] The death of the two brothers in so short an interval was a great tragedy — especially as they were aged only 19. The twins were born at Middlesborough early in 1898. The fact that the condemned soldier was a twin came to light from the details supplied by the parents for inclusion in the register pertaining to the cemetery in which the executed soldier was buried. Details about the twins' birth were obtained from the General Register Office, London. Charles Nicholson is buried at St Omer, where the inscription on his grave reads:

*'Loved by all in life, lamented in death'.*

Some soldiers who served with the BEF could not have been compelled to enlist had they not wanted to join, yet the supply of such recruits would not seem to have dwindled. Irishmen were the prime source of such volunteers, and amongst the ranks of those executed they formed the bulk of the men who had enlisted under false names. The reasons for such falsehoods rarely come to light, although in the case of **Private Stephen Byrne** it must be assumed that good reason did exist as he also appears to have stated a false age when enlisting.[45] Byrne served as Private Monaghan, in No.1 Company, 1 Royal Dublin Fusiliers, part of 29 Division. Scant detail has emerged about his crime, except that on the day of his offence he had been fed-up, having served without leave for eight months. He also stated that he had gone absent as he was feeling cold and ill.[46] Private Byrne (alias Monaghan) was shot on 28 October, although the place of execution remains a mystery, as the soldier is commemorated on the Arras Memorial to the Missing.

The month of October which had opened with a soldier being executed also closed with such unpleasantness, the difference being that at the end of the month there were two victims who were shot at separate locations. One victim was the third man from the King's Royal Rifle Corps to be shot that month. **Rifleman Thomas Donovan** was a conscript serving in 16 Battalion, also known as the Church Lads Brigade. The soldier's conduct, however, was far from angelic, and after the end of the Battle of the Somme he was convicted of desertion, receiving a sentence of six months' detention. 18 months later, whilst again serving on the Somme, Donovan went missing only to be arrested shortly afterwards in Amiens. Three days after his conviction for this offence the rifleman escaped from the guardroom, being arrested in the same city over a month later. Although the prisoner was safely returned to his battalion, which was now serving in the northernmost sector of the Western Front, the Londoner escaped once more on 22 August. He attacked his guard and threw him to the ground before gagging and tying him up. It had been some time since an escapologist of such skill had successfully fled military custody, but his freedom was short-lived. On 1 September the deserter was arrested, masquerading as a Belgian labourer.[47] A six week delay followed before he was brought to trial; quite why it took so long is not clear.

Eventually the trial was held on 17 October when the 20 year old told the court that his sister had begged him to return home after two of his brothers had been killed on the Somme.[48] Of course it was difficult to verify his sister's wishes, but Donovan might well have been telling the truth about his brothers. There is a record of a Rifleman Patrick Donovan, also from London, who was also serving in 16 King's Royal Rifle Corps, and who died of wounds on 5 November 1916. Whilst it is noteworthy that yet again a young soldier of bad character had chosen to be unrepresented at his trial, the likelihood is that the outcome would have remained the same even if he had been represented, having regard to the series of offences.

One of the few Regular soldiers to be shot during the Flanders offensive was a private from 2 King's Own Yorkshire Light Infantry. **Private Henry Webb** had enlisted in the army in 1913 and consequently had served on the Western Front for a considerable period. The soldier's downfall came about when a heavy enemy barrage had been more than he could stand. Webb's platoon commander had been sympathetic and sent the soldier to see the battalion doctor. Unfortunately the doctor prescribed medicine and duty, and consequently the private went absent without leave. For two months the Yorkshireman remained missing, until the theft of a French civilian's wallet led to the soldier's arrest and detection.[49] Webb, who was under a suspended sentence of five years' imprisonment for a previous crime, was shot in the remote village of Lederzeele.

As has previously been stated details of capital crimes together with sentences of death were periodically read out on parade, supposedly to deter others. However, the information that was disclosed did not always give a true representation of the circumstances under which a soldier had committed a crime. On 5 November, the entry in an Irish battalion's war diary was just such an example.

*'The death sentence on No.12609,* **Private G Hanna** *was promulgated at Barrosa Hall, Metz (-en-Couture) by Captain and Adjutant W Scott, MC. This was the first death sentence ordered to be carried out in this Battn. since its arrival in France. Private Hanna was only about five hours with the Battn. he having joined with a draft, but when warned for the trenches, disappeared.'*[50]

In fact Private Hanna had seen action in the Dardanelles whilst serving in 10 Division, the soldier having landed at Suvla Bay on 7 August

1915.[51] Following the evacuation of the Peninsula, Hanna had soldiered in Salonika (with 2 Royal Irish Fusiliers) until the spring of 1917 when he had returned to the Western Front. In the course of his army service Hanna had twice previously been convicted of desertion, being sentenced to death on the second occasion.[52] Seemingly this punishment was commuted to 7 years' penal servitude before being suspended.[53] 26 year old Private Hanna was shot on 6 November by a firing squad from his battalion, commanded by Lieutenant G Reeve, MC.

Very few Regular soldiers were shot during the closing months of 1917, and those who were had served abroad for some considerable time. One such man was **Private John Taylor** who was serving in 2 South Staffs. Had it not been for the war, Taylor would have been transferred to the Reserve in the summer of 1916. Unfortunately the private mistakenly believed that on this anniversary he was entitled to a month's leave. Perhaps this grievance was the root cause of his disaffection, for Taylor had deserted twice, before a third and final conviction terminated the matter.[54] Private Taylor was shot at Lapugnoy − near Lens − on 6 November.

A man who had joined the army during Lord Derby's final call and before the introduction of conscription, died in front of his comrades some two years after joining up. **Private John Milburn** had enlisted for service in the Northumberland Fusiliers and served in France with a Tyneside Irish battalion − which was ultimately amalgamated to form 24/27 Northumberland Fusiliers. Milburn was serving under a suspended sentence of 2 years' imprisonment when he deserted in order to avoid serving in the trenches opposite the Hindenburg Line.[55]

During the raising of Kitchener's New Armies by the creation of units known as Service Battalions, existing Territorial units were also doubled-up to form second-line formations. Certain regiments even went as far as raising third-line formations. Such battalions used fractional notations to indicate their lineage, the first number being the 'line number' and the second the battalion number. Most of the third-line formations were amalgamated, but a few did go to France.

In early 1917, 66 Division was sent to France and amongst its units was 3/5 Lancashire Fusiliers. The battalion was comprised of many pre-war Territorials who had re-enlisted after the outbreak of war, and naturally the unit consisted of older men, although younger reinforcements were drafted in. Amongst the first orders issued when the battalion arrived in France was one that today seems absurd, but it highlights just how seriously the threat of spies was taken at the time. The soldiers were instructed that, if asked, they did not know the name of any other person serving in the battalion.[56]

Although the division had been abroad for some months, the official history of the war recorded that it was not seriously engaged until the Battle of Poelcappelle. On that day (9 October) the Fusiliers' objective was a line just 700 yards short of Passchendaele village. The official account continued that during the war, no previous attack mounted by Second Army had had such an unfavourable start.[57] Details recorded by the diarist of 3/5 Lancashire Fusiliers confirmed that statement.[58]

Instructions regarding the forthcoming operations had reached the battalion just before midnight on 4 October, an order to move being issued for 9 am the following day. Initially the battalion's destination had been Brandhoek, a village between Ypres and Poperinghe, but this was later altered while the Territorials moved up by bus. The eventual billets on the Frezenberg Ridge proved far from hospitable, but there the Fusiliers remained for four days. On 8 October orders were issued to move up at 6 pm that evening — ready for the attack next morning. An Australian soldier from an Engineering Company had been detailed to guide the party to the trenches; the commanding officer, however, and the signal officer set out during the afternoon in order to see the new positions during daylight. The precaution came to naught, as owing to the mud the two men were unable to reach the trenches in the available time.

The battalion's departure for the trenches was delayed by German shelling, and half-an-hour late the Fusiliers set off — the whole unit strung-out in single file. Bringing up the rear was the battalion medical officer, Captain H A Sandiford, with his party of stretcher bearers and medical assistants. After the battle the doctor wrote an account of his experiences.

'The Battalion was in single file, ploughing through mud. I had gone about 500 yards when an urgent call for the MO was passed down the line. I went forward to investigate, hurrying past the long winding column and collecting most of the Frezenburg Ridge [mud] on the way, to find an exhausted soldier in a shell hole. I gave him some advice and halted there while the Battalion filed past . . . I had only proceeded about 50 yards further when another urgent message was received for the MO. Nothing doing. I eventually overtook this second casualty, a lance-corporal stuck in the mud. My carrying party now proceeded to collapse and slowly settle down into the mud during the next 200 yards. I watched them whilst doing some heavy thinking. I decided to jettison the blankets and such kit as could be most conveniently spared . . . We fought our way along "F" track slowly with the aid of an electric torch, following the tape, where it existed, and looking for whitened props where it did not. NB Why does somebody lay a tape across large shell holes containing water instead of round them? . . . the "pillbox" on the railway was not Battalion HQrs so

*I decided to form my Regimental Aid Post there. The pillbox consisted of two strong dugouts . . . slightly wounded cases could crawl into them.*[59]

Although the doctor makes mention of certain difficulties, the night in fact was inky black, and it was the rain that was causing the ground to turn to mud.[60] Whilst the doctor struggled at the rear of the column, events at the head had gone wrong too. Half way to the trenches the Australian guide had abandoned the battalion, leaving them to find their own way. He had told them that the tape was almost continuous all the way to their destination, and that guides were stationed at all the doubtful points to assist the group.

The commanding officer, who had gone ahead, searched the trenches but was unable to locate the CO of 2/7 Manchesters, the battalion he was to relieve. He noted that at 5 am, 15 minutes before zero, there was still no sign of his battalion. With his whole command apparently absent, and no sign of the other two attacking brigades, the Fusiliers' colonel telephoned from his dugout to report on the situation. Amidst such chaos, with the CO oblivious in his dugout, the battalion arrived in the forward trench exactly at zero hour, and went straight into the attack.

For at least one man the strain was too great, and on the way to the trenches he opted out with a self-inflicted wound. Perhaps surprisingly, on the day of battle only one man was evacuated with shellshock, although Captain Sandiford, the battalion MO, had no available men to assist such cases. The casualties that day were recorded as 316 — with one or two men (stretcher cases) dying outside the pillbox that was being used as a Regimental Aid Post, when enemy shells rained down.

Three men however had decided to avoid the carnage of this battle and they absconded, remaining absent for three days. Surprisingly the trio gave themselves up at one of the Channel ports. When Privates Brookes, North and Smith were brought to trial the expected sentences were imposed. Quite why **Private William Smith** from Pendleton in Manchester, was singled out to be the scapegoat is unknown. Captain Sandiford had been awarded the Military Cross for his gallantry during the operations of 9 October, but there was one more job that he had to undertake, and one that he would not find to his liking.

On 14 November, 20 year old Private Smith faced a firing squad from his battalion. Commanding the squad was Second-Lieutenant Dunn and in attendance was Captain Sandiford who had worked so valiantly during the Battle of Poelcappelle. The doctor's sentiments are not difficult to imagine, and a week after the execution, Sandiford went sick.

In the aftermath of the execution, deserters Brookes and North pondered their fates. Undoubtedly the two were kept waiting as a deterrent. Twelve days after the death of their comrade the news came. Both death sentences had been commuted to 15 years' penal servitude and suspended. The two men had been spared. It seems likely that Smith's parents were not told the true cause of their son's death, as information volunteered to the War Graves Commission for publication stated that the boy had 'died of wounds'.

Although in a number of previous executions the condemned men had served in a number of different battalions within their own regiment, very few men who faced a firing squad had served with more than one regiment. Such a transfer was not of course, a disciplinary measure, but simply part of the policy adopted after the enormous casualties suffered on the Somme to prevent the annihilation of the entire male population from closely defined recruitment areas.

**Private Richard Davies** had enlisted in the Northamptonshire Regiment in 1915 and had been sent to the Western Front in November of that year as a reinforcement to 7 Battalion, which had landed two months previously.[61] At an unknown date Private Davies had been transferred to the Sherwood Foresters, who, in the summer of 1917, were serving in Belgium. Davies' battalion, 11 Foresters, were in action on the first day of the Battle of Messines, where, on the extreme left they had a stiff fight at Mount Sorrel. At the end of September the battalion was again heavily engaged, this time near Tower Hamlets on the Menin Road. The Foresters were holding newly captured ground when the enemy counter-attacked, using flamethrowers.[62] It is not known when Private Davies deserted, but during the month of October the unit did alternate duty in and out of the line. Davies was a bad character, already being under a suspended sentence of death for a similar offence, [63] and on 15 November 1917 he was shot at Wizernes, near St Omer, just a short while before his division – the Twenty-Third – went to Italy.

A soldier from the north of England who was seemingly of previous good character was shot on 21 November. **Private Thomas Foulkes** had been sent to the Western Front as a reinforcement to a Manchester Pals battalion, the 21st.[64] At a later date he transferred to 1/10 Manchesters from whom he deserted with fatal result. Many years after the war a serving officer from the battalion wrote an account of the shooting of a deserter, and it is believed that the condemned man was Private Foulkes. As another man from the battalion was shot in 1918 it is not possible to be absolutely certain that Foulkes was the victim.

Henry Lawton, a young subaltern with the Manchesters, was not an eyewitness to the shooting, but heard of the event from a fellow officer. The battalion was out of the line at the time and preparations for the ritual were made in secret. Early the following morning the soldier had been taken to a rifle range and tied in a chair with a piece of white paper pinned to his chest as a target. The story continued that in the aftermath of the volley the firing squad turned and fled, unable to look upon the consequence of their actions.

If Lawton's account can be believed, then the shooting had little deterrent value as he maintained that less than 10 per cent of the battalion knew about the killing.[65] Although the execution was recorded by the adjutant-general, 42 Division, as having taken place at Zermezeele,[66] after the war Foulkes' remains were not identified, and the private is commemorated on the Loos Memorial.

Lawton's account of life on the Western Front maintains that he (together with two other officers) received a dressing down from the divisional commander for not having imposed a death sentence during a previous court martial case. A number of irregularities are disclosed in Lawton's account of this trial, which must throw some doubt on the strictness of its accuracy. The lieutenant recorded that the charge was sleeping at his post, and that the charming 19 year old defendant was unrepresented. The story continues that after the finding, no details were disclosed to the court about the individual's character or length of service. Lawton also commented that there was no written record of the trial, and that in the ensuing arguments he never did discover whether the imposition of a death sentence was a mandatory requirement for such an offence!

Although written records were required to be kept of courts martial held in the field, one particular battalion kept an impromptu account of acts of indiscipline in its own war diary. At the end of July 1915, 7 Queen's (Royal West Surreys) had crossed to France, and with them had gone volunteer **Private Thomas Hawkins.** In the following month the battalion had moved to the Somme where the BEF was in the process of taking over trenches from the French. When the Somme

battle opened the battalion was in action, and during the following month a private accidentally shot and wounded his sergeant. The man was only sentenced to seven days' field punishment, although it would seem to have been the prerogative of the battalion to show mercy, as during the same month the case of a private charged with sleeping on his post was dismissed.

On 12 June 1917 Private Hawkins was tried for cowardice resulting from his conduct during the Messines offensive. At some time prior to this date Hawkins must also have been convicted of desertion and sentenced to death − the sentence having been suspended. The private heard no more about his cowardly behaviour, but two months later an inquiry was held at Brigade HQ, concerning men who had gone missing on 10 August during an attack on Inverness Copse. Hawkins was not amongst the offenders, but a week later a sergeant, a lance-corporal and a private, all from the battalion, found themselves on trial for desertion. A month passed before the sentences on the two NCOs were promulgated, leaving Private Hawkins still unaware of his punishment for the offence of cowardice. Both NCOs were reduced to the ranks, and surprisingly the junior NCO got the severest sentence — ten years as opposed to two years.

In mid-September, some three months after his trial, Private Hawkins eventually learned that he had been sentenced to two years' with hard labour, which had then been suspended. Despite a flurry of court martial activity during September the battalion diarist recalled the period with an optimistic note.

*'September has been a most enjoyable month. The battalion has been out of the line the whole period, and the greater part has been spent in the agricultural country which lies north of St Omer. The weather has been most favourable and has greatly facilitated the work of reorganising the battalion. Work and pleasure have been inter-mixed with a regular frequency. Numbers of officers and men have been sent on leave to England.'*[67]

Certainly this officer seemed to have been enjoying himself. However, whether the leave allocation had been equally distributed between the officers and the other ranks was not disclosed; and consequently whether the rankers' lot was equally convivial is questionable; however, they had notched up one achievement that month, when they thrashed the New Zealanders 7 -1 at football.

The following month (October) brought the renewal of military activity, and with it a ten year sentence for one private — although in fairness, two under-age soldiers had also been returned to the UK. On 12 October the battalion took part in the battle for Passchendaele, although Private Hawkins had opted out by going missing. In November, news came of several courts martial held on battalion members. The first, a private, having his death sentence commuted to five years before being suspended. Habitual offender Thomas Hawkins, however, had chanced his luck once too often, and was executed at 6.53 am on 22 November. Before the month was out another soldier's death sentence was commuted, yet the battalion diarist seemed to think nothing was amiss. Clearly the officer was oblivious to the ordinary soldier's lot, as in the end of month summary he recorded, *'the morale of the men has improved considerably'.*[68]

A brigadier who had added a damning comment to the court martial transcript of a coward in 1915 (Private Oliver Hodgetts) repeated the injustice again in the winter of 1917. The unfortunate victim was **Private Ernest Lawrence** serving with 2 Devons.

At the soldier's trial the written statement supplied to the court about the private's character stated that Lawrence had been a constant source of trouble in the battalion and that he was of no fighting value. The author, Lieutenant, but in fact acting Lieutenant-Colonel, A Tillett DSO MC, was in fact quite right, although the gallant officer was only to survive the private by a fortnight, the colonel being mortally wounded at Passchendaele on 2 December.

 Private Lawrence had gone absent on 5 May 1917 when he had been sent back from the support line to fetch rations from a dump. Instead the soldier had made his way to Rouen, where he reported himself and told a fabricated story. On 8 May prisoner Lawrence was detailed to work in the front line, but again he absconded to Rouen, where he was arrested whilst trying to borrow money, using a false name. In his possession was a false paybook and also a movement order. Shortly after his arrest Lawrence escaped from his escort. Whereupon the shrewd soldier took up employment in the Royal Flying Corps repair workshops in Rouen. For two-and-a-half months he worked for the RFC until arrested again on 9 August.[69] It is not perhaps surprising that, with three convictions recorded against him, ultimately Private Lawrence was sentenced to death. However, after Brigadier-General G W St G Grogan, VC, had added his speculative opinion to the proceedings, stating that Lawrence's undesirable influence was likely to infect the fighting troops with whom he came in contact, it is not surprising that no mercy was shown.[70] The 21 year old Londoner was shot at the prison in Ypres on same day as Private Hawkins – 22 November. Private Lawrence's grave carries the inscription:

*'In loving memory of my dear son gone but not forgotten'*

On the same day a third and separate execution took place. The soldier was a young pre-war Regular, who on account of his youth had been prevented from going to France until September 1915. His overseas departure followed just five days after his marriage, and the private was posted as a reinforcement to 8 South Wales Borderers.[71] In the course of his service **Private Harry Rigby** deserted, and upon conviction

 received a three year suspended prison sentence. Rigby was transferred to 10 Battalion, and in August 1917 whilst serving as a brigade runner he went absent. A week later the private was arrested in Calais, where he pretended to be attached to a base camp.[72]

Private Rigby's flight from the newly captured German trenches in the Ypres Salient is perhaps not surprising, as his battalion recorded that during the August attack, 50 other ranks had to be evacuated with

shellshock.[73] However, at his court martial, Rigby offered an alternative explanation for his behaviour. He told the court that he was worried about his wife's health. Seemingly the private's concern was not without foundation for his unfortunate spouse died a few years after the war. 21 year old Private Rigby was shot at Armentières on 22 November.

On the last day of October the final case of cowardice that resulted in an execution was tried. The victim was **Private J S Adamson** a 30 year old volunteer in 7 Cameron Highlanders, part of 15 (Scottish) Division. The circumstances of the offence are unknown, but a graphic description of the execution exists, the eyewitness having been newly posted to the Mounted Military Police at Arras.

*'What a setup. The APM beneath contempt. The sergeant-major a cowardly vindictive rat (Sergeant Major Brigham Young) and the senior sergeant a loud mouthed shyster, and for the men themselves with the exception of about seven they were a proper shower . . . Soon after I joined the unit we had to turn out one night and fall in outside the hut, and I wondered what it was for. Then along came two of the police with a prisoner and they stood backs to the hut and we faced them; next came a file of men with an officer and they stood at ease in front of us. We had an old soldier who looked after things at night time and he came along with a lighted lantern. Then the APM walked up with a paper in his hand and stood facing the prisoner. The old boy stood at the back of him holding up the lantern to shine over the APM's shoulder. We were called to attention and the APM began to read. Private 'so and so', you have been charged and found guilty of cowardice and desertion in the face of the enemy. The verdict of the Court Martial is that you are to be shot at dawn, signed Sir Douglas Haig. Next morning the sun was shining and a touch of frost [was] in the air. I was sent up the road to stop any traffic and high up I had a bird's-eye view. I saw the man brought out to the post, the firing squad march into positions turn right and take up stand. I heard the report as they fired and saw the smoke from their rifles. They then turned and marched off. The officer with revolver in hand inspected the body then turned away. The dead man was then taken away on a blanket and buried in the small cemetery in the next field, it was over, I came down but it did not seem real.'[74]*

On the same day (23 November) a young volunteer was executed in the Ypres Salient. The private was serving in 18 Division, which only the day before had had a man executed. The condemned man's battalion − 8 East Surreys − had become famous on the opening day of the Battle of the Somme, when the men had gone into action kicking footballs.[75] In 1917 Londoner **Private Arthur Westwood** had been sentenced to 90 days' field punishment for desertion, and later that year the battalion moved into the shell torn morass that passed for trenches near Poelcappelle. Reluctant youngster Westwood was not present, however, and on 27 October his case came to trial, when the undefended private was unable to make out a defence.[76] After the execution, 20 year old Westwood was buried in Bleuet Farm Cemetery, where his grave now carries the inscription:

'*Resting with loved ones far away in God's great universe mother*'.

Thirty-five soldiers were executed during the final quarter of 1917, and after the largest ever monthly total in October of 20, the figures had decreased to eleven in November and in December, only four. The half-yearly statistics showed that by far the largest number of executions had taken place in New Army divisions or in units specifically raised for the war. Although only seven executions during the six months ending in December had been in Regular divisions, a sizeable number (a dozen) had been in Territorial units. It is noteworthy that half of these men were conscripts.

For some reason that is probably not significant, three of the four men executed during December 1917 were serving in Territorial divisions. The exception to the rule was the first man, who was also a conscript.

**Private Joseph Bateman** was serving in 2 South Staffs, a unit which

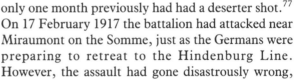

only one month previously had had a deserter shot.[77] On 17 February 1917 the battalion had attacked near Miraumont on the Somme, just as the Germans were preparing to retreat to the Hindenburg Line. However, the assault had gone disastrously wrong, as the Germans had been alerted by a British soldier who had deserted to the enemy.[78]

At the end of June the battalion had moved into the line at Givenchy, where it served until moving into rest at the beginning of October. Consequently Private Bateman had not experienced the horrors of the Ypres Salient when later that month he chose to go absent. As was common in capital cases the soldier had deserted when warned for the trenches — only to be arrested the next day. Candidly Bateman admitted he was an absentee, although he had been arrested at a PoW camp wearing a sergeant's stripes.[79] Had the private not escaped from the guardroom only to be arrested six days later at Boulogne, he might well have avoided the extreme penalty. The reluctant soldier was shot at a remote spot between Bapaume and Peronne on 3 December.

Two of the executions during December took place in London Territorial divisions. The first case happened in 58 Division. In October 1917 a soldier (Sinizki) serving in a Canadian unit had been executed for cowardice, after refusing to march up to the trenches; the Londoner shot in December had committed the same crime, but was, however, shot for disobedience.

**Private Frederick Slade** was serving in 2/6 London Regiment as a stretcher bearer, and had been in France since the beginning of 1917. After eight months' good service the soldier had been sentenced to 90 days' field punishment for disobedience. In the following month the battalion was involved in the Battle of the Menin Road, and in the month after, was engaged in the second drive towards Passchendaele. On that day (26 October) Slade had refused to parade prior to moving up to the line. Neither his sergeant nor the adjutant could persuade him, and as a result he was arrested, pending a court martial. Slade stood trial on 14 November when he told the court that the horrors of battle had affected his mind.[80] However, an RAMC captain denied that the soldier was mentally unfit, and as a consequence the 24 year old was sentenced to death.

It seems possible that Frederick Slade may have lied about his age during the 1915 National Registration census. Slade's death certificate, comprising details supplied from army records, states that the soldier was aged 28. However, records at the General Register Office, London, show his true age to have been 24.

Very recently the recollections of a member of the firing squad that shot Private Slade were published. Private Sidney Suffield had newly arrived on the Western Front when selected for the gruesome task. His account recalled details of how the execution took place. The soldiers filed out and collected their rifles, whereupon the officer commanding the firing squad took up his position to the front and to the right of the squad – clearly in their view. The soldier was then brought out, tied to a post and blindfolded. When the officer raised his sword in silence without a word of command being spoken, the squad raised their rifles and took aim – the target being a white card, attached over the condemned man's heart. As the sword was lowered the squad fired. Immediately afterwards they turned away and marched off. [81]

A week before Christmas, Under-Secretary of State Macpherson was asked in the House whether it might not be a kindness to relatives at home not to promulgate details of men executed to soldiers serving abroad. The ritual of reading out details to men on parade, of the offence, sentence and shooting being an established practice.[82] Mr Macpherson refused, although his decision was somewhat at odds with the doings of the War Cabinet.

Four weeks previously the War Cabinet had decided that, in future, relatives of soldiers executed for military crimes would receive a pension in the same manner as soldiers dying honourably. This pension right was also made retrospective. And they also decided to alter the formal notification sent to next-of-kin after an execution.[83]

Although the army's blunt form for notifying next-of-kin of a relative's execution was in a number of cases not utilised, it was not until December 1916 that it had been toned down somewhat. The modified form conveyed very deep regret, but went on to stipulate the offence and date of execution. It is noted however that the message of sympathy from the King and Queen was always omitted.

The November 1917 alteration suggested that the notification should read that the soldier had 'died in service'. The expression of very great regret was also diluted to read great regret. Hence, the intention was not to give the next-of-kin any hint that their relative had been executed. A cursory comparison between the 'covert' notification and the pro forma used for an honorable death might reveal discrepancies, but there was no obvious hint or suggestion that anything was amiss.

However, the War Cabinet's suggestion did not find favour with the War Office; and on 7 January 1918 Lord Derby replied that such a policy might increase relatives' distress — should they find out the truth inadvertently. He continued that such a deception in the past had resulted in the production of memorial cards, and other such methods of marking the honourable passing of a loved one.

Nevertheless the War Cabinet had its way, and on 12 February 1918 instructions were issued for the use of the new form. The final design of Army Form B 104-149, was in fact altered, but the ambiguous phrase 'died in service', did remain. However, because of an alteration to the normal form — used for men who were killed in action — the form began by using different phraseology. The message conveyed was that the authorities had the painful duty to inform the next-of-kin that information from the War Office reported that Number, Rank, Name and Regiment had died in service — on the date given.[84] The charade was complete, but whether it was effective is questionable. (The same form was also used in World War Two — 500 were printed in October 1939.)

The circumstances of a second soldier shot in a London Territorial division were not dissimilar from the case a fortnight earlier. **Private Harry Williams** was, however, a volunteer who had enlisted in a Middlesex Territorial battalion in 1915. His transfer from 1/8 Middlesex to Queen Victoria's Rifles took place during the Battle of the Somme. He was already under a 15 year suspended sentence for absence when in November 1917 he had fallen out from his company and refused orders.[85] A German attack was in progress and reinforcements were required, but, sick with fear, the private remained immovable.[86] Strangely, the private was charged with desertion, when perhaps cowardice might have seemed a more likely charge. What Williams required however was rest, away from the carnage of war. His treatment, like so many others, was despicable. Private Williams, the fourth and final volunteer to be shot in 56 Division, was executed near Arras on 28 December.

Another volunteer shot that day might well have had other medical problems besides shellshock. **Private Charles McColl** enlisted into 11 East Yorks in 1914, and at the end of the following year sailed to Egypt before the battalion was recalled to the Western Front. In September 1916 his unit had been holding the line at the Rue du Bois, near Neuve Chapelle when Private McColl was wounded by a shell.

The Yorkshireman was invalided home with heart failure and shattered nerves, he later told the court.[87] Upon his return to France, however, McColl was posted to 4 East Yorks, a Territorial battalion. No longer able to stand the strain the soldier soon went absent, receiving a sentence of ten years' imprisonment. On 28 October 1917 Private McColl absconded from his platoon who were in brigade support near Houlthulst Forest in the Ypres Salient, leaving his rifle and equipment behind. Four days later McColl was arrested in Calais after enquiring about a rest camp and stating that he was on his way to England.[88]

McColl's court martial proved an absolute farce. Undefended, the soldier detailed his nervous condition and his inability to control himself when in the trenches. He told the court that under such conditions he shook all over. The court martial panel were clearly indifferent, as they did not even take the trouble to order a medical examination, merely sentencing the private to death.[89]

Until recently two ex-soldiers with knowledge of the case were still alive. The two were Cecil M Slack, one time captain and commander of McColl's company, and Len Cavinder, once a sergeant in the battalion. Slack and Cavinder were agreed on their opinion about the soldier. They described him as unstable and slow, and that there was something wrong with him.[90]

Prior to the execution Sergeant Cavinder and another soldier went to the military prison at Brandhoek and escorted Private McColl to the prison at Ypres. With the private still unaware of his fate, the two soldiers attempted to ply the victim with drink, but he became suspicious. At around midnight on the eve of the execution a number of staff officers entered the condemned cell and promulgated the finding and sentence. In the aftermath Private McColl was reported to have acted like a maniac for a while. As the dawn approached, two military policemen entered the cell, manacling Private McColl and blindfolding him with a reversed gas mask. Outside the prison the battalion firing squad waited, whilst McColl was strapped into a chair. The squad comprised ten men, five kneeling and five standing. On the command of 'Fire', the volley rang out, killing the 26 year old. Len Cavinder and the other guard were then left to bury the body[91]

Captain Slack wrote to McColl's mother, who, he recalled, was a widow. He told her that her son had been killed in action, however it seems likely that the unfortunate woman would have learnt the truth from an official notification sent by an Army Records Office.

As well as on the Western Front, executions had been taking place in other theatres of operations during 1917. At least eleven sentences of death had been confirmed, and the first related to events early in the year.

In February 1917, 13 Division, which had last had a man executed over a year previously just prior to the evacuation of the Gallipoli peninsula, had to furnish firing squads to shoot three men. At this time the division was serving in Mesopotamia, and the trio all came from the same battalion.

The men were all volunteers who were serving in 6 South Lancs. The first offender – but last to be shot – was **Private Richard Jones**, a married man aged 40 who had been convicted of desertion. His execution on 21 February was exactly one month after the date that he had gone missing. In an earlier narrative in this book, details of procedural irregularities were disclosed concerning Sergeant Robins who had been executed at Gallipoli – whilst also serving in a unit in 13 Division; and events repeated themselves in the case of Jones, when a written statement was submitted by a prosecution witness who should have given evidence in person. Needless to say, although the judge-advocate spotted this error, the Commander-in-Chief took no steps to correct the irregularity.[92]

**Private Robert Burton** and **Private Thomas Downing** had both been convicted of an offence that was very prevalent on the Western Front – that of sleeping at their post – and, unusually, the two had been tried very shortly after the commission of their offences; Burton being tried the very same day, and Downing the day after. The pair were of good character, although neither received a recommendation to mercy. Opinion amongst the reviewing officers differed – the battalion and divisional commanders favouring commutation, whilst brigade and corps commander recommended the sentences be carried out.[93]

An old soldier later recalled what he had heard about all three men and the circumstances surrounding the cases. The Commander-in-Chief in Mesopotamia was General Maude, and the NCO related how the General had soon become unpopular.[94] The account maintained that prior to the offences 6 South Lancs had had to march for over 30 miles, and Burton and Downing were unlucky when they were selected for sentry duty. The NCO continued that two days prior to the executions the colonel of the South Lancs had pleaded in vain with the

Commander-in-Chief for the men's lives. In consequence of this refusal, it was stated that the whole army seethed with indignation and never forgave General Maude. The account of events given by ex-Sergeant Crutchlow must be treated with a certain amount of suspicion, as his book also recalls that 30 Chinese Labourers had been sentenced to death in Basra for murdering two Arab dancing girls, the insinuation being that the Chinamen had also cooked and devoured the females!

At 7 am on 19 February 1917, 22 year old Private Downing was shot alongside 24 year old Private Burton, and although the executions, including that of Private Jones, were recorded as having taken place at Bassouia,[95] none of the three graves were located after the war. Consequently the trio are commemorated on the Basra Memorial to the Missing.

A fourth executed private is also commemorated on the Basra Memorial, the Scotsman being the last soldier to have been shot in Mesopotamia during the war. **Private George Cutmore** was a volunteer serving in 2 Black Watch − part of 7 Indian Division − and had deserted early in 1917. After an absence of four months the private was arrested and then tried on 2 July, when he stated to the court that the reason he had gone missing was that he had won a sum of money playing cards and was intent on spending his winnings.[96] The pleading did not find favour with the military authorities, and on 25 July Private Cutmore was shot.[97]

Earlier in 1917 another soldier from the Gold Coast Regiment had been shot. With characteristic haste for events away from the Western Front, the soldier had been tried and then very soon afterwards shot. In April 1917 **Lance-Corporal Allassan Mamprusi's** unit had been engaged in ambushing German patrols, a venture in which they had enjoyed a considerable amount of success. However, the NCO had found the stress of combat all too much, and on 25 April he was tried for cowardice at Rumbo in German East Africa.[98] Surprisingly the battalion had a very large establishment of 1,302 men, with only nine officers − assisted by seven NCOs.[99] Considering that the rate of sickness in the Gold Coast Regiment was high, especially amongst officers, the death of Lance-Corporal Mamprusi just three days after his trial further depleted those in authority.

Towards the end of 1915 a British Expeditionary Force, together with French allies, landed at Salonika − part of Greece. Their arrival, however, had been too late to save the Serbians, who had been forced by the Bulgarians to withdraw through Albania. Ultimately the intervention proved very wasteful, as maintaining an allied presence tied up some half a million allied troops with no tangible result.

In the summer of 1917 a British soldier serving on the Macedonian

Front was shot for desertion. However, a number of details recounted by Judge Babington do not tally with those ascertained by the authors. **Private Archibald Brown** enlisted in the Black Watch in September 1914, and in mid-month was posted to 10 Battalion which was formed at Perth.[100] Anthony Babington comments that for 18 months Private Brown served on the Western Front;[101] however, although Brown went to France in September 1915[102] his battalion passed briefly through France on its way to Salonika.

What is clear however is that Brown deserted the day before a most disastrous British attack, when on 8 May 1917, 600 men from 10 Black Watch had attacked the Bulgars. The casualties were recorded as ten men killed, 58 missing, 212 wounded, and another 100 wounded who had remained at duty – making a total of 380. Private Brown was tried at Reselli on 20 May. The court heard that the Scotsman was serving under a suspended sentence of one year's hard labour for striking a superior officer.[103] Strangely Anthony Babington's examination of the court martial transcript suggests that no previous convictions had been recorded against the soldier. The Scotsman was shot by a firing squad from his battalion at 4.30 am on 1 June.

Although the previously executed soldier was the first victim to be executed in Salonika, another serious disciplinary matter was under consideration at the same time. The incident involved the killing of a muleteer in the Macedonian Mule Corps. The Corps was mainly comprised of recruits who had been enlisted in Cyprus, although the ranks did also include a number of local men. The muleteers were attached to the Army Service Corps and their duties involved the transportation of supplies and provisions.

Early in the morning of 14 May 1917 a doctor from 79 Field Ambulance (part of 26 Division) went to Yenikoj to investigate the death of muleteer Markou Christolis. The officer reported that murder was suspected, a finding that was also returned by a Court of Inquiry that sat at 11 am the same day. At four in the afternoon the APM with an interpreter inspected the scene of the crime and interviewed the witnesses. Yet over two weeks were to pass before Lieutenant Stormont Darling of 10 Black Watch took a summary of the evidence. Presumably language problems were a considerable difficulty as the summary took three days to complete. On 9 June a FGCM was convened to sit the next day, but eventually this was postponed twice, ultimately sitting on 12 June. **Foreman 'E' (Nicolas)** was the accused, and seemingly language problems again caused considerable difficulties, as the trial took five days – probably the longest of the war. After the finding of guilty and the passing of a sentence of death events again happened slowly. Eventually on 6 July the APM called at 79 Field Ambulance to make arrangements for the execution. At 6 pm the staff of the Field Ambulance, together with the muleteers paraded to hear the promulgation of the court's finding and sentence. An hour later Foreman 'E' was shot.[104]

Three days after this execution Muleteer Nicola Polykarbos was murdered.[105] However, the authors have been unable to determine whether his death was connected with the previous case. Neither have we been able to identify his murderer, or details about what subsequently happened. The authors have discovered five names of executed murderers, all of whom it is believed were muleteers;[106] however, it is thought that these men were probably executed after the end of the war. Unfortunately details about these muleteers, their victims and their crimes have not been unearthed, and in fact it is possible that one man on this list might have been shot whilst serving in a Black Sea Labour Company.

In July 1917 another shooting took place in 26 Division, again involving a Scottish regiment, as well as the same fateful attack that had taken place in May. **Lance-Sergeant Harry Ashton** was a Lancashire lad who had enlisted in the Cameronian (Scottish Rifles) in September 1914. He had served on the Western Front twice, and been wounded on both occasions.[107]

In the attack of 8 May 1917, the situation with regard to the battalion's plight at first remained a mystery, until 2.15 am the following morning when the battalion diarist recorded, *'A great deal of confusion was also occasioned by the dust and smoke of the bombardment.'* And he recorded the Cameronians' losses as 13 killed, 102 missing and 134 wounded.[108] During the attack, Lance-Sergeant Ashton and another NCO had both missed the battalion's departure into action.

In the case of the sergeant it was later stated that he had made no attempt to re-join his unit — and in fact had deliberately avoided doing so.[109] Although Ashton had an admirable record and denied the charge, he was shot on 8 July.

On 28 July the sergeant's picture appeared in his home town's newspaper — although the details given showed that his mother has been deceived as to the real cause of her son's demise. During the war, Ashton was the only NCO from the Cameronians to be executed, Lance-Sergeant Harry Ashton but together with the other unfortunate individuals he was commemorated in the official casualty records for his regiment. As usual no cause of death was given.[110]

On 27 July 1917 another solder was executed in German East Africa. The offender was **Private Samuel Sabongidda** who was serving in 3 Nigerian Regiment. The exact nature of his crime is unknown, however Sabongidda was shot for an offence involving violence.[111] The condemned man had served in the army since September 1914, and was the only soldier from his regiment to be executed during the war.[112]

In the second half of 1917 two other soldiers were also shot for offences of violence. Both men were from the same regiment whose battalions were serving in the Middle East. The unit concerned was the British West Indies Regiment, and the first offender was a particularly rebellious and vicious individual.

 **Private Hubert Clarke** of the second battalion was serving a prison sentence in the Kantara Field Punishment Compound (by the Suez Canal) when a disturbance from within caused the intervention of the Military Police. As a police sergeant approached Clarke the private punched the NCO in the face before recommencing his assault with a three-foot-long piece of wood. When the club struck the sergeant in the face it knocked him to the ground; however, a lance-corporal came to his colleague's assistance, whereupon the attacker drew a razor. Undaunted the lance-corporal advanced on the prisoner who lashed out with his razor viciously, wounding the junior NCO in the stomach.[113]

The RAMC doctor on duty that day recalled that the lance-corporal — a heavily built individual — had a ten inch cut across his abdomen, and that the man's intestines were having to be prevented from protruding from the wound.[114] The doctor incorrectly recalled that the injured man was a sergeant, but he continued to give a detailed account of the events that followed.

'*Well, we sewed him up and he recovered. But at the court martial the negro was condemned to be shot at dawn* [Private Clarke was sentenced to death after being found guilty on two charges of striking his superior officer]*; and I found it was part of my unpleasant duty as a field officer to be present with the Assistant Provost-Marshal to certify death.*

'*The day of execution came. I can remember every detail of that morning still. Daylight comes rapidly in the tropics. At a quarter to six it is quite dark. At six the sun rises. At six-fifteen it is clear morning. We started in the darkness to drive across the desert sand in a battered old Ford — my quartermaster in front with the driver, the Baptist chaplain and myself behind. None of us spoke during the entire journey. The APM, the prisoner and the firing-party had marched in front to the place of execution, the mud wall of a disued rifle range alongside the Suez Canal. We got there just before dawn. The prisoner was standing close to the wall, a magnificent bronze Hercules, clad in a pair of khaki shorts only, his hands fastened behind his back. The firing-party, men of a Labour Battalion, stood huddled*

230

some twenty feet away. *Their faces looked white and drawn in the gathering light. I glanced at my little Quartermaster. His face, usually ruddy, was blanched. I turned towards the APM. He was nervously fingering his revolver. We were all in a state of extreme tension. Then I looked at the prisoner. The light was now coming up from the East. It glistened on his bronze skin and the white of his eyes, and I was startled to see there was a smile of beatitude on his face. His white teeth sparkled. He was completely at ease.*

'The Baptist chaplain went over to him. *They conversed in quiet tones for a minute. The man's eyes seemed to glow with an inner joy.*

'The APM standing beside me stamped his feet, for the dawn was chilly and he was getting more and more edgy. Still the prisoner and the padre talked quietly. I watched them, fascinated. At length the chaplain stepped back. He nodded towards our group. "That means he's ready," I thought. Someone was whispering behind me to the APM. It was the NCO in charge of the firing-party. The APM turned to me.

"He says, Major, that the men are afraid they mayn't kill him at the first volley, and they'd like you to mark where his heart is. Do you mind?" Evidently my Quartermaster had been told of this beforehand, for he straight away produced a roll of sticking-plaster and a pair of scissors. Together, then we walked up to the prisoner, and with strips of plaster I marked a star the size of my palm on his chest. It stood out clearly on his dark skin in the brightening morn. Once I looked up at the man. His soft brown eyes were gazing at me, soft as a gazelle's. Finally I stepped back, and someone produced a handkerchief to blindfold him.

"'May I die with my eyes open?" he said in the educated tones so surprising to those who do not know the West Indian negro. "Better not," I said gently. "All right, Doctor," he answered submissively; and they slipped it over.

'A few seconds later the quick word of command rang out; then came the volley; and then the great, beautiful body crumpled and suddenly fell. It didn't seem real, somehow. The APM and I ran forward. "Is he dead?" he gasped, drawing his revolver, for his gruesome duty was to finish the job if the rifle fire had failed, and he was not as accustomed to death as I. We turned the body over, and I looked at the chest with the holes in it. "Quite dead," I answered.

'The chaplain and I got into the Ford again. The quartermaster slipped in beside the driver, and we drove back to camp. It was now broad daylight. No one spoke until we passed a gang of coolies putting up wire fencing. That broke the spell. I turned to the padre. "The courage of the man! I was surprised," I said. The padre looked at me. "You needn't have been. I have never known anyone so ready to meet his Maker," he answered quietly. And then it was all clear to me. The padre had been with him almost hourly during the previous week. He had repented of his sins, and *believed he had been forgiven. He was ready, therefore, to face his God, "fortified by the rites of Holy Church".*[115]

Towards the end of 1917 another soldier from the British West Indies Regiment was executed. **Private James Mitchell** was serving with 1 Battalion in Palestine and was shot for murder following an attempted sexual assault. The soldier had somewhat crudely asked a young married Arab girl to have sex with him, and when rejected tried to force himself upon her. When the husband came to his wife's assistance Mitchell shot him before making off. However, the offender was later detained following a massive identification parade.[116] The private was convicted of murder on 15 December and shot by his battalion one week later.[117]

**NOTES**

1 WO93/49, Summary of First World War capital court martial cases.
2 WO95/2422, Battalion War Diary.
3 *Soldiers Died in the Great War*, part 31.
4 William Allison & John Fairley, *The Monocled Mutineer.*
5 Edwin T Woodhall, *Detective & Secret Service Days.*
6 Gill & Dallas, *The Unknown Army.*
7 Anthony Babington, *For the Sake of Example.*
8 Ibid.
9 WO97/5895, Soldier's Documents 1900-1913.
10 Anthony Babington, op cit.
11 WO329/697, *British War & Victory Medal Roll.*
12 Ibid.
13 WO93/49, op cit.

14 Canadian Army Service Records.
15 Desmond Morton, 'The Supreme Penalty: Canadian Deaths by Firing Squad in the First World War', *Queen's Quarterly* 1972, Volume 79.
16 WO95/3842, War Diary of the Adjutant-General, 3 Canadian Division. The entry has been partly 'weeded' and the original page removed into a file of such extractions − WO154/113.
17 Anthony Babington, op cit.
18 WO95/4040, War Diary, Marseilles Base.
19 Anthony Babington, op cit.
20 The account here has been compiled from details in WO95/4040, op cit, and the description of events given by Anthony Babington.
21 Op cit. Anthony Babington, op cit.
22 WO97/4245, Soldier's Documents 1900-1913.
23 Canadian Expeditionary Force, Nominal Roll of Officers, Non-Commissioned Officers and Men.
24 Desmond Morton, op cit.
25 Canon F G Scott, *The Great War as I saw It.*
26 The events are described in Chapter 22 of Scott's book. Chapter 21 deals with everyday life during August and September 1917, and Chapter 23 tells of visits to Rome and Passchendaele in October and November of 1917. Hence the deduction that William Alexander was the victim − as he was the only soldier to be executed in 1 Canadian Division during 1917.
27 Guy Empey, *Over the Top.*
28 WO95/3731, War Diary of Adjutant-General, 1 Canadian Division. An abortive attempt at 'weeding' details of the case caused the removal of the entry relating to the promulgation (to the 'closed' class WO154/105) but left the record of the execution itself.
29 WO329/1, Index to the *Great War Medal Rolls.*
30 WO329/1494, *British War & Victory Medal Roll.*
31 WO93/49, op cit.
32 *The Times*, 15 December 1917.
33 Anthony Babington, op cit.
34 WO95/2829, Battalion War Diary.
35 WO93/49, op cit.
36 *Soldiers Died in the Great War*, part 10.
37 MH106/2161, Soldier's Medical History Records from the Great War.
38 *The Times*, op cit.
39 WO93/49, op cit.
40 Records of the General Register Office, London.
41 Page from the company crime book − private collection of Peter T Scott.
42 Anthony Babington, op cit.
43 WO93/49, op cit.
44 Private John Nicholson of 2 Battalion, Essex Regiment, is buried in Poelcappelle British Cemetery.
45 Anthony Babington in his book, *For the Sake of Example*, states that the Irishman was 27; however, information volunteered to the Commonwealth War Graves Commission in post-war years, gives his age as 30.
46 Anthony Babington, op cit.
47 WO93/49, op cit.
48 Anthony Babington, op cit.
49 Ibid.
50 WO95/2502, War Diary, 1 Royal Irish Fusiliers.
51 WO329/1, op cit.
52 WO93/49, op cit.
53 Anthony Babington, op cit.
54 Ibid.
55 WO95/2467, Battalion War Diary.
56 WO95/3137, Battalion War Diary.
57 Brigadier Sir J E Edmonds, *Military Operations France & Belgium, 1917*, Volume 2.
58 WO95/3137, op cit.
59 The battalion war diary, ibid., contains this account.
60 Brigadier Sir J E Edmonds, op cit.

61 WO329/2751, *1915 Star Medal Roll*, Sherwood Foresters.
62 Brigadier Sir J E Edmonds, op cit.
63 WO93/49, op cit.
64 WO329/1, op cit.
65 Henry Lawton, *Vignettes of the Western Front.*
66 WO95/2647, War Diary of the Adjutant-General, 42 Division.
67 WO95/2051, Battalion War Diary.
68 Ibid.
69 WO93/49, op cit.
70 Anthony Babington, op cit.
71 WO329/2695, *1915 Star Medal Roll.*
72 WO93/49, op cit.
73 WO95/2562, Battalion War Diary.
74 Memoirs of G S Chaplin, Imperial War Museum, reference 74/100/1 & PP/MCR/63.
75 WO95/2050, The battalion war diary records the event.
76 WO93/49, op cit.
77 Ibid.
78 WO95/1362, Battalion War Diary.
79 WO93/49, op cit.
80 Anthony Babington, op cit.
81 Sidney M J Suffield, 'One Man's War', *Stand To!*, *(Journal of the Western Front Association)*, Winter 1987, number 21.
82 *The Times*, 19 December 1917.
83 War Cabinet Meeting no.279, (21 November 1917.) WO32/4675.
84 WO32/4675, op cit.
85 WO93/49, op cit.
86 Anthony Babington, op cit.
87 Ibid.
88 WO93/49, op cit.
89 Anthony Babington, op cit.
90 Dr A J Peacock, *Gunfire*, No.1.
91 Ibid.
92 Anthony Babington, op cit.
93 Ibid.
94 Ex-Sergeant Crutchlow DCM, *Tale of an Old Soldier.*
95 WO95/5155, War Diary of 38 Brigade HQ.
96 Anthony Babington, op cit.
97 WO93/49, op cit.
98 Ibid.
99 WO95/5321, Battalion War Diary.
100 Records of Black Watch Regimental Museum.
101 Anthony Babington, op cit.
102 WO329/2741, *1915 Star Medal Roll.*
103 WO93/49, op cit.
104 WO95/4867, War Diary of 79 Field Ambulance, RAMC.
105 WO329/2357, Medal Roll of the Macedonian Mule Corps.
106 WO93/49, op cit.
107 *The Blackburn Times*, 28 July 1917.
108 WO95/4870, Battalion War Diary.
109 Anthony Babington, op cit.
110 *Soldiers Died in the Great War*, part 31.
111 WO93/49, op cit.
112 WO329/2333, Nigerian Regiment Medal Roll.
113 WO93/49, op cit.
114 J Johnston Abraham, *Surgeon's Journey.*
115 Ibid. The execution took place on 11 August 1917.
116 Anthony Babington, op cit.
117 WO95/4410, Battalion War Diary.

# Chapter Eight

## *With our backs to the wall.*

Following a trend started in December 1917, the opening months of the new year saw very few capital sentences put into effect. In fact, during January only one soldier was shot. He was an Irishman serving on the Western Front with the Royal Inniskilling Fusiliers, having landed in August 1914. However, **Private John Seymour's** subsequent service had not all been creditable, and the soldier was already serving under a suspended sentence of death.[1] He was shot near Ypres on 24 January.

The majority of soldiers who faced a firing squad during 1918 were already serving under suspended sentences for previous offences; and one such was shot on 9 February. **Private Wilfred Clarke,** a volunteer with the Durham Light Infantry, had deserted during the previous winter. The private was serving with 2 Battalion, a unit to which he had been posted no less than three times.[2] The story of his crime was a familiar one. Two hours prior to departure for the trenches, he had made off, only to be arrested two months later in Calais.[3] By the time that the notification of the soldier's death reached the Durham's Record Office, the War Cabinet's new 'cover-up' form — for just such cases — was available. A copy was sent to the soldier's parents in South Shields, and at the beginning of March the local paper referred to Clarke's death. The journal reported that the 23 year old had died on active service in France, and that he was deeply mourned by father, mother, sisters and brothers.[4]

The case of a 26 year old soldier shot during February would suggest that military expediency received more consideration than any aspect of justice or fair play. The victim was variously described as a vagrant, a lunatic, mentally deficient as well as criminally degenerate.[5] Surprisingly perhaps, the man was married.

**Private Thomas Hopkins** was in 1/8 Lancashire Fusiliers, and while serving on the Western Front had spent the majority of his time wearing handcuffs for a variety of crimes.

In September 1917 Hopkins absconded from the trenches during a gas attack and remained absent for eight days, and following his trial most of the reviewing officers would seem to have been in favour of carrying out the sentence. The delay in shooting Hopkins was only caused by the requirement to have the man examined by a specialist doctor.[6] In due course the doctor's damning report virtually amounted to a signature authorising the shooting. Hopkins, a one time petty criminal and 'mental defective', was executed on 13 February. The crime for which the soldier had been sentenced to death was for leaving his post. For the remander of the war all other executions on the Western Front — that did not involve murder — were for desertion. The Index to the *Great War Medals Roll* (WO329/1.) states that Hopkins' medals were forfeited under article 1236B of the Royal Pay Warrant as amended by Army Order no.298 of 1920.

Another soldier shot shortly after Private Hopkins was also described as being mentally weak. The man in question, a conscript, had been executed on the day that his battalion was disbanded. Of course, the execution had no bearing on the disbandment of the unit but in the aftermath of the event, questions were asked in the House. The soldier, identified only as Private E.H. No.46127, West Yorkshire Regiment, had been shot on 17 February. Had the War Cabinet's directive to use the newly printed form for notifying such a death been followed, then the issue would never have arisen. As it turned out, Number 2 Infantry Record Office at York had blundered by following the old established practice, and as a result the soldier's mother had had her allowance cut. In the ensuing Parliamentary debate, comment was made that the man was regarded by many to be mentally weak, and the House questioned the soldier's mental condition at the time. An assurance was given, however, that both before and after his trial the 26 year old had been specially examined. One further revelation was that the soldier's whereabouts as a deserter had been traced with the assistance of his mother. Whilst at liberty **Private Ernest Horler** had written to his mother in Yeovil, who in turn had passed the envelopes to the military authorities. As a consequence the soldier was traced. [7] It is not difficult to imagine the grief felt by the dead soldier's relative.

The last New Zealander to be shot during the war was a private in 1 Battalion, Otago Regiment, and was probably well educated, as he was an engineer by trade.

**Private Victor Spencer** enlisted in April 1915, and did brief service in the Dardanelles before being sent to the Western Front. His service career then took a turn for the worse when he received a short sentence of field punishment for missing a defaulters' roll call. A month later in July, Spencer was admitted to hospital with shellshock after having been blown-up by a type of German trench mortar called a *minenwerfer*.[8] However, on the day of his discharge, two-and-half- weeks later, he went missing. A fortnight's absence resulted in an 18 month prison sentence, which surprisingly was put into effect. He served only half his sentence before being released and returned to his battalion on 19 June 1917.[9]

Accounts differ concerning the date on which the soldier went absent for the last time, but in any event he had gone missing during August 1917, at a time when his battalion was supplying wiring parties. For over four months Spencer evaded the military authorities, until 2 January 1918 when the military police caught him, still in bed, in a small house by the railway at Morebeque in a rear area. It would seem likely that French civilians had been harbouring the absentee, as such persons were also resident at the place of capture.[10] The Reverend Hoani Parata attended the 23 year old during his last moments, and recalled that the deserter met his end bravely.[11] Spencer was shot on 24 February at Dickebusch, in the Ypres Salient.

Over sixty years after the shooting information was published that Private Spencer had deserted because he was serving in a Pakeha battalion, whereas he had been brought up with Maoris and wished to serve with them. The suggestion was also made that the soldier was illiterate and hardly knew right from wrong; however, this disclosure would seem to be at odds with his declared pre-war trade in engineering. The account recalled that an attempt had been made to stop the execution, and this was undoubtedly true.[12] Further details stated that a senior New Zealand Army officer, Major James Hargest, had tried to halt the execution because he regarded the punishment as monstrous. However, the attempt was unsuccessful, and following the shooting a wave of revulsion spread throughout the dead man's battalion.[13]

At the beginning of March two more Canadians were shot, the first to die being a 22 year old native of Ontario who was shot on 2 March. **Private Fairburn** was buried near Vimy Ridge, where the headstone on his grave now carries the inscription, *'Sleeping in our father's arms'*. His fellow countryman was shot four days later in the last execution of the war to take place in the abbatoir at Mazingarbe. **Private Welsh** was already serving under a suspended sentence of death for desertion, when prior to the Passchendaele attack he had absconded. However, ten weeks later when he was arrested, the objective had been taken. Like the previous case of the New Zealand soldier, Welch was arrested in a private house − on this occasion in Poperinghe.[14]

The first case of murder during 1918 was, like previous cases, typical in terms of the irrational behaviour displayed by the killer. 28 year old **Lance-Sergeant Wickings** had served on the Western Front for three years, and at the time of his offence was serving with 9 Rifle Brigade. His crime, the murder of a prostitute in Le Havre, would seem to have had little motive, unless either the soldier did not want to pay, or he had killed his victim before searching her property for money.

Whatever his reason, he did not disclose it, maintaining his innocence at the trial. However, the noise that had emanated from her room prior to her killing, together with scratch marks on the suspect's face, were consistent with the cause of death – strangulation.[15] Sergeant Wickings was shot at Le Havre on 7 March.

The ranks of the British Expeditionary Force were filled with as diverse a selection of nationalities as could be found, but in March 1918 a French-Canadian serving in a Scottish regiment, was shot by firing squad. **Private Hector Dalande** had enlisted early in the war and was posted to the Western Front just before the end of 1915.[16] For over a year the soldier served with 8 Seaforth Highlanders with distinction and credit.

However, in early 1917 he committed the first of a number of offences, going absent without leave. His offence resulted in a three year sentence, but in the following August Dalande was invalided with shellshock. For two months he received treatment, but later that year when back with his battalion, he again went absent, compounding his crime by escaping after his arrest. Private Dalande was finally arrested in January 1918 having discarded his army uniform.[17] His execution took place at Arras on 9 March, and an eyewitness later recalled the event.

'My battalion was out of the line when the senior chaplain called at my billet one evening to tell me that a man, belonging to another brigade of my division, was to be shot next morning for desertion, and that he had asked for a priest . . . I found the condemned man in an improvised cell at the APM's quarters. He was sitting in a corner, his head bowed on his manacled hands, holding a wretched rag or handkerchief to his eyes. He was sobbing brokenly, and I confess that the words which had vaguely occurred to me as I hurried along, died upon my lips . . .

'English was only his second language; and rightly or wrongly, he believed that his comrades laughed at and made a butt of him, chiefly on account of his noticeably foreign accent and unfamiliar ways. He seemed to be rather exceptionally sensitive, and his dread of incurring further ridicule by making mistakes in speech, made him awkward and unready in repartee . . .

'[Serving in the army he was] . . . soon profoundly unhappy, his one desire, which rapidly became an obsession, was to join the French Army, in which he believed that he would find himself at home. There were insuperable technical difficulties in the way of a legalised transfer, so he madly resolved to take the matter into his own hands . . .

'A few minutes more and the door opened to admit the APM, accompanied by a medical officer, the prisoner's own company sergeant-major, and three military policemen. The prisoner came at once to attention and saluted the officers. The sergeant-major then formally identified him; the policeman tied a bandage over his eyes and fastened his hands behind him, and the medical *officer pinned a small square of lint over his heart, to serve as mark for the firing party . . . I kept my hand upon his arm as we walked, and I can vouch for it that he never faltered nor trembled . . . At a sign from the APM, the firing party, which up till then had stood with their backs to the condemned man, faced about to him. At a second sign they took aim, at a third they fired: and the bound figure crumpled and slid down as far as the ropes would let him go . . . I ask no better than that I may meet my death, when I must, as gallantly as did that Deserter.'*[18]

Private Dalande's wife had an inscription put upon her husband's grave. It reads:

*'The Lord looked upon him and said go in this thy might'.*

The percentage of Dominion soldiers executed in the early part of 1918 was higher than at any other time during the war. No apparent reason explains why this was so, but in mid-March two more Canadians were shot.

**Private Lodge** was serving with 19 Battalion CEF, when on 3 November 1917 he asked permission to 'fall out'. At the time his unit were on their way towards Passchendaele. The requested was refused, but nevertheless he fell out and made off. Over a month later Lodge was arrested in Boulogne whilst masquerading as a corporal in the Red Cross. After eight days in custody the resourceful Canadian escaped, only to be arrested in the new year whilst stowed away in the forward part of a ship that was about to sail. Indicating his desperate plight, four days later Lodge jumped from a train to escape his escort. Predictably he was arrested once again in Boulogne. On the day that Private Lodge suffered the extreme penalty, on hand to witness the event was the assistant provost-marshal and the deputy assistant adjutant-general of 2 Canadian Division.[19] Perhaps they were concerned that once again the nimble soldier might try to escape.

The second victim serving with the CEF was in fact an American who had joined the Canadian Army immediately after hostilities had been declared. The soldier had been born at New Bedford, Massachusetts, USA. In the forces he had followed his pre-war occupation as a cook, and had been posted to No.1 Canadian General Hospital which in September 1914 was based at Quebec. The following month **Private Arthur Dagesse** sailed for England, and in March of the following year he twice suffered loss of pay together with detention for being absent. Whilst still serving at No.1 General Hospital with the Canadian Army Medical Corps Dagesse went to France.[20]

For most of his active service career Private Dagesse alternated between going absent and receiving treatment for venereal disease.[21] Undoubtedly the two were connected, and after five months in France

239

an aggressive infection set in. Ironically the cook was admitted to his own hospital unit, but recurring problems over the month caused him to be transferred for specialist treatment, first in Le Havre and then in Etaples. At the end of 1915, and again in February 1916 he was in trouble for absence, although the penalties were comparatively light as he was serving on the coast and not at the front. During March Dagesse returned to the hospital in Le Havre as a syphilitic infection with complications again troubled the soldier. During his hospitalisation Private Dagesse only received half-pay.

Assuming that the soldier's venereal problem was one of re-infection, rather than a recurring problem, then when Private Dagesse was posted to a Stationary Hospital in Paris, it was almost as if the military were tempting the man to commit a self-inflicted wound. However, perhaps past treatment, which would have been unpleasant in the extreme, had taught him a lesson, for in spite of three absences in the summer of 1916 while stationed in Paris, no further infection was contracted.

The reason for Private Dagesse's eventual transfer to a fighting unit is not known. It might have been a disciplinary measure, or it may just have been a 'combing out' operation, designed to produce more fighting men. But for whatever reason, Dagesse was transferred to the French-speaking 22 Battalion – at the end of October 1916. Surprisingly, for over six months the soldier would seem to have behaved, until May 1917, when he went absent for a final time. At the time of going absent Dagesse had been under arrest, and his battalion had just been warned for the trenches.[22]

Confirming his affinity for Paris life, the soldier was arrested in the capital five months later, while masquerading as a sergeant of the RAMC. Again for a reason that is not clear Arthur Dagesse spent over four months in custody before being brought to trial on 21 February 1918.[23] He had already been tried less than a month previously, on 28 January 1918, although the offence is not known. The 32 year old was shot on 15 March, just two days after the execution of his comrade, who was also serving in a unit of the Second Canadian Division.

On 21 March 1918, the day that the Germans launched their spring offensive, a doctor in the Royal Army Medical Corps was tried by General Court Martial. His offence is unknown, but the matter must have been serious, because when the captain was found guilty he was dismissed from the service, and later his medal entitlement was refused.[24]

Ludendorff's ambitious offensive was launched on a 50 mile battlefront which then increased on subsequent days. The Germans had been lucky on the opening day of the attack, as fog had rendered them considerable assistance in obscuring their advancing troops. The main thrust of the Germans armies fell against the British Fifth Army and in the aftermath the commander, General Sir Hubert Gough, was dismissed. The removal was ordered on instructions from the government, although it was soon acknowledged that Gough had been a scapegoat.

By the end of April the Germans had made enormous territorial gains; and although it is acknowledged that the establishments of the British units were considerably under strength at the time, when the official history of the war came to be written, it would seem that the seriousness of the situation in 1918 was played down. Brigadier Sir J E Edmonds (the official historian) made the somewhat puzzling comment that the British Army was untrained in retreat, and he continued, *'The splendid young manhood which filled the ranks was never beaten, never demoralised by retreat.'*[25] To quote a modern day expression the historian was being somewhat economical with the truth, as in fact contingency plans had been drawn-up for the evacuation of the Western Front − over twenty years before the realities of 'Dunkirk'.

After the war at least two officers described desperate measures that they had taken during the retreat. Brigadier-General F P Crozier recorded that he had ordered rifle and machine gun fire to be opened on the fleeing Portuguese troops. And he also recounted how he personally had shot, with his own revolver, a young British officer who was running away from the enemy.[26] Effective though such a shooting might have been in stemming the rout, such actions were not lawful. The second such incident was recalled by Lieutenant-Colonel G Seton-Hutchinson. On 13 April, at a location very near to the scene of Crozier's summary execution, Hutchinson ordered machine guns to be turned on British soldiers who were throwing down their weapons and surrendering to the enemy. The colonel maintained that of the party of 40 who held up their hands, 38 were shot down.[27]

In the midst of the German onslaught only two British soldiers were executed. They were both from the north of England, one from Yorkshire and the other from Lancashire. The Yorkshireman was a 27 year old conscript who, during his brief time of the Western Front, had already been sentenced to death in the previous December.[28] **Private Henry Hughes** was serving in a Territorial battalion, 1/5 Yorks & Lancs, part of 49 (West Riding) Division, which to date had had no man executed. Hughes was shot on 10 April, and significantly he was the third native of Sheffield to face a firing squad.

The Lancastrian shot that month was a volunteer, and discrepancies concerning his age suggest that he might have advanced his true age in order to enlist in 1914. **Private Albert Holmes** had seen considerable service and had been wounded, but additionally he had been convicted of two offences of desertion.[29] However, a repeat offence committed shortly after his sentence of death had been suspended, proved to be his undoing.[30] The 22 year old married man from 8 Royal Lancaster Regiment was shot on 22 April.

On the day of Private Holmes' execution the House of Commons was debating the annual Army Act, and in order to ease the bill's passage a concession was made. Henceforth, it was decided, after a conviction where a sentence of death was imposed, then the penalty would be made known to the prisoner – at the time. In order to facilitate this a special form was drawn up – Army Form W3996. Included in the wording was an entry indicating whether or not mercy had been recommended, and if so on what grounds. Also included was a declaration to the effect that the sentence was subject to confirmation.[31] The new procedure was introduced in May 1918, but did not always find favour with the military, and in at least one case was the cause of a tragedy.

The second case of murder during 1918 is interesting mainly because of its similarities with the first murder of the war. Once again, out-of-character and irrational behaviour were in evidence – the offender in this case being a 39 year old private in 2 Welsh Regiment. Just like his battalion predecessor in 1915, he had shot and killed his sergeant,  and similarly **Private James Skone** had claimed to be drunk. The incident had occurred on 13 April in the trenches at Gorre, near Béthune, when the Welshman had been placed under arrest for a brief absence – with the result that he killed Lance-Sergeant Edwin Williams who was just a few years his senior. The crime had no other motive, and Skone had formerly been of good character.[32]

The battalion, 2 Welsh, the rank of the victim and the circumstances were the same as the first murder of the war – that had been committed in 1915. Private James Skone was the fifth member of his battalion to die in this inglorious way during the war. His division, the 1st, showed a curious pattern of executions. Following the execution of the two murderers from 2 Welsh in February 1915, a stream of seventeen further shootings had paused when the Somme offensive opened in July 1916. The execution of Private Skone, nearly two years later, was the final execution in 1 Division. Skone, a married man from Pembroke, was shot in the mining village of Hersin, France, on 10 May.

 The only NCO shot for a military offence during 1918, was also the last of the pre-war Regular soldiers to face a firing squad. Long service had taken its toll, both in terms of wounds and the commission of offences. Had **Corporal James Reid** not escaped from arrest during October 1917, only to remain absent for four months, then once again his former good service might have saved him. Unfortunately, the 26 year old corporal from 6 Cameron Highlanders, was shot near Arras on 11 May. (The War Office recorded Corporal Reid's age as 30.) His grave now carries the inscription, *'Gone but not forgotten'*.

The thirty-first and last soldier to be unrepresented at his trial before being executed was tried on 26 April 1918. 24 year old **Private Frank O'Neill** was also the last soldier to be executed in 8 Division. It comes as no surprise, however, to hear that the soldier's past offences were of a serious nature. Two convictions were recorded against the private, one for desertion and the other for violence. O'Neill had absconded from his battalion, 1 Sherwood Foresters, whilst his section was digging trenches, and when arrested four days later was wearing civilian clothing.[33] Although his previous sentences had been comparatively lenient − two years, and then 18 months − it was decided to confirm a sentence of death for O'Neill's third offence.

A doctor from the Royal Army Medical Corps later recorded in his diary details of an execution at which he had officiated. Captain M S Esler had originally served in Salonika in 1915, but in early 1918 he joined a field ambulance in 8 Division, and in April of that year was transferred to 2 Middlesex.[34] It has been assumed that as no other death sentences were carried out in this division during 1918, then the execution that Captain Esler recorded must have been that of Private O'Neill. The doctor recalled that he had offered the condemned man half a pint of brandy, in order that the soldier might render himself oblivious to events. The soldier refused, and consequently the dawn ritual proceeded in sobriety.[35] The shooting took place at the remote village of Hermonville on 16 May.

Another volunteer shot that month was also serving in a Regular Army division. **Private Robert Simmers** had joined the Royal Scots and was attached to the second battalion, part of 3 Division. The 25 year old was shot on 19 May, becoming the twenty-third victim of the firing squad in this the bloodiest of all the army's divisions, as far as death sentences were concerned.

Two days later a Canadian soldier of a similar age was shot, and it is suggested that the former labourer might not have been too bright. When the man enlisted, either he did not know how old he was, or he did not know his correct date of birth. Army records of the soldier's stated age and his date of birth do not tally. **Private Leopold Delisle**, a native of Montreal, had enlisted in April 1915 and sailed for England the following month. Shortly after his arrival in the UK a drunken spree coupled with absence and insubordination resulted in his detention and loss of pay. Later that month, in addition to a fortnight's detention, Delisle again had his pay docked, this time to as little at 10 per cent, for refusing to obey orders.

At the beginning of September 1915 Delisle was again fined for drunkenness, as well as for being absent from parade. Any further truancy was soon curtailed when the soldier was posted to France – just before the Battle of Loos. However, the young offender soon incurred the wrath of the commanding officer of 22 Battalion CEF, who on three occasions in quick succession had to deal with matters of insubordination, absence from parade and refusing to parade. The latter offence had occurred early in 1916, when the private received a sentence of 28 days' field punishment no.1 for his defiance.

However, the punishment did not deter the Canadian, and soon afterwards he was in trouble for striking a superior officer. Although the offence was a capital crime, Delisle escaped with a sentence of one year's imprisonment with hard labour, which was immediately put into effect. The punishment was served in full, and on 22 March 1917 Private Delisle was released from No.3 Military Prison at Le Havre and returned to his unit.

The next entry on the soldier's record states that at the beginning of September the private was admitted to a field ambulance suffering from convulsions.[36] It is a matter for speculation whether the soldier was truly ill or feigning, but the fact that Delisle was discharged the next day tends to suggest that he could have been malingering. Shortly afterwards the village of Passchendaele was assaulted, and in the absence of evidence to the contrary it must be assumed that for the following six months the soldier behaved.

On 29 March 1918 Private Delisle absconded until arrested eight days later. The crime proved fatal, as at the beginning of May he was tried for desertion and sentenced to death. On 20 May the deputy assistant adjutant-general together with the assistant provost-marshal of 2 Canadian Division, called at the advanced HQ of the Military Police in connection with the execution; and at 4 pm the sentence was promulgated to the prisoner.[37] Just over twelve hours later Private Delisle was shot.

On 17 April a third case of murder in 1918 occurred. Yet again the victim was serving in the same unit as the murderer, and on this occasion the deceased was a second-lieutenant. Once again the killing was irrational, and no motive has been disclosed. During a rifle  inspection at Senlis on the afternoon of the day in question, **Sapper Bell** shot Second Lieutenant Wynell Lloyd. Immediately the offender was place under arrest and taken into custody at Contay. The next day a Court of Inquiry sat to consider the shooting, whilst in the afternoon Lloyd was buried. The findings suggested murder, and the next day a summary of evidence was taken. Sapper Bell, of 123 Field Company, Royal Engineers, stood trial at Toutencourt on 4 May.

In the middle of May the penalty was confirmed, and Sapper Bell, who had been detained in the German PoW camp in Toutencourt, was shot on the 22nd of the month.[38]

On the same day an execution at Poperinghe took place. The victim was a 27 year old pre-war Territorial soldier who had served on the Western Front for three years.[39] The death of **Private John McFarlane** of 4 King's (Liverpool) Regiment is recorded in the official casualty rolls, and the cause of death is stated as 'died of wounds'.[40] Although McFarlane was the sixth and final soldier from the regiment to suffer the extreme penalty, only one other was recorded in the official returns − his cause of death being given simply as 'died'. (Private J Tongue − shot 8 January 1917.) Perhaps the recent War Cabinet directive concerning notification to the next-of-kin in the cases of death sentences was the reason that it was required that McFarlane's record be 'fudged'.

On 26 May 1918, a second soldier who claimed both a personal and family history of mental illness, was shot. The private, who had enlisted as a volunteer in the Argyll & Sutherland Highlanders before transferring to the Gordon Highlanders,[41] had shown himself to be an adept escaper. **Private Malcolm Richmond** had escaped from the guardroom at Etaples on 14 October 1917, only a short while after the Etaples disturbances had died down. A month later he had been arrested in nearby Boulogne, when he had given false particulars. Richmond proved a slippery customer and he escaped again in December, gaining yet another month's liberty. Early in 1918 he was again arrested in Boulogne after trying to bluff his way free. The matter did not end there however, as a fortnight later he escaped again, only to be arrested a day later masquerading as a driver in the Army Service Corps.[42] Yet another false story would suggest that Private Richmond was an inveterate liar, and Anthony Babington comments that enquiries made by the military failed to determine that the soldier had ever been an inmate of an asylum.[43] 22 year old Richmond, who was serving in 1/6 Gordon Highlanders, part of 51 Division, was shot near Arras. His death was the final execution in the Highland Division.

Another 22 year old from the north of England was shot the next day. **Private William Earl** was a conscript in 1/7 Lancashire Fusiliers, and he came from an area of Manchester that had already had a number of men executed. Strangely the road that the soldier lived in bore his family surname, and just one road away from

245

his home once lived another man who had been executed after deserting from another battalion of the Lancashire Fusiliers. (Private William Smith executed on 14 November 1917.) Earl had absented himself from his battalion during April 1918 when they were serving on the Somme.[44] His freedom was short-lived because he was captured, tried and shot before the end of May. The inscription on the headstone of Earl's grave reads: *'Those miss him most who loved him best'*.

The next soldier to face a firing squad had been serving in the same division as Private Earl – the forty second. The victim, **Private Thomas Brigham,** was also aged 22, but there the similarities ended. Brigham had enlisted in the Territorials prior to the war, and had landed in Egypt at the end of September 1914.[45] In May of the following year he had gone ashore at Gallipoli[46] where the youngster endured his first ordeal in battle.

In 1917 the division had transferred to the Western Front, where later in the year the soldier twice deserted. Brigham's sentences included a suspended sentence of death, yet in 1918 he repeated his crime.[47] He was shot near Warlincourt (an area adjoining the Arras front) at the beginning of June.

A few days later another soldier who had served at Gallipoli was executed. Londoner **Private William Spry** had enlisted in the Royal Fusiliers early in the war, before serving with 2 Battalion (part of 29 Division) in the Dardanelles. In the following year the Fusiliers had again been heavily engaged, when they were involved in the unsuccessful Somme attack on 1 July. Consequently by 1918 Spry had seen much action. Perhaps under more charitable circumstances, when he had started to go absent, inquiries might have been made into his mental state. Instead Spry was court martialled. At the time of his fatal crime the soldier was serving under two suspended sentences, including one of death. However, at stand-to, one day in May, the Londoner had absconded, only to be arrested four days later in Boulogne. Unfortunately he compounded his crime by lying.[48]

On 14 June, 2 Royal Fusiliers paraded in the village of Morbecque while the death sentence was carried out.[49] Unfortunately the 29 year old victim, a veteran of many battles, was also a married man with two dependent children.[50]

In the summer of 1918 a Canadian who had joined his country's army in 1916 was shot for desertion. **Private Stephen Fowles** was a volunteer, serving in 44 Battalion, part of the 4th Canadian Division.[51] The soldier's service had not been unblemished, because Fowles was serving under a suspended sentence of death for a previous offence of desertion.[52]

The Canadian was shot near the village of Villers behind Vimy Ridge, on 19 June.

In the last week of June an ex-machine gunner who had served with a number of different units was shot by his comrades. **Private Walter Dossett** from Sheffield may well have been a volunteer, although he did not serve abroad until 1916. Once on the Western Front the soldier served in three different Machine Gun Companies — 143rd, part of 48 Division, 118th, part of 39 Division, and 63rd, part of 21 Division — before being transferred to 1/4 battalion, Yorks & Lancs.[53]

Private Dossett had gone absent from his battalion during the Ludendorff Offensive in 1918 and had been sentenced to death. Following the usual procedure, arrangements were made to carry out the sentence. A soldier from 49 Division Ammunition Column recorded the events in his diary. Private Scullin had not been a witness to the execution, but the details he noted in his diary, based on the recollection of a colleague, are consistent with other accounts of such a scene.

An ambulance drew up and Private Dossett was brought out under escort. The prisoner was then taken to a nearby rifle range where he was bound in a chair. The blindfold was then applied and a piece of white paper pinned over Dossett's heart. The firing squad had been selected from machine gunners in 21 Division.[54] The events took place near Vlamertinghe in the Ypres Salient on 25 June, and Scullin speculated whether the soldier's next-of-kin would be notified that their relative was 'missing'. This was apparently not the case, because the grave was identified and an inscription recorded: '*Until we meet again*'.

In July 1917 a Routine Order had been published stating that by virtue of Section 176, subsection 9, Chinese Labourers were subject to the Army Act.[55] The section mentioned was, in fact, an all-embracing provision that declared that any person not subject to other provisions, and who was employed by the armed forces on active service, was subject to the Army Act.

The order continued that when the Chinese arrived in France, the principles of military law had been explained, together with procedures for lodging complaints. In describing the requirements to convene a court martial it was stated that the officer commanding the Chinese Labour Corps would carry out such tasks, and would appoint a president and two other officers to sit on the panel, including one member who must be an officer from the Corps.

The directive went on to state that Chinese were reluctant witnesses, as such testimony might endanger their own lives. It was suggested that Chinese witnesses should not take the oath but be sworn according to their native customs. It was added that the oath had no moral weight with a Chinaman. A further requirement was that officers from the Corps should be used as interpreters, the suggestion being that natives could not be relied on. One further direction was that in the event of a death sentence being carried out, the body should be returned to the man's company for burial. These instructions had been issued nearly a year in advance of such an event.

The authors have been unable to discover much, other than what Anthony Babington has revealed, about the Chinese labourers who were executed, although the judge would seem to have been mistaken about when the first execution took place. Babington states that two labourers were executed after murdering a French woman during a robbery at her estaminet.[56] As only one double execution involving the Chinese took place at the time, and these were the first such executions, then it must be assumed that **En Jung Wang** and **Ch'ing Shan Yang** were the two robbers and murderers. The two Chinamen were executed near Calais on 26 June, but only their numbers not their names appear on the tombstones.[57] The grave of Labourer Wang carries the inscription, '*Faithful unto death*', and that of Labourer Yang, '*A noble duty bravely done*'. However, these phrases were placed by the War Graves Commission, who were unaware of the dead men's activities. A total of four different phrases are repeated upon all the graves of Chinese labourers buried on the Western Front, or elsewhere; the inscriptions represent a gesture on behalf of a grateful employer.[58]

No executions took place in the first two weeks of July, but on the 18th the ritual recommenced. During a trial in the previous month the officer commanding 13 Middlesex had volunteered to the court the most damning of statements about the accused. The commander had stated that in the face of any danger, then **Private David Stevenson** could always be relied upon to run away. [59]

Whilst in a forward area Stevenson had absconded and remained absent for seven weeks. Details of the offence were posted at the Cyclist Base Depot at Rouen on 2 August 1918. Private Stevenson was next seen in a village in a back area, leading a pony. True to his commander's prediction, when sensing danger the soldier had run off, as the military officials approached. When questioned the private had lied, saying that he was working for the town major.[60] Unfortunately for Stevenson he was already under a suspended sentence for a previous offence of desertion.

During the review procedure Sir Henry Horne, commanding First Army, commented on the soldier's age. His opinion was that although the soldier was young – in fact 23 – so were a good number of other soldiers who were serving creditably.[61] The army commander was indeed correct on this point, although Private Stevenson would seem to have been a little younger than most men who were executed at this time.

During the first six months of 1918, the average age of those soldiers shot by firing squad was just under twenty-six-and-a-half years. This statistic is based on a sample embracing twenty of the twenty-six soldiers shot during the first six months of 1918.

The recollections of an ex-sergeant, who had been in charge of the firing squad who shot Private Stevenson, were published after the war.

'. . . It was a terrible scene, being that I knew him made it worse for me. The ten men were selected [for the firing squad] from a few details left out of the line. They were nervous wrecks themselves, and two of them had not the nerve to fire. Of course, they were tried [by court martial] but they were found to be medically unfit − their nerves had gone . . . The last words the lad said were: "What will my mother say?".'[62]

The grim ritual had taken place at 3.57 am on 18 July, in the mining village of Bully-Grenay, near Lens.

On the following day one of the most tragic cases of the war was concluded. The victim was a 27 year old volunteer from the north of England. **Private Arthur Briggs** had enlisted in the Notts & Derby Regiment early in 1915, and later that year he was sent to Gallipoli as a reinforcement to 9 Battalion.[63] Like so many of the soldiers who served on the Peninsula, he had fallen ill with dysentery, and in Briggs' case he had been returned home. Surprisingly he had not been sent to the Western Front until the end of 1916, and in departing had left his 18 year old girlfriend pregnant. Briggs' parents strongly opposed the couple getting married, but nevertheless the two remained determined to be wed.[64]

For over a year Private Briggs had to wait for UK leave, which was eventually granted in January 1918.[65] When the soldier returned he found his mother still in an uncompromising mood, but in spite of her threat to shun the couple, the marriage went ahead. Briggs had only been granted seven days' leave, and consequently became desperate to find a home for his wife and child. He maintained at his court martial that he had applied for an extension of leave, but in any event he had overstayed his furlough and taken his family to Scotland. In the summer of 1918 Briggs received an emotional letter from his mother informing him that both his father and brother had been killed in action. However, before he had had time to consider assistance, Briggs was arrested in Edinburgh, dressed in civilian clothing.[66]

Events followed their usual pattern, with the soldier being escorted back to France to face a court martial. Surprisingly in view of the fact that the soldier had no previous convictions, the sentence of death carried no recommendation to mercy. Once again however the uncompromising statement of a commanding officer decided the outcome, when Briggs' CO derided his value as a fighting soldier.[67] Private Briggs was shot on 19 July, in the mining village of Hersin. His grave carries the inscription from his wife, *'Gone but not forgotten'*.

In July a third Chinese Labourer was executed. **Cheng Shan Kung**  had murdered one of his fellow countrymen,[68] but no details, other than the date of his death on 23 July have emerged. [69] It would however be safe to assume from Cheng's service number that he had served on the Western Front for about a year.

At the end of July another soldier from 49 (West Riding) Division was shot. **Private George Ainley** was aged 20 and served in the King's Own Yorkshire Light Infantry at the time of his death, and judging by his young age it is presumed that he must have been a conscript. Ainley had been tried on 28 January 1918 for a self-inflicted wound. Yet his plight was to prove even more desperate, as before the end of the summer he had deserted no less than three times. Ainley's commanding officer submitted a written statement for the court's attention, and his comments must be considered fair. *'Private Ainley appears to be lacking a sense of responsibility, and his military character in consequence is not good'*.[70] The Yorkshireman (from Sheffield)[71] was shot behind the Ypres Salient on 30 July.

Two Scottish soldiers who were executed at the beginning of August could not have been returned to their unit for court martial without considerable difficulty. **Private Frederick Johnson** and **Private Harry McClair** had enlisted together in the Border Regiment. Towards the end of 1915 the two men had been posted to 2 Battalion on the Western Front.[72] The date when they absconded is not known, but when they were arrested in the summer of 1918, they must have been absent for some considerable time, because their division (the 7th) had been transferred to Italy at the end of 1917. Between their trial and confirmation of their sentences, the two middle-aged Scots were held at Caserne Pepinière in Paris. On 31 July they were enjoying a boisterous game of football with other soldiers when they were informed by a cavalry officer that they would be executed on the following day.

By arrangement with the French authorities, the pair were transferred to Vincennes, where the former had already executed 27 spies and traitors. Their final hours were critically recalled by a French officer who had witnessed many executions.

*'The two condemned had passed the night separately incarcerated in candlelit cells, preached at by a huge padre of alcoholic appearance.*

*'They were tied up from head to toe like sausages. A thick bandage hid*

*their faces. And, a horrible thing, on their chests a square of fabric was placed over their hearts . . . The unfortunate duo could not move. They had to be carried like two dummies on the open-backed lorry which bore them to the rifle range. It is impossible to articulate the sinister impression the sight of those two living parcels made on me.*

*'The padre mumbled some words and then went off to eat! Two six-strong platoons appeared, lined up with their backs to the firing posts. The guns lay on the ground.*

*'When the condemned had been attached, the men of the platoon who had not been able to see events, responding to a silent gesture, picked up their guns, abruptly turned about, aimed and opened fire.*

*'They then turned their backs on the bodies and the sergeant ordered "Quick march!"*

*'The men marched right past them, without inspecting their weapons, without turning a head.*

*'No military compliments, no parade, no music, no march past; a hideous death without drums or trumpets.'*[73]

## NOTES

1 WO93/49, Summary of First World War capital court martial cases.
2 WO329/1605, *British War & Victory Medal Roll*.
3 WO93/49, op cit.
4 *Shields Daily Gazette*, 1 March 1918.
5 Anthony Babington, *For the Sake of Example*.
6 Ibid.
7 *Hansard*, 17 April 1918, and *The Yeovil Leader*, 22 April 1918.
8 Christchurch Star, 8 October 1988.
9 New Zealand Army Service Records.
10 WO93/49, op cit.
11 *Christchurch Star*, 24 October 1987.
12 *New Zealand Listener*, 29 May 1982.
13 *The Christchurch Star*, 29 April 1987.
14 WO93/49, op cit.
15 Anthony Babington, op cit.
16 WO329/1, Index to the *Great War Medal Rolls*.
17 Anthony Babington, op cit.
18 R H J Steuart, *March Kind Comrade*.
19 WO95/3789, War Diary of the Adjutant-General, 2 Canadian Division.

20 Canadian Army Service Records.
21 Soldier's Medical Record.
22 WO93/49, op cit.
23 WO93/43, Nominal Roll of Canadian Soldiers' courts martial.
24 WO329/2284, *British War & Victory Medal Roll.*
25 Brigadier Sir J E Edmonds, Military Operations France & Belgium, 1918, Volume 1.
26 Brigadier-General F P Crozier, *The Men I Killed.*
27 Lieutenant-Colonel G Seton Hutchinson, *History and Memoir of the 33rd Battalion, Machine Gun Corps.*
28 WO93/49, op cit.
29 Ibid.
30 Anthony Babington, op cit.
31 WO32/3989, Records relating to the announcement of sentences of death in open court.
32 Anthony Babington, op cit.
33 WO93/49, op cit.
34 WO95/1703, War Diary of 24 Field Ambulance, RAMC.
35 Diary of Captain M S Esler, RAMC, Imperial War Museum, reference 74/102/1.
36 Canadian Army Service Records.
37 WO95,3789, op cit.
38 WO95/2547, War Diary of 123 Field Company, Royal Engineers.
39 WO329/1, op cit.
40 *Soldiers Died in the Great War,* part 13.
41 WO329/1, op cit.
42 WO93/49, op cit.
43 Anthony Babington, op cit.
44 WO95/2655, Battalion War Diary.
45 WO329/1, op cit.
46 WO329/2777, *1915 Star Medal Roll.*
47 WO93/49, op cit.
48 Ibid.
49 WO95/2301, Battalion War Diary.
50 Records of General Register Office, London.
51 Canadian Expeditionary Force, *Nominal Roll of Officers,* Non-Commissioned Officers and Men.
52 WO93/49, op cit.
53 WO329/1600, *British War & Victory Medal Roll.*
54 Diary of Private E Scullin, Royal Field Artillery, Imperial War Museum, reference PP/MCR/137.
55 WO95/184, War Diary of Adjutant-General First Army, has a copy of this order – No.1306.
56 Anthony Babington, op cit.
57 WO329/2375, Medal Roll of Chinese Labour Corps – states the names of all coolies.
58 Michael Summerskill, *China on the Western Front.*
59 Anthony Babington, op cit.
60 WO93/49, op cit.
61 Anthony Babington, op cit.
62 Ernest Thurtle, *Shootings at Dawn.*
63 Another soldier who had served at Gallipoli with 9 Sherwood Foresters, Private W Randle, was shot towards the end of 1916.
64 Anthony Babington, op cit.
65 WO93/49, op cit.
66 Ibid.
67 Anthony Babington, op cit.
68 Ibid.
69 WO93/49, op cit. & WO329/2379, Chinese Labour Corps Medal Roll.
70 WO93/49, op cit.
71 Records of the General Register Office, London.
72 WO329/1, op cit.
73 E Massard, *Les Espions à Paris.*

# Chapter Nine

*Lord, let us now thy servants depart in peace.*

The 8th of August 1918 was later described as General Ludendorff's 'Black Day'.[1] The tables were turned and henceforth the German armies fell back in retreat. On that day the fifth and last guardsman was executed. **Private Benjamin O'Connell,** who was serving in 1 Irish Guards, had already been convicted of two offences involving absence. Initially he had been sentenced to two years, and for a second offence ten years.[2] Following his further offence the 23 year old was shot at Bailleulmont.

On the following day a Chinese Labourer, **Chao Hsing I**, was shot near Calais for murder.[3] Quite why this sudden increase in labourers murdering one another should come about is unclear. The Chinamen were known to be keen gamblers,[4] and it is of course possible that gambling was the cause.

斩 鞠
瘁 盡

On 10 August a 25 year old soldier was shot, and he was almost certainly a conscript. Ernest Thurtle later stated that **Private William Scholes** was not a coward, and a braver man never went on active service;[5] nevertheless the northerner had not chosen to volunteer – although he could have. Consequently the testimony of Thurtle's informant must be treated with some scepticism, especially in view of the fact that Private Scholes was already serving under a suspended sentence of death for a previous offence of desertion.[6] The motive suggested for Scholes' repeated absences was that he was the sole support of his widowed mother, and as such went missing in protest at what he considered to be the small allowance paid to her.[7] Scholes was ultimately executed by a firing squad from his battalion – 2 South Wales Borderers – becoming the only conscript to face a firing squad in 29 Division. The inscription on Scholes' grave leaves an uncertainty about whether the soldier's mother learned of the true circumstances of her son's death. The epitaph reads, *'Nothing to us can ever repay the sacrifice he made that day'.*

Another conscript, shot the following day, also had an unenviable reputation. **Private John Swain** was serving in 5 Royal Berks under two suspended sentences. Nevertheless, after being warned for the trenches he absconded and was found the next day, several miles away hiding in a cornfield. As was so often the case the soldier gave a false name, although his attempted precaution of removing his regimental badges of identification proved counter-productive, as in fact it attracted attention.[8] Swain was shot on 11 August, and was buried in the small cemetery in the village of Montigny, where his grave is quite separate from those soldiers who died honourably.

The last Canadian soldier to be executed was a young volunteer from 1915 who had been sentenced to death for desertion on a previous occasion. **Private Wilson Ling** joined up in May 1915, leaving Canada  before the end of the year.[9] During his first year on the Western Front he was treated leniently when he had a sentence of death for desertion suspended. However, on 21 June 1917, when ordered to report to 2 Battalion which was in reserve, he absconded. The Canadian enjoyed considerable liberty, and was not arrested until nearly a year later, when he was detained by the Military Police in Mazingarbe.[10] Private Ling was tried on 8 July 1918, but the 22 year old was not executed until 12 August. His headstone in Cerisy-Gailly Military Cemetery carries the inscription:

*'Ever remembered by loved ones at home'.*

The execution of Private Ling was the fifth consecutive daily shooting during August. As regards military executions, August was the bloodiest month during 1918, with a total of ten soldiers and a Chinaman being shot. With the exception of May, during which nine men had been shot, no other month had seen more than half-a-dozen executions, although the sanction would at best seem to have been used somewhat haphazardly. After Ling's death there was a twenty-four-hour lull before the next execution took place.

 The victim was **Private William Baker**, a volunteer with 26 Royal Fusiliers. Baker was already under arrest when, on 22 April 1918, he had absented himself. Interestingly, on 8 May he had reported for work at the Army Post Office at Boulogne, stating that he had been sent there for duty. However, he had soon disappeared again. Ten days later his motives became clear, when he was arrested near the mail boat at Boulogne docks. As usual, a false name and particulars were given. Later that month he escaped and invoked a different plan when he tried to gain admittance to a hospital at Etaples using a false name.[11] Other details of Baker's military service are unknown, but the weary soldier was shot at Poperinghe on 14 August.

On 23 August the oldest soldier to be shot during the war was executed. The man was an American who had volunteered for service with an Irish Regiment. **Private Henry Hendricks** had enlisted in the summer of 1917 and was serving in 2 Battalion Leinster Regiment. After

the court martial Hendrick's brigade commander appended a somewhat forceful opinion to the proceedings. Brigadier-General B C Freyberg VC commented that the American was a defiant offender who deliberately committed crime, and that the soldier was one of the worst characters in the British army.[12] It comes therefore as no surprise that the 46 year old was shot. Henry Hendricks was at least the third American to be shot under the (British) Army Act. Lance-Bombardier Arnold had been shot in July 1916, and Private Dagesse in March 1918. At least four other soldiers over forty had been shot. The second eldest being 44 year old Welshman Private Thomas, shot in May 1916.

On the same day that Hendricks died, a volunteer in 1 Battalion Leicestershire Regiment was shot for desertion. During his four years' service **Private Joseph Nisbet** had accrued two convictions, one for violence for which he had received a four year sentence, and another for disobedience for which he had been sentenced to death.

During the summer of 1918 Nisbet had reported sick at a time when the battalion had been warned for the front line. He was ordered to attend the next sick parade, but instead he absconded. Three days later he was arrested in Calais without his equipment. [13] In confirming the sentence of death, no doubt the Commander-in-Chief took into consideration the opinion of the man's CO, who had reported that the private's behaviour might well prove infectious.[14]

The final execution in August was that of a man from Kent. **Private Frederick Butcher** had enlisted in the East Kent Regiment in October 1915, before serving on the Western Front in 7 Battalion, part of 18 Division. Few details (that can be verified with absolute accuracy) have emerged about the soldier's offence. However, a newspaper report, written by a doctor who had served in the RAMC, was published a year after the execution. It contains a number of clues which suggest that the individual described was Private Butcher.

*'I shall call him Jim. He had been out three years. He had been wounded, but he was wounded at a time when the wounded were cared for in France and were back in the line in six weeks. There was nothing about Jim which attracted special attention. He was the average happy-go-lucky sort of a lad who did the day's work in the average way. War had become normal to him, and he had settled down to that fatalism which characterised so many of our men when they said, "If it's to be it will, and if it ain't it won't."*

*'As if he had suddenly been hit in the mind, he stood stock still one night and point blank refused to go over with a raiding party. In an instant he became a marked man. His comrades could not quite determine whether it was bravery or idiocy. Perhaps some string had snapped, something somewhere*

*had gone wrong, but Jim just refused. He was exceedingly nervous, but such a breach of discipline was in itself sufficient to account for that. By the time he stood on the mat before the Court he had partly regained his normal composure, but the seriousness of the situation had washed away the colour from his face, and there was a dull leaden look in his blue eyes.*

*'His record saved him. It was good and his judges tempered judgement with mercy and consideration. He had had many platoon commanders – many captains, and with all he had done his bit. The Court gave him a chance. He made no excuse whatever, but when asked the question, he promised that it would not occur again.*

*'A week later it did occur again, and the next court sentenced him to death. Blindfolded, with his hands tied behind him, he was to be shot at dawn the following day.* [The account is flawed at this point because it makes no reference to review and confirmation procedures.]

*'From the death sentry Jim learned the names of the officer and men who were to send him West next morning. They were all his friends. Two or three officers who had known him for years went into the death hut and said good-bye. Somehow, none of them could quite catalogue Jim as a coward. The sentry saw some men hovering around, and gauging the situation by intuition, turned his back, while through the open window old pals whispered, 'Au revoir, Jim' . . .*

*'Terrible things happen in war, but nothing perhaps is more terrible than to send one of your own out of life when you are not quite sure whether he is a coward or a martyr. The world will never know the real truth. There was no psychologist there to give an opinion. Even if there had been it might not have altered the course of events. Discipline even then might have won an unfair victory over science.*

*'In the mechanism of Jim's mentality a cog slipped and the wheels revolved irregularly. From what the CO and Jim's pals told me I am fully persuaded that Jim died as a martyr to discipline . . .*

*'Jim was blindfolded, his hands were bound together behind him, as he stood there, calm and steady as a rock, the orders were given. "Good-bye sir – Good-bye boys!", he said, just as if he were off on 10 days furlough. There was no reply. The subaltern was choked with emotion and the firing squad, as heartrent as he, dared not reply. The sharp crack of a volley, smothered sighs of relief from the squad, and all was over – all save laying him beneath the soil of France. And there, where Jim lies, there shall remain for ever a little bit of England.'* [15]

The reason for the appearance of the doctor's article in the press arose because of a question raised in the House of Commons. Colonel L Ward had sought an undertaking from the Secretary of State for War that no distinction would be made between those soldiers who died honourably, and those executed for military offences.[16] In the case of Private Butcher it mattered not, for after the war the soldier's grave was not identified.

Colonel Ward had made his request during the debate on Army estimates and made some interesting observations. He stated that:

*'In the early winter of 1914, it was my unfortunate duty to sit on a court martial at which five men were sentenced to death . . . during the whole sitting of that court I had the uncomfortable feeling that, even with my limited knowledge of the law, I could have got those men off on a technicality if I had been in a position to act as their friend . . . They were not cowards in the accepted meaning of the word . . .'*[17]

In the case of Private Butcher the official notification, covering up the true cause of the soldier's death, was sent to his mother who lived in Folkestone. After the war the town commenced to commemorate its dead, and details were requested from the bereaved. Mrs Butcher complied, stating that her son had been killed in action, and she requested one of the municipal Certificates of Glory. The commemorative scroll was issued by the Borough of Folkestone to the next-of-kin of those killed — should they so request such an issue. Mrs Butcher opted to have one.[18] Consequently, on Folkestone's War Memorial appears the name of F C Butcher. The memorial is very appropriately located at the top of the 'Hill of Remembrance', down which marched countless thousands of soldiers who embarked from the port, many never to return.

All of the soldiers executed during September and October 1918 were volunteers. The first was a Yorkshireman who had served in 49 (West Riding) Division with King's Own Yorkshire Light Infantry. **Private Frank Bateman** had originally been posted to 1/4 KOYLIs at the end of June 1915, shortly after the Division had arrived in France.[19] The battalion had served at Ypres during the autumn before transferring to the Somme in the following year. That summer Private Bateman was wounded, and after recovering from his injuries he was posted to 1/5 Battalion.[20] During 1917 the Yorkshireman committed his first offence of going absent, and for this he received a sentence of one year's imprisonment — although the punishment was suspended.[21] However, the soldier did not behave, and subsequently Bateman was sent to England suffering from a self-inflicted wound.[22]

In 1918 Private Bateman deserted from his original battalion (1/4 KOYLI) to which he had been returned. A 15 year sentence resulted, although suspension meant that the soldier could be returned to duty. During July 1918 the battalion, together with American allies, was taking turns in manning the trenches, when Bateman yet again went absent.[23] The offence proved fatal and on 10 September, 28 year old Bateman was shot. His death was the fourth execution in 49 Division, all shootings having taken place in 1918. Bateman was the sixth (and final) native of Sheffield to be shot. A month after the execution a newspaper entry indicated that the soldier's relatives had been successfully deceived, the 'deaths column' carrying the following entry:

'*BATEMAN. – In loving memory of Private Frank Bateman, Yorks and Lancs., died on service, September 10th, 1918, after three-and-half years' service. Deeply regretted. – From Father, Brother and Sister.*'[24]

The tell-tale phrase 'died on service' concealed the true cause, the phraseology having been copied from the official army notification.

On 12 September another machine gunner was executed. The soldier was serving in 47 Battalion Machine Gun Corps – part of the London Territorial division of the same number. **Private Patrick Murphy** had served for most of the war, and perhaps surprisingly two written accounts exist to recall his final hours. Both these recollections portray the victim and the assistant provost-marshal in a manner other than would be expected.

Captain M L Walkinton wrote after the war that,

'*If you desert and let your friends down, and left them to do your fighting for you, you deserved what you got . . . It came as a great shock, however, when the colonel sent for me and told me that I had to provide a firing party from my company to shoot a man who had been convicted of desertion on three separate occasions. No one in the company could remember him. It seemed that on the final occasion he had joined it one day and deserted it the next, when on the way up to the line.*'[25]

The chaplain detailed to attend Private Murphy also recorded the events. Father Benedict Williamson related that he had been summoned because the victim was a Roman Catholic. (Father Benedict Williamson was Roman Catholic Padre to 47 Division.)

'*I saw the APM, a kindly-hearted man who was really much distressed over the affair, as indeed I think everyone was; for there is an immense difference between seeing a number of men slain in battle and seeing one shot with all the cold deliberation that follows in such a case as this . . . The shelter was closed with a door of open ironwork; outside the guards were mounted with fixed bayonets.... We talked together some time, and as I was going away he said very earnestly, "Father, I am glad I am a Catholic, and I am not afraid to die." I promised to come back and see how he was later on . . . When I arrived [back] the boy was asleep . . . I spend some time encouraging him for the fiery ordeal he would soon pass through. The scene almost carried one back to the days of the martyrs, the boy was so wonderfully calm and resigned.*'[26]

The firing squad was comprised of six men, and according to Walkinton, one allegedly had a rifle loaded with a blank round. Walkinton continued his account, although he recorded that the information he received had come from the officer in charge of the firing squad, and that he himself had not been present. The execution took place at the Monastery at Labeuvrière.

*'Six men with long service at the front were chosen and although they all hated the job they loyally obeyed their orders. The shooting took place at dawn . . . The only people present were the deserter, a chaplain, who read some prayers, a doctor, the provost-marshal and an escort of Military Police, and the firing party. The officer in charge told me when he returned that the condemned man "a nice quiet friendly sort of chap" smiled on the firing party and assured them that he bore them no ill will and realised that they had to obey orders. He was then blindfolded,* [although Father Williamson recorded that the victim had requested not to have to wear a blindfold], *a bit of white paper was pinned near his heart, the escort stepped aside and the order to fire was given. The man fell dead and after a very brief prayer the firing party marched away leaving the Military Police to deal with the body.'*[27]

Father Williamson also bore witness to the condemned man's spirit. He recalled, *'The boy's death and his fine courage made a great impression on all who assisted at that sorrowful scene . . .'*[28]

On the same day yet another Chinese Labourer, one **Hui I He** paid the price for killing a comrade.[29]

On 24 September the last soldier to be arrested in the UK, before being returned to France to face trial, was brought before a firing squad. **Private David Gibson** had enlisted voluntarily for service in the Royal Scots and had served on the Western Front with 12 Battalion. In 1918 Gibson failed to return from leave, and was eventually arrested by the police at his home in Glasgow.[30]

When Gibson was returned to his unit in France an attack involving the battalion was shortly due to be carried out. It was therefore suggested to the Scotsman that if he served creditably in battle, then the outcome of his forthcoming court martial might be more favourable than otherwise. Foolishly he ignored the advice and absconded instead, remaining absent for two days — and in doing so sealed his own fate. At his court martial the soldier explained that the cause of his distraction was his wife's infidelity. In due course neither the court nor the confirming authorities were moved by the plea, and the 25 year old was shot in a rear area of the Ypres Salient. (Army records suggest that Private Gibson was 27; however, information given to the War Graves Commission, suggests that he was two years younger.)

The third and last officer to be executed during the war was shot for murder. **Second-Lieutenant John Paterson** had been commissioned from the ranks, and as Anthony Babington has already commented, mystery surrounds the case.

Paterson had originally enlisted into the Middlesex Regiment, and the prefix of his army number, F/1239, indicates that he had joined the 'Footballers' battalion'. This fact is confirmed by medal records which show that he went to France with 17 Middlesex in November 1915.[31] It is reported that twice in the following year Paterson was wounded on the Somme, and that in March 1917 he was returned home for officer training.[32] In September 1917 Paterson was commissioned into the Essex Regiment, before returning to France towards the end of the year.

At the end of March 1918 Second-Lieutenant Paterson had deserted from 1 Battalion Essex Regiment who were then in reserve trenches near Ypres. As a result of the cashing of a number of forged cheques by an officer of Paterson's description the Military Police were detailed to try and arrest the offender.[33] As it turned out, the policemen detailed for the task were no ordinary 'red caps', but detectives from the GHQ Detective Staff.[34]

On the evening of 3 July, forty year old Sergeant Harold Collison, DCM, MSM, a big man, five feet ten inches tall, was on duty near Calais together with a fellow corporal of the force.[35] The two policemen saw Paterson walking down the road with a French girl, and realising that he resembled the wanted officer approached him. Without proof of identity, and with Paterson giving what turned out to be a false name, the NCOs decided to follow the couple. On the outskirts of the village Paterson admitted his true identity to the policemen, and asked to be able to speak to the French girl whilst having a cup of tea in a nearby house. After refreshments he maintained that he would surrender to their custody. Sergeant Collison agreed, and later permitted an extension, although by then the NCOs had been waiting for over an hour. As a precaution the corporal had been keeping watch at the front whilst Collison maintained a vigil at the rear.[36]

In failing light Second-Lieutenant Paterson emerged from the rear of the building, and after an alarmed shout from Collison that summoned his colleague, the officer shot the sergeant three times. Inadvertently the second-lieutenant had also wounded himself in the groin. In the confusion, as the corporal went to fetch assistance, Paterson and the girl escaped.[37] In the shooting Collison had not been killed outright, but was mortally wounded. Consequently, the corporal had come to his assistance and had not been able to arrest Paterson. Sergeant Collison died of his wounds the next day,[38] and the hunt for the missing officer began.

Paterson remained at liberty for over two weeks until arrested by the French police at St Omer. When brought to trial he faced charges of both murder and desertion. As it turned out the General Court Martial panel only considered the murder charge, returning a verdict of guilty.[39]

In his examination of the proceedings Judge Babington concluded that much remains undisclosed about the case of Second-Lieutenant

Paterson. For example, it is possible to speculate that Paterson was involved in more complex, illicit activities, possibly involving drug dealing — perhaps deploying pre-war business skills acquired as a West African trader. It could well be that it was Paterson's involvement in such activities that that caused him to enter into extended mysterious discussions with the French woman [prior to his dash for freedom by way of the back door], before the shooting occurred.[40]

Second-Lieutenant Paterson was executed at Boulogne on 24 September and with somewhat unusual attention to precise detail, his death was recorded as having occurred at seven-and-a-half minutes past six in the morning.[41]

In the final week of September Major-General S W Hare, commanding 54 Division — a force that had never had a man executed — wrote to complain about the recent policy change which required that the sentence of a court martial be disclosed to the prisoner, before such a sentence had been confirmed (or otherwise). And the General went on to relate an incident that had occurred after a private in 1/5 Suffolk Regiment had been told that he had been sentenced to death. At the time 54 Division was in Palestine.

*'He seems to be a man of a highly nervous temperament, the anxiety worked upon him, there was considerable delay before a decision was arrived at and on 20 September 1918 he cut his own throat. The very same day the Division was informed that Private W.........'s Court Martial had been quashed on a legal point.*

*'It so happens that in forwarding the Court Martial (papers), I had recommended that the sentence be commuted.'*[42]

As it turned out Private W......... was unsuccessful in his attempt to kill himself.

As the war drew towards a close the number of soldiers being executed dropped dramatically, and during the final two months, only two soldiers per month were shot.

**Private Harry Knight** was the first deserter to die in October. The soldier, one of the earliest of volunteers from 1914, had served on the Western Front for over three years. Knight had a series of previous convictions 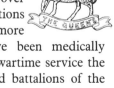 for disobedience and had also been wounded.[43] In more charitable circumstances the soldier might have been medically examined and treated more leniently. During his wartime service the private had served with both the first and second battalions of the Queen's (Royal West Surrey Regiment).[44] At the time of his death Knight was serving with the first battalion.

The last Scotsman to be executed was typical of those shot at this period. Like many others who were executed, the soldier had a poor disciplinary record and had also been wounded.

Like the previous soldier, **Private Lawrence Elford** was a volunteer,  and in his case was serving in 7/8 King's Own Scottish Borderers. Amongst the soldier's previous convictions was a sentence of 15 years' penal servitude which had been imposed for an offence of striking a superior officer.[45]

Following his desertion Elford was arrested at Boulogne, which together with Calais would seem to have been an obvious place to look for absent soldiers. At his trial the Scotsman told the court that his wife was ill and that his concern for her had caused his flight.[46] Although Elford's illicit attempt to return home might have been unrealistic, for a soldier with his bad record the prospects of compassionate leave were nil. The 28 year old was shot at Noeux-les-Mines on 11 October.

Private Louis Harris

Four days before the Armistice two deserters were executed in separate shootings. The younger of the two soldiers was a London-born Jew who was serving in the West Yorkshire Regiment. **Private Louis Harris** had volunteered for service in 1915, but had been rejected on medical grounds.[47] It was ironic therefore that when medical requirements were lowered the Londoner should be conscripted, and later face a firing squad. Harris was 23 at the time of his death, and was serving in 10 West Yorks. The Commonwealth War Graves Commission records show that the soldier's parents lived in Leeds.[48]

The other soldier shot that day was also a Londoner, and like a number of previous men he claimed at his trial that his family had a history of mental illness. However, conscript **Private Ernest Jackson** was already serving under a suspended sentence – although the two year penalty was comparatively light when compared to some offenders' punishments. Had the soldier not escaped after deserting in September 1918[49] he might well have avoided the extreme penalty. The 32 year old private was serving in 24 Battalion Royal Fusiliers and faced a firing squad in the isolated village of Romeries.

In the final months of the war two soldiers were shot in distant theatres of operations. The first was a conscript deserter shot in Salonika (Greece) in September 1918. **Private Robert Young,** who was serving with 11 Worcestershire Regiment, was already serving under a two year suspended sen-tence for absence and striking a superior officer, when again he went missing.[50] The soldier's offence had been committed just two months before the end of hostilities – when the private had found himself in action for the first time. During heavy shelling, in which it is reported that the soldier's dugout had been blown in, Young had made his way to the rear.[51] Although he was convicted of desertion, the suggestion is that had evidence been available a charge of cowardice might have been preferred. As usual, little or no regard was paid to statements made by the soldier in defence of his actions. 21 year old Private Young was executed by firing squad on 18 September.

The second shooting was for a murder committed in German East Africa. The condemned soldier was **Private Dezari Barama,** serving with the Gold Coast Mounted Infantry Regiment. Although details of the offence have not come to light, Barama was tried on 21 October 1918 and shot on 10 November.[52] The execution was the third and final case in the Gold Coast Regiment.

Four days after the signing of the Armistice a secret letter commanded that no further executions were to be carried out, except for murder, without the sanction of the War Office. The policy decision had come about after a letter of enquiry from the Commander-in-Chief in Salonika. General Milne enquired whether soldiers who had been convicted by post-war courts of deliberate desertion to the enemy, might suffer the extreme penalty.[53] It may be presumed that, after a reply in the negative, trials did not proceed with much conviction; and William Moore has stated that post-war reports, that had to be furnished by returned British POWs, resulted in no disciplinary action.[54]

Although the Armistice on the Western Front came into effect on the eleventh hour of the eleventh day of the eleventh month, this was not the case in German East Africa. In this theatre of operations hostilities ceased on 14 November and the German Forces did not surrender until 25 November.[55] In the following month the case of an African soldier convicted of murder was referred to the War Office in Great Britain. Private Oyouda Kiiberenge of 2/3 King's African Rifles had gone absent and then been arrested. In his subsequent escape the soldier shot and killed an intelligence department scout. The outcome of his case is unknown, although a surprising reply from the War Office, dated 4 January 1919, stated that the death sentence could be imposed if the conviction was justified![56] No confirmation has been found that the sentence was carried out and for this reason the soldier does not appear amongst the statistics quoted in this volume.

Early in 1919 a fourth and final execution of a British West Indies soldier took place. The condemned man was **Private Albert Denny** who was serving in 8 Battalion in Italy. For some reason that is not clear three months had passed between Denny committing his crime – bayoneting a fellow soldier whilst drunk – and his case being brought to trial.[57] The private was tried by General Court Martial towards the end of 1918, and in the new year Denny was shot by a firing squad from his battalion.[58] A neighbouring unit, 7 British West Indies Regiment, recorded in its war diary most matters relating to discipline, and an unusual entry exists for 16 January 1919. On that day Acting Sergeant Robert Richards had been charged with the manslaughter of Private Pinnock, in that he had shot and killed the man. Surprisingly the NCO, in contrast to Denny, had been found not guilty, but had been convicted of a lesser charge of conduct to the prejudice of good order and military discipline. Furthermore the initial sentence of six months' imprisonment with hard labour was later commuted to just two months.[59]

During 1919 a number of individuals continued to be shot for murder, and in February, Chinese Labourer **Wan Fa Yu** was shot at Rouen.[60] And in May of that year **Wang Ch'un Ch'ih** was shot at Poperinghe. Visitors to the Town Hall at Poperinghe are permitted to view the execution post which was used in this shooting. The previous execution post at Poperinghe presumably had been destroyed.

A week after the death of Coolie Wang an army instruction declared that the Suspension of Sentences Act did not apply to Chinese Labourers.[61] Quite why this was so, and by what authority was not disclosed. However, some specific disciplinary matters amongst the labourers must have arisen.

The diary also detailed another problem that was rapidly escalating. France and Belgium were overflowing with servicemen, who, released from their gruelling tasks, were eager to return home. The diary recorded that the more indisciplined of them had taken to looting supply trains, and that the problem was quite widespread. Even the mounting of armed guards on the trains did not entirely alleviate the problem.

In the United Kingdom a number of soldiers who had behaved satisfactorily in action found themselves penalised for post-war crimes. A cursory examination of just one regiment shows that soldiers from the Northumberland Fusiliers lost their medal entitlement owing to having been convicted of theft and handling stolen goods.[62]

Although the sanction of the death penalty was not imposed for post-war offences of desertion, an artilleryman was executed in 1919 as a result of a murder he committed in an attempt to avoid being arrested whilst absent without leave. **Gunner Frank Wills** had gone missing from his Trench Mortar Battery after the Armistice, and in March 1919 Wills had been detained by the Military Police in Paris. In a ploy calculated to facilitate his escape the gunner had managed to draw a revolver before shooting dead one NCO and then wounding another. However, while trying to get away the soldier had been detained by a crowd of Parisians.[63] Not surprisingly the senseless crime attracted the extreme penalty; the 20 year old was executed at Le Havre on 27 May 1919.

Shortly after the signing of the Peace Treaty in June 1919 a number of troops were executed for mutiny. Although the condemned men were neither British, Colonial, nor labourers, it is thought that the death sentences were imposed under authority of the British Army Act. The executed men were in fact Russians who were serving in the Slavo-British Penal Battalion. It is believed that the reason that the men were subject to British jurisdiction was the fact the unit had been financially dependent on Britain.

The Russians were shot following a mutiny at Topsa and details of the individuals are included here only for the reason of completeness. A tabulation naming the men and their sentences is included below.

Those tried on 13 July 1919 were:

Private Lasheff − Acquitted; Private Kanieff − Acquitted; Private Terenfieff − Acquitted; Private Shouliatieff − Death, sentence commuted to 10 years' penal servitude; Private Deriagin − Death; Private Sakharoff − Death; Sergeant Pesochnikoff − Death.

Those tried on the following day were:

Private Artemento − Acquitted; Private Petontioff − Death, sentence commuted to 10 years' penal servitude; Private Posdjeef Death; Private Elisaieff − Death; Private Volkoff − Death; Private Taratin − Death; Private Cherbukin − Death; Private Lashkoff − Death; Private

Kameff — Death; Private Bitel — Death; Private Maroochin (outcome unknown — died 14 July 1920).

Tried and acquitted on 15 July 1919 was Second-Lieutenant A M Zouer.

Further trials for mutiny occurred on 17 July.

Private Piasooky — Acquitted; Private Roond — Acquitted; Private Kolhin — Acquitted; Private Bykoff — Death, sentence commuted to 10 years' penal servitude; Private Evskatoff — Death, sentence commuted to 10 years' penal servitude; Private Mianid — Death, sentence commuted to 10 years' penal servitude; Private Sharoff Death, sentence commuted to 10 years' penal servitude; Private Tonkikh — Death, sentence commuted to 10 years' penal servitude.

Also tried on that day, but for sedition, were:

Private Savin — Acquitted; Private P Babourkin — Death, sentence commuted to 10 years' penal servitude.

Also tried on the same date, but for desertion, was Private Kozmitcheef. His death sentence was also commuted to ten years' penal servitude.

Just after these offences a number of Russians who were serving in a separate unit — the Russian Disciplinary Battalion — had mutinied. At least five executions followed.[64] Details of the cases do not appear amongst British records as the unit was financed by White Russia.

In the summer of 1919 another British soldier in France was shot for murder. The crime was particularly distasteful, and had occurred the previous year. Involved were four soldiers from the Lincolnshire Regiment who had carried out a number of burglaries in Calais. **Private Joseph Chandler,** suspicious that one gang member had concealed an additional share of the booty, killed the man — albeit with some assistance from the others. A fortnight later Chandler was arrested, although the cunning criminal feigned mental illness until June of the following year.[65] On 11 August 1919 the private finally paid the price for his violent ways.

Towards the end of August two native labourers were shot for murdering Belgian women. 23 year old **Willie Harris** and 24 year old **Abraham Davids** were both serving in 1 Battalion Cape Coloured Labour Corps.[66] A detailed, if somewhat gory, account exists of the two men's execution which took place at Lille.

*'One afternoon, about a couple of weeks after my arrival* [at Lille], *I received instructions from Worthington* [Assistant Director of Medical Services at V Army HQ] *to report to his office. In his greeting, "Ha! Ha! Here you are", there was just enough offhandedness to make me suspicious at once, for I knew my Worthington, [and] had heard the tone of this approach before. It was a sure indication that an unsavoury job lay ahead.*

Without preamble he handed it to me: "Two prisoners will be executed tomorrow morning and a Medical Officer must be present. The APM complains that the last MO supplied to him fainted during the proceedings. He wants me to provide one who won't. I am therefore detailing you..."

'The executions were to take place on the filled-in moat before the Ramparts at the NW corner of Vauban's ancient fortifications. The APM and his party met me. The party looked ill at ease. Two thick stakes, some six feet apart, stood side-by-side on the old moat's site. The condemned men were, of course, elsewhere at this stage. No chaplain was in attendance. The Ramparts formed a grim background. The early morning was grey. Lazily stirring along the filled moat, a thin chill mist caressed the twin stakes and passed on . . . I was told that I might give each victim a heavy dose of morphia, "but the prisoners must be capable of walking with assistance and on no account will be carried . . ."

'The firing party, of twelve I think, then took up their positions facing the stakes. They were given final instructions, and words of encouragement which manifestly they needed. The loaded rifles were grounded. The party filed out of sight. A sergeant loaded some of the rifles with blanks — he said — no man would know whether he was partly responsible for the killing. He assured me that, in the row made by the simultaneous shots, no man could tell if he used live or blank; I had thought the kick would be different.

'As he [the sergeant] picked up one rifle it went off. The bullet zipped by my head; it passed, so I estimated, precisely just over my left shoulder where that structure joins the neck. A stray piece of wire, with one end fixed in the ground, had in some way discharged the rifle. "My God, sir!" the scared sergeant shouted, 'it nearly got you!' He then conducted me to the condemned men, seated with their guards in a small, forbidding compartment of the Ramparts.

'They watched my preparations without evident interest. I remember having some misgivings about the morphia injections. People vary in their reactions to that drug, both as to the reaction and the time necessary to produce it. I gave each victim a large enough dose to ensure the required result. The men did not speak except when addressed. We waited silently, hidden away in the grim Rampart's guts. When I saw that the drug was taking effect I produced two square envelopes, and I now worked rapidly. Of the many distasteful professional duties which have inevitably come my way, what followed stayed in my mind as the worst.

'The men were clothed in thin shirts, tight, close fitting intentionally. I had to percuss out cardiac areas, identify apex-beats, pin envelopes to [the] shirts. The envelopes were the targets. To do this while meeting these men's eyes looking into my eyes was humiliating and shocking. I blindfolded them. Nodding to the escorts. A guard on each side of each victim supported. Their arms were not tied. Our dreadful walk to the waiting stakes began.

'As we moved from the Ramparts slowly, towards the filled-in moat, we

267

*could see the firing squad in position. The APM and a warrant officer stood on their right. Prisoners were tied to the stakes without a moment's loss of time. A sergeant with a revolver took up his position on their right flank, facing the squad. I stood on their left. My instructions were to stand as near the stakes, and line of fire, as was compatible with safety, and literally dash in immediately after the volley to pronounce the men dead or not. I thought this a needless refinement of dispatch, but grasped its object later when I attended another execution. The signal to fire came as soon as I was clear. I cannot recall what the signal was. The Ramparts behind flung back the noise of the volley. The noise was surprisingly loud, and perhaps seemed louder because I was facing the rifles. The two heads fell forward. The bodies could not. I had hardly expected to see such copious gushing of blood. I could hear it splashing while quickly examining the victims. The firing squad was marched off at once.'[67]*

The further execution that Captain Gameson made mention of was that of yet another Cape Coloured Labourer. The young South African had enlisted under a false name – perhaps not surprising as his true surname was Boos. However, the supposed **Private F 'Alberts'** had on 13 May murdered one of his battalion comrades – Private Barend De Vries.[68] Once again the execution took place at Lille, with Captain Gameson in attendance.

*'This execution followed the pattern of killings I had seen before, with the same solemn, shocking formalities. Again the crime was murder. Again I came unpleasantly near to being shot myself; this time, with a revolver.*

*'Omitting all preliminaries, one deals with the end. The squad's aiming had been bad. I dashed in immediately after the volley and at once told the sergeant on the opposite side of the moribund victim that the man still lived. With a revolver, he shot the man through the skull at its side's thinnest part. I repeat that I stood on the opposite flank of the victim. The sergeant fired before I had any chance to remove myself. The bullet went clean through and buzzed by my head as I bent over the semi-unconscious man tied to his stake. It was a messy, disturbing business. I told the sergeant it was much to his credit that he was so rattled by our sordid work as to be irresponsibly careless; perhaps the firing squad had been rattled. I kept the blindfolding bandage. In it were two bullet holes – not made by the revolver bullet. This was pretty wild shooting of presumably selected men. My target over the victim's heart had been plain to see at the prescribed short range.'[69]*

The three bodies were buried in Mouvaux Cemetery on the outskirts of Lille, but after a few years they were re-interred in 'Y' Farm Military Cemetery at Bois Grenier, near Armentières.

The final three men to face British Army firing squads in France were executed in February 1920. They were part of a hundred-thousand-strong Chinese workforce recruited by the British during the war, mainly for labouring tasks on the Western Front. Personal details

Chang Ju Chih

about Labourer **Chang Ju Chih** were chronicled beneath his photograph on the Military Police record, reproduced on page 351. On the back of the card, Captain W T Munday, Deputy Assistant Provost-Marshal laconically detailed the main features of the case and, rather unusually, his own role in executing Chih:

'*This coolie murdered a woman and her three children November 1918 near Amiens. Was arrested April 19 and sentenced to death by Court Martial. Escaped 12.5.19. Left Marseilles August 1919 for China; was not allowed to land at Shanghi owing to not having any papers and was sent back to Marseilles. Since then he has been all over France trafficing in cocaine until arrested near Calais 1.2.20. I visited him on 2.2.20 and felt certain that he was No.16174. He denied this until 8.2.20 when he admitted to being the man wanted on 12.2.20 . . . Execution which I arranged for dawn 14th inst. I stayed with him all night 13/14 Feb. He confessed all.*

鞠躬盡瘁

*The sentence was carried out at 6.41 a.m. 14th Feb. A chaplain, a doctor and myself were present. Six police formed the firing party. The MO seemed in doubt as to his death. I finished him with a .45 Colt revolver . . . He died bravely, asked me not to bandage his eyes and to allow him to sing a hymn just before he died. Both these requests were granted.*[70]

The other two Chinese were also convicted of murder. Labourer **K'ung Ch'ing Hsing** arrived in France in mid-1917, a short while before his comrade **Hei Chi Ming**.[71] Their execution at Rouen on 21 February 1920 was attended by two officers from the town's detention hospital.[72]

斩　鞠

瘁　盡

Little is known of the man of 3 Black Sea Labourer Company, shot for murder shortly after the two Chinese. However, circumstantial evidence suggests that he may be Labourer T Jegoroff, who died on 17 March and was buried in Constantinople.

The last two soldiers to be executed in 1920 were Irish. The first was **Private James Joseph Daly**, aged 20, shot for his part in the much-chronicled mutiny by 1 Connaught Rangers, who were protesting about the British Army counter-insurgency in Ireland. The mutiny took place at Jullundur and Solon cantonments and ended when officers shot some mutineers. Sixty-nine were later tried at Dagshai cantonment and did not have defending officers – most were harshly punished. However, of the 14 death sentences inflicted by the court martial only Daly's was confirmed. He was shot on 2 November at Dagshai prison and buried nearby. His remains and those of his two comrades killed during the mutiny, were repatriated to Ireland in 1968, Daly being re-interred in Tyrellspass Churchyard, County Westmeath.[73]

In contrast to the publicity posthumously accorded Daly, few details have emerged about the case of convicted murderer **Private Richard Flynn**, a Regular with 5 Dublin Fusiliers (part of the British occupation forces in Turkey). Flynn was shot for murder on 6 November 1920 and buried in Haidar Pasha Cemetery, Constantinople.[74]

British generals of the period never publicly revised their endorsement of any military death sentences carried out between 1914 and 1920. Nevertheless, the easy confidence invested in wartime courts martial was soon grudgingly eroded. Field-Marshal Sir Douglas Haig, writing a couple of months before the first anniversary of the Armistice, commented:

*'It has frequently happened during the war that officers and men have been properly sentenced by Courts Martial for offences which were either purely military in character or became of greatly increased importance owing to war conditions. I might perhaps quote an example that has been brought to my notice. In this case an officer was cashiered by court martial for*

*presenting an unloaded revolver at a Frenchman who threatened him in a village where he [the officer] was stationed. The officer, who was a public schoolboy, a volunteer with a good military record, finds his future peace career ruined by the disgrace of a sentence which, although very proper and necessary at the time, has today lost much of its significance.*[75]

Haig suggested the establishment of special tribunals to review wartime sentences of imprisonment and penal servitude — but he could not personally intervene because (by virtue of the Army Act, section 58) soldiers transferred to the UK to serve prison sentences were subject to civil authority.

The immediate post-war period also witnessed the establishment of two Parliamentary bodies charged with reviewing courts martial procedures. In 1919 a senior judge, Sir Charles Darling, chaired a committee composed of senior military officers and five MPs (including Horatio Bottomley who had publicised Dyett's case).

The evidence they heard was never published and its conclusions were embodied in two final reports. The majority report concluded that the courts martial were well conducted and standards of justice inspired confidence in their fairness by the rank-and-file! The dissenting minority report, signed by three MPs, including Bottomley, was critical of the army's judicial practices, and suggested soldiers sentenced to death be allowed to appeal, possibly to the Court of Criminal Appeal.[75]

As Parliamentary interest stirred, another fifteen-member committee, including eleven doctors, began inquiring into the condition known as shellshock. Their final report attempted to crowd all nerve disorders under three headings; obliquely conceded that the medical profession had failed in its duties and concluded that shellshock was not a new form of nervous illness. Although the Shellshock Committee glossed over a good deal, it identified 18-25 year-olds as being most vulnerable to war neurosis.[76] The body would have been better served to have heeded sentiments later expressed by Lord Moran:

*'Courage is the will-power, whereof no man has an unlimited stock; and when in war it is used up, he is finished. A man's courage is his capital and he is always spending. The call on the bank may be only the daily drain of the front line or it may be a sudden draft which threatens to close the account.'*[77]

During the 1920s Westminster's attention waxed and waned about punishment under military law, usually rèceiving consideration during the annual Army and Air Force Act debate.

Interest heightened (appropriately) on 1 April 1925, when the report of the Interdepartmental Committee on proposed amendments to the Army and Air Force Acts was published. Unsurprisingly, the high-ranking officials who composed the Committee maintained that no miscarriages of justice could be attributed to unreasonable treatment of defendants during trials, nor were there failures to identify soldiers who had suffered breakdowns.[78] Nevertheless, the Committee proposed abolishing capital sentences for some offences punishable on active service with death. A futile gesture since Parliament remained unmoved.

The leader of the parliamentary campaign to abolish capital punishment for military crimes was Labour MP, Ernest Thurtle. Although son-in-law of the celebrated pacifist, George Lansbury MP, Thurtle immediately joined up in 1914 as a private in 7 Londons. Commissioned from the ranks Thurtle was wounded in the throat while serving in France.

After he was discharged from the Army in May 1919, Thurtle became involved in campaigning on a variety of issues affecting former serving soldiers. He was prominent in successful National Federation of Discharged Sailors and Soldiers' agitation to persuade Winston Churchill to release soldiers still imprisoned after the war for offences committed during hostilities. Thurtle became a staunch opponent of military conscription and the death penalty for military crimes – forcefully arguing his case in *Military Discipline and Democracy*.

After a couple of abortive attempts, Thurtle eventually became an MP in 1923. His House of Commons campaign to abolish the death penalty for military crimes became especially noticeable with the annual debate on the Army Bill but it was two years before his efforts bore fruit. In 1915, with official Labour Party support, Thurtle's motion on abolition was narrowly defeated. The debate provoked considerable publicity outside Parliament and deeply embarrassed the War Office. Thurtle demanded to know why the War Office felt it necessary to retain the death penalty for Canadians, New Zealanders and British troops, in order to ensure that they would fight effectively, when it was unnecessary to do so in the case of Australians, who had fought so magnificently? The War Office blustered but could not present any effective answer to Thurtle's sniping.

In 1928 the Government conceded an interim measure which abolished the death penalty for eight offences. The crimes included striking superior officers, disobedience and sleeping on posts. Very few soldiers had been shot during the war for these crimes and the death penalty still remained for the two controversial offences of cowardice and desertion.[79]

Abolition finally came about partly because the 1929 General Election brought Labour to power but also because of Thurtle's effective lobbying of MPs. The Bill to abolish military capital punishment was initially restricted to offences involving cowardice and quitting of posts but Thurtle persuaded his colleagues to include desertion.

However, the drama was not fully played out, for the House of Lords, after speeches from various retired senior military figures, including Lord Allenby, rejected the proposals. Nevertheless, the Tory dinosaurs in both Houses were conclusively defeated when the Commons overrode the Lords' rejection and the Royal Assent was given on 29 April 1930. The death penalty for mutiny and treachery was retained and both offences generated executions in the Second World War — although the total was only four.

News of the abolition of the death penalty for crimes of cowardice and desertion seemed to take some while to percolate into the corridors of power. In an astonishing letter from the Ministry of Pensions to the War Office, an enquiry was made about the details and type of notification to be forwarded to relatives after a soldier had been executed. The letter only made reference to those shot for cowardice and 'other crimes in the field' — it was dated 14 August 1939.[80] Britain's involvement in the Second World War had not even begun, yet the Ministry of Pensions was attempting to make provision for future victims of the firing squad, and that for at least one offence that was no longer punishable by death.

## NOTES

1 Brigadier Sir J E Edmonds, *Military Operations France & Belgium, 1918*, Volume 4.
2 WO93/49, Summary of First World War capital court martial cases.
3 Ibid. & WO329/2378, Chinese Labour Corps Medal roll.
4 Michael Summerskill, *China on the Western Front*.
5 Letter to Ernest Thurtle MP, and quoted in his pamphlet, *Shootings at Dawn*.
6 WO93/49, op cit.
7 Ernest Thurtle, op cit.
8 WO93/49, op cit.
9 Canadian Expeditionary Force, Nominal Roll of Officers, Non-Commissioned Officers and Men.
10 WO93/49, op cit.
11 Ibid.
12 Anthony Babington, *For the Sake of Example*.
13 WO93/49, op cit.
14 Anthony Babington, op cit.
15 Dr Alexander Irvine, *Lincolnshire Chronicle*, 9 August 1919, article entitled Coward or Martyr?
16 *Hansard*, 29 July 1919.
17 Ibid.
18 *Roll of Honour* Index, Folkestone Reference Library.
19 WO329/1, Index to the *Great War Medal Rolls*.
20 WO329/1600, *British War & Victory Medal Roll*.
21 WO93/49, op cit.
22 Anthony Babington, op cit.
23 WO95/2805, Battalion War Diary.
24 *Sheffield Weekly News*, 12 October 1918.
25 Diary of Captain M L Walkinton, (written in 1927), Imperial War Museum, reference DS/MISC/41.
26 Benedict Williamson, *Happy Days in France and Flanders*.
27 Captain Walkinton, op cit.
28 Benedict Williamson, op cit.
29 WO93/49, op cit. & WO329/2378, op cit.
30 *The Scotsman*, 24 September 1988.
31 WO329/1, op cit.
32 Anthony Babington, op cit.
33 Ibid.

34 Information about the Military Police comes from the Commonwealth War Graves Commission Cemetery register, Les Baraques Military Cemetery.

35 Sergeant Collison had originally enlisted in the Artillery in 1896. He had completed his time on the reserve and had re-enlisted during the (First World) War — WO97/4561 — Soldiers Documents. Collison had been awarded the Distinguished Conduct Medal earlier in 1918, and has a most unusual citation for his endeavours. 'For conspicuous gallantry and devotion to duty. He has served at the front during many engagements. His duties, which mainly consisted in making inquiries into alleged looting of the dead, took him frequently into positions of great personal danger.'

36 Anthony Babington, op cit.

37 Ibid.

38 *Soldiers Died in the Great War*, part 80.

39 Anthony Babington, op cit.

40 Details of drug addiction in World War One were recently published by Dr A J Peacock in *Gunfire*, No.8.

41 Records of the General Register Office, London.

42 WO32/3990, Objections to the announcement of death sentences in open court.

43 Anthony Babington, op cit.

44 WO329/657, *British War & Victory Medal Roll*.

45 WO93/49, op cit.

46 Anthony Babington, op cit.

47 Ibid.

48 Commonwealth War Graves Commission register, Ghissignies British Cemetery.

49 Anthony Babington, op cit.

50 WO93/49, op cit.

51 Anthony Babington, op cit.

52 WO95/5328, Battalion War Diary.

53 WO32/5479, Papers relating to the imposition of the extreme penalty after the Armistice.

54 William Moore, *The Thin Yellow Line*.

55 WO95/5327, War Diary of 2/3 King's African Rifles.

56 WO32/5479, op cit.

57 Anthony Babington, op cit.

58 WO95/4262, War Diary of 8 Battalion British West Indies Regiment.

59 WO95/4262, War Diary of 7 Battalion British West Indies Regiment.

60 WO93/49, op cit., & WO329/2374, Chinese Labour Corps Medal Roll.

61 WO95/531, War Diary of Adjutant-General, V Army, carries a copy of this instruction — V Army Administrative Instruction No.8.

62 WO329/2624, *British War & Victory Medal Roll*.

63 Anthony Babington, op cit.

64 Ronald Lewin, *Man of Armour* — biography of General V Pope.

65 Anthony Babington, op cit.

66 Details of the duo come from WO329/2346, Medal Roll, Cape Coloured Labour Corps.

67 Diary of Captain L Gameson. Imperial War Museum, reference P.395-7.

68 WO329/2346, op cit.

69 Captain L Gameson, op cit.

70 Details from the original card: Steve Knight Collection.

71 WO329/2382; WO329/2378 Medal Rolls, Chinese Labour Corps.

72 WO95/4114 War Diary, Detention Hospital, Rouen.

73 T P Kilfeather, *The Connaught Rangers*; S Pollock, *Mutiny for the Cause*; A Babington, *The Devil to Pay*.

74 WO93/49 op cit.; Commonwealth War Graves Commission Register.

75 Report of the Darling Committee.

76 Report of the Shellshock Committee.

77 Lord Moran, *The Anatomy of Courage*.

78 Report of the Interdepartmental Committee on Proposed Disciplinary Amendments to the Army and Air Force Acts.

79 Army and Air Force (Annual) Act, 1928.

80 WO32/4676 Papers relating to the notification sent to next-of-kin in the case of a sentence of death.

# Acknowledgements

A book like this has taken many years to research and thanks are due to many individuals who have given assistance. The majority of those who have helped are members of the Western Front Association including, Tony Spagnoly, Paul Reed, John Hide, Dr Alf Peacock (editor of *Gunfire* magazine) and Bob Elliston (who gave advice on medical matters). We would also like to acknowledge assistance given by Julie Wheelwright, Craig Liddle (no relation of Peter Liddle) and Bridget England.

Our thanks go to the staff of the Imperial War Museum, including Clive Hughes, Rod Suddaby, Peter Thwaites and Mike Willis. Thanks also to Bob Cotton, a New Zealand journalist on the staff of the *Christchurch Star*, as well as Darrell Waight, in Australia. We are also grateful for the co-operation of the staff of the Public Archives of Canada (Ottawa) and the staff of the Public Record Office at Kew, who have been burdened with the tasks of fetching hundreds of records for our consultation.

Acknowledgement is also made to the Controller of Her Majesty's Stationery Office for permission to reproduce Crown-copyright material in the Public Record Office. The authors are also grateful to relatives of soldiers whose diaries and papers are deposited in the Imperial War Museum, for permission to quote extracts from such material.

Acknowledgement is also made to the following publishers for permission to quote their copyright material:

C W Daniel Company Limited: *Shootings at Dawn* and *Military Discipline & Democracy* both by Ernest Thurtle;
Constable Publishers: *Anatomy of Courage* by Lord Moran;
A M Dent: *Tommy Goes to War* by Malcom Brown;
Sherwood Press Limited: *Blast of War* by M Bacon and D Langley;
Sheed & Ward Limited: *March Kind Comrade* by R H J Steuart;
Thorsons Publishing Group Limited: *Johnny Get Your Gun* by J F Tucker and *From the Somme to the Armistice* by Captain Stormont-Gibbs.
Extracts from *Surgeon's Journey* by J J Abraham are reprinted by permission of William Heinemann Limited.

Special thanks are also due to Peter T Scott, editor of *The Great War Journal, 1914-1918*. Also to David Evans and John Garwood for background research. Finally, one person has been invaluable in dealing with numerous enquiries, and has carried out these lengthy and difficult tasks without complaint. A special thank you goes to Geoff Bridger for all his efforts in this respect.

*The authors have made every attempt to obtain copyright permission for material quoted in this book. In the event that we have inadvertently infringed anyone's copyright then we would request that person to contact the publishers.*

# Bibliography

## PUBLISHED SOURCES

Abraham, Johnston, *Surgeon's Journey*, Heinemann, 1957.

Allison, Sydney, *The Bantams*, Howard Baker, 1981.

Allison, William, & John Fairley, *The Monocled Mutineer*, Quartet, 1978.

Babington, Anthony, *For the Sake of Example*, Leo Cooper, 1983.

Bacon, Maurice, & David Langley, *The Blast of War, Nottingham's Bantams*, Sherwood Press Ltd, Nottingham, 1977.

Blackburne, Harry W, *This Also Happened on the Western Front*, Hodder & Stoughton Ltd, 1932.

Brown, Malcolm, *Tommy Goes To War*, Dent, 1978.

Bruce, Brigadier-General C D, *The History of The Duke of Wellington's Regiment 1881 – 1923*, Medici Society, 1927.

Chapman, Guy, *Vain Glory*, Cassell, 1937.

Childs, Major-General Sir Wyndham, *Episodes and Reflections*, Cassell, 1930.

Coombs, Rose E B, *Before Endeavours Fade*, After the Battle, 1976.

Crozier, FP, *A Brass Hat in No Man's Land*, Jonathan Cape, 1930.

Crozier, FP, *The Men I Killed*, Michael Joseph, 1937.

Crutchlow, Ex-Sergeant, *Tale of an Old Soldier*, Hale, 1937.

Dallas, Gloden, & Douglas Gill, *The Unknown Army*, Verso, 1985.

Dunn, Private J R, *Diary of the late*.

The Burgoyne Diaries, Thomas Harmsworth Publishing, 1985.

Empey, Arthur G, *Over the Top*, Putnam's, 1917.

Gleichen, Brigadier-General Count, *The Doings of the Fifteenth Infantry Brigade*.

Graham, Stephen, *A Private in the Guards*, Macmillan, 1919.

Graves, Robert, *Goodbye To All That*, Jonathan Cape, 1929.

Herbert, AP, *The Secret Battle*, Methuen, 1919.

Hutchison, Lieutenant-Colonel G Seton, *History and Memoir of the 33rd Battalion, Machine Gun Corps 1915-19*, Waterloo, 1921.

Jerrold, Douglas, *A Georgian Adventure (Autobiography)*, Collins, 1937.

Lawton, Henry, *Vignettes of the Western Front*, Positif Press, Oxford, 1979.

Lewin, Ronald, *Man of Armour – biography of General V Pope*, Leo Cooper, 1976.

Macready, Lieutenant-General Sir Gordon, *In The Wake Of The Great*, Clowes, 1965.

Middlebrook, Martin, *The First Day on the Somme*, Lane, 1971.

Montague, CE, *Rough Justice* (novel), Chatto & Windus, 1936.

Moore, William, *The Thin Yellow Line*, Leo Cooper, 1974.

Moran, Lord, *The Anatomy of Courage*, Constable, 1945.

Pankhurst, Sylvia, *The Home Front*, Hutchinson, 1932.

Paassen, Pierre van, *Days of Our Years*, Hillman Curl, New York, 1939.

Pollock, Sam, *Mutiny For The Cause*, Leo Cooper, 1969.

Pound, Reginald, *A P Herbert*, Michael Joseph, 1976.

Pugsley, Christopher, *Gallipoli – The New Zealand Story*, Hodder & Stoughton, 1984.

Scott, Canon FG, *The Great War as I saw It*, Clarke & Stuart, Vancouver, 1934.

Steuart, R H J, *March Kind Comrade*, Sheed & Ward, 1931.

Stormont-Gibbs, Captain, *Memoirs of, From the Somme to the Armistice*.

Summerskill, Michael, *China on the Western Front*, Summerskill, 1982.

Swinton, Major-General Sir Ernest (editor), *Twenty Years After*, *(3 vols.)*, Newnes, 1936-8.

Thurtle, Ernest, *Military Discipline and Democracy*, C W Daniels, 1920.

Tucker, John F, *Johnny Get Your Gun*, William Kimber, 1978.

Williamson, Benedict, *Happy Days in France and Flanders with the 47th & 48th Divisions*, Harding & Moore, 1921.

Williamson, Henry, *Love and the Loveless* (novel), Macdonald, 1958.

Woodhall, Edwin T, *Detective & Secret Service Days*, Mellifont, 1937.

# REPORTS & OTHER SPECIALISED RECORD SOURCES

Adler, M (editor), *British Jewry Book of Honour*, Caxton, 1922.

*Army Lists.*

Becke, Major AF, *Order of Battle of Divisions, Part 1*, HMSO, 1934.

Bell, Ernest W, *Soldiers Killed on the First Day of the Somme*, E W Bell, Bolton, 1977.

*Bristol & the Great War.*

*Canadian Army Service Records.*

Craig-Brown, Brigadier E, *Army Quarterly*, Volume 102, No.1.

Indices of births, marriages & deaths, at the General Register Offices, England & Wales, and Scotland.

General Routine Orders: copies included in the war diary of 1 Royal Welsh Fusiliers – WO95/1665.

General Routine Orders: copies included in the war diary of the Adjutant-General at GHQ – WO95/25 & 26.

Canadian Expeditionary Force, Nominal Roll of Officers, Non-Commissioned Officers and Men.

Official List of Casualties to Members of the Canadian Expeditionary Force. Ottawa: Government Printing Bureau: 1914, etc.

Commonwealth War Graves Commission cemetery and memorial registers.

*Hansard,* – Official Parliamentary Reports.

*Statistics of the Military Effort of the British Empire during the Great War 1914-20*, HMSO, 1922.

Report of the Committee constituted by the Army Council to inquire into the Law and Rules of Procedure regulating Military Courts Martial, HMSO, 1919. – (Darling Committee.)

*Report of the War Office Committee of Enquiry into Shell-Shock*, HMSO, 1922. – (Southborough Report.)

*Report of the Interdepartmental Committee on Proposed Disciplinary Amendments to the Army and Air Force Acts*, HMSO, 1925.

*Soldiers Died in the Great War*, HMSO, Re-printed J B Hayward, 1988.

James, Brigadier EA, *British Regiments 1914-18*, Samson Books, 1974.

*King's Regulations 1914*, HMSO.

MacMillan, Leading Seaman T, *unpublished memoirs of.*

*Manchester City Battalions Book of Honour*, Sherratt & Hughes, 1916.

*Manual of Military Law 1914*, HMSO.

Morton, Desmond, 'The Supreme Penalty: Canadian Deaths by Firing Squad in the First World War', *Queen's Quarterly*, 1972, Volume 79.

*Alphabetical roll of New Zealand Expeditionary Force.*

*The Great War 1914-18*, New Zealand Expeditionary Force Roll of Honour.

New Zealand Army Service Records.

Nova Scotia, Street Directory, 1907/8.

Official Histories of the War – various theatres.

Thurtle, Ernest, *Shootings at Dawn* – pamphlet – 1924.

*Public Record Office classes CAB, MH & WO.*

White, Colonel H A, *Report of the Judge Advocate-General, GHQ, American Expeditionary Force, US War Dept. Washington, 1919.*

Anglia Television.

BBC Television.

Newspapers & Journals

## NEWSPAPERS & JOURNALS

Blackburn Times.
Blackwood's Magazine.
Bradford Telegraph & Argus.
Bradford Weekly Telegraph.
Bristol Gazette.
John Bull.
Christchurch Star (*New Zealand newspaper*).
Daily Telegraph.
Dover Standard.
The Dreadnought.
Hornsey Journal.
Keighley News.
Lincolnshire Chronicle.
London Gazette.
Manchester Evening Chronicle.
Manchester Evening News.
New Zealand Listener.
Northwich Chronicle.
Northwich Guardian.
North West Kent Family Historical Journal.
Past and Present.
The Scotsman.
Sheffield Weekly News.
Shields Daily Gazette.
Stand To!, *Journal of the Western Front Association*.
The Sunday Examiner (*Tasmanian newspaper*).
The Times.
Wairarapa Times-Age (*NZ*).
The Yeovil Leader.

## PUBLISHED ACCOUNTS OF EXECUTIONS WHERE THE VICTIM(S) HAVE NOT BEEN IDENTIFIED.

Bragg, Melvyn, *Speak for England*, Secker & Warburg, 1976.
Snook, J F, *Gun Fodder*, George Allen & Unwin, 1930.
Plater, Charles (editor), *Catholic Soldiers by sixty chaplains & many others*, Longmans,
        1919.
McNeile, Herman C, ('Sapper'), *The Lieutenant and Others* (novel),
        Hodder & Stoughton, 1916.
Williamson, Henry, *A Fox Under My Cloak* (novel), Macdonald, 1955.
Coppard, George, *With a Machine Gun to Cambrai*, Imperial War Museum, 1970.
Ashurst, George, *My Bit*, Bird Crowood, 1987.
Lamont, H P, alias Wilfred Saint-Maude, *War, Wine and Women*,
        New York, 1926.
Richardson, Sue (editor), *The Recollections of Three Manchesters in the Great War*,
        Richardson, Manchester, 1985. (Re: Soldier in Royal West Kents.)
Silvester, Victor, 'Victor's Deadly Secret', *Daily Express*, 16 August 1978.

# Appendix

### Place of Burial or Commemoration of Executed Men
### Executions in Regimental or Unit Order
### Executions on the Western Front
### Executions in 'Other Theatres'

# PLACE OF BURIAL OR COMMEMORATION OF EXECUTED MEN

| Cemetery or Memorial | Plot/Row/Grave | Regt. No. | Rank | Name | | Offence | Unit | Date of death | | |
|---|---|---|---|---|---|---|---|---|---|---|
| Acheux Brit Cem | 1/B/8 | 14387 | Pte | W B | Nelson | desertion | 14/DLI | 11 | 8 | 16 |
| Achicourt Road Cem | C/11 | 492050 | Pte | J | Mayers | desertion | 1/13 R Fus. (Kens'ton) | 16 | 6 | 17 |
| Achicourt Road Cem | B/16 | 474371 | Rfn | W | Yeoman | desertion | 1/12 R Fus. (Rangers) | 3 | 7 | 17 |
| Achiet-le-Grand Com Cem Ex | 4/R/3 | 240678 | Pte | A | Mitchell | desertion | 1/6 Lancs Fus. | 20 | 8 | 17 |
| Aeroplane Cem | 2/A/6 | 7625 | Pte | A D | Thompson | desertion | 3/Worcs | 26 | 7 | 15 |
| Aeroplane Cem | 2/A/7 | 7377 | Pte | J | Robinson | desertion | 3/Worcs | 26 | 7 | 15 |
| Aeroplane Cem | 2/A/8 | 8164 | Pte | B | Hartells | desertion | 3/Worcs | 26 | 7 | 15 |
| Agenvillers Chyd (Somme) | NE corner | 11850 | Pte | J | Tongue | desertion | 1/King's (L'pool) | 8 | 1 | 17 |
| Aix-Noulette Com Cem Ex | 1/F/20 | 448160 | Pte | G | Comte | desertion | 22/CEF | 3 | 7 | 17 |
| Aix-Noulette Com Cem Ex | 1/F/21 | 672604 | Pte | J | LaLancette | desertion | 22/CEF | 3 | 7 | 17 |
| Albert Com Cem Ex | 1/P/65 | 3057 | Pte | H | Palmer | desertion | 1/5 N. Fus. | 27 | 10 | 16 |
| Albert Com Cem Ex | 1/R/43 | 89173 | Pnr | E | Beeby | desertion | 212 Coy RE | 9 | 12 | 16 |
| Arras Memorial | - | 7711 | Pte | J. | Fox | striking a S.O. | 2/HLI | 12 | 5 | 16 |
| Arras Memorial | - | 40422 | Pte | S | Byrne | desertion | 1/R Dublin Fus. | 28 | 10 | 17 |
| Arras Road Cem | 3/O/1 | 9970 | Pte | A L | Jefferies | desertion | 6/SLI | 1 | 11 | 16 |
| Auchel Com Cem | 4 graves | 10874 | Pte | J G | Carr | desertion+ | 2/Welsh | 7 | 2 | 16 |
| Bailleul Com Cem Ex | 2/B/110 | 2408 | Pte | W W | Roberts | desertion+ | 4/R Fus. | 29 | 5 | 16 |
| Bailleul Com Cem Ex | 3/A/219 | 17790 | LCpl | W A | Moon | desertion | 11/Cheshire | 21 | 11 | 16 |
| Bailleul Com Cem Ex | 3/A/3 | 26028 | Pte | J | Rogers | desertion | 2/S Lancs | 9 | 3 | 17 |
| Bailleulmont Com Cem | A/7 | 1957 | Pte | W G | Hunt | desertion | 18/Manchesters | 14 | 11 | 16 |
| Bailleulmont Com Cem | B/13 | 10502 | Pte | A | Longshaw | desertion | 18/Manchesters | 1 | 12 | 16 |
| Bailleulmont Com Cem | B/12 | 10495 | Pte | A | Ingham | desertion | 18/Manchesters | 1 | 12 | 16 |
| Bailleulmont Com Cem | C/7 | 10686 | Pte | B | O'Connell | desertion | 1/Irish Guards | 8 | 8 | 18 |
| Bancourt British Cem | 1/D/18 | 11606 | Pte | W | Clarke | desertion | 2/DLI | 9 | 2 | 18 |
| Barlin Com Cem Ex | 2/D/43 | 20726 | CQMS | W | Alexander | desertion | 10/CEF | 18 | 10 | 17 |
| Barly French Mil Cem | 2/A/11 | 3563 | Pte | J. | Sloan | desertion | 1/4 King's Own | 16 | 7 | 16 |
| Barly French Mil Cem | 2/A/13 | 4567 | Pte | J | Brennan | desertion | 1/8 King's (L'pool) | 16 | 7 | 16 |
| Basra Memorial | - | 10912 | Pte | R | Burton | sleeping at post | 6/S Lancs | 19 | 2 | 17 |
| Basra Memorial | - | 10555 | Pte | T | Downing | sleeping at post | 6/S Lancs | 19 | 2 | 17 |
| Basra Memorial | - | 10764 | Pte | R M | Jones | desertion | 6/S Lancs | 21 | 2 | 17 |
| Basra Memorial | - | S/13248 | Pte | G | Cutmore | desertion | 2/B Watch | 25 | 7 | 17 |
| Beauval Com Cem | G/1 | 5715 | Pte | C | Depper | desertion | 1/4 R Berks | 13 | 9 | 16 |
| Bedford House Enclosure No.4 | 4/A/18 | 266120 | Pte | F | Turner | desertion | 1/6 N. Fus. | 23 | 10 | 17 |
| Bellacourt Mil Cem | 2/J/6 | 62218 | Pte | L | Delisle | desertion | 22/CEF | 21 | 5 | 18 |
| Berneville Com Cem | 3 graves | 9552 | Dmr | F | Rose | desertion | 2/Yorks | 4 | 3 | 17 |
| Berneville Com Cem | 3 graves | 26685 | Pte | E | Holt | desertion | 19/Manchesters | 4 | 3 | 17 |
| Bertrancourt Mil Cem | 1/J/12 | L/11710 | Pte | A T | Ansted | desertion | 4/R Fus. | 15 | 11 | 16 |
| Bertrancourt Mil Cem | 2/A/15 | 27555 | Pte | J | Taylor | desertion | 15/Lancs Fus. | 27 | 1 | 17 |
| Bertrancourt Mil Cem | 2/A/17 | 12384 | Pte | A | Reid | desertion | 16/HLI | 31 | 1 | 17 |
| Bertrancourt Mil Cem | 2/A/19 | 251482 | Rfn | W | Murphey | desertion | 5/6 R Scots | 7 | 2 | 17 |
| Béthune Town Cem | 4/A/17 | 11967 | Pte | R | Morgan | murder | 2/Welsh | 15 | 2 | 15 |
| Béthune Town Cem | 4/A/18 | 12942 | LCpl | W | Price | murder | 2/Welsh | 15 | 2 | 15 |
| Béthune Town Cem | 6/H/3 | 20101 | Pte | E | Bryant | desertion | 10/Cheshire | 27 | 10 | 17 |
| Beuvry Com Cem Ex | 2/D/15 | 25531 | Pte | J | Archibald | desertion | 17/R Scots | 4 | 6 | 16 |
| Blaringhem Chyd | north side | 11225 | Pte | E | Mackness | desertion | 1/Cameronians | 1 | 10 | 17 |
| Bleuet Farm Cem | 2/B/12 | G/1533 | Pte | T | Hawkins | desertion | 7/R W Surrey | 22 | 11 | 17 |
| Bleuet Farm Cem | 2/B/13 | L/11661 | Pte | A H | Westwood | desertion | 8/Queen's | 23 | 11 | 17 |
| Bleuet Farm Cem | 2/B/33 | 322497 | Rfn | F W | Slade | disobedience | 2/6 R Fus. | 14 | 12 | 17 |
| Borre Cem | 2/G/11 | 44174 | Pte | W | Scholes | desertion | 2/S Wales Borderers | 10 | 8 | 18 |
| Boulogne Eastern Cem | 8/B/81 | 18603 | Pte | G | Mills | desertion+ | 2/DCLI | 29 | 9 | 15 |
| Boulogne Eastern Cem | 8/A/137 | C/40124 | L/Bmdr | F S | Arnold | desertion | 1 Bde CFA | 25 | 7 | 16 |
| Boulogne Eastern Cem | 8/A/154 | 107526 | Pte | J W | Roberts | desertion+ | 2/Can Mount Rif | 30 | 7 | 16 |
| Boulogne Eastern Cem | 8/I/43 | 26/626 | A/Cpl | J R | Short | mutiny | 24/N. Fus. | 4 | 10 | 17 |
| Bouzincourt Com Cem Ex | 1/C/25 | 2676 | Pte | A G | Earp | quitting post+ | 1/5 Warwicks | 22 | 7 | 16 |
| Bray Mil Cem | 2/K/11 | 23972 | Cpl | J | Wilton | quitting post | 15/S'wood For. | 17 | 8 | 16 |
| Brown's Road Mil Cem | 4/D/19 | 5/3119 | Rfn | W. | Bellamy | cowardice | 1/KRRC | 16 | 7 | 15 |
| Brown's Road Mil Cem | 5/G/13 | 15251 | Pte | G H | Lawton | cowardice+ | 17/S'wood For. | 30 | 7 | 16 |
| Brown's Road Mil Cem | 5/B/16 | 31821 | Pte | B | McCubbin | cowardice+ | 17/S'wood For. | 30 | 7 | 16 |
| Bucquoy Rd Cem | 2/C/8 | 45688 | Pte | J B | Milburn | desertion | 24/27 N. Fus. | 8 | 11 | 17 |

| Cemetery or Memorial | Plot/Row/Grave | Regt. No. | Rank | Name | | Offence | Unit | Date of death |
|---|---|---|---|---|---|---|---|---|
| Bucquoy Rd Cem | 2/L/14 | 46127 | Pte | E | Horler | desertion | 12/W Yorks | 17 2 18 |
| Bully-Grenay Com Cem Brit Ex | 2/A/9 | 2506 | Pte | J | Smith | desertion | 1/Loyals | 2 7 16 |
| Bully-Grenay Com Cem Brit Ex | 2/B/14 | 67882 | Pte | E | Young | desertion | 25/CEF | 29 10 16 |
| Bully-Grenay Com Cem Brit Ex | 5/G/1 | G/52128 | Pte | D | Stevenson | desertion | 13/Middx | 18 7 18 |
| Bully-Grenay Com Cem French Ex | B/6 | 86872 | Dvr | J W | Swaine | desertion | 54 Bty 39 Bde RFA | 9 6 16 |
| Cabaret-Rouge BC/Fleurbaix Ch | Sp Mem 41 | 8225 | LCpl | P | Sands | desertion | 1/R Irish Rifles | 15 9 15 |
| Cabaret-Rouge BC/Merris Chyd | Sp.Mem.51 | 26248 | Pte | J. | Wishard | desertion | 7/R Inniskilling Fus. | 15 6 17 |
| Canadian Cem No.2 | 19/A/14 | 43619 | Pte | C M | Milligan | desertion | 10/Cameronians | 3 6 17 |
| Carnoy Mil Cem | Z/11 | 23992 | Pte | E W | Harris | desertion | 10/Lancs Fus. | 3 2 17 |
| Carnoy Mil Cem | Z/10 | 96498 | Dvr | R | Murray | desertion | 81 Bde RFA | 3 2 17 |
| Cavillon Com Cem | NW corner | 13167 | Pte | W H | Randle | desertion | 10/S'wood For. | 25 11 16 |
| Cavillon Com Cem | NW corner | 8534 | Pte | H | Poole | desertion | 7/Yorks | 9 12 16 |
| Cerisy- Gailly Mil Cem | 2/N/20 | 454610 | Pte | W N | Ling | desertion | 2/CEF | 12 8 18 |
| Chap.d'Armentieres Com Cem | E/1 | 62971 | Gnr | W | Jones | desertion | 43 Bty RFA | 20 4 15 |
| Chap.d'Armentieres Old Mil Cem | B/8 | 8014 | LCpl | A | Atkinson | desertion | 1/W Yorks | 2 3 15 |
| Chap.d'Armentieres Old Mil Cem | B/9 | 7981 | Pte | E | Kirk | desertion | 1/W Yorks | 6 3 15 |
| Chap.d'Armentieres Old Mil Cem | B/27 | 14780 | A/Cpl | A | Chisholm | murder | 20 Army Troop Coy RE | 17 5 15 |
| Chatby War Mem Cem Egypt | Grave 3 | 494 | Pte | N. | Matthews | murder | 3rd S African Infty | 3 4 16 |
| Choques Mil Cem | 3/C/10 | 18143 | Pte | A | Holmes | desertion | 8/King's Own | 22 4 18 |
| Choques Mil Cem | 3/A/19 | 20808 | Pte | R W | Simmers | desertion | 2/R Scots | 19 5 18 |
| Cité Bonjean Mil Cem | 9/G/94 | 14357 | Pte | F C H | Bladen | desertion | 10/York & Lancs | 23 3 16 |
| Cité Bonjean Mil Cem | 1/A/18 | 15469 | Pte | A H | Robinson | desertion | 9/N. Fus. | 10 5 16 |
| Cité Bonjean Mil Cem | 1/F/22 | 2057 | Pte | J | Higgins | desertion | 1/9 Argylls | 26 8 16 |
| Cité Bonjean Mil Cem | 2/A/3 | 11490 | Pte | T H B | Rigby | desertion | 10/S Wales Borderers | 22 11 17 |
| Corbie Com Cem Ex | 2/C/86 | 21373 | Pte | J | Carey | desertion | 7/R Irish Fusiliers | 15 9 16 |
| Côte 80 French Nat Cem | B/2 | 71502 | Dvr | J | Spencer | desertion | 65 Bty 8 Bde RFA | 29 9 15 |
| Coxyde Mil Cem | 3/G/6 | 2064 | Pte | W | Wycherley | desertion | 2/Manchesters | 12 9 17 |
| Coxyde Mil Cem | 4/G/23 | R/24441 | Rfn | F W | Cheeseman | desertion | 18/KRRC | 20 10 17 |
| Coxyde Mil Cem | 4/G/24 | 94236 | Spr | A P | Oyns | desertion | 50 Search Light Coy RE | 20 10 17 |
| Dartmoor Cem | 2/B/1 | 8/1384 | Pte | J J | Sweeney | desertion | 1/Otago (NZ) | 2 10 16 |
| Dickebusch New Mil Cem | D/15 | 8992 | LCpl | J S V | Fox | desertion | 1/Wilts att.3/Div Cy Coy | 20 4 15 |
| Dranoutre Mil Cem | 2/J/24 | 17402 | Pte | F | Broadrick | desertion | 11/Warwicks | 1 8 17 |
| Duhallows ADS Cem | 3/F/10 | 10603 | Pte | J | Seymour | desertion | 2/R Inniskilling Fus. | 24 1 18 |
| Duisans British Cem | 5/G/46 | 7674 | Cpl | J | Reid | desertion | 6/Camerons | 11 5 18 |
| Ecoivres Mil Cem | 2/E/17 | 13857 | LCpl | J | Holland | cowardice+ | 10/Cheshire | 30 5 16 |
| Ecoivres Mil Cem | 6/C/7 | 416008 | Pte | E | Perry | desertion | 22/CEF | 11 4 17 |
| Ecoivres Mil Cem | 6/K/19 | 830020 | Pte | D | Sinizki | cowardice | 52/CEF | 9 10 17 |
| Ecoivres Mil Cem | 5/L/8 | 285031 | Pte | M R | Richmond | desertion | 1/6 Gordons | 26 5 18 |
| Englebelmer Com Cem Ex | D/5 | 12396 | Pte | J | Cassidy | desertion | 1/R Inniskilling Fus. | 23 7 16 |
| Esquelbecq Com Cem | 1 of 2 | 9694 | Pte | J H | Abigail | desertion | 8/Norfolk | 12 9 17 |
| Esquelbecq Mil Cem | 1/B/1A | 4/9170 | Pte | G | Hunter | desertion+ | 2/DLI | 2 7 16 |
| Estaires Communal Cem | 3/D/ | 10853 | Pte | A | Troughton | desertion+ | 1/R Welsh Fus. | 22 4 15 |
| Estaires Communal Cem | 3/D/ | 10958 | Pte | M | Penn | desertion+ | 1/R Welsh Fus. | 22 4 15 |
| Faubourg d'Amiens Cem | 4/J/16 | G10474 | Pte | R G | Pattison | desertion | 7/Queen's | 4 7 17 |
| Faubourg d'Amiens Cem | 4/J/17 | G/4495 | Pte | J E | Barnes | desertion | 7/R Sussex | 4 7 17 |
| Favreuil British Cem | 1/B/20 | R/28638 | Rfn | A E | Allsop | desertion | 12/KRRC | 15 6 17 |
| Ferme-Olivier Cem | 3/C/12 | 8139 | Pte | G | Watkins | desertion | 13/Welsh | 15 5 17 |
| Ferme-Olivier Cem | 3/G/12 | 23726 | Pte | R | Hope | desertion | 1/R Inniskilling Fus. | 5 7 17 |
| Fienvillers Brit Cem | D/22 | 20062 | Pte | J A | Anderson | cowardice+ | 12/King's (L'pool) | 12 9 16 |
| Fins New Brit Cem | 6/E/20 | G/6565 | Pte | H J | Knight | desertion | 1/R W Surrey | 6 10 18 |
| Forceville Com Cem | 3/E/2 | 15094 | Pte | J | Lewis | desertion | 5/Dorset | 19 4 17 |
| Gezaincourt Com Cem Ex | 1/P/1 | 9828 | Pte | W E | Anderson | desertion+ | 5/Dorset | 31 3 17 |
| Ghissignies British Cem | B/34 | 43055 | Pte | L | Harris | desertion | 10/W Yorks | 7 11 18 |
| Gorre British Cem | 5/D/13 | 307350 | Pte | T | Hopkins | leaving his post | 1/8 Lancs Fus. | 13 2 18 |
| Green Hill Cem Gallipoli | 1/G/26 | 16734 | Pte | H | Salter | desertion+ | 6/E Lancs | 11 12 15 |
| HAC Cem | 8/C/23 | R/15325 | Rfn | J | Woodhouse | desertion | 12/KRRC | 4 10 17 |
| Habarcq Com Cem Ex | 8/J/7 | 5626 | Pte | J | McQuade | desertion | 18/HLI | 6 11 16 |
| Habarcq Com Cem Ex | 8/G/7 | 5323 | Pte | H | Flynn | desertion | 18/HLI | 15 11 16 |
| Hagle Dump Cem | 1/E/7 | 45980 | Pte | W | Dossett | desertion | 1/4 York & Lancs | 25 6 18 |
| Hagle Dump Cem | 2/D/5 | 202893 | Pte | G | Ainley | desertion | 1/4 KOYLI | 30 7 18 |
| Haidar Pasha Cem | 1/J/5 | 7076018 | Pte | R | Flynn | murder | 2/R Dublin Fus. | 6 11 20 |
| Hallencourt Com Cem | 2 graves | 24/2008 | Pte | F | Hughes | desertion | 2/Cant (NZ) | 25 8 16 |
| Ham British Cem | 1/G/8 | 17137 | Pte | T | Hogan | desertion | 2/R Inniskilling Fus. | 14 5 17 |

*281*

| Cemetery or Memorial | Plot/Row/Grave | Regt. No. | Rank | Name | | Offence | Unit | Date of death |
|---|---|---|---|---|---|---|---|---|
| Hazebrouck Com Cem | 1/A/13 | 2063 | Dvr | B | De Fehr | murder | 1/Res. Pk (Can.ASC) | 25 8 16 |
| Hermonville Mil Cem | 3/G/6 | 13612 | Pte | F | O'Neill | desertion | 1/S'wood For. | 16 5 18 |
| Hersin Com Cem Ex | 3/B/1 | 36224 | Pte | J | Skone | murder | 2/Welsh | 10 5 18 |
| Hersin Com Cem Ex | 3/E/2 | 21801 | Pte | A | Briggs | desertion | 9/S'wood For. | 19 7 18 |
| Hyde Park Corner Cem | A/17 | 5009 | Rfn | S | McBride | desertion | 2/R Irish Rifles | 7 12 16 |
| Kantara War Memorial Cem Egypt | D/60 | 4881 | Pte | H A | Clarke | striking a S.O. | 2/Brit W Indies | 11 8 17 |
| Karasouli Mil Cem Greece | A/22 | S/5470 | Pte | A | Brown | desertion | 10/B Watch | 1 6 17 |
| Karasouli Mil Cem Greece | C/487 | 13827 | L/Sgt | H | Ashton | desertion | 11/Cameronians | 8 7 17 |
| Karasouli Mil Cem Greece | D/885 | 204232 | Pte | R | Young | desertion | 11/Worcs | 18 9 18 |
| Kemmel Château Mil Cem | G/66 | A/6730 | Pte | S | Stewart | desertion | 2/R Scots Fus. | 29 8 17 |
| Kemmel Château Mil Cem | M/25 | 52929 | Pte | J | Smith | desertion+ | 17/King's (L'pool) | 5 9 17 |
| Kirkee Memorial | - | 7144396 | Pte | JJ | Daly | mutiny | 1/Conn Rangers | 2 11 20 |
| Kumasi Mem German East Africa | - | 7560 | Pte | A | Frafra | cast'g away arms | Gold Coast | 28 9 16 |
| Kumasi Mem German East Africa | - | A/2600 | Pte | D | Barama | murder | Gold Coast Mtd.Inf.Coy | 10 11 18 |
| La Clytte Mil Cem | 3/A/2 | 31184 | Pte | L | Mitchell | desertion | 8/York & Lancs | 19 9 17 |
| La Ferté-sous-Jouarre Memorial | - | L/10061 | Pte | T J | Highgate | desertion | 1/R W Kent | 8 9 14 |
| La Ferté-sous-Jouarre Memorial | - | 9641 | Pte | G | Ward | cowardice | 1/R Berks | 26 9 14 |
| La Kreule Mil Cem | 3/C/1 | 4519 | Pte | H | Hendricks | desertion | 2/Leinster | 23 8 18 |
| Labourse Com Cem | B/3 | 21161 | Pte | H | Martin | desertion | 9/Essex | 20 3 16 |
| Labourse Com Cem | B/5 | 11/1799 | Pte | A | Beverstein | desertion | 11/Middx | 20 3 16 |
| Labourse Com Cem | B/4 | G/7547 | Pte | W L | Thompson | desertion | 6/Buffs | 22 4 16 |
| Lapugnoy Mil Cem | 7/A/11 | 8793 | Pte | J | Taylor | desertion | 2/S Staffs | 6 11 17 |
| Lapugnoy Mil Cem | 8/B/8 | 34453 | Pte | A C | Dagesse | desertion | 22/CEF | 15 3 18 |
| Le Cauroy Com Cem | 1 of 4 | 43359 | Sgt | G E | Gleadow | desertion | 1/W Yorks | 6 4 17 |
| Le Cauroy Com Cem | 4 graves | 251797 | Pte | W | Benham | desertion | 1/3 R Fus. | 12 7 17 |
| Le Crotoy Com Cem | - | | Sub/Lt | E L A | Dyett | desertion | Nelson Bn RND | 5 1 17 |
| Le Grand Beaumont Brit Cem | 3/H/19 | 2710 | L Cpl | W J | Irvine | desertion+ | 1/King's Own | 20 4 15 |
| Le Grand Beaumont Brit Cem | 3/H/20 | 8136 | Pte | J | Kershaw | desertion+ | 1/King's Own | 26 4 15 |
| Le Grand Hasard Mil Cem | 3/B/9 | 15437 | Pte | C W | Knight | murder | 10/R Welsh Fus. | 15 11 15 |
| Le Touret Memorial | - | 5919 | Pte | E | Tanner | desertion | 1/Wilts | 27 10 14 |
| Le Touret Memorial | - | L/14164 | Pte | F | Sheffield | desertion | 2/Middx | 12 1 15 |
| Le Touret Memorial | - | L/14232 | Pte | J | Ball | desertion | 2/Middx | 12 1 15 |
| Le Touret Memorial | - | 2222 | Pte | T | Cummings | desertion | 1/Irish Guards | 28 1 15 |
| Le Touret Memorial | - | 3379 | Pte | A | Smythe | desertion | 1/Irish Guards | 28 1 15 |
| Le Touret Memorial | - | 5231 | Pte | J | Briggs | desertion | 2/Borders | 6 3 15 |
| Le Touret Memorial | - | 6584 | Pte | J | Duncan | desertion | 1/Camerons | 7 3 15 |
| Le Touret Memorial | - | 70304 | Dvr | J | Bell | desertion | 57 Bty 43 How.Bde RFA | 25 4 15 |
| Lederzeele Chyd | 1 of 3 | 11046 | Pte | H J | Webb | desertion | 2/KOYLI | 31 10 17 |
| Les Baraques Mil Cem | 9/C | 10272 | Coolie | C H | Yang | murder | Chin Lab Corps | 26 6 18 |
| Les Baraques Mil Cem | 9/C | 10299 | Coolie | E J | Wang | murder | Chin Lab Corps | 26 6 18 |
| Les Baraques Mil Cem | 9/C | 46090 | Coolie | H I | Chao | murder | Chin Lab Corps | 9 8 18 |
| Les Baraques Mil Cem | | 50079 | Pte | J | Chandler | murder | Lincs | 11 8 19 |
| Les Baraques Mil Cem | 9/C | 16174 | Collie | J C | Chang | murder x4 | Chin Lab Coy | 14 2 20 |
| Lijssenthoek Mil Cem | 25/B/22 | 22635 | Pte | W | Baker | desertion | 26/R Fus. | 14 8 18 |
| Lillers Com Cem | 4/E/16 | 6807 | Pte | JJ | Dennis | desertion | 1/N'hamptons | 30 1 16 |
| Locre Chyd | 1/A/1 | 15576 | Pte | J | Byers | desertion | 1/R Scots Fus. | 6 2 15 |
| Locre Chyd | 1/A/2 | 7177 | Pte | A | Evans | desertion | 1/R Scots Fus. | 6 2 15 |
| Locre Chyd | 1/B/1 | 9618 | Pte | G E | Collins | desertion | 1/Lincs | 15 2 15 |
| Locre Hospice Cem | 1/A/22 | 40435 | Pte | D J | Blakemore | desertion | 8/N Staffs | 9 7 17 |
| Locre Hospice Cem | 1/C/4 | 15954 | Pte | W | Jones | desertion | 9/R Welsh Fus. | 25 10 17 |
| R Fus. Cem Neuville-Vitasse | 1/C/1 | 1529 | Pte | S H | Cunnington | desertion | 2/Warwicks | 19 5 17 |
| Longuenesse (Souvenir) Cem | 1/A/68 | 7552 | L/Sgt | W | Walton | desertion | 2/KRRC | 23 3 15 |
| Longuenesse (Souvenir) Cem | 3/B/26 | 8752 | Pte | I | Reid | desertion | 2/Scots Guards | 9 4 15 |
| Longuenesse (Souvenir) Cem | 5/F/71 | 9/28719 | Pte | J | Cuthbert | disobedience | 9/Cheshire | 6 5 16 |
| Longuenesse (Souvenir) Cem | 4/A/39 | 404436 | Pte | E J | Reynolds | desertion | 3/CEF | 23 8 16 |
| Longuenesse (Souvenir) Cem | 4/E/66 | 32559 | Pte | C B | Nicholson | desertion | 8/York & Lancs | 27 10 17 |
| Loos Memorial | - | G/12341 | Pte | W | Bowerman | desertion | 1/Queen's | 24 3 17 |
| Loos Memorial | - | 43499 | Pte | T | Foulkes | desertion | 1/10 Manchesters | 21 11 17 |

| Cemetery or Memorial | Plot/Row/Grave | Regt. No. | Rank | Name | | Offence | Unit | Date of death | | |
|---|---|---|---|---|---|---|---|---|---|---|
| Louez Mil Cem | 2/F/6 | 10018 | Pte | P | Giles | desertion | 14/N. Fus. | 24 | 8 | 16 |
| Louvencourt Mil Cem | 1/D/17 | 43665 | Pte | H | MacDonald | desertion | 12/W Yorks | 4 | 11 | 16 |
| Louvencourt Mil Cem | 1/D/20 | 10758 | Rfn | F M | Barratt | desertion | 7/KRRC | 10 | 7 | 17 |
| Mailly-Maillet Com Cem | C/21 | 15/13211 | Rfn | J E | McCracken | desertion | 15/R Irish Rifles | 19 | 3 | 16 |
| Mailly-Maillet Com Cem | C/20 | 15/890 | Rfn | J | Templeton | desertion | 15/R Irish Rifles | 19 | 3 | 16 |
| Maple Leaf Cem | K/4 | 42467 | Pte | A | Parry | desertion | 2/W Yorks | 30 | 8 | 17 |
| Maroc British Cem | 1/B/38 | 10710 | Pte | W | Hunter | desertion+ | 1/Loyals | 21 | 2 | 16 |
| Maroc British Cem | 1/H/39 | 1214 | Pte | W | Watts | desertion+ | 1/Loyals | 5 | 5 | 16 |
| Maroc British Cem | 1/H/6 | 10161 | Pte | J | Molyneaux | desertion | 1/Loyals | 15 | 6 | 16 |
| Mazingarbe Com Cem | 42 | 9948 | Pte | J | Graham | desertion+ | 2/R Munster Fus. | 21 | 12 | 15 |
| Mazingarbe Com Cem | 3 | S/9672 | Pte | J | Docherty | desertion | 9/B Watch | 15 | 2 | 16 |
| Mazingarbe Com Cem | 104 | 9840 | Pte | J T | Jones | desertion+ | 1/ N'hamptons | 24 | 2 | 16 |
| Mazingarbe Com Cem | 103 | 4437 | Pte | A | Dale | murder | 13/R Scots | 3 | 3 | 16 |
| Mazingarbe Com Cem | 98 | B/21000 | Cpl | C. | Lewis | desertion | 12/HLI | 11 | 3 | 16 |
| Mazingarbe Com Cem Ex | 1/A/12 | 1/15134 | Pte | A | O'Neil | desertion | 1/S Wales Borderers | 30 | 4 | 16 |
| Mazingarbe Com Cem Ex | 1/B/5 | L/36251 | Dvr | J W | Hasemore | disobedience+ | 180 Bde RFA | 12 | 5 | 16 |
| Mazingarbe Com Cem Ex | 1/D/2 | 12727 | Pte | J. | Thomas | desertion | 2/Welsh | 20 | 5 | 16 |
| Mazingarbe Com Cem Ex | 1/D/3 | L/10414 | Pte | W H | Burrell | desertion | 2/Sussex | 22 | 5 | 16 |
| Mazingarbe Com Cem Ex | 1/D/7 | R/19333 | Rfn | E A | Card | desertion | 20/KRRC | 22 | 9 | 16 |
| Mazingarbe Com Cem Ex | 3/B/12 | A/38119 | Pte | C. | Welsh | desertion | 8/CEF | 6 | 3 | 18 |
| Mendingham British Cem | 5/A/29 | R/27615 | Rfn | J J | Hyde | desertion | 10/KRRC | 5 | 9 | 17 |
| Mendingham British Cem | 7/F/36 | 200757 | Pte | C | Britton | desertion | 1/5 Warwicks | 12 | 9 | 17 |
| Mendingham British Cem | 10/E/19 | 38332 | Pte | D | Gibson | desertion | 12/R Scots | 24 | 9 | 18 |
| Menin Gate Memorial | - | S/6922 | Pte | W | Scotton | desertion | 4/Middx | 3 | 2 | 15 |
| Menin Gate Memorial | - | 10459 | Cpl | G H | Povey | leaving his post | 1/Cheshire | 11 | 2 | 15 |
| Menin Gate Memorial | - | T4/040862 | Dvr | T | Moore | murder | 24 Division Train ASC | 26 | 2 | 16 |
| Mikra British Cem Salonika | G/9 | 6/227 | Pte | P J | Downey | disobedience | 6/Leinster | 27 | 12 | 15 |
| Montigny Com Cem Ex | A/21 | 39463 | Pte | J | Swain | desertion | 5/R Berks | 11 | 8 | 18 |
| Morbecque British Cem | 1/G/19 | 305 | Pte | W T | Spry | desertion | 2/R Fus. | 14 | 6 | 18 |
| Neuville-Bourjonval Brit Cem | E/16 | 12609 | Pte | G | Hanna | desertion | 1/R Irish Fusiliers | 6 | 11 | 17 |
| Nine Elms British Cem Belgium | 11/A/2 | 265427 | Pte | J | McFarlane | desertion | 4/King's (L'pool) | 22 | 5 | 18 |
| Nine Elms British Cem Belgium | 15/C/21 | 11682 | Pte | J | Nisbet | desertion | 1/Leics | 23 | 8 | 18 |
| Noeux-les-Mines Com Cem | 1/P/2 | S/2889 | Pte | F | Murray | murder | 9/Gordons, att.RE | 1 | 10 | 16 |
| Noeux-les-Mines Com Cem | 1/P/17 | 39213 | Pte | A | Hamilton | desertion | 14/DLI | 27 | 3 | 17 |
| Noeux-les-Mines Com Cem | 1/P/18 | 13224 | Spr | F | Malyon | desertion | 12 Coy RE att.RFA | 4 | 4 | 17 |
| Noeux-les-Mines Com Cem | 4/B/5 | 2095 | Pte | H E J | Lodge | desertion | 19/CEF | 13 | 3 | 18 |
| Noeux-les-Mines Com Cem Ex | 5/A/19 | 21654 | Pte | L D | Elford | desertion | 7/8 KOSB | 11 | 10 | 18 |
| Norfolk Cem | 1/D/85 | 8037 | Pte | J | Jennings | desertion | 2/S Lancs | 26 | 6 | 16 |
| Norfolk Cem | 1/D/86 | 549 | Pte | G | Lewis | desertion | 2/S Lancs | 26 | 6 | 16 |
| Peronne Com Cem Ex | 3/B/22 | 70715 | Pte | W | Robinson | desertion | 1/S'wood For. | 10 | 4 | 17 |
| Perth (China Wall) Cem | 6/K/20 | 3/1433 | Pte | G E | Roe | desertion | 2/KOYLI | 10 | 6 | 15 |
| Perth (China Wall) Cem | 5/K/14 | L/10132 | Pte | T | Harris | desertion | 1/R W Kent | 21 | 6 | 15 |
| Perth (China Wall) Cem | 6/E/1 | 11559 | Pte | T | Docherty | desertion | 2/KOSB | 16 | 7 | 15 |
| Perth (China Wall) Cem | 1/G/41 | 12295 | Cpl | F | Ives | desertion | 3/Worcs | 26 | 7 | 15 |
| Perth (China Wall) Cem | 5/K/13 | 9722 | Pte | E | Fellows | desertion | 3/Worcs | 26 | 7 | 15 |
| Perth (China Wall) Cem | Sp Mem C/8 | 11653 | Pte | E | Fraser | desertion+ | 2/R Scots | 2 | 8 | 15 |
| Perth (China Wall) Cem | 6/K/1 | 10315 | Pte | L R | Phillips | desertion | 6/SLI | 19 | 8 | 15 |
| Ploegsteert Memorial | - | 8278 | Pte | A | Browne | desertion+ | 2/Essex | 19 | 12 | 14 |
| Ploegsteert Memorial | - | 8747 | Pte | A. | Pitts | desertion | 2/ Warwicks | 8 | 2 | 15 |
| Ploegsteert Memorial | - | 9689 | Pte | T | Hope | desertion+ | 2/Leinster | 2 | 3 | 15 |
| Pont d'Achelles Mil Cem | 1/F/3 | G/8857 | Pte | E | Worsley | desertion | 2/Middx | 22 | 10 | 17 |
| Poperinghe New Mil Cem | 2/H/2 | 10701 | Pte | J H | Wilson | desertion | 4/CEF | 9 | 7 | 16 |
| Poperinghe New Mil Cem | 2/H/3 | 416874 | Pte | C | LaLiberte | desertion | 3/CEF | 4 | 8 | 16 |
| Poperinghe New Mil Cem | 2/J/7 | 3/4071 | Pte | J | Bennett | cowardice | 1/Hants | 28 | 8 | 16 |
| Poperinghe New Mil Cem | 2/F/7 | 12772 | Pte | A | Botfield | cowardice | 9/S Staffs | 18 | 10 | 16 |
| Poperinghe New Mil Cem | 2/H/9 | 2554 | Pte | R | Stevenson | desertion | 1/4 Loyals | 25 | 10 | 16 |
| Poperinghe New Mil Cem | 2/D/9 | 2974 | Pte | B | McGeehan | desertion | 1/8 King's (L'pool) | 2 | 11 | 16 |
| Poperinghe New Mil Cem | 2/F/9 | SD/4242 | Pte | R T | Tite | cowardice | 13/Sussex | 25 | 11 | 16 |
| Poperinghe New Mil Cem | 2/E/9 | G/11296 | Pte | W H | Simmonds | desertion | 23/Middx | 1 | 12 | 16 |
| Poperinghe New Mil Cem | 2/A/11 | - | 2/Lt | E S | Poole | desertion | 11/W Yorks | 10 | 12 | 16 |
| Poperinghe New Mil Cem | 2/B/14 | 34595 | Pte | J | Crampton | desertion | 9/York & Lancs | 4 | 2 | 17 |
| Poperinghe New Mil Cem | 2/D/14 | 16120 | Pte | J W | Fryer | desertion | 12/Queen's | 14 | 6 | 17 |
| Poperinghe New Mil Cem | 2/H/24 | 23686 | Pte | J S | Michael | desertion | 10/Cameronians | 24 | 8 | 17 |

| Cemetery or Memorial | Plot/Row/Grave | Regt. No. | Rank | Name | | Offence | Unit | Date of death | | |
|---|---|---|---|---|---|---|---|---|---|---|
| Poperinghe New Mil Cem | 2/F/41 | 88378 | Pte | J | Stedman | desertion | 117 Coy MGC | 5 | 9 | 17 |
| Poperinghe New Mil Cem | 2/F/42 | 13216 | Sgt | J T | Wall | desertion | 3/Worcs | 6 | 9 | 17 |
| Poperinghe New Mil Cem | 2/F/44 | 8833 | Pte | G | Everill | desertion | 1/N Staffs | 14 | 9 | 17 |
| Poperinghe New Mil Cem | 2/F/45 | 7429 | Pte | H | Morris | desertion | 6/Brit W Indies | 20 | 9 | 17 |
| Poperinghe New Mil Cem | 2/J/34 | G/15605 | Pte | F C | Gore | desertion | 7/Buffs | 16 | 10 | 17 |
| Poperinghe Old Mil Cem | 2/O/54 | 44735 | Coolie | C C | Wang | murder | 107 Chin Lab Coy | 8 | 5 | 19 |
| Quatre Vent Mil Cem | 2/A/6 | 11528 | Pte | F | Harding | desertion | 1/KRRC | 29 | 6 | 16 |
| Quatre Vent Mil Cem | 2/A/9 | 12182 | Pte | A | Murphy | desertion | 9/Cameronians | 17 | 8 | 16 |
| Quatre Vent Mil Cem | 3/A/9 | 457241 | Pte | H H | Kerr | desertion | 7/CEF | 21 | 11 | 16 |
| Quatre Vent Mil Cem | 1/B/2 | 177753 | Pte | J M | Higgins | desertion | 1/CEF | 7 | 12 | 16 |
| Ramleh Cem Palestine | AA/71 | 9191 | Pte | J A | Mitchell | murder+ | 1/Brit W Indies | 22 | 12 | 17 |
| Reninghelst New Mil Cem | 2/E/15 | 1731 | Rfn | R L | Barker | cowardice | 6/R Fus. (City of Lond.) | 4 | 11 | 16 |
| Reninghelst New Mil Cem | 3/B/14 | 683458 | Pte | F | Loader | desertion | 1/22 R Fus. (The Queen's) | 19 | 8 | 17 |
| Reninghelst New Mil Cem | 4/B/28 | 204455 | Pte | W | Smith | desertion | 3/5 Lancs Fus. | 14 | 11 | 17 |
| Ribemont Com Cem Ex | 4/M/5 | 541 | Tpr | A | Butler | murder | R Can Dragoons | 2 | 7 | 16 |
| Ribemont Com Cem Ex | 3/K/5 | 67440 | Dvr | T G | Hamilton | striking a S.O. | 72 Bty 38 Bde RFA | 3 | 10 | 16 |
| Ribemont Com Cem Ex | 3/K/4 | 64987 | Dvr | J | Mullany | striking a S.O. | 72 Bty 38 Bde RFA | 3 | 10 | 16 |
| Ribemont Com Cem Ex | 2/A/7 | 5/1791 | Pte | J | Cameron | desertion | 1/5 N. Fus. | 4 | 12 | 16 |
| Roclincourt Mil Cem | 2/F/4 | 393923 | Rfn | H | Williams | desertion | 1/9 R Fus. (QVR) | 28 | 12 | 17 |
| Roclincourt Valley Cem | 2/F/7 | 10263 | Pte | E | Bolton | desertion | 1/Cheshire | 14 | 4 | 16 |
| Rocquigny-Equancourt Rd Br Cem | 6/A/27 | 200945 | Pte | J | Bateman | desertion | 2/S Staffs | 3 | 12 | 17 |
| Romeries Com Cem Ex | 4/C/20 | G/46730 | Pte | E | Jackson | desertion | 24/R Fus. | 7 | 11 | 18 |
| Royal Irish Rifles Graveyard | 4/D/2 | 8662 | Pte | O W | Hodgetts | cowardice | 1/Worcs | 4 | 6 | 15 |
| Sailly-Labourse Com Cem | O/2 | G/335 | Pte | H | Carter | desertion | 11/Middx | 26 | 4 | 16 |
| Sailly-sur-la-Lys Can Cem | 1/E/87 | S/9405 | Rfn | W | Smith | desertion | 2/Rifle Bde | 3 | 10 | 15 |
| Sailly-sur-la-Lys Can Cem | 1/E/86 | S/9560 | Rfn | G A | Irish | desertion | 2/Rifle Bde | 3 | 10 | 15 |
| Sand Pits Cem | 4/E/5 | 15161 | Pte | P | Murphy | desertion | 47 Bn MGC | 12 | 9 | 18 |
| St Nicolas British Cem | 2/C/17 | S/15240 | Pte | T | Ward | desertion | 8/10 Gordons | 16 | 10 | 17 |
| St Nicolas British Cem | 2/C/16 | S/15954 | Pte | N H | Taysum | desertion | 9/B Watch | 16 | 10 | 17 |
| St Nicolas British Cem | 2/C/18 | S/17688 | Pte | J S | Adamson | cowardice | 7/Camerons | 23 | 11 | 17 |
| St Nicolas British Cem | 2/D/1 | S/9696 | Pte | H | Dalande | desertion | 8/Seaforths | 9 | 3 | 18 |
| St Pol Com Cem Ex | D/2 | 19/158 | LCpl | P | Goggins | quitting post | 19/DLI | 18 | 1 | 17 |
| St Pol Com Cem Ex | D/3 | 19/420 | LCpl | J | McDonald | quitting post | 19/DLI | 18 | 1 | 17 |
| St Pol Com Cem Ex | D/1 | 19/647 | L/Sgt | J W | Stones | cast'g away arms | 19/DLI | 18 | 1 | 17 |
| St Sever Cem Ex | O/1/M/8 | 52081 | Gnr | W E | Lewis | mutiny | 124 Bde RFA/Details RFA | 29 | 10 | 16 |
| St Sever Cem Ex | O/1/K/10 | 24/1521 | Pte | J | Braithwaite | mutiny | 2/Otago (NZ) | 29 | 10 | 16 |
| St Sever Cem Ex | S/1/E/2 | 5884 | Coolie | F Y | Wan | murder | Chin Lab Corps | 15 | 2 | 19 |
| St Sever Cem Ex | S/1/F/1 | 97170 | Coolie | C M | Hei | murder | Chin Lab Corps | 21 | 2 | 20 |
| St Sever Cem Ex | S/1/F/6 | 44340 | Coolie | C H | K'ung | murder | Chin Lab Corps | 21 | 2 | 20 |
| St Vaast Post Mil Cem | 1/G/1 | 8710 | Pte | E A | Beaumont | desertion | 2/Leics | 24 | 6 | 15 |
| Ste Catherine British Cem | E/32 | 14813 | Pte | T W | Watts | desertion | 7/E Yorks | 30 | 8 | 17 |
| Ste Catherine British Cem | E/33 | 19445 | Pte | W | Neave | desertion | 10/W Yorks | 30 | 8 | 17 |
| Ste Catherine British Cem | F/1 | 7423 | Pte | C H | Kirman | desertion | 7/Lincs | 23 | 9 | 17 |
| Ste Marie Cem | Div62/1/K3 | 3019 | L/Sgt | A | Wickings | murder | 9/Rifle Bde | 7 | 3 | 18 |
| Ste Marie Cem | Div64/6/E5 | 253617 | Gnr | F O | Wills | murder | X50th TMB RFA | 27 | 5 | 19 |
| Sucrerie Mil Cem | 1/A/5 | 14218 | Rfn | J | Crozier | desertion | 9/R Irish Rifles | 27 | 2 | 16 |
| Suzanne Mil Cem No.3 | 1/C/7 | S/6778 | Pte | F | Wright | desertion | 1/R W Surrey | 28 | 1 | 17 |
| Suzanne Mil Cem No.3 | 1/C/10 | 1763 | Pte | B A | Hart | desertion | 1/4 Suffolk | 6 | 2 | 17 |
| Suzanne Mil Cem No.3 | 2/C/1 | 3/10390 | Pte | F | Stead | desertion | 2/Duke of Wellington's | 12 | 2 | 17 |
| Taranto Town Cem Ex Italy | 6/D/4 | 11080 | Pte | A | Denny | murder | 8/Brit W Indies | 20 | 1 | 19 |
| Terlincthun Brit Mil Cem | 4/B/48 | - | 2/Lt | J H | Paterson | murder | 3/Essex att. 1st | 24 | 9 | 18 |
| The Huts Cem | 15/B/10 | 8/2733 | Pte | V M | Spencer | desertion | 1/Otago (NZ) | 24 | 2 | 18 |
| The Huts Cem | 15/D/15 | 242904 | Pte | H | Hughes | desertion | 1/5 York & Lancs | 10 | 4 | 18 |
| Thiepval Memorial | - | 8871 | Pte | H T | Farr | cowardice | 1/W Yorks | 18 | 10 | 16 |
| Thiepval Memorial | - | SR/9629 | Pte | C W F | Skilton | desertion | 22/R Fus. | 26 | 12 | 16 |
| Thiepval Memorial | - | 40806 | Pte | P | Cairnie | desertion | 1/R Scots Fus. | 28 | 12 | 16 |
| Toutencourt Com Cem | 2/A/9 | 62536 | Spr | R | Bell | murder | 123 Field Coy RE | 22 | 5 | 18 |
| Trois Arbres Cem | 2/F/17 | 2267 | Cpl | G W | Latham | desertion+ | 2/Lancs Fus. | 22 | 1 | 15 |

284

| Cemetery or Memorial | Plot/Row/Grave | Regt. No. | Rank | | Name | Offence | Unit | Date of death |
|---|---|---|---|---|---|---|---|---|
| Trois Arbres Cem | 3/H/5 | 23621 | Pte | F | Auger | desertion | 14/CEF | 26 3 16 |
| Trois Arbres Cem | 1/B/1 | 6744 | Pte | P | Black | desertion | 1/4 B Watch | 18 9 16 |
| Trois Arbres Cem | 1/Z/23 | 6/1598 | Pte | J | King | desertion | 1/Cant (NZ) | 19 8 17 |
| Twelve Tree Copse Cem Gallipoli | SpMemC259 | 9610 | Sgt | J | Robins | disobedience+ | 5/Wilts | 2 1 16 |
| Vieille Chapelle New Mil Cem | 5/F/9 | 18/313 | Pte | H | Crimmins | desertion | 18/W Yorks | 5 9 16 |
| Vieille Chapelle New Mil Cem | 5/F/6 | 18/356 | Pte | A | Wild | desertion | 18/W Yorks | 5 9 16 |
| Vieille Chapelle New Mil Cem | 6/F/5 | 7595 | Pte | J A | Haddock | desertion | 12/York & Lancs | 16 9 16 |
| Villers Station Cem | 10/A/7 | 454482 | Pte | H G | Carter | desertion | 73/CEF | 20 4 17 |
| Villers Station Cem | 11/B/23 | 227098 | Pte | E. | Fairburn | desertion | 18/CEF | 2 3 18 |
| Villers Station Cem | 13/B/1 | 718566 | Pte | S McD | Fowles | desertion | 44/CEF | 19 6 18 |
| Villers Station Cem | 12/C/4 | 203313 | Pte | F | Bateman | desertion | 1/4 York & Lancs | 10 9 18 |
| Vincennes New Com Cem (Paris) | NE corner | 20035 | Pte | F | Johnson | desertion | 2/Borders | 1 8 18 |
| Vincennes New Com Cem (Paris) | NE corner | 20037 | Pte | H | McClair | desertion | 2/Borders | 1 8 18 |
| Vis-en-Artois Memorial | - | G/18469 | Pte | F C | Butcher | desertion | 7/Buffs | 27 8 18 |
| Vlamertinghe Mil Cem | 2/E/12 | 29219 | Dvr | A | Lamb | desertion | 21 Bty 2 Bde RFA | 2 10 15 |
| Vlamertinghe Mil Cem | 4/D/7 | 12923 | Pte | A | Rickman | desertion | 1/R Dublin Fus. | 15 9 16 |
| Vlamertinghe New Mil Cem | 9/H/19 | 335727 | Pte | E | Delargey | desertion | 1/8 R Scots | 6 9 17 |
| Wanquetin Com Cem | 1/C/13 | 10930 | Pte | J | Ferguson | desertion | 1/R Scots Fus., att. RE | 20 4 17 |
| Warlincourt Halte British Cem | 12/C/8 | 9541 | LCpl | F | Hawthorne | cowardice+ | 1/5 S Staffs | 11 8 16 |
| Warlincourt Halte British Cem | 12/B/10 | 41643 | Pte | W J | Earl | desertion | 1/7 Lancs Fus. | 27 5 18 |
| Warlincourt Halte British Cem | 11/C/15 | 300199 | Pte | T | Brigham | desertion | 1/10 Manchesters | 4 6 18 |
| Warloy-Baillon Com Cem Ex | 6/D/18 | 11257 | LCpl | G E | Hughes | desertion | 7/King's Own | 23 11 16 |
| Warlus Com Cem | only grave | A/1579 | Rfn | A E | Parker | desertion+ | 7/KRRC | 15 5 16 |
| Westhof Farm Cem | 2/D/14 | A/201225 | Rfn | T | Donovan | desertion | 16/KRRC | 31 10 17 |
| White House Cem | 3/P/1 | 2779 | Pte | H H | Chase | cowardice | 2/Lancs Fus. | 12 6 15 |
| White House Cem | 2/C/24 | G/7171 | Pte | W J | Turpie | desertion | 2/Queen's | 1 7 15 |
| White House Cem | 3/L/9 | L/10098 | Pte | R W | Gawler | desertion | 1/Buffs | 24 2 16 |
| White House Cem | 3/L/10 | L/8107 | Pte | A E | Eveleigh | desertion | 1/Buffs | 24 2 16 |
| Wizernes Com Cem | 1 of 3 | 73372 | Pte | R M | Davies | desertion | 11/S'wood For. | 15 11 17 |
| Wormhoudt Com Cem | in NW part | 9197 | Pte | H T W | Phillips | desertion | 1/Coldstream Guards | 30 5 16 |
| Y Farm Mil Cem | A/15 | 1239 | Pte | A | Davids | murder | 1 Cape Col Lab Regt | 26 8 19 |
| Y Farm Mil Cem | A/14 | 49 | Pte | W P | Harris | murder | 1 Cape Col Lab Regt | 26 8 19 |
| Y Farm Mil Cem | A/16 | 1454 | Pte | F | Boos | murder | 1 Cape Col Lab Regt | 15 10 19 |
| Ypres Reservoir Cem | 1/H/76 | 443288 | Pte | T L | Moles | desertion | 54/CEF | 22 10 17 |
| Ypres Reservoir Cem | 1/I/145 | 3/20279 | Pte | E | Lawrence | desertion | 2/Devon | 22 11 17 |
| Ypres Reservoir Cem | 4/A/6 | 11/81 | Pte | C F | McColl | desertion | 1/4 E Yorks | 28 12 17 |
| not commemorated | | 1/9804 | Pte | T | Davis | quitting post | 1/R Munster Fus. | 2 7 15 |
| not commemorated | | 2479 | Pte | | Fatoma | cowardice+ | West African Regt | 19 7 15 |
| not commemorated | | 3832 | Pte | H F | Burden | desertion | 1/N. Fus. | 21 7 15 |
| not commemorated | | 5538 | LCpl | A | Mamprusi | cowardice | Gold Coast | 28 4 17 |
| not commemorated | | 3972 | Pte | S | Sabongidda | violence | 3/Nigerian | 27 7 17 |
| not commemorated | | 385 | Lab | M M | Ahmed | mutiny | Egypt Lab Corps | 10 10 17 |
| not commemorated | | | | N | Thaourdis | murder | Muleteers | |
| not commemorated | | | | K | ---Ili | murder | Muleteers | |
| not commemorated | | | | Y | Antonio | murder | Muleteers | |
| not commemorated | | | | Y H | Louka | murder | Muleteers | |
| not commemorated | | | | S | Simeoni | murder | Muleteers | |
| grave not identified | | 53497 | Coolie | S K | Cheng | murder | Chin Lab Corps | 23 7 18 |
| grave not identified | | 42476 | Coolie | I H | Hui | murder | Chin Lab Corps | 12 9 18 |
| not known | | | Pte | | Deriagin | mutiny | Slavo-British Penal Bn | 7 19 |
| not known | | | Pte | | Sàkharoff | mutiny | Slavo-British Penal Bn | 7 19 |
| not known | | | Pte | | Posdjeef | mutiny | Slavo-British Penal Bn | 7 19 |
| not known | | | Pte | | Elisaieff | mutiny | Slavo-British Penal Bn | 7 19 |
| not known | | | Pte | | Volkoff | mutiny | Slavo-British Penal Bn | 7 19 |
| not known | | | Sgt | | Pesochnikoff | mutiny | Slavo-British Penal Bn | 7 19 |
| not known | | | Pte | | Taratin | mutiny | Slavo-British Penal Bn | 7 19 |
| not known | | | Pte | | Cherbukin | mutiny | Slavo-British Penal Bn | 7 19 |
| not known | | | Pte | | Lashkoff | mutiny | Slavo-British Penal Bn | 7 19 |
| not known | | | Pte | | Kameff | mutiny | Slavo-British Penal Bn | 7 19 |
| not known | | | Pte | | Bitel | mutiny | Slavo-British Penal Bn | 7 19 |

(It is believed that the commemoration of these Russian soldiers is not the responsibility of the Commonwealth War Graves Commission.)

*285*

# EXECUTIONS IN REGIMENTAL OR UNIT ORDER

| Regt. No. | Rank | | Name | Age | Offence | Unit | Division | Date of death | | |
|---|---|---|---|---|---|---|---|---|---|---|
| 29219 | Dvr | A | Lamb | | desertion | 21 Bty 2 Bde RFA | 6 | 2 | 10 | 15 |
| 62971 | Gnr | W | Jones | | desertion | 43 Bty RFA | 6 | 20 | 4 | 15 |
| 253617 | Gnr | FO | Wills | 20 | murder | X50th TMB RFA | BEF | 27 | 5 | 19 |
| 86872 | Dvr | J W | Swaine | | desertion | 54 Bty 39 Bde RFA | 1 | 9 | 6 | 16 |
| 70304 | Dvr | J | Bell | | desertion | 57 Bty 43 How. Bde RFA | 1 | 25 | 4 | 15 |
| 71502 | Dvr | J | Spencer | | desertion | 65 Bty 8 Bde RFA | 5 | 29 | 9 | 15 |
| 67440 | Dvr | T G | Hamilton | 22 | striking a S.O. | 72 Bty 38 Bde RFA | 6 | 3 | 10 | 16 |
| 64987 | Dvr | J | Mullany | | striking a S.O. | 72 Bty 38 Bde RFA | 6 | 3 | 10 | 16 |
| 96498 | Dvr | R | Murray | | desertion | 81 Bde RFA | 17 | 3 | 2 | 17 |
| 52081 | Gnr | WE | Lewis | 30 | mutiny | 124 Bde RFA/ Details RFA | 37 | 29 | 10 | 16 |
| L/36251 | Dvr | J W | Hasemore | 23 | disobedience+ | 180 Bde RFA | 16 | 12 | 5 | 16 |
| 13224 | Spr | F | Malyon | | desertion | 12 Coy RE att RFA | 6 | 4 | 4 | 17 |
| 14780 | A/Cpl | A | Chisholm | 31 | murder | 20 Army Troop Coy RE | II Army | 17 | 5 | 15 |
| 94236 | Spr | A P | Oyns | 31 | desertion | 50 Search Light Coy RE | IV Army | 20 | 10 | 17 |
| 62536 | Spr | R | Bell | 29 | murder | 123 Field Coy RE | 38 | 22 | 5 | 18 |
| 89173 | Pnr | E | Beeby | | desertion | 212 Coy RE | 33 | 9 | 12 | 16 |
| 9197 | Pte | H T W | Phillips | 24 | desertion | 1/Coldstream Guards | Guards | 30 | 5 | 16 |
| 8752 | Pte | I | Reid | 20 | desertion | 2/Scots Guards | 7 | 9 | 4 | 15 |
| 2222 | Pte | T | Cummings | 27 | desertion | 1/Irish Guards | 2 | 28 | I | 15 |
| 3379 | Pte | A | Smythe | 22 | desertion | 1/Irish Guards | 2 | 28 | 1 | 15 |
| 10686 | Pte | B | O'Connell | 23 | desertion | 1/Irish Guards | Guards | 8 | 8 | 18 |
| 11653 | Pte | E | Fraser | 19 | desertion+ | 2/R Scots | 3 | 2 | 8 | 15 |
| 20808 | Pte | R W | Simmers | 25 | desertion | 2/R Scots | 3 | 19 | 5 | 16 |
| 251482 | Rfn | W | Murphey | | desertion | 5/6 R Scots | 32 | 7 | 2 | 17 |
| 335727 | Pte | E | Delargey | 19 | desertion | 1/8 R Scots | 51 | 6 | 9 | 17 |
| 38332 | Pte | D | Gibson | 25 | desertion | 12/R Scots | 9 | 24 | 9 | 18 |
| 4437 | Pte | A | Dale | | murder | 13/R Scots | 15 | 3 | 3 | 16 |
| 25531 | Pte | J | Archibald | 20 | desertion | 17/R Scots | 35 | 4 | 6 | 16 |
| S/6778 | Pte | F | Wright | | desertion | 1/R W Surrey | 33 | 28 | 1 | 17 |
| G/6565 | Pte | HJ | Knight | | desertion | 1/R W Surrey | 33 | 6 | 10 | 18 |
| G/1533 | Pte | T | Hawkins | | desertion | 7/R W Surrey | 18 | 22 | 11 | 17 |
| L/10098 | Pte | R W | Gawler | 20 | desertion | 1/Buffs | 6 | 24 | 2 | 16 |
| L/8107 | Pte | A E | Eveleigh | 27 | desertion | 1/Buffs | 6 | 24 | 2 | 16 |
| G/7547 | Pte | W L | Thompson | 27 | desertion | 6/Buffs | 12 | 22 | 4 | 16 |
| G/15605 | Pte | F C | Gore | 19 | desertion | 7/Buffs | 18 | 16 | 10 | 17 |
| G/18469 | Pte | F C | Butcher | 26 | desertion | 7/Buffs | 18 | 27 | 8 | 18 |
| 2710 | LCpl | WJ | Irvine | 19 | desertion+ | 1/King's Own | 4 | 20 | 4 | 15 |
| 8136 | Pte | J | Kershaw | | desertion+ | 1/King's Own | 4 | 26 | 4 | 15 |
| 3563 | Pte | J | Sloan | | desertion | 1/4 King's Own | 55 | 16 | 7 | 16 |
| 11257 | LCpl | G E | Hughes | | desertion | 7/King's Own | 19 | 23 | 11 | 16 |
| 18143 | Pte | A | Holmes | 22 | desertion | 8/King's Own | 3 | 22 | 4 | 18 |
| 3832 | Pte | HF | Burden | 17 | desertion | 1/N. Fus. | 3 | 21 | 7 | 15 |
| 3057 | Pte | H | Palmer | | desertion | 1/5 N. Fus. | 50 | 27 | 10 | 16 |
| 5/1791 | Pte | J | Cameron | | desertion | 1/5 N. Fus. | 50 | 4 | 12 | 16 |
| 266120 | Pte | F | Turner | 31 | desertion | 1/6 N. Fus. | 50 | 23 | 10 | 17 |
| 15469 | Pte | A H | Robinson | | desertion | 9/N. Fus. | 17 | 10 | 5 | 16 |
| 10018 | Pte | P | Giles | | desertion | 14/N. Fus. | 21 | 24 | 8 | 16 |
| 26/626 | A/Cpl | J R | Short | 31 | mutiny | 24/N. Fus. | 34 | 4 | 10 | 17 |
| 45688 | Pte | J B | Milburn | | desertion | 24/27 N. Fus. | 34 | 8 | 11 | 17 |
| 8747 | Pte | A | Pitts | | desertion | 2/ Warwicks | 7 | 8 | 2 | 15 |
| 1529 | Pte | S H | Cunnington | 20 | desertion | 2/ Warwicks | 7 | 19 | 5 | 17 |
| 2676 | Pte | A G | Earp | | quitting post+ | 1/5 Warwicks | 48 | 22 | 7 | 16 |
| 200757 | Pte | C | Britton | | desertion | 1/5 Warwicks | 48 | 12 | 9 | 17 |
| 17402 | Pte | F | Broadrick | | desertion | 11/ Warwicks | 37 | 1 | 8 | 17 |
| 305 | Pte | W T | Spry | 29 | desertion | 2/R Fus. | 29 | 14 | 6 | 18 |
| 2408 | Pte | W W | Roberts | 34 | desertion+ | 4/R Fus. | 3 | 29 | 5 | 16 |
| L/11710 | Pte | A T | Ansted | 29 | desertion | 4/R Fus. | 3 | 15 | 11 | 16 |
| SR/9629 | Pte | C W F | Skilton | 20 | desertion | 22/R Fus. | 2 | 26 | 12 | 16 |
| G/46730 | Pte | E | Jackson | 32 | desertion | 24/R Fus. | 2 | 7 | 11 | 18 |
| 22635 | Pte | W | Baker | | desertion | 26/R Fus. | 41 | 14 | 8 | 18 |

| Regt. No. | Rank | | Name | Age | Offence | Unit | Division | Date of death |
|---|---|---|---|---|---|---|---|---|
| 251797 | Pte | W | Benham | | desertion | 1/3 R Fus. | 56 | 12 7 17 |
| 1731 | Rfn | R L | Barker | 21 | cowardice | 6/R Fus. (City of Lond.) | 47 | 4 11 16 |
| 322497 | Rfn | F W | Slade | 24 | disobedience | 2/R Fus. | 58 | 14 12 17 |
| 393923 | Rfn | H | Williams | | desertion | 1/9 R Fus. (QVR) | 56 | 28 12 17 |
| 474371 | Rfn | W | Yeoman | 22 | desertion | 1/12 R Fus. (Rangers) | 56 | 3 7 17 |
| 492050 | Pte | J | Mayers | 25 | desertion | 1/13 R Fus. (Kens'ton) | 56 | 16 6 17 |
| 683458 | Pte | F | Loader | | desertion | 1/22 R Fus. (The Queen's) | 47 | 19 8 17 |
| 11850 | Pte | J | Tongue | | desertion | 1/King's (L'pool) | 2 | 8 1 17 |
| 265427 | Pte | J | McFarlane | 27 | desertion | 4/King's (L'pool) | 33 | 22 5 18 |
| 4567 | Pte | J | Brennan | | desertion | 1/8 King's (L'pool) | 55 | 16 7 16 |
| 2974 | Pte | B | McGeehan | | desertion | 1/8 King's (L'pool) | 55 | 2 11 16 |
| 20062 | Pte | J A | Anderson | 30 | cowardice+ | 12/King's (L'pool) | 25 | 12 9 16 |
| 52929 | Pte | J | Smith | 26 | desertion+ | 17/King's (L'pool) | 30 | 5 9 17 |
| 9694 | Pte | J H | Abigail | 20 | desertion | 8/Norfolk | 18 | 12 9 17 |
| 50079 | Pte | J | Chandler | | murder | Lincs | BEF | 11 8 19 |
| 9618 | Pte | G E | Collins | 20 | desertion | 1/Lincs | 3 | 15 2 15 |
| 7423 | Pte | C H | Kirman | 32 | desertion | 7/Lincs | 17 | 23 9 17 |
| 3/20279 | Pte | E | Lawrence | 21 | desertion | 2/Devon | 8 | 22 11 17 |
| 1763 | Pte | B A | Hart | 22 | desertion | 1/4 Suffolk | 33 | 6 2 17 |
| 10315 | Pte | L R | Phillips | 23 | desertion | 6/SLI | 14 | 19 8 15 |
| 9970 | Pte | A L | Jefferies | | desertion | 6/SLI | 14 | 1 11 16 |
| 8014 | LCpl | A | Atkinson | 24 | desertion | 1/W Yorks | 6 | 2 3 15 |
| 7981 | Pte | E | Kirk | 24 | desertion | 1/W Yorks | 6 | 6 3 15 |
| 8871 | Pte | H T | Farr | 23 | cowardice | 1/W Yorks | 6 | 18 10 16 |
| 43359 | Sgt | G E | Gleadow | | desertion | 1/W Yorks | 6 | 6 4 17 |
| 42467 | Pte | A | Parry | | desertion | 2/W Yorks | 8 | 30 8 17 |
| 19445 | Pte | W | Neave | | desertion | 10/W Yorks | 17 | 30 8 17 |
| 43055 | Pte | L | Harris | 23 | desertion | 10/W Yorks | 17 | 7 11 18 |
| - | 2/Lt | E S | Poole | 31 | desertion | 11/W Yorks | 23 | 10 12 16 |
| 43665 | Pte | H | MacDonald | 32 | desertion | 12/W Yorks | 3 | 4 11 16 |
| 46127 | Pte | E | Horler | 26 | desertion | 12/W Yorks | 3 | 17 2 18 |
| 18/313 | Pte | H | Crimmins | 32 | desertion | 18/W Yorks | 31 | 5 9 16 |
| 18/356 | Pte | A | Wild | 24 | desertion | 18/W Yorks | 31 | 5 9 16 |
| 11/81 | Pte | C F | McColl | 26 | desertion | 1/4 E Yorks | 50 | 28 12 17 |
| 14813 | Pte | T W | Watts | 21 | desertion | 7/E Yorks | 17 | 30 8 17 |
| 11682 | Pte | J | Nisbet | 26 | desertion | 1/Leics | 6 | 23 8 18 |
| 8710 | Pte | E A | Beaumont | 27 | desertion | 2/Leics | 7/Indian | 24 6 15 |
| 9552 | Dmr | F | Rose | 23 | desertion | 2/Yorks | 30 | 4 3 17 |
| 8534 | Pte | H | Poole | | desertion | 7/Yorks | 17 | 9 12 16 |
| 2267 | Cpl | G W | Latham | 23 | desertion+ | 2/Lancs Fus. | 4 | 22 1 15 |
| 2779 | Pte | H H | Chase | 21 | cowardice | 2/Lancs Fus. | 4 | 12 6 15 |
| 204455 | Pte | W | Smith | 20 | desertion | 3/5 Lancs Fus. | 66 | 14 11 17 |
| 240678 | Pte | A | Mitchell | | desertion | 1/6 Lancs Fus. | 42 | 20 8 17 |
| 41643 | Pte | W J | Earl | 22 | desertion | 1/7 Lancs Fus. | 42 | 27 5 18 |
| 307350 | Pte | T | Hopkins | 26 | leaving his post | 1/8 Lancs Fus. | 42 | 13 2 18 |
| 23992 | Pte | E W | Harris | 20 | desertion | 10/Lancs Fus. | 17 | 3 2 17 |
| 27555 | Pte | J | Taylor | | desertion | 15/Lancs Fus. | 32 | 27 1 17 |
| 15576 | Pte | J | Byers | 17 | desertion | 1/R Scots Fus. | 3 | 6 2 15 |
| 7177 | Pte | A | Evans | | desertion | 1/R Scots Fus. | 3 | 6 2 15 |
| 40806 | Pte | P | Cairnie | | desertion | 1/R Scots Fus. | 3 | 28 12 16 |
| 10930 | Pte | J | Ferguson | 21 | desertion | 1/R Scots Fus. att.RE | 3 | 20 4 17 |
| A/6730 | Pte | S | Stewart | 21 | desertion | 2/R Scots Fus. | 30 | 29 8 17 |
| 10459 | Cpl | G H | Povey | 23 | leaving his post | 1/Cheshire | 5 | 11 2 15 |
| 10263 | Pte | E | Bolton | | desertion | 1/Cheshire | 5 | 14 4 16 |
| 9/28719 | Pte | J | Cuthbert | 20 | disobedience | 9/Cheshire | 19 | 6 5 16 |
| 13857 | LCpl | J | Holland | 31 | cowardice+ | 10/Cheshire | 25 | 30 5 16 |
| 20101 | Pte | E | Bryant | 33 | desertion | 10/Cheshire | 25 | 27 10 17 |
| 17790 | LCpl | W A | Moon | 20 | desertion | 11/Cheshire | 25 | 21 11 16 |
| 10853 | Pte | A | Troughton | 22 | desertion+ | 1/R Welsh Fus. | 7 | 22 4 15 |
| 10958 | Pte | M | Penn | 21 | desertion+ | 1/R Welsh Fus. | 7 | 22 4 15 |
| 15954 | Pte | W | Jones | | desertion | 9/R Welsh Fus. | 19 | 25 10 17 |
| 15437 | Pte | C W | Knight | 28 | murder | 10/R Welsh Fus. | 3 | 15 11 15 |
| 1/15134 | Pte | A | O'Neil | | desertion | 1/S Wales Borderers | 1 | 30 4 16 |

# EXECUTIONS IN REGIMENTAL OR UNIT ORDER
## (continued)

| Regt. No. | Rank | | Name | Age | Offence | Unit | Division | Date of death |
|---|---|---|---|---|---|---|---|---|
| 44174 | Pte | W | Scholes | 25 | desertion | 2/S Wales Borderers | 29 | 10 8 18 |
| 11490 | Pte | THB | Rigby | 21 | desertion | 10/S Wales Borderers | 38 | 22 11 17 |
| 11559 | Pte | T | Docherty | 20 | desertion | 2/KOSB | 5 | 16 7 15 |
| 21654 | Pte | LD | Elford | 28 | desertion | 7/8 KOSB | 15 | 11 10 18 |
| 11225 | Pte | E | Mackness | 25 | desertion | 1/Cameronians | 33 | 1 10 17 |
| 12182 | Pte | A | Murphy | 27 | desertion | 9/Cameronians | 9 | 17 8 16 |
| 43619 | Pte | CM | Milligan | 20 | desertion | 10/Cameronians | 15 | 3 6 17 |
| 23686 | Pte | JS | Michael | | desertion | 10/Cameronians | 15 | 24 8 17 |
| 13827 | L/Sgt | H | Ashton | 20 | desertion | 11/Cameronians | 26 | 8 7 17 |
| 12396 | Pte | J | Cassidy | | desertion | 1/R Inniskilling Fus. | 29 | 23 7 16 |
| 23726 | Pte | R | Hope | 23 | desertion | 1/R Inniskilling Fus. | 29 | 5 7 17 |
| 17137 | Pte | T | Hogan | 31 | desertion | 2/R Inniskilling Fus. | 32 | 14 5 17 |
| 10603 | Pte | J | Seymour | | desertion | 2/R Inniskilling Fus. | 32 | 24 1 18 |
| 26248 | Pte | J | Wishard | 24 | desertion | 7/R Inniskilling Fus. | 16 | 15 6 17 |
| 8662 | Pte | OW | Hodgetts | 19 | cowardice | 1/Worcs | 8 | 4 6 15 |
| 12295 | Cpl | F | Ives | 30 | desertion | 3/Worcs | 3 | 26 7 15 |
| 7625 | Pte | AD | Thompson | 25 | desertion | 3/Worcs | 3 | 26 7 15 |
| 7377 | Pte | J | Robinson | 31 | desertion | 3/Worcs | 3 | 26 7 15 |
| 8164 | Pte | B | Hartells | 32 | desertion | 3/Worcs | 3 | 26 7 15 |
| 9722 | Pte | E | Fellows | 29 | desertion | 3/Worcs | 3 | 26 7 15 |
| 13216 | Sgt | JT | Wall | 22 | desertion | 3/Worcs | 25 | 6 9 17 |
| 204232 | Pte | R | Young | 21 | desertion | 11/Worcs | 26 | 18 9 18 |
| 16734 | Pte | H | Salter | 24 | desertion+ | 6/E Lancs | 13 | 11 12 15 |
| G/12341 | Pte | W | Bowerman | 38 | desertion | 1/Queen's | 5 | 24 3 17 |
| G/7171 | Pte | WJ | Turpie | 24 | desertion | 2/Queen's | 28 | 1 7 15 |
| G/10474 | Pte | RG | Pattison | 23 | desertion | 7/Queen's | 12 | 4 7 17 |
| L/11661 | Pte | AH | Westwood | 20 | desertion | 8/Queen's | 18 | 23 11 17 |
| 16120 | Pte | JW | Fryer | 23 | desertion | 12/Queen's | 41 | 14 6 17 |
| 18603 | Pte | G | Mills | 21 | desertion+ | 2/DCLI | 27 | 29 9 15 |
| 3/10390 | Pte | F | Stead | 20 | desertion | 2/Duke of Wellington's | 4 | 12 2 17 |
| 5231 | Pte | J | Briggs | | desertion | 2/Borders | 7 | 6 3 15 |
| 20035 | Pte | F | Johnson | | desertion | 2/Borders | 7 | 1 8 18 |
| 20037 | Pte | H | McClair | | desertion | 2/Borders | 7 | 1 8 18 |
| L/10414 | Pte | WH | Burrell | 21 | desertion | 2/Sussex | 1 | 22 5 16 |
| G/4495 | Pte | JE | Barnes | 24 | desertion | 7/R Sussex | 12 | 4 7 17 |
| SD/4242 | Pte | RT | Tite | 27 | cowardice | 13/Sussex | 39 | 25 11 16 |
| 3/4071 | Pte | J | Bennett | 19 | cowardice | 1/Hants | 4 | 28 8 16 |
| 8793 | Pte | J | Taylor | 24 | desertion | 2/S Staffs | 2 | 6 11 17 |
| 200945 | Pte | J | Bateman | | desertion | 2/S Staffs | 2 | 3 12 17 |
| 9541 | LCpl | F | Hawthorne | 22 | cowardice+ | 1/5 S Staffs | 46 | 11 8 16 |
| 12772 | Pte | A | Botfield | 28 | cowardice | 9/S Staffs | 23 | 18 10 16 |
| 9828 | Pte | WE | Anderson | 21 | desertion+ | 5/Dorset | 11 | 31 3 17 |
| 15094 | Pte | J | Lewis | 21 | desertion | 5/Dorset | 11 | 19 4 17 |
| 8037 | Pte | J | Jennings | | desertion | 2/S Lancs | 25 | 26 6 16 |
| 549 | Pte | G | Lewis | | desertion | 2/S Lancs | 25 | 26 6 16 |
| 26028 | Pte | J | Rogers | | desertion | 2/S Lancs | 25 | 9 3 17 |
| 10912 | Pte | R | Burton | 24 | sleeping at post | 6/S Lancs | 13 | 19 2 17 |
| 10555 | Pte | T | Downing | 22 | sleeping at post | 6/S Lancs | 13 | 19 2 17 |
| 10764 | Pte | RM | Jones | 40 | desertion | 6/S Lancs | 13 | 21 2 17 |
| 11967 | Pte | R | Morgan | 32 | murder | 2/Welsh | 1 | 15 2 15 |
| 12942 | LCpl | W | Price | 41 | murder | 2/Welsh | 1 | 15 2 15 |
| 10874 | Pte | JG | Carr | 21 | desertion+ | 2/Welsh | 1 | 7 2 16 |
| 12727 | Pte | J | Thomas | 44 | desertion | 2/Welsh | 1 | 20 5 16 |
| 36224 | Pte | J | Skone | 39 | murder | 2/Welsh | 1 | 10 5 18 |
| 8139 | Pte | G | Watkins | 31 | desertion | 13/Welsh | 38 | 15 5 17 |
| S/13248 | Pte | G | Cutmore | | desertion | 2/B Watch | 7/Indian | 25 7 17 |
| 6744 | Pte | P | Black | | desertion | 1/4 B Watch | 51 | 18 9 16 |
| S/9672 | Pte | J | Docherty | 20 | desertion | 9/B Watch | 15 | 15 2 16 |

| Regt. No. | Rank | | Name | Age | Offence | Unit | Division | Date of death |
|---|---|---|---|---|---|---|---|---|
| S/15954 | Pte | N H | Taysum | 25 | desertion | 9/B Watch | 15 | 16 10 17 |
| S/5470 | Pte | A | Brown | | desertion | 10/B Watch | 26 | 1 6 17 |
| - | 2/Lt | J H | Paterson | 28 | murder | 3/Essex att.1st | 37 | 24 9 18 |
| 8278 | Pte | A | Browne | 26 | desertion+ | 2/Essex | 4 | 19 12 14 |
| 21161 | Pte | H | Martin | | desertion | 9/Essex | 12 | 20 3 16 |
| 70715 | Pte | W | Robinson | | desertion | 1/S'wood For. | 8 | 10 4 17 |
| 13612 | Pte | F | O'Neill | 24 | desertion | 1/S'wood For. | 8 | 16 5 18 |
| 21801 | Pte | A | Briggs | 27 | desertion | 9/S'wood For. | 11 | 19 7 18 |
| 13167 | Pte | W H | Randle | | desertion | 10/S'wood For. | 17 | 25 11 16 |
| 73372 | Pte | R M | Davies | | desertion | 11/S'wood For. | 23 | 15 11 17 |
| 23972 | Cpl | J | Wilton | 40 | quitting post | 15/S'wood For. | 35 | 17 8 16 |
| 15251 | Pte | G H | Lawton | 36 | cowardice+ | 17/S'wood For. | 39 | 30 7 16 |
| 31821 | Pte | B | McCubbin | 22 | cowardice+ | 17/S'wood For. | 39 | 30 7 16 |
| 10710 | Pte | W | Hunter | 20 | desertion+ | 1/Loyals | 1 | 21 2 16 |
| 1214 | Pte | W | Watts | 29 | desertion+ | 1/Loyals | 1 | 5 5 16 |
| 10161 | Pte | J | Molyneaux | | desertion | 1/Loyals | 1 | 15 6 16 |
| 2506 | Pte | J | Smith | | desertion | 1/Loyals | 1 | 2 7 16 |
| 2554 | Pte | R | Stevenson | 23 | desertion | 1/4 Loyals | 55 | 25 10 16 |
| 6807 | Pte | J J | Dennis | 19 | desertion | 1/N'hamptons | 1 | 30 1 16 |
| 9840 | Pte | J T | Jones | 21 | desertion+ | 1/N'hamptons | 1 | 24 2 16 |
| 9641 | Pte | G | Ward | 20 | cowardice | 1/R Berks | 2 | 26 9 14 |
| 5715 | Pte | C | Depper | 30 | desertion | 1/4 R Berks | 48 | 13 9 16 |
| 39463 | Pte | J | Swain | | desertion | 5/R Berks | 12 | 11 8 18 |
| L/10061 | Pte | T J | Highgate | 19 | desertion | 1/R W Kent | 5 | 8 9 14 |
| L/10132 | Pte | T | Harris | 21 | desertion | 1/R W Kent | 5 | 21 6 15 |
| 3/1433 | Pte | G E | Roe | 19 | desertion | 2/KOYLI | 5 | 10 6 15 |
| 11046 | Pte | H J | Webb | | desertion | 2/KOYLI | 32 | 31 10 17 |
| 202893 | Pte | G | Ainley | 20 | desertion | 1/4 KOYLI | 49 | 30 7 18 |
| L/14164 | Pte | F | Sheffield | 26 | desertion | 2/Middx | 8 | 12 1 15 |
| L/14232 | Pte | J | Ball | 20 | desertion | 2/Middx | 8 | 12 1 15 |
| G/8857 | Pte | E | Worsley | | desertion | 2/Middx | 8 | 22 10 17 |
| S/6922 | Pte | W | Scotton | 19 | desertion | 4/Middx | 3 | 3 2 15 |
| 11/1799 | Pte | A | Beverstein | 21 | desertion | 11/Middx | 12 | 20 3 16 |
| G/335 | Pte | H | Carter | 18 | desertion | 11/Middx | 12 | 26 4 16 |
| G/52128 | Pte | D | Stevenson | 23 | desertion | 13/Middx | 24 | 18 7 18 |
| G/11296 | Pte | W H | Simmonds | 23 | desertion | 23/Middx | 41 | 1 12 16 |
| 5/3119 | Rfn | W | Bellamy | 34 | cowardice | 1/KRRC | 2 | 16 7 15 |
| 11528 | Pte | F | Harding | 21 | desertion | 1/KRRC | 2 | 29 6 16 |
| 7552 | L/Sgt | W | Walton | 26 | desertion | 2/KRRC | 1 | 23 3 15 |
| A/1579 | Rfn | A E | Parker | 35 | desertion+ | 7/KRRC | 14 | 15 5 16 |
| 10758 | Rfn | F M | Barratt | 23 | desertion | 7/KRRC | 14 | 10 7 17 |
| R/27615 | Rfn | J J | Hyde | | desertion | 10/KRRC | 20 | 5 9 17 |
| R/28638 | Rfn | A E | Allsop | 21 | desertion | 12/KRRC | 20 | 15 6 17 |
| R/15325 | Rfn | J | Woodhouse | | desertion | 12/KRRC | 20 | 4 10 17 |
| A/201225 | Rfn | T | Donovan | 20 | desertion | 16/KRRC | 33 | 31 10 17 |
| R/24441 | Rfn | F W | Cheeseman | 29 | desertion | 18/KRRC | 41 | 20 10 17 |
| R/19333 | Rfn | E A | Card | 23 | desertion | 20/KRRC | 3 | 22 9 16 |
| 5919 | Pte | E | Tanner | 33 | desertion | 1/Wilts | 3 | 27 10 14 |
| 8992 | LCpl | J S V | Fox | 20 | desertion | 1/Wilts att.3/Div Cy Coy | 3 | 20 4 15 |
| 9610 | Sgt | J | Robins | | disobedience+ | 5/Wilts | 13 | 2 1 16 |
| 2064 | Pte | W | Wycherley | 24 | desertion | 2/Manchesters | 32 | 12 9 17 |
| 43499 | Pte | T | Foulkes | 21 | desertion | 1/10 Manchesters | 42 | 21 11 17 |
| 300199 | Pte | T | Brigham | 22 | desertion | 1/10 Manchesters | 42 | 4 6 18 |
| 1957 | Pte | W G | Hunt | 20 | desertion | 18/Manchesters | 30 | 14 11 16 |
| 10502 | Pte | A | Longshaw | 21 | desertion | 18/Manchesters | 30 | 1 12 16 |
| 10495 | Pte | A | Ingham | 24 | desertion | 18/Manchesters | 30 | 1 12 16 |
| 26685 | Pte | E | Holt | 22 | desertion | 19/Manchesters | 30 | 4 3 17 |
| 8833 | Pte | G | Everill | 30 | desertion | 1/N Staffs | 24 | 14 9 17 |
| 40435 | Pte | D J | Blakemore | 28 | desertion | 8/N Staffs | 19 | 9 7 17 |
| 45980 | Pte | W | Dossett | 22 | desertion | 1/4 York & Lancs | 49 | 25 6 18 |
| 203313 | Pte | F | Bateman | 28 | desertion | 1/4 York & Lancs | 49 | 10 9 18 |
| 242904 | Pte | H | Hughes | 27 | desertion | 1/5 York & Lancs | 49 | 10 4 18 |
| 31184 | Pte | L | Mitchell | | desertion | 8/York & Lancs | 23 | 19 9 17 |

| Regt. No. | Rank | | Name | Age | Offence | Unit | Division | Date of death |
|---|---|---|---|---|---|---|---|---|
| 32559 | Pte | C B | Nicholson | 19 | desertion | 8/York & Lancs | 23 | 27 10 17 |
| 34595 | Pte | J | Crampton | 42 | desertion | 9/York & Lancs | 23 | 4 2 17 |
| 14357 | Pte | F C H | Bladen | 26 | desertion | 10/York & Lancs | 21 | 23 3 16 |
| 7595 | Pte | J A | Haddock | 32 | desertion | 12/York & Lancs | 31 | 16 9 16 |
| 4/9170 | Pte | G | Hunter | | desertion+ | 2/DLI | 6 | 2 7 16 |
| 11606 | Pte | W | Clarke | 23 | desertion | 2/DLI | 6 | 9 2 18 |
| 14387 | Pte | W B | Nelson | 24 | desertion | 14/DLI | 6 | 11 8 16 |
| 39213 | Pte | A | Hamilton | 31 | desertion | 14/DLI | 6 | 27 3 17 |
| 19/158 | LCpl | P | Goggins | 21 | quitting post | 19/DLI | 35 | 18 1 17 |
| 19/420 | LCpl | J | McDonald | 28 | quitting post | 19/DLI | 35 | 18 1 17 |
| 19/647 | L/Sgt | J W | Stones | 25 | cast'g away arms | 19/DLI | 35 | 18 1 17 |
| 7711 | Pte | J | Fox | | striking a S.O. | 2/HLI | 2 | 12 5 16 |
| B/21000 | Cpl | C | Lewis | | desertion | 12/HLI | 15 | 11 3 16 |
| 12384 | Pte | A | Reid | 30 | desertion | 16/HLI | 32 | 31 1 17 |
| 5626 | Pte | J | McQuade | | desertion | 18/HLI | 35 | 6 11 16 |
| 5323 | Pte | H | Flynn | | desertion | 18/HLI | 35 | 15 11 16 |
| S/9696 | Pte | H | Dalande | | desertion | 8/Seaforths | 15 | 9 3 18 |
| 285031 | Pte | M R | Richmond | 22 | desertion | 1/6 Gordons | 51 | 26 5 18 |
| S/15240 | Pte | T | Ward | 23 | desertion | 8/10 Gordons | 15 | 16 10 17 |
| S/2889 | Pte | F | Murray | | murder | 9/Gordons att RE | 15 | 1 10 16 |
| 6584 | Pte | J | Duncan | | desertion | 1/Camerons | 1 | 7 3 15 |
| 7674 | Cpl | J | Reid | 26 | desertion | 6/Camerons | 15 | 11 5 18 |
| S/17688 | Pte | J S | Adamson | 30 | cowardice | 7/Camerons | 15 | 23 11 17 |
| 8225 | LCpl | P | Sands | 27 | desertion | 1/R Irish Rifles | 8 | 15 9 15 |
| 5009 | Rfn | S | McBride | | desertion | 2/R Irish Rifles | 25 | 7 12 16 |
| 14218 | Rfn | J | Crozier | 18 | desertion | 9/R Irish Rifles | 36 | 27 2 16 |
| 15/13211 | Rfn | J E | McCracken | 19 | desertion | 15/R Irish Rifles | 36 | 19 3 16 |
| 15/890 | Rfn | J | Templeton | | desertion | 15/R Irish Rifles | 36 | 19 3 16 |
| 12609 | Pte | G | Hanna | 26 | desertion | 1/R Irish Fusiliers | 36 | 6 11 17 |
| 21373 | Pte | J | Carey | | desertion | 7/R Irish Fusiliers | 16 | 15 9 16 |
| 7144396 | Pte | J J | Daly | 21 | mutiny | 1/Conn Rangers | India | 2 11 20 |
| 2057 | Pte | J | Higgins | | desertion | 1/9 Argylls | 51 | 26 8 16 |
| 9689 | Pte | T | Hope | 20 | desertion+ | 2/Leinster | 6 | 2 3 15 |
| 4519 | Pte | H | Hendricks | 46 | desertion | 2/Leinster | 29 | 23 8 18 |
| 6/227 | Pte | P J | Downey | 20 | disobedience | 6/Leinster | 10 | 27 12 15 |
| 1/9804 | Pte | T | Davis | 21 | quitting post | 1/R Munster Fus. | 29 | 2 7 15 |
| 9948 | Pte | J | Graham | 21 | desertion+ | 2/R Munster Fus. | 1 | 21 12 15 |
| 12923 | Pte | A | Rickman | 27 | desertion | 1/R Dublin Fus. | 29 | 15 9 16 |
| 40422 | Pte | S | Byrne | 30 | desertion | 1/R Dublin Fus. | 29 | 28 10 17 |
| 7076018 | Pte | R | Flynn | | murder | 2/R Dublin Fus. | MEF | 6 11 20 |
| S/9405 | Rfn | W | Smith | 37 | desertion | 2/Rifle Bde | 8 | 3 10 15 |
| S/9560 | Rfn | G A | Irish | 30 | desertion | 2/Rifle Bde | 8 | 3 10 15 |
| 3019 | L/Sgt | A | Wickings | 28 | murder | 9/Rifle Bde | 14 | 7 3 18 |
| 15161 | Pte | P | Murphy | 20 | desertion | 47 Bn MGC | 47 | 12 9 18 |
| 88378 | Pte | J | Stedman | 25 | desertion | 117 Coy MGC | 39 | 5 9 17 |
| T4/040862 | Dvr | T | Moore | 23 | murder | 24 Division Train ASC | 24 | 26 2 16 |
| - | Sub/Lt | E L A | Dyett | 21 | desertion | Nelson Bn RND | 63 | 5 1 17 |
| 541 | Tpr | A | Butler | | murder | R Can Dragoons | 3/Can | 2 7 16 |
| 107526 | Pte | J W | Roberts | 20 | desertion+ | 2/Can Mount Rif | 3/Can | 30 7 16 |
| 177753 | Pte | J M | Higgins | 24 | desertion | 1/CEF | 1/Can | 7 12 16 |
| 454610 | Pte | W N | Ling | 22 | desertion | 2/CEF | 1/Can | 12 8 18 |
| 416874 | Pte | C | LaLiberte | 25 | desertion | 3/CEF | 1/Can | 4 8 16 |
| 404436 | Pte | E J | Reynolds | | desertion | 3/CEF | 1/Can | 23 8 16 |
| 10701 | Pte | J H | Wilson | | desertion | 4/CEF | 1/Can | 9 7 16 |
| 457241 | Pte | H H | Kerr | | desertion | 7/CEF | 1/Can | 21 11 16 |
| A/38119 | Pte | C | Welsh | | desertion | 8/CEF | 1/Can | 6 3 18 |
| 20726 | CQMS | W | Alexander | 37 | desertion | 10/CEF | 1/Can | 18 10 17 |
| 23621 | Pte | F | Auger | 25 | desertion+ | 14/CEF | 1/Can | 26 3 16 |

| Regt. No. | Rank | | Name | Age | Offence | Unit | Division | Date of death | |
|---|---|---|---|---|---|---|---|---|---|
| 227098 | Pte | E | Fairburn | 22 | desertion | 18/CEF | 2/Can | 2 3 | 18 |
| 2095 | Pte | HEJ | Lodge | | desertion | 19/CEF | 2/Can | 13 3 | 18 |
| 416008 | Pte | E | Perry | 21 | desertion | 22/CEF | 2/Can | 11 4 | 17 |
| 448160 | Pte | G | Comte | 22 | desertion | 22/CEF | 2/Can | 3 7 | 17 |
| 672604 | Pte | J | LaLancette | 21 | desertion | 22/CEF | 2/Can | 3 7 | 17 |
| 34453 | Pte | AC | Dagesse | 32 | desertion | 22/CEF | 2/Can | 15 3 | 18 |
| 62218 | Pte | L | Delisle | 26 | desertion | 22/CEF | 2/Can | 21 5 | 18 |
| 67882 | Pte | E | Young | 19 | desertion | 25/CEF | 2/Can | 29 10 | 16 |
| 718566 | Pte | S McD | Fowles | 21 | desertion | 44/CEF | 4/Can | 19 6 | 18 |
| 830020 | Pte | D | Sinizki | 22 | cowardice | 52/CEF | 3/Can | 9 10 | 17 |
| 443288 | Pte | TL | Moles | 28 | desertion | 54/CEF | 4/Can | 22 10 | 17 |
| 454482 | Pte | HG | Carter | 21 | desertion | 73/CEF | 4/Can | 20 4 | 17 |
| C/40124 | L/Bmdr | FS | Arnold | 26 | desertion | 1 Bde CFA | 1/Can | 25 7 | 16 |
| 2063 | Dvr | B | De Fehr | | murder | 1/Res.Pk (Can.ASC) | GHQ | 25 8 | 16 |
| 8/1384 | Pte | JJ | Sweeney | 37 | desertion | 1/Otago (NZ) | NZ | 2 10 | 16 |
| 8/2733 | Pte | VM | Spencer | 23 | desertion | 1/Otago (NZ) | NZ | 24 2 | 18 |
| 24/1521 | Pte | J | Braithwaite | 33 | mutiny | 2/Otago (NZ) | NZ | 29 10 | 16 |
| 6/1598 | Pte | J | King | 32 | desertion | 1/Cant (NZ) | NZ | 19 8 | 17 |
| 24/2008 | Pte | F | Hughes | 28 | desertion | 2/Cant (NZ) | NZ | 25 8 | 16 |
| 494 | Pte | N | Matthews | | murder | 3rd S African Infty | SA Bde | 3 4 | 16 |
| 9191 | Pte | JA | Mitchell | 18 | murder+ | 1/Brit W Indies | GHQ Pal | 22 12 | 17 |
| 4881 | Pte | HA | Clarke | | striking a S.O. | 2/Brit W Indies | Pal LoC | 11 8 | 17 |
| 7429 | Pte | H | Morris | 17 | desertion | 6/Brit W Indies | IV Army | 20 9 | 17 |
| 11080 | Pte | A | Denny | | murder | 8/Brit W Indies | It LoC | 20 1 | 19 |
| 7560 | Pte | A | Frafra | | cast'g away arms | Gold Coast | 1/E Afr | 28 9 | 16 |
| 5538 | LCpl | A | Mamprusi | | cowardice | Gold Coast | HANforce | 28 4 | 17 |
| A/2600 | Pte | D | Barama | | murder | Gold Coast Mtd.Inf.Coy | EDforce | 10 11 | 18 |
| 2479 | Pte | | Fatoma | | cowardice+ | West African Regt | WAHQ | 19 7 | 15 |
| 3972 | Pte | S | Sabongidda | | violence | 3/ Nigerian | Nig Bde | 27 7 | 17 |
| 385 | Lab | MM | Ahmed | | mutiny | Egypt Lab Corps | BEF LoC | 10 10 | 17 |
| 10299 | Coolie | EJ | Wang | | murder | Chin Lab Corps | BEF LoC | 26 6 | 18 |
| 10272 | Coolie | CH | Yang | | murder | Chin Lab Corps | BEF LoC | 26 6 | 18 |
| 53497 | Coolie | SK | Cheng | | murder | Chin Lab Corps | BEF LoC | 23 7 | 18 |
| 46090 | Coolie | HI | Chao | | murder | Chin Lab Corps | BEF LoC | 9 8 | 18 |
| 42476 | Coolie | IH | Hui | | murder | Chin Lab Corps | BEF LoC | 12 9 | 18 |
| 5884 | Coolie | FY | Wan | | murder | Chin Lab Corps | BEF LoC | 15 2 | 19 |
| 44735 | Coolie | CC | Wang | | murder | 107 Chin Lab Coy | BEF LoC | 8 5 | 19 |
| 97170 | Coolie | CM | Hei | | murder | Chin Lab Corps | BEF LoC | 21 2 | 20 |
| 44340 | Coolie | CH | K'ung | | murder | Chin Lab Corps | BEF LcC | 21 2 | 20 |
| 16174 | Collie | JC | Chang | | murder x4 | Chin Lab Coy | BEF LoC | 14 2 | 20 |
| 1239 | Pte | A | Davids | 24 | murder | 1 Cape Col Lab Regt | BEF LoC | 26 8 | 19 |
| 49 | Pte | WP | Harris | 23 | murder | 1 Cape Col Lab Regt | BEF LoC | 26 8 | 19 |
| 1454 | Pte | F | Boos | 19 | murder | 1 Cape Col Lab Regt | BEF LoC | 15 10 | 19 |
| | | N | Thaourdis | | murder | Muleteers | MEF LoC | | |
| | | K | ---lli | | murder | Muleteers | MEF LoC | | |
| | | Y | Antonio | | murder | Muleteers | MEF LoC | | |
| | | YH | Louka | | murder | Muleteers | MEF LoC | | |
| | | S | Simeoni | | murder | Muleteers | MEF LoC | | |
| | Pte | | Deriagin | | mutiny | Slavo- British Penal Bn | N Russia | 7 | 19 |
| | Pte | | Sakharoff | | mutiny | Slavo-British Penal Bn | N Russia | 7 | 19 |
| | Pte | | Posdjeef | | mutiny | Slavo- British Penal Bn | N Russia | 7 | 19 |
| | Pte | | Elisaieff | | mutiny | Slavo- British Penal Bn | N Russia | 7 | 19 |
| | Pte | | Volkoff | | mutiny | Slavo-British Penal Bn | N Russia | 7 | 19 |
| | Sgt | | Pesochnikoff | | mutiny | Slavo-British Penal Bn | N Russia | 7 | 19 |
| | Pte | | Taratin | | mutiny | Slavo-British Penal Bn | N Russia | 7 | 19 |
| | Pte | | Cherbukin | | mutiny | Slavo-British Penal Bn | N Russia | 7 | 19 |
| | Pte | | Lashkoff | | mutiny | Slavo-British Penal Bn | N Russia | 7 | 19 |
| | Pte | | Kameff | | mutiny | Slavo-British Penal Bn | N Russia | 7 | 19 |
| | Pte | | Bitel | | mutiny | Slavo- British Penal Bn | N Russia | 7 | 19 |

# EXECUTIONS ON THE WESTERN FRONT IN CHRONOLOGICAL ORDER

| Regt. No. | Rank | | Name | Age | Offence | Unit | Division | Div. Type | Type of Soldier | Date of death | | |
|---|---|---|---|---|---|---|---|---|---|---|---|---|
| L/10061 | Pte | T J | Highgate | 19 | desertion | 1/R W Kent | 5 | R | Regular | 8 | 9 | 14 |
| 9641 | Pte | G | Ward | 20 | cowardice | 1/R Berks | 2 | R | Regular | 26 | 9 | 14 |
| 5919 | Pte | E | Tanner | 33 | desertion | 1/Wilts | 3 | R | Regular | 27 | 10 | 14 |
| 8278 | Pte | A | Browne | 26 | desertion+ | 2/Essex | 4 | R | Regular | 19 | 12 | 14 |
| L/14232 | Pte | J | Ball | 20 | desertion | 2/Middx | 8 | R | Regular | 12 | 1 | 15 |
| L/14164 | Pte | F | Sheffield | 26 | desertion | 2/Middx | 8 | R | Regular | 12 | 1 | 15 |
| 2267 | Cpl | G W | Latham | 23 | desertion+ | 2/Lancs Fus. | 4 | R | Regular | 22 | 1 | 15 |
| 2222 | Pte | T | Cummings | 27 | desertion | 1/Irish Gds | 2 | R | Volunteer | 28 | 1 | 15 |
| 3379 | Pte | A | Smythe | 22 | desertion | 1/Irish Gds | 2 | R | Volunteer | 28 | 1 | 15 |
| S/6922 | Pte | W | Scotton | 19 | desertion | 4/Middx | 3 | R | Regular | 3 | 2 | 15 |
| 15576 | Pte | J | Byers | 17 | desertion | 1/R Scots Fus. | 3 | R | Kitchener | 6 | 2 | 15 |
| 7177 | Pte | A | Evans | | desertion | 1/R Scots Fus. | 3 | R | Reservist | 6 | 2 | 15 |
| 8747 | Pte | A. | Pitts | | desertion | 2/Warwicks | 7 | R | Regular | 8 | 2 | 15 |
| 10459 | Cpl | G H | Povey | 23 | leaving his post | 1/Cheshire | 5 | R | Regular | 11 | 2 | 15 |
| 9618 | Pte | G E | Collins | 20 | desertion | 1/Lincs | 3 | R | Regular | 15 | 2 | 15 |
| 11967 | Pte | R | Morgan | 32 | murder | 2/Welsh | 1 | R | Regular | 15 | 2 | 15 |
| 12942 | LCpl | W | Price | 41 | murder | 2/Welsh | 1 | R | Regular | 15 | 2 | 15 |
| 8014 | LCpl | A | Atkinson | 24 | desertion | 1/W Yorks | 6 | R | Regular | 2 | 3 | 15 |
| 9689 | Pte | T | Hope | 20 | desertion+ | 2/Leinster | 6 | R | Volunteer | 2 | 3 | 15 |
| 5231 | Pte | J | Briggs | | desertion | 2/Borders | 7 | R | Regular | 6 | 3 | 15 |
| 7981 | Pte | E | Kirk | 24 | desertion | 1/W Yorks | 6 | R | Regular | 6 | 3 | 15 |
| 6584 | Pte | J | Duncan | | desertion | 1/Camerons | 1 | R | Regular | 7 | 3 | 15 |
| 7552 | L/Sgt | W | Walton | 26 | desertion | 2/KRRC | 1 | R | Regular | 23 | 3 | 15 |
| 8752 | Pte | I | Reid | 20 | desertion | 2/Scots Guards | 7 | R | Regular | 9 | 4 | 15 |
| 8992 | LCpl | J S V | Fox | | desertion | 1/Wilts att.3/Div Cy. Coy | 3 | R | Regular | 20 | 4 | 15 |
| 2710 | LCpl | W J | Irvine | 19 | desertion+ | 1/King's Own | 4 | R | Regular | 20 | 4 | 15 |
| 62971 | Gnr | W | Jones | | desertion | 43 Bty, RFA | 6 | R | Regular | 20 | 4 | 15 |
| 10958 | Pte | M | Penn | 21 | desertion+ | 1/R Welsh Fus. | 7 | R | Regular | 22 | 4 | 15 |
| 10853 | Pte | A | Troughton | 22 | desertion+ | 1/R Welsh Fus. | 7 | R | Regular | 22 | 4 | 15 |
| 70304 | Dvr | J | Bell | | desertion | 57 Bty, 43, How.Bde, RFA | 1 | R | Regular | 25 | 4 | 15 |
| 8136 | Pte | J | Kershaw | | desertion+ | 1/King's Own | 4 | R | Regular | 26 | 4 | 15 |
| 14780 | A/Cpl | A | Chisholm | 31 | murder | 20 Army Tp Coy RE | II Army | N | Regular | 17 | 5 | 15 |
| 8662 | Pte | O W | Hodgetts | 19 | cowardice | 1/Worcs | 8 | R | Regular | 4 | 6 | 15 |
| 3/1433 | Pte | G E | Roe | 19 | desertion | 2/KOYLI | 5 | R | Regular | 10 | 6 | 15 |
| 2779 | Pte | H H | Chase | 21 | cowardice | 2/Lancs Fus. | 4 | R | Regular | 12 | 6 | 15 |
| L/10132 | Pte | T | Harris | 21 | desertion | 1/R W Kent | 5 | R | Regular | 21 | 6 | 15 |
| 8710 | Pte | E A | Beaumont | 27 | desertion | 2/Leics | 7/Indian | R | Reservist | 24 | 6 | 15 |
| G/7171 | Pte | W J | Turpie | 24 | desertion | 2 Queen's | 28 | R | Kitchener | 1 | 7 | 15 |
| 5/3119 | Rfn | W | Bellamy | 34 | cowardice | 1/KRRC | 2 | R | Reservist | 16 | 7 | 15 |
| 11559 | Pte | T' | Docherty | 20 | desertion | 2/KOSB | 5 | R | Regular | 16 | 7 | 15 |
| 3832 | Pte | H F | Burden | 17 | desertion | 1/N.Fus. | 3 | R | Kitchener | 21 | 7 | 15 |
| 9722 | Pte | E | Fellows | 29 | desertion | 3/Worcs | 3 | R | Reservist | 26 | 7 | 15 |
| 8164 | Pte | B | Hartells | 32 | desertion | 3/Worcs | 3 | R | Regular | 26 | 7 | 15 |
| 12295 | Cpl | F | Ives | 30 | desertion | 3/Worcs | 3 | R | Regular | 26 | 7 | 15 |
| 7377 | Pte | J | Robinson | 31 | desertion | 3/Worcs | 3 | R | Regular | 26 | 7 | 15 |
| 7625 | Pte | A D | Thompson | 25 | desertion | 3/Worcs | 3 | R | Regular | 26 | 7 | 15 |
| 11653 | Pte | E | Fraser | 19 | desertion+ | 2/R Scots | 3 | R | Kitchener | 2 | 8 | 15 |
| 10315 | Pte | L R | Phillips | 23 | desertion | 6/SLI | 14 | N | Kitchener | 19 | 8 | 15 |
| 8225 | LCpl | P | Sands | 27 | desertion | 1/R Irish Rifles | 8 | R | Volunteer | 15 | 9 | 15 |
| 18603 | Pte | G | Mills | 21 | desertion+ | 2/DCLI | 27 | R | Kitchener | 29 | 9 | 15 |
| 71502 | Dvr | J | Spencer | | desertion | 65 Bty, 8 Bde, RFA | 5 | R | Regular | 29 | 9 | 15 |
| 29219 | Dvr | A | Lamb | | desertion | 21 Bty, 2 Bde, RFA | 6 | R | Regular | 2 | 10 | 15 |
| S/9560 | Rfn | G A | Irish | 30 | desertion | 2/2 RTS/Rifle Bde | 8 | R | Kitchener | 3 | 10 | 15 |
| S/9405 | Rfn | W | Smith | 37 | desertion | 2/2 RTS/Rifle Bde | 8 | R | Kitchener | 3 | 10 | 15 |
| 15437 | Pte | C W | Knight | 28 | murder | 10/R Welsh Fus. | 3 | R | Kitchener | 15 | 11 | 15 |
| 9948 | Pte | J | Graham | 21 | desertion+ | 2/R MunsteR Fus.. | 1 | R | Volunteer | 21 | 12 | 15 |
| 6807 | Pte | J J | Dennis | 19 | desertion | 1/N'hamptons | 1 | R | Regular | 30 | 1 | 16 |
| 10874 | Pte | J G | Carr | 21 | desertion+ | 2/Welsh | 1 | R | Regular | 7 | 2 | 16 |
| S/9672 | Pte | J | Docherty | 20 | desertion | 9/B Watch | 15 | N | Kitchener | 15 | 2 | 16 |

| Regt. No. | Rank | | Name | Age | Offence | Unit | Division | Div. Type | Type of Soldier | Date of death |
|---|---|---|---|---|---|---|---|---|---|---|
| 10710 | Pte | W | Hunter | 20 | desertion+ | 1/Loyals | 1 | R | Regular | 21 2 16 |
| L/8107 | Pte | A E | Eveleigh | 27 | desertion | 1/Buffs | 6 | R | Regular | 24 2 16 |
| L/10098 | Pte | R W | Gawler | 20 | desertion | 1/Buffs | 6 | R | Regular | 24 2 16 |
| 9840 | Pte | J T | Jones | 21 | desertion+ | 1/N'hamptons | 1 | R | Regular | 24 2 16 |
| T4/040862 | Dvr | T | Moore | 23 | murder | 24 Division Train ASC | 24 | N | Kitchener | 26 2 16 |
| 14218 | Rfn | J | Crozier | 18 | desertion | 9/R Irish Rifles | 36 | N | Volunteer | 27 2 16 |
| 4437 | Pte | A | Dale | | murder | 13/R Scots | 15 | N | Kitchener | 3 3 16 |
| B/21000 | Cpl | C | Lewis | | desertion | 12/HLI | 15 | N | Kitchener | 11 3 16 |
| 15/13211 | Rfn | J E | McCracken | 19 | desertion | 15/R Irish Rifles | 36 | N | Volunteer | 19 3 16 |
| 15/890 | Rfn | J | Templeton | | desertion | 15/R Irish Rifles | 36 | N | Volunteer | 19 3 16 |
| 11/1799 | Pte | A | Beverstein | 21 | desertion | 11/Middx | 12 | N | Kitchener | 20 3 16 |
| 21161 | Pte | H | Martin | | desertion | 9/Essex | 12 | N | Kitchener | 20 3 16 |
| 14357 | Pte | F C H | Bladen | 26 | desertion | 10/York & Lancs | 21 | N | Kitchener | 23 3 16 |
| 23621 | Pte | F | Auger | 25 | desertion | 14/CEF | 1/Can | C | Volunteer | 26 3 16 |
| 10263 | Pte | E | Bolton | | desertion | 1/Cheshire | 5 | R | Regular | 14 4 16 |
| G/7547 | Pte | W L | Thompson | 27 | desertion | 6/Buffs | 12 | N | Kitchener | 22 4 16 |
| G/335 | Pte | H | Carter | 18 | desertion | 11/Middx | 12 | N | Kitchener | 26 4 16 |
| 1/15134 | Pte | A | O'Neil | | desertion | 1/S Wales Bor | 1 | R | Kitchener | 30 4 16 |
| 1214 | Pte | W | Watts | 29 | desertion+ | 1/Loyals | 1 | R | Regular | 5 5 16 |
| 9/28719 | Pte | J | Cuthbert | 20 | disobedience | 9/Cheshire | 19 | N | Kitchener | 6 5 16 |
| 15469 | Pte | A H | Robinson | | desertion | 9/N.Fus. | 17 | N | Kitchener | 10 5 16 |
| 7711 | Pte | J | Fox | | striking a S.O. | 2/HLI | 2 | R | Regular | 12 5 16 |
| L/36251 | Dvr | J W | Hasemore | 23 | disobedience+ | 180 Bde, RFA | 16 | N | Kitchener | 12 5 16 |
| A/1579 | Rfn | A E | Parker | 35 | desertion+ | 7/KRRC | 14 | N | Kitchener | 15 5 16 |
| 12727 | Pte | J | Thomas | 44 | desertion | 2/Welsh | 1 | R | Reservist | 20 5 16 |
| L/10414 | Pte | W H | Burrell | 21 | desertion | 2/Sussex | 1 | R | Regular | 22 5 16 |
| 2408 | Pte | W W | Roberts | 34 | desertion+ | 4/R Fus. | 3 | R | Regular | 29 5 16 |
| 13857 | LCpl | J | Holland | 31 | cowardice+ | 10/Cheshire | 25 | N | Kitchener | 30 5 16 |
| 9197 | Pte | H T W | Phillips | 24 | desertion | 1/Coldstream | Guards | R | Regular | 30 5 16 |
| 25531 | Pte | J | Archibald | 20 | desertion | 17/R Scots | 35 | N | Kitchener | 4 6 16 |
| 86872 | Dvr | J W | Swaine | | desertion | 54 Bty, 39 Bde, RFA | 1 | R | Reservist | 9 6 16 |
| 10161 | Pte | J | Molyneaux | | desertion | 1/Loyals | 1 | R | Regular | 15 6 16 |
| 8037 | Pte | J | Jennings | | desertion | 2/S Lancs | 25 | N | Reservist | 26 6 16 |
| 549 | Pte | G | Lewis | | desertion | 2/S Lancs | 25 | N | Reservist | 26 6 16 |
| 11528 | Pte | F | Harding | 21 | desertion | 1/KRRC | 2 | R | Kitchener | 29 6 16 |
| 541 | Tpr | A | Butler | | murder | R Can Dragoons | 3/Can | C | Volunteer | 2 7 16 |
| 4/9170 | Pte | G | Hunter | | desertion+ | 2/DLI | 6 | R | Kitchener | 2 7 16 |
| 2506 | Pte | J | Smith | | desertion | 1/Loyals | 1 | R | Reservist | 2 7 16 |
| 10701 | Pte | J H | Wilson | | desertion | 4/CEF | 1/Can | C | Volunteer | 9 7 16 |
| 4567 | Pte | J | Brennan | | desertion | 1/8 King's (L'pool) | 55 | T | Kitchener | 16 7 16 |
| 3563 | Pte | J | Sloan | | desertion | 1/4 King's Own | 55 | T | Territorial | 16 7 16 |
| 2676 | Pte | A G | Earp | | quitting post+ | 1/5 Warwicks | 48 | T | Kitchener | 22 7 16 |
| 12396 | Pte | J | Cassidy | | desertion | 1/R Inniskilling Fus. | 29 | R | Volunteer | 23 7 16 |
| C/40124 | L/Bmdr | F S | Arnold | 26 | desertion | 1 Bde, Can.FA | 1/Can | C | Volunteer | 25 7 16 |
| 15251 | Pte | G H | Lawton | 36 | cowardice+ | 17/S'wood For | 39 | N | Kitchener | 30 7 16 |
| 31821 | Pte | B | McCubbin | 22 | cowardice+ | 17/S'wood For | 39 | N | Kitchener | 30 7 16 |
| 107526 | Pte | J W | Roberts | 20 | desertion+ | 2/Can Mount Rif | 3/Can | C | Volunteer | 30 7 16 |
| 416874 | Pte | C | LaLiberte | 25 | desertion | 3/CEF | 1/Can | C | Volunteer | 4 8 16 |
| 9541 | LCpl | F | Hawthorne | 22 | cowardice+ | 1/5 S Staffs | 46 | T | Regular | 11 8 16 |
| 14387 | Pte | W B | Nelson | 24 | desertion | 14/DLI | 6 | R | Kitchener | 11 8 16 |
| 12182 | Pte | A | Murphy | 27 | desertion | 9/Cameronians | 9 | N | Kitchener | 17 8 16 |
| 23972 | Cpl | J | Wilton | 40 | quitting post | 15/S'wood For | 35 | N | Kitchener | 17 8 16 |
| 404436 | Pte | E J | Reynolds | | desertion | 3/CEF | 1/Can | C | Volunteer | 23 8 16 |
| 10018 | Pte | P | Giles | | desertion | 14/N.Fus. | 21 | N | Kitchener | 24 8 16 |
| 2063 | Dvr | B. | De Fehr | | murder | 1/Res Pk (Can.ASC) | GHQ | C | Volunteer | 25 8 16 |
| 24/2008 | Pte | F | Hughes | 28 | desertion | 2/Cant (NZ) | NZ | | Volunteer | 25 8 16 |
| 2057 | Pte | J | Higgins | | desertion | 1/9 Argylls | 51 | T | Territorial | 26 8 16 |
| 3/4071 | Pte | J | Bennett | 19 | cowardice | 1/Hants | 4 | R | Regular | 28 8 16 |
| 18/313 | Pte | H | Crimmins | 32 | desertion | 18/W Yorks | 31 | N | Kitchener | 5 9 16 |
| 18/356 | Pte | A | Wild | 24 | desertion | 18/W Yorks | 31 | N | Kitchener | 5 9 16 |
| 20062 | Pte | J A | Anderson | 30 | cowardice+ | 12/King's (L'pool) | 25 | N | Kitchener | 12 9 16 |
| 5715 | Pte | C | Depper | 30 | desertion | 1/4 R Berks | 48 | T | Kitchener | 13 9 16 |

| Regt. No. | Rank | | Name | Age | Offence | Unit | Division | Div. Type | Type of Soldier | Date of death | | |
|---|---|---|---|---|---|---|---|---|---|---|---|---|
| 21373 | Pte | J | Carey | | desertion | 7/R Irish Fusiliers | 16 | N | Volunteer | 15 | 9 | 16 |
| 12923 | Pte | A | Rickman | 27 | desertion | 1/R Dublin Fus. | 29 | R | Volunteer | 15 | 9 | 16 |
| 7595 | Pte | J A | Haddock | 32 | desertion | 12/York & Lancs | 31 | N | Regular | 16 | 9 | 16 |
| 6744 | Pte | P | Black | | desertion | 1/4 B Watch | 51 | T | Territorial | 18 | 9 | 16 |
| R/19333 | Rfn | E A | Card | 23 | desertion | 20/KRRC | 3 | R | Kitchener | 22 | 9 | 16 |
| S/2889 | Pte | F | Murray | | murder | 9/Gordons (att.RE) | 15 | N | Reservist | 1 | 10 | 16 |
| 8/1384 | Pte | J J | Sweeney | 37 | desertion | 1/Otago (NZ) | NZ | | Volunteer | 2 | 10 | 16 |
| 67440 | Dvr | T G | Hamilton | 22 | striking a S.O. | 72 Bty, 38 Bde, RFA | 6 | R | Regular | 3 | 10 | 16 |
| 64987 | Dvr | J | Mullany | | striking a S.O. | 72 Bty, 38 Bde, RFA | 6 | R | Regular | 3 | 10 | 16 |
| 12772 | Pte | A | Botfield | 28 | cowardice | 9/S Staffs | 23 | N | Kitchener | 18 | 10 | 16 |
| 8871 | Pte | H T | Farr | 23 | cowardice | 1/W Yorks | 6 | R | Regular | 18 | 10 | 16 |
| 2554 | Pte | R | Stevenson | 23 | desertion | 1/4 Loyals | 55 | T | Kitchener | 25 | 10 | 16 |
| 3057 | Pte | H | Palmer | | desertion | 1/5 N.Fus. | 50 | T | Kitchener | 27 | 10 | 16 |
| 24/1521 | Pte | J | Braithwaite | 33 | mutiny | 2/Otago (NZ) | NZ | | Volunteer | 29 | 10 | 16 |
| 52081 | Gnr | W E | Lewis | 30 | mutiny | 124 Bde, RFA/Details RFA | 37 | N | Regular | 29 | 10 | 16 |
| 67882 | Pte | E | Young | 19 | desertion | 25/CEF | 2/Can | C | Volunteer | 29 | 10 | 16 |
| 9970 | Pte | A L | Jefferies | | desertion | 6/SLI | 14 | N | Kitchener | 1 | 11 | 16 |
| 2974 | Pte | B | McGeehan | | desertion | 1/8 King's (L'pool) | 55 | T | Territorial | 2 | 11 | 16 |
| 1731 | Rfn | R L | Barker | 21 | cowardice | 6/R.Fus. (City of London) | 47 | T | Territorial | 4 | 11 | 16 |
| 43665 | Pte | H | MacDonald | 32 | desertion | 12/W Yorks | 3 | R | Regular | 4 | 11 | 16 |
| 5626 | Pte | J | McQuade | | desertion | 18/HLI | 35 | N | Kitchener | 6 | 11 | 16 |
| 1957 | Pte | W G | Hunt | 20 | desertion | 18/Manchesters | 30 | N | Regular | 14 | 11 | 16 |
| L/11710 | Pte | A T | Ansted | 29 | desertion | 4/R Fus. | 3 | R | Reservist | 15 | 11 | 16 |
| 5323 | Pte | H | Flynn | | desertion | 18/HLI | 35 | N | Kitchener | 15 | 11 | 16 |
| 457241 | Pte | H H | Kerr | | desertion | 7/CEF | 1/Can | C | Volunteer | 21 | 11 | 16 |
| 17790 | LCpl | W A | Moon | 20 | desertion | 11/Cheshire | 25 | N | Kitchener | 21 | 11 | 16 |
| 11257 | LCpl | G E | Hughes | | desertion | 7/King's Own | 19 | N | Kitchener | 23 | 11 | 16 |
| 13167 | Pte | W H | Randle | | desertion | 10/S'wood For | 17 | N | Kitchener | 25 | 11 | 16 |
| SD/4242 | Pte | R T | Tite | 27 | cowardice | 13/Sussex | 39 | N | Kitchener | 25 | 11 | 16 |
| 10495 | Pte | A | Ingham | 24 | desertion | 18/Manchesters | 30 | N | Kitchener | 1 | 12 | 16 |
| 10502 | Pte | A | Longshaw | 21 | desertion | 18/Manchesters | 30 | N | Kitchener | 1 | 12 | 16 |
| G/11296 | Pte | W H | Simmonds | 23 | desertion | 23/Middx | 41 | N | Kitchener | 1 | 12 | 16 |
| 5/1791 | Pte | J | Cameron | | desertion | 1/5 N.Fus. | 50 | T | Territorial | 4 | 12 | 16 |
| 177753 | Pte | J M | Higgins | 24 | desertion | 1/CEF | 1/Can | C | Volunteer | 7 | 12 | 16 |
| 5009 | Rfn | S | McBride | | desertion | 2/R Irish Rifles | 25 | N | Volunteer | 7 | 12 | 16 |
| 89173 | Pnr | E | Beeby | | desertion | 212 Coy RE | 33 | N | Kitchener | 9 | 12 | 16 |
| 8534 | Pte | H | Poole | | desertion | 7/Yorks | 17 | N | Regular | 9 | 12 | 16 |
| - | 2/Lt | E S | Poole | 31 | desertion | 11/W Yorks | 23 | N | Kitchener | 10 | 12 | 16 |
| SR/9629 | Pte | C W F | Skilton | 20 | desertion | 22/R Fus. | 2 | R | Reservist | 26 | 12 | 16 |
| 40806 | Pte | P | Cairnie | | desertion | 1/R Scots Fus. | 3 | R | Conscript | 28 | 12 | 16 |
| - | Sub/Lt | E L A | Dyett | 21 | desertion | Nelson Bn, RND | 63 | | Volunteer | 5 | 1 | 17 |
| 11850 | Pte | J | Tongue | | desertion | 1/King's (L'pool) | 2 | R | Regular | 8 | 1 | 17 |
| 19/158 | LCpl | P | Goggins | 21 | quitting post | 19/DLI | 35 | N | Kitchener | 18 | 1 | 17 |
| 19/420 | LCpl | J | McDonald | 28 | quitting post | 19/DLI | 35 | N | Kitchener | 18 | 1 | 17 |
| 19/647 | L/Sgt | J W | Stones | 25 | cast'g away arms | 19/DLI | 35 | N | Kitchener | 18 | 1 | 17 |
| 27555 | Pte | J | Taylor | | desertion | 15/Lancs Fus. | 32 | N | Kitchener | 27 | 1 | 17 |
| S/6778 | Pte | F | Wright | | desertion | 1/R W Surrey | 33 | N | Kitchener | 28 | 1 | 17 |
| 12384 | Pte | A | Reid | 30 | desertion | 16/HLI | 32 | N | Kitchener | 31 | 1 | 17 |
| 23992 | Pte | E W | Harris | 20 | desertion | 10/Lancs Fus. | 17 | N | Kitchener | 3 | 2 | 17 |
| 96498 | Dvr | R | Murray | | desertion | 81 Bde, RFA | 17 | N | Kitchener | 3 | 2 | 17 |
| 34595 | Pte | J | Crampton | 42 | desertion | 9/York & Lancs | 23 | N | Reservist | 4 | 2 | 17 |
| 1763 | Pte | B A | Hart | 22 | desertion | 1/4 Suffolk | 33 | N | Territorial | 6 | 2 | 17 |
| 251482 | Rfn | W | Murphey | | desertion | 5/6 R Scots | 32 | N | Kitchener | 7 | 2 | 17 |
| 3/10390 | Pte | F | Stead | 20 | desertion | 2/Duke of Wellington's | 4 | R | Regular | 12 | 2 | 17 |
| 26685 | Pte | E | Holt | 22 | desertion | 19/Manchesters | 30 | N | Kitchener | 4 | 3 | 17 |
| 9552 | Dmr | F | Rose | 23 | desertion | 2/Yorks | 30 | N | Regular | 4 | 3 | 17 |
| 26028 | Pte | J | Rogers | | desertion | 2/S Lancs | 25 | N | Kitchener | 9 | 3 | 17 |
| G/12341 | Pte | W | Bowerman | 38 | desertion | 1/Queen's | 5 | R | Kitchener | 24 | 3 | 17 |

| Regt. No. | Rank | | Name | Age | Offence | Unit | Division | Div. Type | Type of Soldier | Date of death | | |
|---|---|---|---|---|---|---|---|---|---|---|---|---|
| 39213 | Pte | A | Hamilton | 31 | desertion | 14/DLI | 6 | R | Kitchener | 27 | 3 | 17 |
| 9828 | Pte | W E | Anderson | 21 | desertion+ | 5/Dorset | 11 | N | Kitchener | 31 | 3 | 17 |
| 13224 | Spr | F | Malyon | | desertion | 12 Coy RE att. RFA | 6 | R | Regular | 4 | 4 | 17 |
| 43359 | Sgt | G E | Gleadow | | desertion | 1/W Yorks | 6 | R | Reservist | 6 | 4 | 17 |
| 70715 | Pte | W | Robinson | | desertion | 1/S'wood For | 8 | R | Conscript | 10 | 4 | 17 |
| 416008 | Pte | E | Perry | 21 | desertion | 22/CEF | 2/Can | C | Volunteer | 11 | 4 | 17 |
| 15094 | Pte | J | Lewis | 21 | desertion | 5/Dorset | 11 | N | Kitchener | 19 | 4 | 17 |
| 454482 | Pte | H G | Carter | 21 | desertion | 73/CEF | 4/Can | C | Volunteer | 20 | 4 | 17 |
| 10930 | Pte | J | Ferguson | 21 | desertion | 1/R Scots Fus (att.RE) | 3 | R | Regular | 20 | 4 | 17 |
| 17137 | Pte | T | Hogan | 31 | desertion | 2/R Inniskilling Fus. | 32 | N | Volunteer | 14 | 5 | 17 |
| 8139 | Pte | G | Watkins | 31 | desertion | 13/Welsh | 38 | N | Reservist | 15 | 5 | 17 |
| 1529 | Pte | S H | Cunnington | 20 | desertion | 2/Warwicks | 7 | R | Regular | 19 | 5 | 17 |
| 43619 | Pte | C M | Milligan | 20 | desertion | 10/Cameronians | 15 | N | Conscript | 3 | 6 | 17 |
| 16120 | Pte | J W | Fryer | 23 | desertion | 12/Queen's | 41 | N | Kitchener | 14 | 6 | 17 |
| R/28638 | Rfn | A E | Allsop | 21 | desertion | 12/KRRC | 20 | N | Conscript | 15 | 6 | 17 |
| 26248 | Pte | J. | Wishard | 24 | desertion | 7/R Inniskilling Fus. | 16 | N | Volunteer | 15 | 6 | 17 |
| 492050 | Pte | J | Mayers | 25 | desertion | 1/13 R Fus. (Kensington) | 56 | T | Kitchener | 16 | 6 | 17 |
| 448160 | Pte | G | Comte | 22 | desertion | 22/CEF | 2/Can | C | Volunteer | 3 | 7 | 17 |
| 672604 | Pte | J | LaLancette | 21 | desertion | 22/CEF | 2/Can | C | Volunteer | 3 | 7 | 17 |
| 474371 | Rfn | W | Yeoman | 22 | desertion | 1/12 R Fus. (Rangers) | 56 | T | Kitchener | 3 | 7 | 17 |
| G/4495 | Pte | J E | Barnes | 24 | desertion | 7/R Sussex | 12 | N | Kitchener | 4 | 7 | 17 |
| G/10474 | Pte | R G | Pattison | 23 | desertion | 7/Queen's | 12 | N | Kitchener | 4 | 7 | 17 |
| 23726 | Pte | R | Hope | 23 | desertion | 1/R Inniskilling Fus. | 29 | R | Volunteer | 5 | 7 | 17 |
| 40435 | Pte | D J | Blakemore | 28 | desertion | 8/N Staffs | 19 | N | Conscript | 9 | 7 | 17 |
| 10758 | Rfn | F M | Barratt | 23 | desertion | 7/KRRC | 14 | N | Regular | 10 | 7 | 17 |
| 251797 | Pte | W | Benham | | desertion | 1/3 R Fus. | 56 | T | Kitchener | 12 | 7 | 17 |
| 17402 | Pte | F | Broadrick | | desertion | 11/Warwicks | 37 | N | Kitchener | 1 | 8 | 17 |
| 6/1598 | Pte | J | King | 32 | desertion | 1/Cant (NZ) | NZ | | Volunteer | 19 | 8 | 17 |
| 683458 | Pte | F | Loader | | desertion | 1/22 R Fus. | 47 | T | Conscript | 19 | 8 | 17 |
| 240678 | Pte | A | Mitchell | | desertion | 1/6 Lancs Fus. | 42 | T | Territorial | 20 | 8 | 17 |
| 23686 | Pte | J S | Michael | | desertion | 10/Cameronians | 15 | N | Kitchener | 24 | 8 | 17 |
| A/6730 | Pte | S | Stewart | 21 | desertion | 2/R Scots Fus. | 30 | N | Reservist | 29 | 8 | 17 |
| 19445 | Pte | W | Neave | | desertion | 10/W Yorks | 17 | N | Kitchener | 30 | 8 | 17 |
| 42467 | Pte | A | Parry | | desertion | 2/W Yorks | 8 | R | Kitchener | 30 | 8 | 17 |
| 14813 | Pte | T W | Watts | 21 | desertion | 7/E Yorks | 17 | N | Kitchener | 30 | 8 | 17 |
| R/27615 | Rfn | J J | Hyde | | desertion | 10/KRRC | 20 | N | Conscript | 5 | 9 | 17 |
| 52929 | Pte | J | Smith | 26 | desertion+ | 17/King's (L'pool) | 30 | N | Regular | 5 | 9 | 17 |
| 88378 | Pte | J | Stedman | 25 | desertion | 117 Coy MGC | 39 | N | Kitchener | 5 | 9 | 17 |
| 335727 | Pte | E | Delargey | 19 | desertion | 1/8 R Scots | 51 | T | Conscript | 6 | 9 | 17 |
| 13216 | Sgt | J T | Wall | 22 | desertion | 3/Worcs | 25 | N | Regular | 6 | 9 | 17 |
| 9694 | Pte | J H | Abigail | 20 | desertion | 8/Norfolk | 18 | N | Regular | 12 | 9 | 17 |
| 200757 | Pte | C | Britton | | desertion | 1/5 Warwicks | 48 | T | Conscript | 12 | 9 | 17 |
| 2064 | Pte | W | Wycherley | 24 | desertion | 2/Manchesters | 32 | N | Regular | 12 | 9 | 17 |
| 8833 | Pte | G | Everill | 30 | desertion | 1/N Staffs | 24 | N | Reservist | 14 | 9 | 17 |
| 31184 | Pte | L | Mitchell | | desertion | 8/York & Lancs | 23 | N | Conscript | 19 | 9 | 17 |
| 7429 | Pte | H | Morris | 17 | desertion | 6/Brit W Indies | IV Army | | Volunteer | 20 | 9 | 17 |
| 7423 | Pte | C H | Kirman | 32 | desertion | 7/Lincs | 17 | N | Reservist | 23 | 9 | 17 |
| 11225 | Pte | E | Mackness | 25 | desertion | 1/Cameronians | 33 | N | Regular | 1 | 10 | 17 |
| 26/626 | A/Cpl | J R | Short | 31 | mutiny | 24/N. Fus. | 34 | N | Kitchener | 4 | 10 | 17 |
| R/15325 | Rfn | J | Woodhouse | | desertion | 12/KRRC | 20 | N | Kitchener | 4 | 10 | 17 |
| 830020 | Pte | D | Sinizki | 22 | cowardice | 52/CEF | 3/Can | C | Volunteer | 9 | 10 | 17 |
| 385 | Lab | M M | Ahmed | | mutiny | Egypt Lab Corps | BEF LoC | | Volunteer | 10 | 10 | 17 |
| G/15605 | Pte | F C | Gore | 19 | desertion | 7/Buffs | 18 | N | Kitchener | 16 | 10 | 17 |
| S/15954 | Pte | N H | Taysum | 25 | desertion | 9/B Watch | 15 | N | Kitchener | 16 | 10 | 17 |
| S/15240 | Pte | T | Ward | 23 | desertion | 8/10 Gordons | 15 | N | Kitchener | 16 | 10 | 17 |
| 20726 | CQMS | W | Alexander | 37 | desertion | 10/CEF | 1/Can | C | Volunteer | 18 | 10 | 17 |
| R/24441 | Rfn | F W | Cheeseman | 29 | desertion | 18/KRRC | 41 | N | Conscript | 20 | 10 | 17 |
| 94236 | Spr | A P | Oyns | 31 | desertion | 50 Search Light Coy RE | IV Army | | Kitchener | 20 | 10 | 17 |
| 443288 | Pte | T L | Moles | 28 | desertion | 54/CEF | 4/Can | C | Volunteer | 22 | 10 | 17 |
| G/8857 | Pte | E | Worsley | | desertion | 2/Middx | 8 | R | Kitchener | 22 | 10 | 17 |
| 266120 | Pte | F | Turner | 31 | desertion | 1/6 N. Fus. | 50 | T | Kitchener | 23 | 10 | 17 |
| 15954 | Pte | W | Jones | | desertion | 9/R Welsh Fus. | 19 | N | Kitchener | 25 | 10 | 17 |

| Regt. No. | Rank | | Name | Age | Offence | Unit | Division | Div. Type | Type of Soldier | Date of death |
|---|---|---|---|---|---|---|---|---|---|---|
| 20101 | Pte | E | Bryant | 33 | desertion | 10/Cheshire | 25 | N | Kitchener | 27 10 17 |
| 32559 | Pte | C B | Nicholson | 19 | desertion | 8/York & Lancs | 23 | N | Conscript | 27 10 17 |
| 40422 | Pte | S | Byrne | 30 | desertion | 1/R Dublin Fus. | 29 | R | Volunteer | 28 10 17 |
| A/201225 | Rfn | | Donovan | 20 | desertion | 16/KRRC | 33 | N | Conscript | 31 10 17 |
| 11046 | Pte | H J | Webb | | desertion | 2/KOYLI | 32 | N | Regular | 31 10 17 |
| 12609 | Pte | G | Hanna | 26 | desertion | 1/R Irish Fusiliers | 36 | N | Volunteer | 6 11 17 |
| 8793 | Pte | J | Taylor | 24 | desertion | 2/S Staffs | 2 | R | Regular | 6 11 17 |
| 45688 | Pte | J B | Milburn | | desertion | 24/27 N. Fus. | 34 | N | Kitchener | 8 11 17 |
| 204455 | Pte | W | Smith | 20 | desertion | 3/5 Lancs Fus. | 66 | T | Conscript | 14 11 17 |
| 73372 | Pte | R M | Davies | | desertion | 11/S'wood For. | 23 | N | Kitchener | 15 11 17 |
| 43499 | Pte | T | Foulkes | 21 | desertion | 1/10 Man | 42 | T | Conscript | 21 11 17 |
| G/1533 | Pte | T | Hawkins | | desertion | 7/R W Surrey | 18 | N | Kitchener | 22 11 17 |
| 3/20279 | Pte | E | Lawrence | 21 | desertion | 2/Devon | 8 | R | Kitchener | 22 11 17 |
| 11490 | Pte | T H B | Rigby | 21 | desertion | 10/S Wales Borderers | 38 | N | Regular | 22 11 17 |
| S/17688 | Pte | J S | Adamson | 30 | cowardice | 7/Camerons | 15 | N | Kitchener | 23 11 17 |
| L/11661 | Pte | A H | Westwood | 20 | desertion | 8/Queen's | 18 | N | Kitchener | 23 11 17 |
| 200945 | Pte | J | Bateman | | desertion | 2/S Staffs | 2 | R | Conscript | 3 12 17 |
| 322497 | Rfn | F W | Slade | 24 | disobedience | 2/6 R Fus. | 58 | T | Conscript | 14 12 17 |
| 11/81 | Pte | C F | McColl | 26 | desertion | 1/4 E Yorks | 50 | T | Kitchener | 28 12 17 |
| 393923 | Rfn | H | Williams | | desertion | 1/9 R Fus. (QVR) | 56 | T | Kitchener | 28 12 17 |
| 10603 | Pte | J | Seymour | | desertion | 2/R Inniskilling Fus. | 32 | N | Volunteer | 24 1 18 |
| 11606 | Pte | W | Clarke | 23 | desertion | 2/DLI | 6 | R | Kitchener | 9 2 18 |
| 307350 | Pte | T | Hopkins | 26 | leaving his post | 1/8 Lancs Fus. | 42 | T | Conscript | 13 2 18 |
| 46127 | Pte | E | Horler | 26 | desertion | 12/W Yorks | 3 | R | Conscript | 17 2 18 |
| 8/2733 | Pte | V M | Spencer | 23 | desertion | 1/Otago (NZ) | NZ | | Volunteer | 24 2 18 |
| 227098 | Pte | E | Fairburn | 22 | desertion | 18/CEF | 2/Can | C | Volunteer | 2 3 18 |
| A/38119 | Pte | C | Welsh | | desertion | 8/CEF | 1/Can | C | Volunteer | 6 3 18 |
| 3019 | L/Sgt | A | Wickings | 28 | murder | 9/Rifle Bde | 14 | N | Regular | 7 3 18 |
| S/9696 | Pte | H | Dalande | | desertion | 8/Seaforths | 15 | N | Kitchener | 9 3 18 |
| 2095 | Pte | H E J | Lodge | | desertion | 19/CEF | 2/Can | C | Volunteer | 13 3 18 |
| 34453 | Pte | A C | Dagesse | 32 | desertion | 22/CEF | 2/Can | C | Volunteer | 15 3 18 |
| 242904 | Pte | H | Hughes | 27 | desertion | 1/5 York & Lancs | 49 | T | Conscript | 10 4 18 |
| 18143 | Pte | A | Holmes | 22 | desertion | 8/King's Own | 3 | R | Kitchener | 22 4 18 |
| 36224 | Pte | J | Skone | 39 | murder | 2/Welsh | 1 | R | Kitchener | 10 5 18 |
| 7674 | Cpl | J | Reid | 26 | desertion | 6/Camerons | 15 | N | Regular | 11 5 18 |
| 13612 | Pte | F | O'Neill | 24 | desertion | 1/S'wood For. | 8 | R | Kitchener | 16 5 18 |
| 20808 | Pte | R W | Simmers | 25 | desertion | 2/R Scots | 3 | R | Kitchener | 19 5 18 |
| 62218 | Pte | L | Delisle | 26 | desertion | 22/CEF | 2/Can | C | Volunteer | 21 5 18 |
| 62536 | Spr | R | Bell | 29 | murder | 123 Field Coy RE | 38 | N | Kitchener | 22 5 18 |
| 265427 | Pte | J | McFarlane | 27 | desertion | 4/King's (L'pool) | 33 | N | Territorial | 22 5 18 |
| 285031 | Pte | M R | Richmond | | desertion | 1/6 Gordons | 51 | T | Kitchener | 26 5 18 |
| 41643 | Pte | W J | Earl | 22 | desertion | 1/7 Lancs Fus. | 42 | T | Conscript | 27 5 18 |
| 300199 | Pte | T | Brigham | 22 | desertion | 1/10 Manchesters | 42 | T | Territorial | 4 6 18 |
| 305 | Pte | W T | Spry | 29 | desertion | 2/R Fus. | 29 | R | Kitchener | 14 6 18 |
| 718566 | Pte | S McD | Fowles | 21 | desertion | 44/CEF | 4/Can | C | Volunteer | 19 6 18 |
| 45980 | Pte | W | Dossett | 22 | desertion | 1/4 York & Lancs | 49 | T | Kitchener | 25 6 18 |
| 10299 | Coolie | E J | Wang | | murder | Chin Lab Corps | BEF LoC | | Volunteer | 26 6 18 |
| 10272 | Coolie | C H | Yang | | murder | Chin Lab Corps | BEF LoC | | Volunteer | 26 6 18 |
| G/52128 | Pte | D | Stevenson | 23 | desertion | 13/Middx | 24 | N | Kitchener | 18 7 18 |
| 21801 | Pte | A | Briggs | 27 | desertion | 9/S'wood For. | 11 | N | Kitchener | 19 7 18 |
| 53497 | Coolie | S K | Cheng | | murder | Chin Lab Corps | BEF LoC | | Volunteer | 23 7 18 |
| 202893 | Pte | G | Ainley | 20 | desertion | 1/4 KOYLI | 49 | T | Conscript | 30 7 18 |
| 20035 | Pte | F | Johnson | | desertion | 2/Border | 7 | R | Kitchener | 1 8 18 |
| 20037 | Pte | H | McClair | | desertion | 2/Border | 7 | R | Kitchener | 1 8 18 |
| 10686 | Pte | B | O'Connell | 23 | desertion | 1/Irish Gds | Guards | R | Volunteer | 8 8 18 |
| 46090 | Coolie | H I | Chao | | murder | Chin Lab Corps | BEF LoC | | Volunteer | 9 8 18 |
| 44174 | Pte | W | Scholes | 25 | desertion | 2/S Wales Borderers | 29 | R | Conscript | 10 8 18 |
| 39463 | Pte | J | Swain | | desertion | 5/R Berks | 12 | N | Conscript | 11 8 18 |

| Regt. No. | Rank | | Name | Age | Offence | Unit | Division | Div. Type | Type of Soldier | Date of death | | |
|---|---|---|---|---|---|---|---|---|---|---|---|---|
| 454610 | Pte | W N | Ling | 22 | desertion | 2/CEF | 1/Can | C | Volunteer | 12 | 8 | 18 |
| 22635 | Pte | W | Baker | | desertion | 26/R Fus. | 41 | N | Kitchener | 14 | 8 | 18 |
| 4519 | Pte | H | Hendricks | 46 | desertion | 2/Leinster | 29 | R | Volunteer | 23 | 8 | 18 |
| 11682 | Pte | J | Nisbet | 26 | desertion | 1/Leics | 6 | R | Kitchener | 23 | 8 | 18 |
| G/18469 | Pte | F C | Butcher | 26 | desertion | 7/Buffs | 18 | N | Kitchener | 27 | 8 | 18 |
| 203313 | Pte | F | Bateman | 28 | desertion | 1/4 York & Lancs | 49 | T | Kitchener | 10 | 9 | 18 |
| 42476 | Coolie | I H | Hui | | murder | Chin Lab Corps | BEF LoC | | Volunteer | 12 | 9 | 18 |
| 15161 | Pte | P | Murphy | 20 | desertion | 47 Bn MGC | 47 | T | Kitchener | 12 | 9 | 18 |
| 38332 | Pte | D | Gibson | 25 | desertion | 12/R Scots | 9 | N | Kitchener | 24 | 9 | 18 |
| - | 2/Lt | J H | Paterson | 28 | murder | 3/Essex att.1st | 37 | N | Kitchener | 24 | 9 | 18 |
| G/6565 | Pte | H J | Knight | | desertion | 1/R W Surrey | 33 | N | Kitchener | 6 | 10 | 18 |
| 21654 | Pte | L D | Elford | 28 | desertion | 7/8 KOSB | 15 | N | Kitchener | 11 | 10 | 18 |
| 43055 | Pte | L | Harris | 23 | desertion | 10/W Yorks | 17 | N | Kitchener | 7 | 11 | 18 |
| G/46730 | Pte | E | Jackson | 32 | desertion | 24/R Fus. | 2 | R | Conscript | 7 | 11 | 18 |
| 5884 | Coolie | F Y | Wan | | murder | Chin Lab Corps | BEF LoC | | Volunteer | 15 | 2 | 19 |
| 44735 | Coolie | C C | Wang | | murder | 107 Chin Lab Coy | BEF LoC | | Volunteer | 8 | 5 | 19 |
| 253617 | Gnr | F O | Wills | 20 | murder | X50th TMB RFA | BEF | | Conscript | 27 | 5 | 19 |
| 50079 | Pte | J | Chandler | | murder | Lincs | BEF | | Conscript | 11 | 8 | 19 |
| 1239 | Pte | A | Davids | 24 | murder | 1 Cape Col Lab Regt | BEF LoC | | Volunteer | 26 | 8 | 19 |
| 49 | Pte | W P | Harris | 23 | murder | 1 Cape Col Lab Regt | BEF LoC | | Volunteer | 26 | 8 | 19 |
| 1454 | Pte | F | Boos | 19 | murder | 1 Cape Col Lab Regt | BEF LoC | | Volunteer | 15 | 10 | 19 |
| 16174 | Collie | J C | Chang | | murder x4 | Chin Lab Coy | BEF LoC | | Volunteer | 14 | 2 | 20 |
| 97170 | Coolie | C M | Hei | | murder | Chin Lab Corps | BEF LoC | | Volunteer | 21 | 2 | 20 |
| 44340 | Coolie | C H | K'ung | | murder | Chin Lab Corps | BEF LoC | | Volunteer | 21 | 2 | 20 |

# EXECUTIONS IN 'OTHER THEATRES' IN CHRONOLOGICAL ORDER

| Regt. No. | Rank | | Name | Age | Offence | Unit | Division | Div. Type | Type of Soldier | Date of death | | |
|---|---|---|---|---|---|---|---|---|---|---|---|---|
| 1/9804 | Pte | T | Davis | 21 | quitting post | 1/R Munster Fus. | 29 | R | Volunteer | 2 | 7 | 15 |
| 2479 | Pte | | Fatoma | | cowardice+ | West African Regt | WAHQ | | Volunteer | 19 | 7 | 15 |
| 16734 | Pte | H | Salter | 24 | desertion+ | 6/E Lancs | 13 | N | Kitchener | 11 | 12 | 15 |
| 6/227 | Pte | PJ | Downey | 20 | disobedience | 6/Leinster | 10 | N | Volunteer | 27 | 12 | 15 |
| 9610 | Sgt | J | Robins | | disobedience+ | 5/Wilts | 13 | N | Regular | 2 | 1 | 16 |
| 494 | Pte | N. | Matthews | | murder | 3rd S African Infty | SA Bde | | Volunteer | 3 | 4 | 16 |
| 7560 | Pte | A | Frafra | | casting away arm | Gold Coast | 1/E Afr | | Volunteer | 28 | 9 | 16 |
| 10912 | Pte | R | Burton | 24 | sleeping at post | 6/S Lancs | 13 | N | Kitchener | 19 | 2 | 17 |
| 10555 | Pte | T | Downing | 22 | sleeping at post | 6/S Lancs | 13 | N | Kitchener | 19 | 2 | 17 |
| 10764 | Pte | RM | Jones | 40 | desertion | 6/S Lancs | 13 | N | Kitchener | 21 | 2 | 17 |
| 5538 | LCpl | A | Mamprusi | | cowardice | Gold Coast | HANforce | | Volunteer | 28 | 4 | 17 |
| S/5470 | Pte | A | Brown | | desertion | 10/B Watch | 26 | N | Kitchener | 1 | 6 | 17 |
| 13827 | L/Sgt | H | Ashton | 20 | desertion | 11/Cameronians | 26 | N | Kitchener | 8 | 7 | 17 |
| S/13248 | Pte | G | Cutmore | | desertion | 2/B Watch | 7/Indian | R | Kitchener | 25 | 7 | 17 |
| 3972 | Pte | S | Sabongidda | | violence | 3/Nigerian | Nig Bde | | Volunteer | 27 | 7 | 17 |
| 4881 | Pte | HA | Clarke | | striking a S.O. | 2/Brit W Indies | Pal LoC | | Volunteer | 11 | 8 | 17 |
| 9191 | Pte | JA | Mitchell | 18 | murder+ | 1/Brit W Indies | GHQ Pal | | Volunteer | 22 | 12 | 17 |
| 204232 | Pte | R | Young | 21 | desertion | 11/Worcs | 26 | N | Conscript | 18 | 9 | 18 |
| A/2600 | Pte | D | Barama | | murder | Gold Coast Mtd.Inf.Coy | EDforce | | Volunteer | 10 | 11 | 18 |
| 11080 | Pte | A | Denny | | murder | 8/Brit W Indies | It LoC | | Volunteer | 20 | 1 | 19 |
| | Pte | | Bitel | | mutiny | Slavo- British Penal Bn | N Russia | | | | 7 | 19 |
| | Pte | | Cherbukin | | mutiny | Slavo- British Penal Bn | N Russia | | | | 7 | 19 |
| | Pte | | Deriagin | | mutiny | Slavo- British Penal Bn | N Russia | | | | 7 | 19 |
| | Pte | | Elisaieff | | mutiny | Slavo- British Penal Bn | N Russia | | | | 7 | 19 |
| | Pte | | Kameff | | mutiny | Slavo- British Penal Bn | N Russia | | | | 7 | 19 |
| | Pte | | Lashkoff | | mutiny | Slavo- British Penal Bn | N Russia | | | | 7 | 19 |
| | Sgt | | Pesochnikoff | | mutiny | Slavo- British Penal Bn | N Russia | | | | 7 | 19 |
| | Pte | | Posdjeef | | mutiny | Slavo- British Penal Bn | N Russia | | | | 7 | 19 |
| | Pte | | Sakharoff | | mutiny | Slavo- British Penal Bn | N Russia | | | | 7 | 19 |
| | Pte | | Taratin | | mutiny | Slavo- British Penal Bn | N Russia | | | | 7 | 19 |
| | Pte | | Volkoff | | mutiny | Slavo- British Penal Bn | N Russia | | | | 7 | 19 |
| 7144396 | Pte | JJ | Daly | 21 | mutiny | 1/Conn Rangers | India | | Regular | 2 | 11 | 20 |
| 7076018 | Pte | R | Flynn | | murder | 2/R Dublin Fus | MEF | | Regular | 6 | 11 | 20 |
| | | K | ---lli | | murder | Muleteers | MEF LoC | | Volunteer | | | |
| | | Y | Antonio | | murder | Muleteers | MEF LoC | | Volunteer | | | |
| | | YH | Louka | | murder | Muleteers | MEF LoC | | Volunteer | | | |
| | | S | Simeoni | | murder | Muleteers | MEF LoC | | Volunteer | | | |
| | | N | Thaourdis | | murder | Muleteers | MEF LoC | | Volunteer | | | |

| | | | | | |
|---|---|---|---|---|---|
| Elisaieff | 298 | Hawkins T | 218 | Kameff | 298 |
| Evans A | 31 | Hawthorne F | 99 | Kerr H H | 135 |
| Eveleigh A E | 63 | Hei C M | 270 | Kershaw J | 41 |
| Everill G | 193 | Hendricks H | 254 | King J | 184 |
| Fairburn E | 237 | Higgins J | 141 | Kirk E | 35 |
| Farr H T | 121 | Higgins J | 105 | Kirman C H | 196 |
| Fatoma | 56 | Highgate T J | 26 | Knight C W | 56 |
| Fellows E | 49 | Hodgetts O W | 43 | Knight H J | 261 |
| Ferguson J | 170 | Hogan T | 172 | LaLancette J | 177 |
| Flynn H | 134 | Holland J | 83 | LaLiberté C | 98 |
| Flynn R | 270 | Holmes A | 241 | Lamb A | 54 |
| Foulkes T | 217 | Holt E | 164 | Lashkoff | 298 |
| Fowles S | 246 | Hope R | 179 | Latham G W | 30 |
| Fox J S V | 78 | Hope T | 36 | Lawrence E | 220 |
| Fox J | 40 | Hopkins T | 235 | Lawton G H | 96 |
| Frafra A | 59 | Horler E | 236 | Lewis C | 69 |
| Fraser E | 51 | Hughes F | 104 | Lewis G | 86 |
| Fryer J W | 174 | Hughes G E | 135 | Lewis J | 170 |
| Gawler R W | 64 | Hughes H | 241 | Lewis W E | 125 |
| Gibson D | 259 | Hui I H | 259 | Ling W N | 254 |
| Giles P | 103 | Hunt W G | 132 | Loader F | 186 |
| Gleadow G E | 167 | Hunter G | 92 | Lodge H E J | 239 |
| Goggins P | 156 | Hunter W | 63 | Longshaw A | 138 |
| Gore F C | 204 | Hyde J J | 189 | Louka Y H | 298 |
| Graham J | 56 | Ingham A | 138 | MacDonald H | 129 |
| Haddock J A | 114 | Irish (Lee) G A | 54 | Mackness E | 198 |
| Hamilton A | 165 | Irvine W J | 41 | Malyon F | 167 |
| Hamilton T G | 118 | Ives F | 49 | Mamprusi A | 227 |
| Hanna G | 213 | Jackson E | 263 | Martin H | 73 |
| Harding F | 88 | Jefferies A L | 127 | Matthews N | 59 |
| Harris E W | 160 | Jennings J | 86 | Mayers J | 176 |
| Harris L | 262 | Johnson F | 250 | McBride S | 141 |
| Harris T | 45 | Jones J T | 65 | McClair H | 250 |
| Harris W P | 266 | Jones R M | 226 | McColl C F | 225 |
| Hart B A | 161 | Jones W | 42 | McCracken J E | 70 |
| Hartells B | 50 | Jones W | 210 | McCubbin B | 96 |
| Hasemore J W | 79 | K'ung C H | 270 | McDonald J | 156 |

| | | | | | |
|---|---|---|---|---|---|
| McFarlane J | 245 | Pesochnikoff | 298 | Simmonds W H | 140 |
| McGeehan B | 128 | Phillips H T W | 84 | Sinizki D | 203 |
| McQuade J | 131 | Phillips L R | 52 | Skilton C W F | 144 |
| Michael J S | 187 | Pitts A | 33 | Skone J | 242 |
| Milburn J B | 214 | Poole E S | 142 | Slade F W | 223 |
| Milligan C M | 174 | Poole H | 142 | Sloan J | 93 |
| Mills G | 53 | Posdjeef | 298 | Smith J | 92 |
| Mitchell A | 187 | Povey G H | 33 | Smith J | 189 |
| Mitchell J A | 232 | Price W | 33 | Smith W | 54 |
| Mitchell L | 194 | Randle W H | 135 | Smith W | 216 |
| Moles T L | 207 | Reid A | 159 | Smythe A | 30 |
| Molyneaux J | 86 | Reid I | 40 | Spencer J | 53 |
| Moon W A | 135 | Reid J | 242 | Spencer V M | 236 |
| Moore T | 65 | Reynolds E J | 102 | Spry W T | 246 |
| Morgan R | 34 | Richmond M R | 245 | Stead F | 161 |
| Morris H | 195 | Rickman A | 113 | Stedman J | 189 |
| Mullany J | 118 | Rigby T H B | 220 | Stevenson D | 248 |
| Murphey W | 161 | Roberts J W | 98 | Stevenson R | 121 |
| Murphy A | 101 | Roberts W W | 82 | Stewart S | 187 |
| Murphy P | 258 | Robins J | 58 | Stones J W | 156 |
| Murray F | 116 | Robinson A H | 78 | Swain J | 253 |
| Murray R | 160 | Robinson J | 50 | Swaine J W | 85 |
| Neave W | 188 | Robinson W | 168 | Sweeney J J | 116 |
| Nelson W B | 101 | Roe G E | 43 | Tanner E | 27 |
| Nicholson C B | 211 | Rogers J | 164 | Taratin | 298 |
| Nisbet J | 255 | Rose F | 163 | Taylor J | 159 |
| O'Connell B | 253 | Sabongidda S | 230 | Taylor J | 214 |
| O'Neil A | 76 | Sakharoff | 298 | Taysum N H | 205 |
| O'Neill F | 243 | Salter H | 57 | Templeton J | 70 |
| Oyns A P | 207 | Sands P | 52 | Thaourdis N | 298 |
| Palmer H | 122 | Scholes W | 253 | Thomas J | 81 |
| Parker A E | 80 | Scotton W | 31 | Thompson A D | 50 |
| Parry A | 189 | Seymour J | 235 | Thompson W L | 75 |
| Paterson J H | 259 | Sheffield F | 29 | Tite R T | 136 |
| Pattison R G | 178 | Short J R | 200 | Tongue J | 156 |
| Penn M | 42 | Simeoni S | 298 | Troughton A | 42 |
| Perry E | 168 | Simmers R W | 243 | Turner F | 208 |